ANTIMICROBIAL RESISTANCE

Global Report on surveillance

2014

WHO Library Cataloguing-in-Publication Data

Antimicrobial resistance: global report on surveillance.

1.Anti-infective agents - classification. 2.Anti-infective agents - adverse effects. 3.Drug resistance, microbial - drug effects. 4.Risk management. 5.Humans. I.World Health Organization.

ISBN 978 92 4 156474 8   (NLM classification: QV 250)

Credits // Cover photo: ©Shutterstock: © Alex011973 / © Allies Interactive / © Fedorov Oleksiy / © Ivan Cholakov / © Michel Borges / © Vlue //

Design and Layout: www.paprika-annecy.com

Printed in France

Contents

SECTION 01

Resistance to antibacterial drugs

1

SECTION 02

Resistance to antibacterial drugs in selected bacteria of international concern

9

SECTION 03

The health and economic burden due to antibacterial resistance

35

SECTION 04 — Surveillance of antimicrobial drug resistance in disease-specific programmes

43

SECTION 05 — Surveillance of antimicrobial resistance in other areas

59

SECTION 06 — Conclusions

69

Foreword

Antimicrobial resistance (AMR) within a wide range of infectious agents is a growing public health threat of broad concern to countries and multiple sectors. Increasingly, governments around the world are beginning to pay attention to a problem so serious that it threatens the achievements of modern medicine. A post-antibiotic era—in which common infections and minor injuries can kill—far from being an apocalyptic fantasy, is instead a very real possibility for the 21st century.

Determining the scope of the problem is essential for formulating and monitoring an effective response to AMR. This WHO report, produced in collaboration with Member States and other partners, provides as accurate a picture as is presently possible of the magnitude of AMR and the current state of surveillance globally.

The report focuses on antibacterial resistance (ABR) in common bacterial pathogens. Why? There is a major gap in knowledge about the magnitude of this problem and such information is needed to guide urgent public health actions. ABR is complex and multidimensional. It involves a range of resistance mechanisms affecting an ever-widening range of bacteria, most of which can cause a wide spectrum of diseases in humans and animals.

One important finding of the report, which will serve as a baseline to measure future progress, is that there are many gaps in information on pathogens of major public health importance. In addition, surveillance of ABR generally is neither coordinated nor harmonized, compromising the ability to assess and monitor the situation.

Nonetheless, the report makes a clear case that resistance to common bacteria has reached alarming levels in many parts of the world indicating that many of the available treatment options for common infections in some settings are becoming ineffective. Furthermore, systematic reviews of the scientific evidence show that ABR has a negative impact on outcomes for patients and health-care expenditures.

Generally, surveillance in TB, malaria and HIV to detect resistance, determine disease burden and monitor public health interventions is better established and experiences from these programmes are described in the report, so that lessons learnt can be applied to ABR and opportunities for collaboration identified.

WHO, along with partners across many sectors, is developing a global action plan to mitigate AMR. Strengthening global AMR surveillance will be a critical aspect of such planning as it is the basis for informing global strategies, monitoring the effectiveness of public health interventions and detecting new trends and threats.

Dr Keiji Fukuda
Assistant Director-General
Health Security

Summary

Antimicrobial resistance (AMR) threatens the effective prevention and treatment of an ever-increasing range of infections caused by bacteria, parasites, viruses and fungi. This report examines, for the first time, the current status of surveillance and information on AMR, in particular antibacterial resistance (ABR), at country level worldwide.

Key findings and public health implications of ABR are:

- Very high rates of resistance have been observed in bacteria that cause common health-care associated and community-acquired infections (e.g. urinary tract infection, pneumonia) in all WHO regions.

- There are significant gaps in surveillance, and a lack of standards for methodology, data sharing and coordination.

Key findings from AMR surveillance in disease-specific programmes are as follows:

- Although multidrug-resistant TB is a growing concern, it is largely under-reported, compromising control efforts.

- Foci of artemisinin resistance in malaria have been identified in a few countries. Further spread, or emergence in other regions, of artemisinin-resistant strains could jeopardize important recent gains in malaria control.

- Increasing levels of transmitted anti-HIV drug resistance have been detected among patients starting antiretroviral treatment.

Surveillance of ABR and sources of data

There is at present no global consensus on methodology and data collection for ABR surveillance. Routine surveillance in most countries is often based on samples taken from patients with severe infections – particularly infections associated with health care, and those in which first-line treatment has failed. Community-acquired infections are almost certainly underrepresented among samples, leading to gaps in coverage of important patient groups.

Nevertheless, it is critical to obtain a broad picture of the international scope of the problem of ABR. To accomplish this, WHO obtained, from 129 Member States, the most recent information on resistance surveillance and data for a selected set of nine bacteria–antibacterial drug combinations of public health importance. Of these, 114 provided data for at least one of the nine combinations (22 countries provided data on all nine combinations).

Some data sets came from individual surveillance sites, or data from several sources rather than national reports. Many data sets were based on a small number of tested isolates of each bacterium (<30), adding to uncertainty about the precision of the data; this reflects a lack of national structures to provide an overview of the situation and limited capacity for timely information sharing. Most data sets, individual sites or aggregated data, were based on hospital data. Non-representativeness of surveillance data is a limitation for the interpretation and comparison of results.

The data compiled from countries indicate where there may be gaps in knowledge and lack of capacity to collect national data. Among WHO regions, the greatest country-level data were obtained from the European Region and the Region of the Americas, where long-standing regional surveillance and collaboration exist.

Current status of resistance in selected bacteria

In the survey forming the basis for this part of the report, information was requested on resistance to antibacterial drugs commonly used to treat infections caused by nine bacteria of international concern. The chosen bacteria are causing some of the most common infections in different settings; in the community, in hospitals or transmitted through the food chain. The main findings are summarized in the following tables:

Bacteria commonly causing infections in hospitals and in the community

Name of bacterium/ resistance	Examples of typical diseases	No. out of 194 Member States providing data	No. of WHO regions with national reports of 50% resistance or more
Escherichia coli/	Urinary tract infections, blood stream infections		
- vs 3rd gen. cephalosporins		86	5/6
- vs fluoroquinolones		92	5/6
Klebsiella pneumoniae/	Pneumonia, blood stream infections, urinary tract infections		
- vs 3rd gen. cephalosporins		87	6/6
- vs 3rd carbapenems		71	2/6
Staphylococcus aureus/	Wound infections, blood stream infections		
- vs methicillin "MRSA"		85	5/6

Bacteria mainly causing infections in the community

Name of bacterium/ resistance	Examples of typical diseases	No. out of 194 Member States providing data	No of WHO regions with national reports of 25% resistance or more
Streptococcus pneumoniae/ - non-susceptible or resistant to penicillin	Pneumonia, meningitis, otitis	67	6/6
Nontyphoidal Salmonella/	Foodborne diarrhoea, blood stream infections		
- vs fluoroquinolones		68	3/6
Shigella species/	Diarrhoea ("bacillary dysenteria")		
- vs fluoroquinolones		35	2/6
Neisseria gonorrhoea/ - vs 3rd gen. cephalosporins	Gonorrhoea	42	3/6

The high proportions of resistance to 3rd generation cephalosporins reported for *E. coli* and *K. pneumoniae* means that treatment of severe infections likely to be caused by these bacteria in many settings must rely on carbapenems, the last-resort to treat severe community and hospital acquired infections. These antibacterials are more expensive, may not be available in resource-constrained settings, and are also likely to further accelerate development of resistance. Of great concern is the fact that *K. pneumoniae* resistant also to carbapenems has been identified in most of the countries that provided data, with proportions of resistance up to 54% reported. The large gaps in knowledge of the situation in many parts of the world further add to this concern. For *E. coli*, the high reported resistance to fluoroquinolones means limitations to available oral treatment for conditions which are common in the community, such as urinary tract infections.

High rates of MRSA imply that treatment for suspected or verified severe *S. aureus* infections, such as common skin and wound infections, must rely on second-line drugs in many countries, and that standard prophylaxis with first-line drugs for orthopaedic and other surgical procedures will have limited effect in many settings. Second-line drugs for *S. aureus* are more expensive; also, they have severe side-effects for which monitoring during treatment is advisable, increasing costs even further.

Reduced susceptibility to penicillin was detected in *S. pneumoniae* in all WHO regions, and exceeded 50% in some reports. The extent of the problem and its impact on patients is not completely clear because of variation in how the reduced susceptibility or resistance to penicillin is reported, and limited comparability of laboratory standards. Because invasive pneumococcal disease (e.g. pneumonia and meningitis) is a common and serious disease in children and elderly people, better monitoring of this resistance is urgently needed.

The resistance to fluoroquinolones among two of the major causes for bacterial diarrhoea, nontyphoidal *Salmonella* (NTS) and *Shigella species* were comparatively lower than in *E. coli*. However, there were considerable gaps in information on these two bacteria, particularly from areas where they are of major public health importance. Some reports of high resistance in NTS are of great concern because resistant strains have been associated with worse patient outcomes.

In *N. gonorrhoeae*, finally, decreased susceptibility to third-generation cephalosporins, the treatment of last resort for gonorrhoea, has been verified in 36 countries and is a growing problem. Surveillance is of poor quality in countries with high disease rates, where there is also a lack of reliable resistance data for gonorrhoea, and where the extent of spread of resistant gonococci may be high.

Health and economic burden due to ABR

Evidence related to the health and economic burden due to ABR in infections caused by *E. coli, K. pneumoniae* and MRSA was examined through systematic reviews of the scientific literature. Patients with infections caused by bacteria resistant to a specific antibacterial drug generally have an increased risk of worse clinical outcomes and death, and consume more health-care resources, than patients infected with the same bacteria not demonstrating the resistance pattern in question. Available data are insufficient to estimate the wider societal impact and economic implications when effective treatment for an infection is completely lost as a result of resistance to all available drugs.

AMR in disease-specific programmes

Tuberculosis

Globally, 3.6% of new TB cases and 20.2% of previously treated cases are estimated to have multidrug-resistant TB (MDR-TB), with much higher rates in Eastern Europe and central Asia. Despite recent progress in the detection and treatment of MDR-TB, the 84 000 cases of MDR-TB notified to WHO in 2012 represented only about 21% of the MDR-TB cases estimated to have emerged in the world that year. Among MDR-TB patients who started treatment in 2010, only 48% (range 46%–56% across WHO regions) were cured after completion of treatment (with 25% lost to follow-up). The treatment success rate was lower among extensively drug-resistant (XDR-TB) cases.

Malaria

Surveillance of antimalarial drug efficacy is critical for the early detection of antimalarial drug resistance, because resistance cannot be detected with routine laboratory procedures. Foci of either suspected or confirmed artemisinin resistance have been identified in Cambodia, Myanmar, Thailand and Viet Nam. Further spread of artemisinin-resistant strains, or the independent emergence of artemisinin resistance in other regions, could jeopardize important recent gains in malaria control.

HIV

HIV drug resistance is strongly associated with failure to achieve suppression of viral replication and thus with increased risk for disease progression. Data collected between 2004 and 2010 in low- and middle-income countries showed increasing levels of transmitted anti-HIV drug resistance among those starting antiretroviral treatment (ART). Available data suggest that 10%–17% of patients without prior ART in Australia, Europe, Japan and the United States of America (USA) are infected with virus resistant to at least one antiretroviral drug.

Influenza

Over the past 10 years, antiviral drugs have become important tools for treatment of epidemic and pandemic influenza, and several countries have developed national guidance on their use and have stockpiled the drugs for pandemic preparedness. However, widespread resistance to adamantanes in currently circulating A(H1N1) and A(H3N2) viruses have left neuraminidase inhibitors as the antiviral agents recommended for influenza prevention and treatment. Although the frequency of oseltamivir resistance in currently circulating A(H1N1)pdm09 viruses is low (1%–2%), the emergence and rapid global spread in 2007/2008 of oseltamivir resistance in the former seasonal A(H1N1) viruses has increased the need for global antiviral resistance surveillance.

AMR in other related areas

Antibacterial resistance in food-producing animals and the food chain

Major gaps exist in surveillance and data sharing related to the emergence of ABR in foodborne bacteria and its potential impact on both animal and human health. Surveillance is hampered by a lack of harmonized global standards. The multisectoral approach needed to contain ABR includes improved integrated surveillance of ABR in bacteria carried by food-producing animals and in the food chain, and prompt sharing of data. Integrated surveillance systems would enable comparison of data from food-producing animals, food products and humans.

Resistance in systemic candidiasis

Systemic candidiasis is a common fungal infection worldwide and associated with high rates of morbidity and mortality in certain groups of patients. Although it is known that antifungal resistance imposes a substantial burden on health-care systems in industrialized countries, the global burden of antifungal-resistant *Candida* is unknown. Resistance to fluconazole, a common antifungal drug, varies widely by country and species. Resistance to the newest class of antifungal agents, the echinocandins, is already emerging in some countries.

Next steps

This report shows major gaps in ABR surveillance, and the urgent need to strengthen collaboration on global AMR surveillance. WHO will therefore facilitate:

- development of tools and standards for harmonized surveillance of ABR in humans, and for integrating that surveillance with surveillance of ABR in food-producing animals and the food chain;

- elaboration of strategies for population-based surveillance of AMR and its health and economic impact; and

- collaboration between AMR surveillance networks and centres to create or strengthen coordinated regional and global surveillance.

AMR is a global health security threat that requires concerted cross-sectional action by governments and society as a whole. Surveillance that generates reliable data is the essential basis of sound global strategies and public health actions to contain AMR, and is urgently needed around the world.

Acknowledgements

We wish to acknowledge staff in all sites performing resistance surveillance; the aggregated results from this surveillance have formed the basis for the report, without which the report would not have been possible.

Collecting and compiling data for this report

Abubakar Abdinasir, David Agyapong, Norazah Ahmad, Yacoub Ould Ahmedou, Arjana Tambic Andrasevic, Honoré Bankole, Christina Bareja, Raquel de Bolaños, Michael Borg, Golubinka Bosevska, Mina Brajovic, Eka Buadromo, Lula Budiak, Manuela Caniça, Celia Carlos, Rosa Sacsaquispe Contreras, Francis Kasolo, Paul Chun Soo, Silviu Ciobanu, Bruno Coignard, Alex Costa, Robert Cunney, Mbary Daba, Nicole Makaya Dangui, Sabine De Greeff, Nerisse Dominguez, Gabriela El Belazi, Mona El-Shokry, Ian Fisher, Belen Aracil Garcia, Eikhan Gasimov, Gayane Ghukasyan, Matt Goossens, Gilbert Guifar, Lincoln Charimari Gwinji, Antti Hakanen, Helen Heffernan, Ole Heuer, Masoumi Asl Hossein, Simsek Husnive, Marina Ivanova, Aurelia Juncq-Attal, Vladimir Jakubu, Al Saman Mohammed Redha Jameela, Carolina Janson, Zora Jelesic, Atek Kagirita, Agha Khaldoun, Baktygul Kambaralieva, Todor Kantardjev, Lonkululeko Khumalo, Lisa Kohler, Yonwoon Kook, Karl Kristinsson, Andreas Kronenberg, Paul Lalita, Kyunwon Lee, Young-Seon Lee, Barbro Liljequist, Eltaib Lina, Jorge Matheu, Jolanta Miciuleviciene, Kentse Moakofhi, Márta Melles, Serifo Meoteiro, Vasil Milo, Li Mingzhou, Issack Mohammad, Dominique Monnet, Karen Nahapetyan, Saskia Nahrgang, Prenesh Naicker, Jarour Hamed Najwa, Christine Ndjabera, Ines Noll, Manuel Neyra, Milan Nikš, Stefan Schytte Olsen, Fandi Osman, Emile Ouedraogo, Annalisa Pantosti, Boris Pavlin, Monique Perrin-Weniger, Uili Peseta, Despo Pieridou-Bagatzouni, Abdur Rashid, Grace E. B. Saguti, Aboubacar Savane, Rasmané Semde, Roxana Serban, Keigo Shibayama, Noikaseumsy Sithivong, Peter Ngalama Songolo, Gianfranco Spiteri, Jeremy Sobel, Al Busaidy Mohamed Suleiman, Johanna Takkinen, Maha Talaat, Israel Tareke, Seth Theoty, Jens Thomsen, Leonid Titov, Teweia Toatu, Sok Touch, Marija Trkov, Litia Tudravu, Marita Van de Laar, Alkiviadis Vatopoulos, Sirenda Vong, Haruro Watanabe, Nicole Werner-Keiss, Therese Westrell, Zhang Xaixing, Xiao Yonghong, Dorota Zabicka, Khatuna Zakhashvili, Sekesai Zinyowera, Frank Zongo.

We also acknowledge additional contributors, focal points and coordinators not listed above providing data for the surveillance networks coordinated by the ECDC (European Centre for Disease Prevention and Control) – EARS-Net (European Antimicrobial Resistance Surveillance Network), FWD-Net (Foodborne and Waterborne Diseases and Zoonoses Network) and EURO-GASP (the European Gonococcal Antimicrobial Surveillance Programme).

The following institutions participating in the networks coordinated by PAHO/AMRO (Pan American Health Organization/WHO Regional Office for the Americas) – ReLAVRA (Latin American Antimicrobial Resistance Surveillance Network) and SIREVA (Sistema de Redes de Vigilancia de los Agentes Responsables de Neumonías y Meningitis Bacterianas) – Carlos G. Malbrán, ANLIS INEI (Administración Nacional de Laboratorios e Institutos de Salud, Instituto Nacional de Enfermedades Infecciosas) Buenos Aires, Argentina; Instituto Nacional de Laboratorios en Salud, Bolivia, Insitituto Adolfo Lutz, Sao Paulo, Brasil; CARA (Canadian Antimicrobial Resistance Alliance), Instituto de Salud Pública, Chile; Instituto Nacional de Salud, Colombia; Instituto Costarricense de Investigación y Enseñanza en Nutrición y Salud, Costa Rica; IPK (Insitituto de Medicina Tropical, Pedro Kouri), La Habana, Cuba; LNS-PDD (Laboratorio Nacional de Salud Pública), Dominican Republic; Instituto Nacional de Salud Pública e Investigación (INSPI), Ecuador; Laboratorio Central, Doctor Max Bloch, El Salvador; ECDC; Laboratorio Nacional de Salud, Guatemala; Laboratorio Nacional de Vigilancia, Doctor Alenjandro Lara, Tegucigalpa D.C Honduras; Instituto de Diagnóstico y Referencia Epidemiológicos, Maxico; CNDR MINSA (Centro Nacional de Diagnostico y renferencia, Ministerio de Salud), Managua, Nicaragua; Laboratorio de Salud Pública, Instituto Conmemorativo Gorgas LCRSP, Panama; Laboratorio Centralde Salud Pública, Paraguay; Instituto Nacional de Salud, Lima, Peru; Office of Antimicrobial Resistance, US Centers for Disease Control and Prevention, United States of America; Instituto Nacional de Higiene, Caracas, Venezuela. Finally, contributors, focal points and coordinators of the international networks ANSORP (Asian Network for Surveillance of Resistant Pathogens) and RusNet, and additional staff in the WHO Country Offices who provided support in the collection of data for this report are acknowledged.

Written contributions

Cecile Torp Anderson, Veli-Jukka Anttila, Maiken Cavling Arendrup, Lena Ros Asmundsdottir, Jhoney Barcarolo, Amy Barette, Silvia Bertagnolio, Terry Gail Besselaar, Arunaloke Chakrabarti, Sharon Chen, Tom Chiller, Anuradha Chowdhary, Angela Ahlquist Cleveland, Arnaldo L. Colombo, Renu Drager, Matthew Falagas, Joveria Farooqi, Cornelia Lass Forl, Peter Gaustad, Nelesh Govender, Christopher Kibbler, Shawn Lockhart, Olivier Lortholary, Ali Mafi, Gérard Moulin, Marcio Nucci,

Patrick Otto, Mike Phaller, Jean-Baptiste Ronat, Aparna Sing Shah, Jong Hee Shin, Shunji Takakura, Anna Martia Tortorano, Magnus Unemo, Teodora Wi, Danilo Lo-Fo Wong, Ali Yahaya

Systematic reviews of burden of resistance

William Cameron, Li Chen, Shannon Kelly, Karen Lee, Meghan Murphy, Joan Peterson, Vijay Shukla, Leigh-Ann Topfer, George A Wells

Medical information and library support

Tomas Allen

Maps Section 2

Katarina Hayek, Florence Rusciano

Review Group

Benedetta Allegranzi, Otto Cars, Liselotte Diaz-Högberg, Sergey Eremin, Washif Khan, Roman Kozlov, Stewart B Levy, Thomas O'Brien, Wantana Pawenkittiporn, Jean Patel, Wing-Hong Seto, Betuel Siguaque, Gunnar Skov Simonsen, Constanza Vallenas, Timothy Walsh, Neil Woodford, Kathleen Young

Developer group and co-authors

Frank Møller Aarestrup, Awa Aidara-Kane, Nienke van de Sande-Bruinsma, Dennis Falzon, Hajo Grundmann, Monica Lahra, Elizabeth Mathai, Manjula Lusti-Narasimhan, Christopher Oxenford, Pilar Ramon Pardo, Pascal Ringwald, Anuj Sharma, John Stelling, Krisantha Weerasuriya, Matteo Zignol

Executive group

Charles Penn, Carmem Pessoa da Silva, Paul Rogers, Johan Struwe

Editing

Hilary Cadman, Lindsay Martinez

Financial support

The Governments of Japan and Sweden

Declaration of Interest (DoI) from experts contributing to the WHO global report on AMR surveillance

DoI forms were submitted by all external experts invited to contribute or to review the report. In the context of the scope of the work to be performed, none of the interest declared were regarded as of sufficient significance to impede the contribution of any expert to the work performed. A summary of the interests declared by the named individuals, the further information received upon follow-up and the outcome of the assessment of acceptability of the individual to contribute to the report development is available on request.

Abbreviations

ABR	antibacterial resistance
AGISAR	Advisory Group on Integrated Surveillance of Antimicrobial Resistance
AMR	antimicrobial resistance
ANSORP	Asian Network for Surveillance of Resistant Pathogens
AST	antibacterial susceptibility testing
CA-MRSA	community-acquired MRSA
CAESAR	Central Asian and Eastern European Surveillance of Antimicrobial Resistance
CC	Collaborating Centre
CDC	US Centers for Disease Control and Prevention
CI	confidence interval
CIPARS	Canadian Integrated Program for Antimicrobial Resistance Surveillance
DALY	disability-adjusted life years
DR-TB	drug-resistant TB
DST	drug susceptibility testing
ECDC	European Centre for Disease Prevention and Control
EARS-Net	European Antimicrobial Resistance Surveillance Network
EFSA	European Food Safety Authority
ESBL	extended spectrum beta-lactamase
ESCMID	European Society of Clinical Microbiology and Infectious Diseases
EQA	external quality assessment
EU	European Union
FAO	Food and Agriculture Organization of the United Nations
FWD-Net	Foodborne and Waterborne Diseases and Zoonoses Network
GASP	Gonococcal Antimicrobial Surveillance Programme
GFN	Global Foodborne Infections Network
GISP	Gonococcal Isolate Surveillance Project
GRASP	Gonococcal Resistance to Antimicrobials Surveillance Programme
ICU	intensive care unit
IDSR	Integrated Disease Surveillance and Response
LOS	length of stay
MD	mean difference
MDR-TB	multidrug-resistant TB
MIC	minimum inhibitory concentration
MRSA	methicillin-resistant *Staphylococcus aureus*
MSSA	methicillin-susceptible *Staphylococcus aureus*
NICD	National Institute for Communicable Diseases
NRL	national reference laboratory

NS	non-susceptible
NTS	nontyphoid *Salmonella*
OIE	World Organisation for Animal Health
PBP	penicillin-binding protein
PICO	population, intervention, comparison, outcome
ReLAVRA	Latin American Antimicrobial Resistance Surveillance Network
RR	relative risk
SA	*Staphylococcus aureus*
SIREVA	Sistema de Redes de Vigilancia de los Agentes Responsables de Neumonías y Meningitis Bacterianas (System of Networks for Surveillance of the Bacterial Agents Responsible for Pneumonia and Meningitis)
SRL	supranational TB reference laboratory
TB	tuberculosis
WHA	World Health Assembly
WHD	World Health Day
WHO	World Health Organization
XDR	extensively drug-resistant (TB)

WHO regions and regional offices

AFR/AFRO	African Region/Regional Office
AMR/AMRO[a]	Region of the Americas/Regional Office
EMR/EMRO	Eastern Mediterranean Region/Regional Office
EUR/EURO	European Region/Regional Office
PAHO	Pan American Health Organization
SEAR/SEARO	South-East Asia Region/Regional Office
WPR/WPRO	Western Pacific Region/ Regional Office

---

[a] The Pan American Sanitary Conference and the Directing Council of the Pan American Health Organization (PAHO) simultaneously serve as the WHO Regional Committee for the Americas, except when the Conference or the Council is considering matters relating to PAHO's Constitution, PAHO's juridical relations with WHO or the Organization of American States, or other questions relating to PAHO's role as an inter-American specialized organization.

Introduction

For several decades antimicrobial resistance (AMR) has been a growing threat to the effective treatment of an ever-increasing range of infections caused by bacteria, parasites, viruses and fungi. AMR results in reduced efficacy of antibacterial, antiparasitic, antiviral and antifungal drugs, making the treatment of patients difficult, costly, or even impossible. The impact on particularly vulnerable patients is most obvious, resulting in prolonged illness and increased mortality. The magnitude of the problem worldwide and the impact of AMR on human health, and on costs for the health-care sector and the wider societal impact, are still largely unknown.

Some estimates of the economic effects of AMR have been attempted, and the findings are disturbing. For example, the yearly cost to the US health system alone has been estimated at US $21 to $34 billion dollars, accompanied by more than 8 million additional days in hospital. Because AMR has effects far beyond the health sector, it was projected, nearly 10 years ago, to cause a fall in real gross domestic product (GDP) of 0.4% to 1.6%, which translates into many billions of today's dollars globally.

AMR is a complex global public health challenge, and no single or simple strategy will suffice to fully contain the emergence and spread of infectious organisms that become resistant to the available antimicrobial drugs. The development of AMR is a natural phenomenon in microorganisms, and is accelerated by the selective pressure exerted by use and misuse of antimicrobial agents in humans and animals. The current lack of new antimicrobials on the horizon to replace those that become ineffective brings added urgency to the need to protect the efficacy of existing drugs.

The development and implementation of effective strategies to curtail the emergence and spread of AMR, and to evaluate the effect of interventions to do so, depend on the collection of accurate representative information on the extent of the problem and its impact. WHO has for many years promoted the global monitoring of AMR and taken steps to raise awareness of the impending public health crisis it will cause. Among a range of WHO initiatives, in 2001 the *Global strategy for containment of antimicrobial resistance (1)* was published, and AMR was the focus of World Health Day in 2011 when a 6-point AMR policy package was issued (*2*). The World Health Assembly, through several resolutions over the years, has called for intensified implementation of the global strategy, stressing the need for strengthened surveillance of AMR and enhanced laboratory capacity to carry it out, and reduction in the inappropriate use of antimicrobial drugs. The capacity to perform antimicrobial susceptibility testing, which can inform surveillance of AMR, also falls within the scope of the *International Health Regulations (3)*, which stipulate the requirement for access by States Parties to capacity for investigation of any disease outbreak that may represent an international public health threat.

Many gaps remain in the efforts to contain AMR. Many diverse bacterial, viral, fungal and parasitic pathogens show resistance, and for some specific diseases (e.g. tuberculosis [TB], HIV, influenza and malaria) there are programmes in place that address resistance, and many of the most immediate and urgent concerns relate to antibiotic resistance in common bacteria. Antibacterial resistance (ABR)[a] involves bacteria that cause many common and life-threatening infections acquired in hospitals and in the community, for which treatment is becoming difficult, or in some cases impossible. Despite the importance of these infections, there are major gaps in information concerning the extent, spread, evolution and impact of ABR. Urgency is added in particular by the lack of new therapeutic options in the development pipeline to replace those that lose their efficacy as bacteria become resistant to them. Thus, the main focus of this report is on ABR, for which knowledge, support and concerted action are inadequate.

Although ABR surveillance has been undertaken for many years in a number of high-income countries, there are still large gaps in knowledge about the status of ABR surveillance capacities worldwide, particularly in resource-limited settings. This report attempts to map ABR surveillance status in Member States, and specifically the availability of data from national official sources.

This is the first attempt by WHO to assemble the accessible information on national ABR surveillance and on ABR data for a set of common pathogenic bacteria, in order to present an analysis of the global situation as it appeared in 2013, together with an examination of the evidence base concerning the health and economic impact of ABR. The information gathered highlights the strengths and weaknesses in both the collection of data and the quality of data collected in Member States, and demonstrates the need for further effort and investment.

In addition to gathering information on ABR surveillance and ABR occurrence, the report also summarizes the situation in major disease-specific control programmes (i.e. HIV, influenza, malaria and TB) and in related fields (i.e. foodborne and fungal infections).

---

[a] Although *Mycobacterium tuberculosis*, the main cause of tuberculosis, is also a bacterium, it has specific features and is described separately in Section 4.1.

The report has the following structure and specific focus:

- **Section I** gives an overview of ABR surveillance in the different WHO regions.

- **Section 2** examines the availability and status of resistance data in Member States for a set of common bacteria of importance to global public health.

- **Section 3** examines the available evidence concerning the health and economic burden due to ABR in a subset of the selected bacteria, based on a systematic review of the scientific literature.

- **Section 4** provides summaries of surveillance and the status of AMR in TB, malaria, HIV and influenza.

- **Section 5** summarizes key issues in surveillance and AMR in foodborne pathogens and fungal infections.

- **Section 6** discusses the main findings from the data and information assembled for the report (noting the main gaps in knowledge), and considers directions for future work in this field.

- **Annexes 1–3** provide:

  - a description of the methods used to obtain data;

  - all of the collected data and sources of information for each of the selected bacteria, country by country in each WHO region; and

  - a detailed technical report on the systematic review of the evidence on health and economic burden due to ABR.

- **Appendices 1–3** provide:

  - the questionnaires used to obtain data on resistance;

  - the available WHO tools to facilitate surveillance of ABR;

  - the list of *International statistical classification of diseases and related health problems* (ICD) codes related to ABR; and

  - a description of some international ABR surveillance networks.

For this first report, for which no common agreed methodology for surveillance of ABR existed, it was not feasible to compare the accuracy of the submitted data. Nonetheless, despite gaps and other shortcomings, the data do give at least an indication of the current worldwide status of ABR at country level. The report also establishes a baseline against which progress in strengthening global surveillance capacities and standards can be measured. It is important to note that the national data on ABR have been compiled for the purpose of a situation analysis of global surveillance, rather than as a basis for decisions on clinical care of patients, for which standard treatment guidelines should be followed.

The report is intended to provide information primarily for public health policy-makers and managers, and for the wider medical and public health community (including pharmaceutical companies), as a support for informing strategic actions and programme planning. It will also be of interest to the other sectors that are directly involved, including veterinary drug and animal husbandry, agriculture and aquaculture.

References

1. *Global strategy for containment of antimicrobial resistance*. Geneva, World Health Organization, 2001. (http://www.who.int/drugresistance/WHO_Global_Strategy_English.pdf, accessed 3 January 2014).

2. *World Health Day policy briefs*. Geneva, World Health Organization, 2011. (http://www.who.int/world-health-day/2011/policybriefs/en/index.html, accessed 27 December 2013).

3. *International Health Regulations*. Geneva, World Health Organization, 2005. (http://www.who.int/ihr/9789241596664/en/index.html, accessed 3 January 2014).

SECTION
01

Resistance to antibacterial drugs

1.1 Background

For more than 60 years, antibacterial drugs[a] have been regarded as the panacea to cure infections, whether or not their use is appropriate, and whether the infection was acquired in the community or in the hospital setting. Already in his Nobel Prize speech in 1945, Alexander Fleming, who discovered penicillin, warned that bacteria could become resistant to these remarkable drugs. Indeed, the development of each new antibacterial drug has been followed by the detection of resistance to it. The development of resistance is a normal evolutionary process for microorganisms, but it is accelerated by the selective pressure exerted by widespread use of antibacterial drugs. Resistant strains are able to propagate and spread where there is non-compliance with infection prevention and control measures.

Use of antibacterial drugs has become widespread over several decades (although equitable access to antibacterial drugs is far from being available worldwide), and these drugs have been extensively misused in both humans and food-producing animals in ways that favour the selection and spread of resistant bacteria. Consequently, antibacterial drugs have become less effective or even ineffective, resulting in an accelerating global health security emergency that is rapidly outpacing available treatment options.

Until the 1970s, many new antibacterial drugs were developed to which most common pathogens were initially fully susceptible, but the last completely new classes of antibacterial drugs were discovered during the 1980s (Figure 1). It is essential to preserve the efficacy of existing drugs through measures to minimize the development and spread of resistance to them, while efforts to develop new treatment options proceed.

Figure 1 Dates of discovery of distinct classes of antibacterial drugs

Illustration of the "discovery void." Dates indicated are those of reported initial discovery or patent.

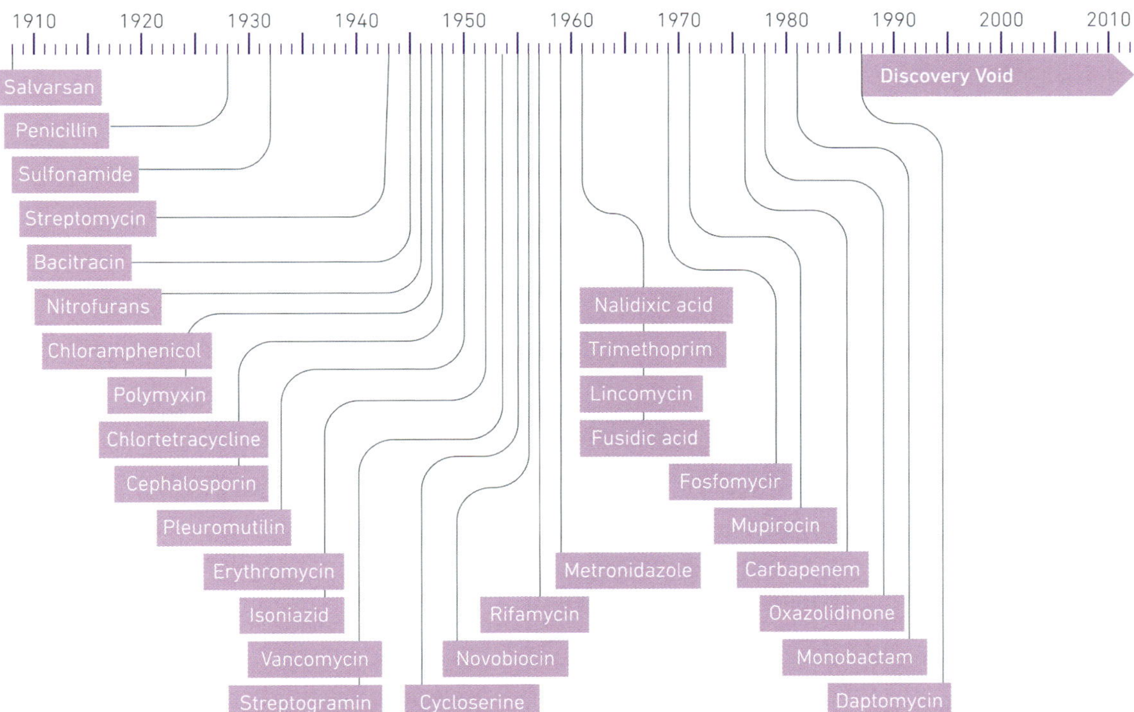

Adapted from Silver 2011 (1) with permission of the American Society of Microbiology Journals Department.

---

[a] Antibacterial drugs act against bacteria and include antibiotics (natural substances produced by microorganisms), and antibacterial medicines, produced by chemical synthesis.

Greater emphasis should be placed on prevention, including strengthening hygiene and infection prevention and control measures, improving sanitation and access to clean water, and exploring a more widespread use of vaccines. Although preventive vaccines have become available for several bacterial infections, their application is still limited.

The pipeline for the development of new antibacterial drugs is now virtually empty, particularly for the treatment of Gram-negative enteric bacteria,[a] and research on treatments to replace antibacterial drugs is still in the early stages. Situations are increasingly arising where bacteria that are resistant to most, or even all, available antibacterial drugs are causing serious infections that were readily treatable until recently. This means that progress in modern medicine, which relies on the availability of effective antibacterial drugs, is now at risk, as exemplified in the following situations:

- Common community-acquired infections such as pneumonia, which used to be readily treatable after the introduction of penicillin, may not respond to available or recommended drugs in many settings, putting the lives of patients at risk.

- Cystitis, one of the most common of all bacterial infections in women, which readily responded to oral treatment in the past, may need to be treated by injected drugs, imposing additional costs for patients and health systems, or become untreatable.

- Common infections in neonatal and intensive care are increasingly becoming extremely difficult, and sometimes impossible, to treat.

- Patients receiving cancer treatment, organ transplants and other advanced therapies are particularly vulnerable to infection. When treatment of an infection fails in such patients, the infection is likely to become life-threatening and may be fatal.

- Antibacterial drugs used to prevent postoperative surgical site infections have become less effective or ineffective.

Major gaps in data on the extent of ABR, and on the types and number of infections caused by bacteria that have become resistant to antibacterial drugs, make it impossible to estimate precisely the global prevalence and impact of the problem. Nevertheless, it is abundantly clear that together, the burden of morbidity and mortality resulting from ABR in many infections and settings has serious consequences for individuals and society in terms of clinical outcomes and added costs.

The collection of reliable information about the ABR situation through well-conducted surveillance is essential to inform strategies and prioritize

interventions to tackle the problem. ABR surveillance should generate data to support action at all levels: local, national, regional and global. Countries with appropriate surveillance systems have the ability to:

- obtain national information on the magnitude and trends in resistance;

- detect emerging problems;

- follow the effect of interventions and countermeasures;

- inform treatment guidelines, decision-making and a research agenda;

- collect information on the public health burden of ABR; and

- participate in international networks for data sharing and monitoring of trends to inform global strategies.

1.1.1 Limitations

This report describes the current situation of ABR surveillance and ABR rates for selected types of bacterial resistance worldwide. The ABR rates presented in this report include a compilation of the available data as reported by countries and surveillance programmes, and in scientific journal articles. The priority was to obtain data from national official sources, such as reports or other compilations at the national level at ministries of health, national reference laboratories, public health institutes or other sources identified by WHO. When data from national official sources were not available or were available in sample sizes that were too small (i.e. fewer than 30 isolates tested), other sources (i.e. non-official networks and scientific journal articles) were sought. The search of scientific journal articles as a complementary source was not intended as a full review of all available publications. Despite the attempt at standardized data collection (methodology described in Annex 1), the compilation of data from various sources proved challenging in this first report.

Given the lack of agreed global standards for ABR surveillance, the reported proportions of resistance should be interpreted with caution. The discrepancies in performance and interpretation of laboratory findings can be such that bacteria considered resistant in one laboratory could be classified as susceptible if tested in another laboratory. The resistance proportions should therefore be regarded as indicators, rather than measures, of the proportion of ABR as it is perceived where the data originate, according to prevailing methodology and the population sampled.

Data from national sources and publications are presented in this report as they were received or obtained from the data source. It was beyond the scope of the report to assess the validity and representativeness of the data. Data from some Member States may not have been obtained for this

---

[a] For example, intestinal bacteria such as *Escherichia coli* and *Klebsiella*, and environmental opportunistic bacteria such as *Pseudomonas* and *Acinetobacter*

report, despite being available at subnational or local levels.

Caution is necessary in interpreting the available data. Limited and skewed patient samples, particularly from hospital patients, are not likely to be representative of the general situation, and could lead to overestimation of the overall resistance problem among all patients in the population. This situation may influence clinicians to make greater use of broad-spectrum antibacterial drugs than is warranted, which in turn will accelerate the emergence and spread of resistance, and add to treatment costs. Therefore, the data presented in this report should not be used to inform local treatment protocols.

The proportions of resistant bacteria are determined based on results from antibacterial susceptibility testing (AST). The methodologies addressing molecular aspects of ABR are not available in most settings. Thus, despite its importance in understanding how bacterial populations and genetic elements spread, molecular epidemiology data has not been included in this report.

The data obtained for this report reveal limitations with regard to heterogeneity of methodology used by the various sources and to representativeness and quality assurance, but nevertheless provide useful insight into the current global status of ABR and surveillance gaps, creating a basis to inform further developments in this field.

1.2 Regional surveillance of antibacterial resistance

1.2.1 WHO African Region

Information concerning the true extent of the problem of AMR in the African Region is limited because surveillance of drug resistance is carried out in only a few countries. There is a scarcity of accurate and reliable data on AMR in general, and on ABR in particular, for many common and serious infectious conditions that are important for public health in the region, such as meningitis, pneumonia and bloodstream infections.

The WHO Member States endorsed the Integrated Disease Surveillance and Response (IDSR) strategy in 1998. Effective implementation of IDSR is a way to strengthen networks of public health laboratories, and thus contribute to effective monitoring of AMR. However, a recent external quality assessment of public health laboratories in Africa revealed weakness in antimicrobial susceptibility testing in many countries (2).

Faced with multiple dimensions of the ABR threat to public health, some countries have established national and regional surveillance collaborations. However, there is no formal framework for collaboration among surveillance programmes across the region. The lack of a regional framework for collaborative surveillance of ABR, with no collection and sharing of information between networks of laboratories, hampers efforts to track and contain the emergence of resistant organisms, and to systematically evaluate trends and resistance-containment activities in the region.

Despite limited laboratory capacity to monitor ABR, available data indicate that the African Region shares the worldwide trend of increasing drug resistance. Significant resistance has been reported for several bacteria that are likely to be transmissible not only in hospitals but also in the community.

To contribute to the improvement of surveillance of ABR at country level, the WHO Regional Office for Africa (AFRO) recently published a guide to facilitate the establishment of laboratory-based surveillance for priority bacterial diseases in the region (3). Collection, sharing and regular dissemination of data can be used by public health policy-makers to regularly update the national AMR policy as necessary.

1.2.2 WHO Region of the Americas

ReLAVRA, the Latin American Antimicrobial Resistance Surveillance Network, was created in 1996 and is led by the WHO Regional Office for the Americas/Pan American Health Organization (AMRO/PAHO), in order to collect aggregated data provided by national reference laboratories (NRLs). At that time, the network involved eight NRLs in the region. The countries agreed to maintain and support the NRLs, which compile information on the identification of the bacterial species isolated and their susceptibility to antibacterial drugs. Also, the NRLs verify the application of the principles of quality assurance in laboratories participating in the national network, and are responsible for performance evaluation. An external quality control programme for the network is carried out by two centres, in Argentina and Canada. Currently, NRLs from 19 countries in Latin America plus Canada and the USA are part of the network. English-speaking Caribbean countries are invited to share their data but do not yet participate directly in the network.

ReLAVRA has increased its ability to detect, monitor and manage data on ABR, based on the growing number of countries participating in the network. As an example, 72 000 bacterial isolates were analysed in 2000, and more than 150 000 in 2010. This increase in the number of isolates studied is due in large part to isolates of hospital origin, reflecting the progressive incorporation of hospitals into the network. More information on the origin of the samples, and their distribution, would enable better assessment of their representativeness.

Coordination by a single agency, AMRO/PAHO, which standardizes the systems for data collection and the use of external quality assurance processes for the network members, has been an important strength of the network. Surveillance protocols are aligned with the WHO recommendations for diarrhoeal disease and respiratory tract infections. The antibacterials selected for the susceptibility tests include those recommended by WHO.

ReLAVRA has not only strengthened national laboratory networks, it has also generated data for decision-making (4); for example, for informing guidelines on the empirical use of antibacterial drugs.

The Sistema de Redes de Vigilancia de los Agentes Responsables de Neumonias y Meningitis Bacterianas – SIREVA II (5) – is a network in Latin America that was initiated by AMRO/PAHO in 1993 to provide a regional monitoring programme for important bacteria causing pneumonia and meningitis. The network is built on sentinel hospitals and laboratories that provide:

- data on serotype distribution and antibacterial susceptibility for *Streptococcus pneumoniae*, *Haemophilus influenzae* and *Neisseria meningitidis*; and

- epidemiological information for estimating the burden of these diseases and the development of increasingly efficient vaccines.

1.2.3 WHO Eastern Mediterranean Region

The collection of resistance information from disease-specific programmes (e.g. TB, HIV and malaria) is relatively advanced in the Eastern Mediterranean Region, but estimates of the magnitude of the wider problem associated with AMR, and the health and socioeconomic burden resulting from it, are hampered by the limited availability of reliable data. Nonetheless, reports and studies from some countries in the region show the geographically extensive emergence of ABR (see Section 2).

Preliminary results obtained through limited country situation analyses in the region have revealed several challenges that need to be tackled as a matter of urgency. Lack of robust functioning national ABR surveillance systems and lack of collaboration with the animal health sector means that insufficient evidence is available for policy-makers to set appropriate policies, strategies and plans to combat ABR. Other challenges include the absence of legislation or the lack of enforcement of laws (where they exist). In countries

currently experiencing complex humanitarian emergencies in the region, there is disruption of basic health services. This also impedes the response to AMR (including ABR) in the affected countries.

Mindful of the public health threats posed by the current trends in AMR, in 2002 and in 2013, the Eastern Mediterranean Regional Committee adopted resolutions addressing AMR (6, 7). However, due to the complexity of the efforts required to tackle AMR and the need to focus on other pressing priorities in the region, the response to the threat of AMR has remained fragmented.

1.2.4 WHO European Region

Currently, most countries of the European Union (EU) have well-established national and international surveillance systems for AMR, whereas countries in other parts of the European Region require strengthening or establishment of such systems. The WHO Regional Office for Europe (EURO) has been supporting these Member States in this endeavour.

The European Antimicrobial Resistance Surveillance Network – EARS-Net (8) – is an international surveillance system that includes all 28 EU countries plus Iceland and Norway. EARS-Net is currently coordinated by the European Centre for Disease Prevention and Control (ECDC). The network includes surveillance of antibacterial susceptibility of eight indicator pathogens causing bloodstream infections and meningitis; it also monitors variations in AMR over time and place. The standardized data collected in EARS-Net have formed the basis for drawing maps of the situation of resistance in the indicator bacteria across Europe in the network's annual report. These maps have been much appreciated and stimulated action to contain AMR in participating countries (9).

The Central Asian and Eastern European Surveillance of Antimicrobial Resistance – CAESAR (10) – is a new joint initiative of EURO, the European Society of Clinical Microbiology and Infectious Diseases (ESCMID) and The Dutch National Institute for Public Health and the Environment (RIVM). The aim is to support all countries of the region that are not part of EARS-Net to develop a network of national surveillance systems for ABR. This initiative strives to enable countries to strengthen AMR epidemiology, as well as laboratory capacity and quality. To facilitate comparison of data throughout the entire European Region, the methodology used in CAESAR adopts the EARS-Net methodology, with the work carried out in close collaboration with ECDC.

The Foodborne and Waterborne Diseases and Zoonoses Network – FWD-Net (11) – is a European network coordinated by the ECDC. AMR data are collected for foodborne bacteria, such as *Salmonella* and *Shigella*, as part of the network's surveillance activities. The data are published annually in a joint report by the ECDC and the European Food Safety Authority (EFSA) on AMR in zoonotic and indicator bacteria from humans, animals and food products in the EU (*12*).

1.2.5 WHO South-East Asia Region

Systematic efforts to collect data on the epidemiology of antimicrobial resistance have not yet been undertaken in the South-East Asia Region. However, information and data available for selected diseases and organisms reveal that AMR is a burgeoning and often neglected problem.

In 2011, the health ministers of the region's Member States articulated their commitment to combat AMR through the Jaipur Declaration on AMR (*13*). Since then, there has been growing awareness throughout the region that containment of AMR depends on coordinated interventions, including appropriate surveillance of drug resistance. All 11 Member States (6 of which already have national systems in place) have agreed to contribute information for a regional database and to participate in a regional consultative process. A more detailed description of the present situation in each country is available in a report from a recent regional workshop (*14*).

1.2.6 WHO Western Pacific Region

In the 1980s, 14 Member States in the Western Pacific Region agreed to share AMR findings for more than 20 key hospital and community pathogens on an annual basis, and annual reports were compiled and distributed to network participants. Unfortunately, the collaboration was interrupted because of a series of other emergencies in the early 2000s. A summary of the experience (*15*) concluded that "*the data reviewed for the Report... reveal serious problems and worsening trends in antimicrobial resistance in various nations of the Region*". Many of the contributing Member States actively used the data and, despite the loss of coordination activities, have continued to develop ABR surveillance at a national level. Recently, the WHO Regional Office for the Western Pacific (WPRO) has taken steps to revive surveillance of AMR in the region.

Most high-income countries in the region have long-established systems for routine surveillance of ABR (including quality assurance), at least in health-care settings, that provide some form of national oversight. There are also links to national and local policies, especially the development of standard treatment guidelines. However, even in some of these high-income countries there are gaps in geographic coverage and lack of surveillance in community settings. Among upper middle-income countries, some have younger AMR surveillance programmes of similar quality to those in most high-income countries, with similar (but larger) gaps. In all these countries there is a high level of technical expertise, which provides an excellent opportunity for further development and collaboration. In the lower middle-income countries there is greater variation in the level and quality of surveillance. The quality of AST may be uncertain in some countries, whereas others have operated fairly extensive and high-quality sentinel AMR surveillance programmes for decades. Some Pacific Island countries face particular challenges given the low sample numbers, lack of human resources and geographic remoteness.

1.3 References

1.	Silver LL. Challenges of antibacterial discovery. *Clin Microbiol Rev*, 2011, 24(1):71-109. doi:10.1128/CMR.00030-10.

2.	Frean J, Perovic O, Fensham V, McCarthy K, von Gottberg A, de Gouveia L et al. External quality assessment of national public health laboratories in Africa, 2002-2009. *Bull WHO*, 2012, 90(3):191-199A. doi:10.2471/BLT.11.091876.

3.	*Guide for establishing laboratory-based surveillance for antimicrobial resistance*. Disease surveillance and response programme area disease prevention and control cluster, Brazzaville, Africa, World Health Organization Regional Office for Africa, 2013. (http://apps.who.int/medicinedocs/documents/s20135en/s20135en.pdf, accessed 2 December 2013).

4.	PAHO. Statistics and maps. Pan American Health Organization. (http://www.paho.org/hq/index.php?option=com_content&view=article&id=8956&Itemid=4335&lang=en, accessed 16 October 2013).

5.	*SIREVA II (Sistema de Redes de Vigilancia de los Agentes Responsables de Neumonias y Meningitis Bacterianas)*. Geneva, World Health Organization, 2013. (http://www.paho.org/hq/index.php?option=com_content&view=category&layout=blog&id=3609&Itemid=3953&lang=pt, accessed 6 December 2013).

6.	*Resolution EM/RC60/R.1*. Regional committee for the Eastern Mediterranean Region, 2013.

7.	*Resolution EM/RC49/R.10 Antimicrobial resistance and rational use of antimicrobial agents*. Regional committee for the Eastern Mediterranean Region, 2001.

8. Antimicrobial resistance interactive database (EARS-Net). European Centre for Disease Prevention and Control, 2013. (http://www.ecdc.europa.eu/en/healthtopics/antimicrobial_resistance/database/Pages/database.aspx, accessed 18 October 2013).

9. *Antimicrobial resistance surveillance in Europe 2012*. European Centre for Disease Prevention and Control, 2012. (http://ecdc.europa.eu/en/publications/Publications/antimicrobial-resistance-surveillance-europe-2012.pdf, accessed 8 April 2014).

10. *Central Asian and Eastern European Surveillance on Antimicrobial Resistance (CAESAR)*. World Health Organization. (http://www.euro.who.int/en/health-topics/disease-prevention/antimicrobial-resistance/antimicrobial-resistance/central-asian-and-eastern-european-surveillance-on-antimicrobial-resistance-caesar, accessed 2 December 2013).

11. Food- and Waterborne Diseases and Zoonoses Programme. European Centre for Disease Prevention and Control (ECDC), 2013. (http://ecdc.europa.eu/en/activities/diseaseprogrammes/fwd/Pages/index.aspx, accessed 29 December 2013).

12. European Food Safety Authority, European Centre for Disease Prevention and Control. The European Union Summary Report on antimicrobial resistance in zoonotic and indicator bacteria from humans, animals and food in 2012. *EFSA Journal*, 2014;12(3):3590. (http://ecdc.europa.eu/en/publications/Publications/antimicrobial-resistance-in-zoonotic-and-indicator-bacteria-summary-report-2012.pdf, accessed 8 April 2014).

13. *Jaipur declaration on antimicrobial resistance*. World Health Organization, 2011. (http://www.searo.who.int/entity/world_health_day/media/2011/whd-11_amr_jaipur_declaration_.pdf, accessed 16 October 2013).

14. *Laboratory based surveillance of antimicrobial resistance*. Report of regional workshop, Chennai, India, World Health Organization Regional Office for South-East Asia, 2013. (http://www.searo.who.int/entity/antimicrobial_resistance/sea_cd_273.pdf, accessed 16 October 2013).

15. *Surveillance of antimicrobial resistance: Western Pacific Region – ten years experience and future directions*. Geneva, World Health Organization Regional Office for the Western Pacific, 2002. (http://apps.who.int/medicinedocs/en/d/Js16877e/, accessed 9 April 2014).

SECTION
02

Resistance to antibacterial drugs in selected bacteria of international concern

For this first WHO report on the global status of ABR and surveillance, information was compiled on resistance to antibacterial drugs commonly used to treat infections caused by nine bacteria of international concern.

- *Escherichia coli*: resistance to third-generation cephalosporins, including resistance conferred by extended spectrum beta-lactamases (ESBLs), and to fluoroquinolones;

- *Klebsiella pneumoniae*: resistance to third-generation cephalosporins, including resistance conferred by ESBLs, and to carbapenems;

- *Staphylococcus aureus:* resistance to beta-lactam antibacterial drugs (methicillin, methicillin-resistant *S. aureus* [MRSA]);

- *Streptococcus pneumoniae*: resistance or non-susceptibility to penicillin (or both);

- Nontyphoidal *Salmonella* (NTS): resistance to fluoroquinolones;

- *Shigella* species: resistance to fluoroquinolones;

- *Neisseria gonorrhoeae:* decreased susceptibility to third-generation cephalosporins.

These types of ABR have a significant public health impact worldwide because they are common etiologies for hospital or community-acquired infections, or both.

A detailed description of the methodology for the data collection is available in Annex 1. In summary, data were collected from the following sources:

- national official sources, such as reports or other compilations at the national level at ministries of health, national reference laboratories, public health institutes or other sources identified by WHO;

- national and international networks for ABR surveillance (if data from national official sources were not available or available in too low sample size; i.e. < 30 isolates tested); and

- scientific journal articles published from 2008 (when data from above sources were not available or available in too low sample size; i.e. < 30 isolates tested).

This section summarizes the main results of the data collection. The details of data obtained are provided in Annex 2.

Interpretation of the data summarized in this report should take account of its precision and representativeness, including the following considerations:

- There is no general agreement on how many bacterial isolates should be tested in order to present a reasonably accurate figure of the resistance proportion. However, the minimum number of tested isolates considered sufficient to present reported proportions of resistance in this section was arbitrarily set at 30.

- The origin of samples is usually skewed towards severely ill hospitalized patients, whose condition did not respond to first-line treatment. This imbalance will generally result in higher proportions of resistance in the collected samples than would be found for a broader, more representative sample of patients in the population.

- Some of the published studies, particularly those on S. *pneumoniae* and MRSA, are based on sampling of healthy carriers without symptoms, which further adds to difficulties in interpretation of public health impact and comparison of resistance proportions.

- It is known that differences exist in the methodology and quality in performance of AST in different countries and regions, which will limit the comparability of results across the various data sources.

2.1 Availability of national resistance data

A response including data, or information that no national data were available, was returned from 129 of the 194 WHO Member States (66%). Of these, 114 provided some data for at least one bacteria–antibacterial drug-resistance combination, as shown in Table 1 and Figure 2.

Table 1 **Information from returned questionnaires, or other sources, on availability of national data on resistance for the requested nine bacteria–antibacterial drug resistance combinations**

	WHO region						Total
	AFR	AMR/ PAHO[a]	EMR	EUR[a]	SEAR	WPR	
No. of Member States returning information (%)	27/47 (57%)	21/35 (60%)	11/21 (52%)	42/53 (79%)	9/11 (82%)	19/27 (70%)	129/194 (66%)
Returned data set(s)/ no. of Member States (%)	23/47 (49%)	21/35 (60%)	7/21 (32%)	38/53 (74%)	6/11 (55%)	19/27 (70%)	114/194 (59%)
Responded "No national data available"	4	–	4	4	3[b]	0[c]	15
No information obtained for this report	20	14	10	11	2	8	65

AFR, African Region; AMR/PAHO; Region of the Americas/Pan American Health Organization; EMR, Eastern Mediterranean Region; EUR, European Region; SEAR, South-East Asia Region; WPR; Western Pacific Region.

a. To avoid duplicate data collection, ECDC, European Centre for Disease Prevention and Control and AMRO forwarded data already collected in their existing surveillance networks.

b. One country responded there was no national data compilation but still returned data.

c. Two countries responded there was no national data compilation but still returned data.

Figure 2 **Availability of data on resistance for selected bacteria–antibacterial drug combinations, 2013**

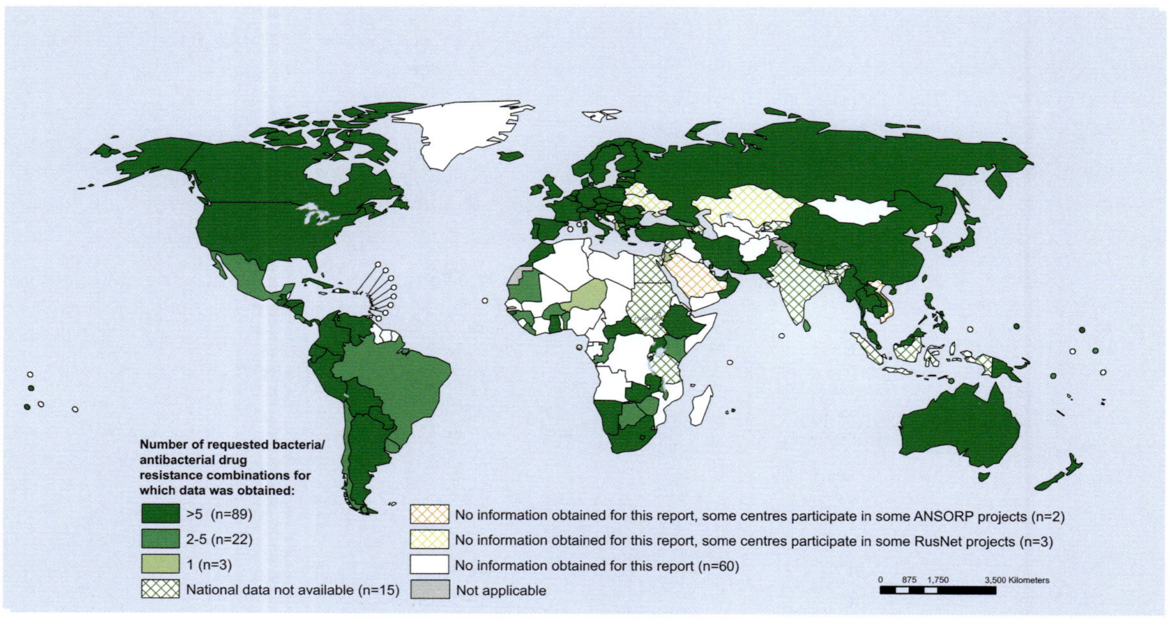

Number of reported bacteria is based on the information obtained based on request to national official sources on antibacterial susceptibility testing of at least one of the requested combinations, regardless of denominator data.
Data from United Arab Emirates originate from Abu Dhabi only.

Table 2 shows that the overall proportion of data sets obtained from national official sources for each bacteria–antibacterial drug combination based on at least 30 tested bacterial isolates was 79%. This proportion ranged from 56% to 92% across the regions, and between 56% and 90% for the different bacteria–antibacterial drug resistance combinations.

Table 2 **Overview of data sets obtained on request to national official sources that included information on at least 1 of the 9 selected bacteria–antibacterial drug resistance combinations based on testing of at least 30 isolates**

	For each bacteria–antibacterial drug-resistance combination[a]: no. of returned data sets[b] based on at least 30 tested isolates/total no. of data sets for each requested combination[c]						
	AFR	AMR/ PAHO	EMR	EUR	SEAR	WPR	Total no. of reports with data sets based on ≥30 tested isolates
E. coli/ 3rd generation cephalosporins[d]	13/19	14/15	5/7	35/36	5/5	14/19	86/101 (85%)
E. coli/ fluoroquinolones[e]	14/19	16/16	5/7	35/35	5/5	17/20	92/102 (90%)
K. pneumoniae/ 3rd generation cephalosporins	13/16	17/17	5/7	33/37	4/5	15/17	87/99 (88%)
K. pneumoniae/ carbapenems[f]	4/7	17/17	5/7	31/35	4/5	10/12	71/83 (86%)
Methicillin-resistant *S. aureus* (MRSA)	9/15	15/17	5/7	36/37	3/4	17/19	85/99 (86%)
S. pneumoniae non-susceptible or resistant to penicillin	5/14	15/21	3/5	31/35	2/5	11/18	67/97 (69%)
Nontyphoidal *Salmonella/* fluoroquinolones	9/19	13/20	4/5	29/30	2/4	11/13	68/91 (75%)
Shigella species/ fluoroquinolones	4/12	14/19	2/3	10/12	0/2	5/9	35/57 (61%)
N. gonorrhoeae/ 3rd generation cephalosporins	2/10	4/12	2/3	17/22	5/7	12/21	42/75 (56%)
Total no. of reports with data sets based on ≥30 tested isolates	73/131 (56%)	125/154 (81%)	36/51 (71%)	257/279 (92%)	30/42 (71%)	112/147 (76%)	Total 636/805 (79%)

AFR, African Region; AMR/PAHO, Region of the Americas/Pan American Health Organization; EDCD, European Centre for Disease Prevention and Control; EMR, Eastern Mediterranean Region; EUR, European Region; SEAR, South-East Asia Region; WPR; Western Pacific Region.

a. Not all countries returned information for all combinations.
b. To avoid duplicate data collection, ECDC and AMRO/PAHO forwarded data already collected in their existing surveillance networks.
c. From countries providing several data sets, one per country and data with highest denominator is included in this table.
d. 3rd generation cephalosporins mentioned in obtained national data are ciprofloxacin; gatifloxacin; levofloxacin; moxifloxacin; norfloxacin; ofloxacin; pefloxacin; refloxacin and sparfloxacin.
e. Fluoroquinolones mentioned in obtained national data are ciprofloxacin, norfloxacin or ofloxacin.
f. Carbapenems mentioned in obtained national data are imipenem, meropenem, doripenem or ertapenem.

Data based on small sample sizes increase the uncertainty of the results. The gaps in data may be indicative of the difficulties in gathering information for this first global report, as well as insufficient capacity in the health systems. Limited health-system capacity may result in insufficiencies in sampling of patients, laboratory capacity for analysis, compilation of results at the laboratory level or collection of aggregated data from laboratories at the national level, as well as other priorities or difficulties. These factors will vary between countries.

2.1.1 Key messages

- Of the 194 Member States, 129 (66%) returned information for the survey forming the basis for this report on national surveillance data. Of these, 114 Member States returned some data on at least one of the requested bacteria–antibacterial drug resistance combinations.

- There is wide variability in the availability of information on ABR at national level, and considerable gaps remain in the capacity of a substantial number of countries to produce national data based on testing of sufficient isolates to obtain reasonably reliable figures for the sampled population.

- The largest gaps in the obtained data were seen in Africa, the Middle East and EUR Member States outside the EU.

2.2 Resistance data on specific pathogens

2.2.1 *Escherichia coli* – resistance to third-generation cephalosporins and to fluoroquinolones

E. coli is part of the normal flora in the intestine in humans and animals. Nevertheless it is:

- the most frequent cause of community and hospital-acquired urinary tract infections (including infections of the kidney);

- the most frequent cause of bloodstream infection at all ages;

- associated with intra-abdominal infections such as peritonitis, and with skin and soft tissue infections due to multiple microorganisms;

- a cause of meningitis in neonates; and

- one of the leading causative agents of foodborne infections worldwide.

Infections with *E. coli* usually originate from the person affected (auto-infection), but strains with a particular resistance or disease-causing properties can also be transmitted from animals, through the food chain or between individuals.

Evolution of antibacterial resistance in *Escherichia coli*

- Resistance in *E. coli* readily develops either through mutations, which is often the case for fluoroquinolone resistance, or by acquisition of mobile genetic elements, which has been the case for broad-spectrum penicillins (e.g. ampicillin or amoxicillin) and resistance to third-generation cephalosporins.

- Resistance to third-generation cephalosporins is mainly conferred by enzymes known as extended spectrum beta-lactamases (ESBLs); these enzymes destroy many beta-lactam antibacterial drugs. ESBLs are transmissible between bacteria and even between bacterial species. Because *E. coli* strains that have ESBL are generally also resistant to several other antibacterial drugs, carbapenems usually remain the only available treatment option for severe infections. A recently emerging threat is carbapenem resistance in *E. coli* mediated by metallo-beta-lactamases, which confers resistance to virtually all available beta-lactam antibacterial drugs.

- This report focuses on available data on proportions of *E. coli* resistant to third-generation cephalosporins, which are widely used for intravenous treatment of severe infections in hospitals, and to fluoroquinolones, which are among the most widely used oral antibacterial drugs in the community.

Resistance to third-generation cephalosporins in *Escherichia coli*

Figure 3 illustrates sources for obtained resistance data in countries according to the methods described in Annex 1.

Figure 3 Sources of data on *Escherichia coli*: Resistance to third-generation cephalosporins[a]

National data refers to requested data returned as described in the methods. The definition does not imply that the data collected are representative for that country as a whole because information gaps are likely. (For details on data see Tables A2.1–A2.6, Annex 2).
a. ceftazidim; cefotaxim; ceftriaxone

Data obtained from Member States are summarized by WHO region in Table 3. Details at country level are provided in Tables A2.1–A2.6, Annex 2.

Table 3 *Escherichia coli:* Resistance to third-generation cephalosporins[a] (summary of reported or published proportions of resistance, by WHO region)

Data sources based on at least 30 tested isolates[b]	Overall reported range of resistant proportion (%)	Reported range of resistant proportion (%) in invasive isolates[c] (no. of reports)
African Region		
– National data (n=13 countries)	2–70	28–36 (n=4)
– Publications (n=17) from 7 additional countries	0–87	0–17 (n=5)
Region of the Americas		
– National data or report to ReLAVRA (n=14 countries)	0–48	
– Publications (n=10) from 5 additional countries	0–68	
Eastern Mediterranean Region		
– National data (n=4 countries)	22–63	41 (n=1)
– Surveillance network in 1 country[d]	39 (caz)–50 (cro)	
– Publications (n=44) from 11 additional countries	2–94	11–33 (n=6)
European Region		
– National data or report to EARS-Net (n=35 countries)	3–82	3–43 (n=32)
– Publications (n=5) from 2 additional countries	0–8	0–8 (n=2)
South-East Asia Region		
– National data (n=5 countries)	16–68	
– Publications (n=26) from 2 additional countries	19–95	20–61 (n=2)
Western Pacific Region		
– National data (n=13 countries)	0–77	
– Institute surveillance (data from 3 hospitals in one country)	4–14	
– Publications (n=4) from 2 additional countries	8–71	

EARS-Net, European Antimicrobial Resistance Surveillance Network; ReLAVRA, Latin American Antimicrobial Resistance Surveillance Network. (For details see Annex 2, Tables A2.1–A2.6).
a. Based on antibacterial susceptibility testing with caz, ceftazidim; cefotaxim or cro, ceftriaxone
b. Reported proportions may vary between compound used for testing and some countries report data for several compounds, or data from more than one surveillance system.
c. Invasive isolates are deep infections, mostly bloodstream infections and meningitis.
d. US Naval Medical Research Unit No 3, Global Disease Detection Program, Egypt.

Resistance to fluoroquinolones in *Escherichia coli*

Figure 4 illustrates sources for obtained resistance data in the countries according to the methods in Annex 1. The major information gaps in national data for *E. coli* resistance to fluoroquinolones were similar to those found for resistance to third-generation cephalosporins.

Figure 4 **Sources of data on *Escherichia coli*: Resistance to fluoroquinolones[a]**

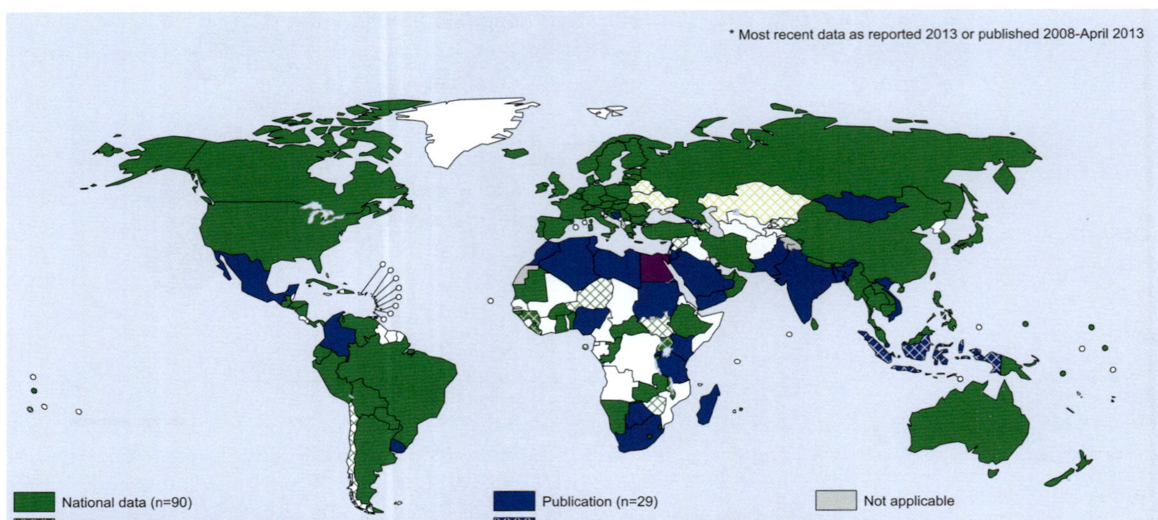

National data refers to requested data returned as described in the methods. The definition does not imply that the data collected are representative for that country as a whole because information gaps are likely. (For details on data see Tables A2.7–A2.12, Annex 2).

a. ciprofloxacin; gatifloxacin; levofloxacin; moxifloxacin; norfloxacin; ofloxacin; pefloxacin; refloxacin; sparfloxacin.

Data obtained from Member States are summarized by WHO region in Table 4, and details at country level are provided in Tables A2.7–A2.12, Annex 2.

Table 4 ***Escherichia coli*: Resistance to fluoroquinolones[a]**

Data sources based on at least 30 tested isolates[b]	Overall reported range of resistant proportion (%)	Reported range of resistant proportion (%) in invasive isolates[c] (no. of reports)
African Region – National data (n=14 countries) – Publications (n=23) from 8 additional countries	 14–71 0–98	 34–53 (n=2) 0–10 (n=4)
Region of the Americas – National data or report to ReLAVRA (n=16 countries) – Publications (n=5) from 4 additional countries	 8–58 2–60	
Eastern Mediterranean Region – National data (n=4 countries) – Surveillance network[d], one additional country – Publications (n=32) from 10 additional countries	 21–62 35 0–91	 54 (n=1) 15–53 (n=5)
European Region – National data or report to EARS-Net (n=35 countries) – Publications (n=3) from 2 additional countries	 8–48 0–18	 8–47 (n=33) 0–18 (n=2)
South-East Asia Region – National data (n=5 countries) – Publications (n=19) from 2 additional countries	 32–64 4–89	
Western Pacific Region – National data (n=16 countries) – Institute surveillance (data from 3 hospitals in 1 country) – Publications (n=5) from 3 additional counties	 3–96 0–14 0.2–65	 7 (n=1) 31 (n=1)

EARS-Net, European Antimicrobial Resistance Surveillance Network; ReLAVRA, Latin American Antimicrobial Resistance Surveillance Network (For details see Annex 2, Tables A2.7–A2.12).

a. Based on antibacterial susceptibility testing with ciprofloxacin, gatifloxacin, levofloxacin, moxifloxacin, norfloxacin, ofloxacin, pefloxacin, refloxacin or sparfloxacin. Where the fluoroquinolone was not specified, ciprofloxacin was used.

b. Reported proportions may vary between compound used for testing and some countries report data for several compounds, or data from more than one surveillance system.

c. Invasive isolates are deep infections, mostly bloodstream infections and meningitis.

d. US Naval Medical Research Unit No 3, Global Disease Detection Program, Egypt.

The reported resistance to fluoroquinolones generally seemed higher than for the third-generation cephalosporins. Similar to the resistance to the third-generation cephalosporins, there were reports of fluoroquinolone resistance in *E. coli* exceeding 50% in five of the WHO regions.

Public health implications

High reported proportions of resistance to third-generation cephalosporins means that treatment for severe infections, for which *E. coli* is a likely cause, may need to be initiated with broader therapy (e.g. carbapenems) in these populations. This implies higher costs and stimulus to the expansion of carbapenem-resistant strains. One review of community-acquired neonatal and infant sepsis in developing countries concluded that, because of resistance, a significant proportion of the causal bacteria were treatable neither by the recommended first-line regimen nor by alternative cephalosporin treatment (*1*).

Quinolones are probably one of the most widely used groups of antibacterial drugs for the treatment of urinary tract infections, of which *E. coli* is the most common cause. Resistance to quinolones may be indicative of resistance to one of the last available oral treatment options in some settings. Data need to be compiled on resistance to other oral antibacterial drugs not included in this report, but which may be useful to treat uncomplicated urinary tract infections (e.g. co-trimoxazole, nitrofurantoin and mecillinam). When oral alternatives are no longer available, treatment by injection may become necessary, with additional costs for the patients and the health systems.

The systematic reviews summarized in Section 3 specifically address the impact on health and economic burden of infections caused by *E. coli* resistant to third-generation cephalosporins and fluoroquinolones. They confirm that patients with infections caused by such resistant *E. coli* strains carry a risk of poorer clinical outcomes and consume more health-care resources than patients with infections by *E. coli* strains susceptible to third-generation cephalosporins or fluoroquinolones.

Key messages

- Data on *E. coli* resistance to third-generation cephalosporins were obtained from 86 (44%) of the Member States, and on resistance to fluoroquinolones from 92 (47%) of the Member States.

- The collection of reports and publications consistently disclosed high resistance rates to the last generation drugs commonly used to treat serious infections, and to oral drugs used for both community and hospital infections.

2.2.2 *Klebsiella pneumoniae* – resistance to third-generation cephalosporins and to carbapenems

Like *E. coli*, bacteria of the genus *Klebsiella* are frequent colonizers of the gut in humans and other vertebrates. Infections with *K. pneumoniae* are particularly common in hospitals among vulnerable individuals such as pre-term infants and patients with impaired immune systems, diabetes or alcohol-use disorders, and those receiving advanced medical care.

Most common are urinary and respiratory tract infections and, in neonates, bloodstream infections. *K. pneumoniae* is a common cause of Gram-negative bloodstream infections. The mortality rates for *K. pneumoniae* hospital-acquired pneumonia depend on the severity of the underlying condition, and can exceed 50% in vulnerable patients, even when treated with appropriate antibacterial drugs.

Like other bacteria in health-care settings *K. pneumoniae* can spread readily between patients, leading to nosocomial outbreaks. This frequently occurs in intensive care units (ITUs) and neonatal care facilities. Spread of *K. pneumoniae* among different hospitals and even across country borders through the transfer of infected or colonized patients has also been documented (*2*).

Evolution of antibacterial resistance in *Klebsiella pneumoniae*

Similar to *E. coli*, *K. pneumoniae* acquires resistance to multiple antibacterial drugs mainly through horizontal transfer of mobile genetic elements such as transposons or plasmids. In contrast to *E. coli*, *K. pneumoniae* carries a resistance gene (chromosomally located beta-lactamase) that naturally renders ineffective penicillins with an extended spectrum, such as ampicillin and amoxicillin. Resistance to other widely used and available oral antibacterial drugs such as co-trimoxazole and fluoroquinolones (e.g. ciprofloxacin) has emerged and spread globally. This means that there are few remaining options for oral treatment of *Klebsiella* infections in many parts of the world.

In 1982, the first ESBL was identified during a hospital outbreak *of K. pneumoniae* infections in Germany (*3*). Since then more than 200 ESBL variants have been identified, some of which have spread rapidly worldwide. Moreover, many ESBL variants initially identified in *K. pneumoniae* have subsequently transferred to *E. coli*. ESBL-positive strains are resistant to all extended beta-lactam antibacterial drugs such as cephalosporins and, for these strains, the carbapenems are the main remaining treatment option.

Section 2

K. pneumoniae is also the main cause of infections caused by carbapenem-resistant bacteria worldwide. All of the most important genes that can confer carbapenem resistance (via carbapenemases) are present in *K. pneumoniae*, thereby rendering almost all available treatment options ineffective. For many patients infected with these bacteria there are no clinically effective treatments.

Given the situation outlined above, this report focuses on resistance in *K. pneumoniae* to third-generation cephalosporins, which have been the standard intravenous treatment for severe *Klebsiella* infections in hospitals, and to carbapenems, which are the last option for treatment of severe infections when cephalosporins are no longer reliable due to a high proportion of ESBL-mediated resistance.

Resistance to third-generation cephalosporins

Figure 5 shows the sources of obtained resistance data in each country, and where major knowledge gaps exist on resistance proportions for *K. pneumoniae* resistant to third-generation cephalosporins.

Figure 5 Sources of data on *Klebsiella pneumoniae*: Resistance to third-generation cephalosporins[a]

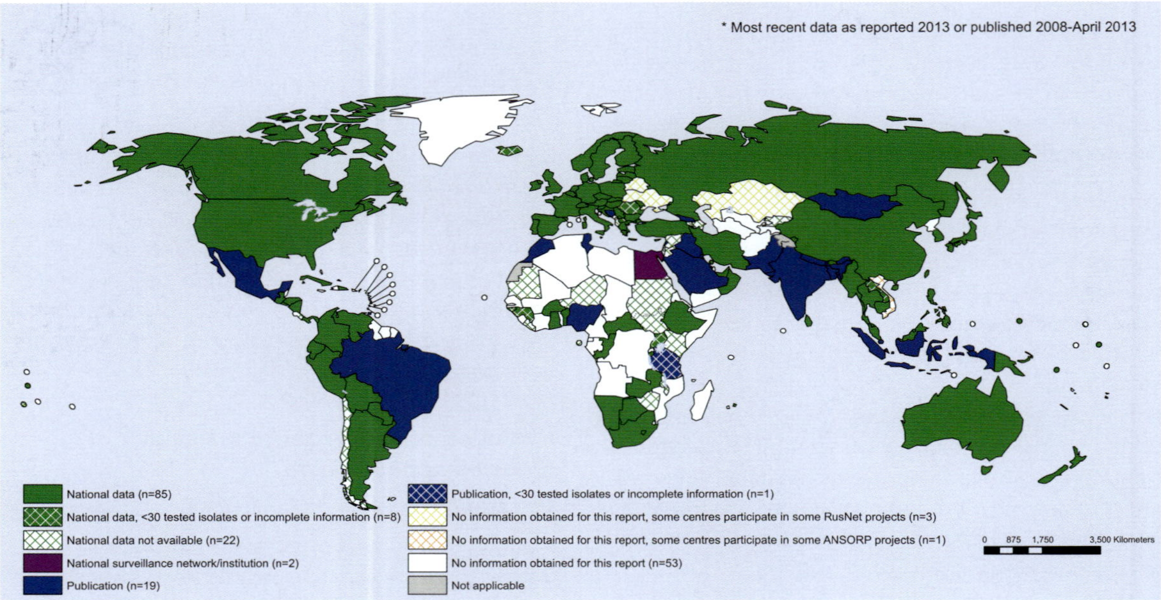

National data refers to requested data returned as described in the methods. The definition does not imply that the data collected are representative for that country as a whole because information gaps are likely. (For details on data see Tables A2.13–A2.18 Annex 2).
a. ceftazidim; cefotaxim; ceftriaxone

Data obtained from Member States are summarized by WHO region in Table 5 (see Tables A2.13–A2.18, Annex 2 for details).

Table 5 *Klebsiella pneumoniae:* **Resistance to third-generation cephalosporins[a] (summary of reported or published proportions of resistance, by WHO region)**

Data sources based on at least 30 tested isolates[b]	Overall reported range of resistant proportion (%)	Reported range of resistant proportion (%) in invasive isolates[c] (no. of reports)
African Region – National data (n=13 countries) – Publications (n=4) from 1 additional country	8–77 9–69	41–62 (n=3)
Region of the Americas – National data or report to ReLAVRA (n=17 countries) – Publications (n=3) from 3 additional countries	4–71 15–56	56 (n=1)
Eastern Mediterranean Region – National data (n=4 countries) – Surveillance network[d] (n=1) in 1 additional country – Publications (n=16) from 7 additional countries	22–50 72 (caz)–82 (cro) 6–75	48 (n=1) 17 (ctx); 43 (caz); 50 (cro) (n=1)
European Region – National data or report to EARS-Net (n=33 countries) – Publications (n=2) from 2 additional countries	2–82 4–61	2–82 (n=31) 11 (cro); 16 (ctx); 18 (caz) (n=1)
South-East Asia Region – National data (n=4 countries) – Publications (n=23) from 4 additional countries	34–81 5–100	53.3–100 (n=4)
Western Pacific Region – National data (n=14 countries) – Institute surveillance (data from 3 hospitals in 1 country) – Publications (n=3) from 2 additional countries	1–72 17–30 27–35	72 (n=1) 27 (n=1)

EARS-Net, European Antimicrobial Resistance Surveillance Network; ReLAVRA, Latin American Antimicrobial Resistance Surveillance Network.

a. caz, ceftazidim; ctx, cefotaxim; cro, ceftriaxone

b. Reported proportions may vary between compound used for testing and some countries report data for several compounds, or data from more than one surveillance system.

c. Invasive isolates are deep infections, mostly bloodstream infections and meningitis.

d. US Naval Medical Research Unit No 3, Global Disease Detection Program, Egypt.

Reported resistance proportions to third-generation cephalosporins were generally higher in *K. pneumoniae* than in *E. coli.* A majority of sources reported more than 30% resistance in *K. pneumoniae* to third-generation cephalosporins in the sampled populations (Annex 2, Tables A2.13–A2.18). Resistance proportions exceeding 50% were reported from all WHO regions.

Resistance to carbapenems

Compiled data on carbapenem resistance in *K. pneumoniae* (Figure 6) show knowledge gaps greater than for cephalosporin resistance in *K. pneumoniae.*

Figure 6 Sources of data on *Klebsiella pneumoniae*: Resistance to carbapenems[a]

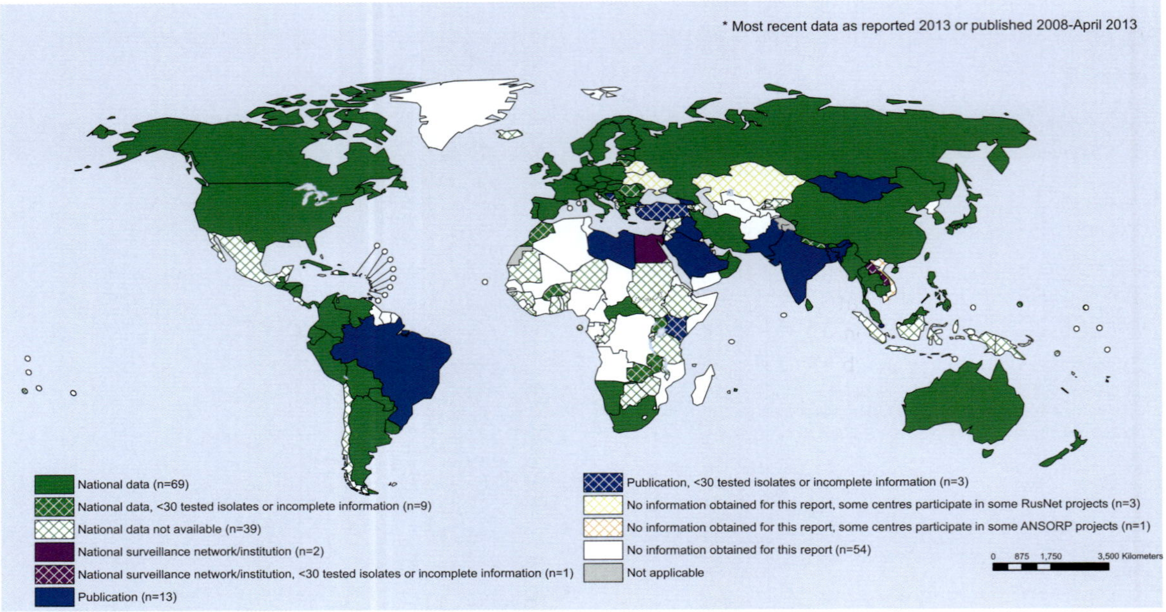

National data refers to requested data returned as described in the methods. The definition does not imply that the data collected are representative for that country as a whole because information gaps are likely. (For details on data see Tables A2.19–A2.24, Annex 2).

a. doripenem, ertapenem, imipenem, meropenem

Data obtained from Member States are summarized by WHO region in Table 6 (see Annex 2, Tables A2.19–A2.24 for details).

Table 6 *Klebsiella pneumoniae*: Resistance to carbapenems[a] (summary of reported or published proportions of resistance, by WHO region)

Data sources based on at least 30 tested isolates[b]	Overall reported range of resistant proportion (%)	Reported range of resistant proportion (%) in invasive isolates[c] (no. of reports)
African Region – National data (n=4 countries) – Publications (n=0)	0–4	
Region of the Americas – National data or report to ReLAVRA (n=17 countries) – Publications (n=2) from 2 additional countries	0–11 0–2	
Eastern Mediterranean Region – National data (n=4 countries) – Surveillance network[d] (n=1) in 1 additional country – Publications (n=9) from 5 additional countries	0–54 6 0–21	54 (n=1) 0 (n=1)
European Region – National data or report to EARS-Net (n=31 countries) – Publications (n=3) from 2 additional countries	0–68 2–7	0–68 (n=30) 2 (n=1)
South-East Asia Region – National data (n=4 countries) – Publications (n=15) from 2 additional countries	0–8 0–55	 0–52 (n=3)
Western Pacific Region – National data (n=9 countries) – Institute surveillance (data from 2 hospitals in 1 country) – Publications (n=2) from 2 additional countries	0–8 0–1 0–11	

EARS-Net, European Antimicrobial Resistance Surveillance Network; PAHO, Pan American Health Organization; ReLAVRA, Latin American Antimicrobial Resistance Surveillance Network.

a. Based on antibacterial susceptibility testing with doripenem, ertapenem, imipenem or meropenem

b. Reported proportions may vary between compound used for testing and some countries report data for several compounds, or data from more than one surveillance system.

c. Invasive isolates are deep infections, mostly bloodstream infections and meningitis.

d. US Naval Medical Research Unit No 3, Global Disease Detection Program, Egypt.

As can be seen in the table, carbapenem-resistant *K. pneumoniae* has now been reported in all WHO regions, with reports in two regions exceeding 50%. There are gaps in information in most WHO regions, because 49 of the 69 datasets came from countries in the Region of the Americas and the European Region.

Public health implications

As for *E. coli* resistant to third-generation cephalosporins, the high proportions of cephalosporin resistance means that treatment for verified or suspected severe *K. pneumoniae* infections in many situations has to rely on carbapenems, if available. This usually involves higher costs and a risk of further expansion of carbapenem-resistant strains. At the same time, and as for *E. coli*, there is a risk that findings based on limited series of skewed patient groups may lead to unnecessarily high usage of broad-spectrum antibacterial drugs, which will exacerbate the resistance problem. Of even greater concern is that infections with carbapenem-resistant strains need to be treated with the last-resort drugs tigecycline or colistin, which are not only less effective but also not widely available.

The systematic review summarized in Section 3 addressed the impact on health and economic burden due to infections caused by *K. pneumoniae* resistant to third-generation cephalosporins and carbapenems. The review confirms that patients with such resistant *K. pneumoniae* infections carry a risk of worse clinical outcomes and consume more health-care resources than patients infected by susceptible strains.

Key messages

- Data on resistance to third-generation cephalosporins were obtained from 87 (45%) of the Member States, and on carbapenem resistance from 71 (37%) of the Member States. Most of the reporting countries are in two WHO regions – Region of the Americas and the European Region – revealing large gaps in knowledge in most parts of the world (including in several non-EU countries in the European Region).

- A majority of sources reported more than 30% resistance in *K. pneumoniae* against third-generation cephalosporins, and some countries more than 60%.

- Alarming rates of carbapenem resistance – exceeding 50% – have been reported in *K. pneumoniae* in some patient groups, for which few if any alternative treatment options are available.

2.2.3 *Staphylococcus aureus* – resistance to methicillin

S. aureus is a Gram-positive bacterium that can be a part of the normal flora on the skin and in the nose, but is another of the most important human pathogens. *S. aureus* can cause a variety of infections, most notably skin, soft tissue, bone and bloodstream infections. It is also the most common cause of postoperative wound infections. Some strains of *S. aureus* produce toxic factors that can cause a variety of specific symptoms, including toxic shock syndrome and food poisoning.

Evolution of antibacterial resistance in *Staphylococcus aureus*

When penicillin was first introduced it was an effective treatment for *S. aureus* infections, but resistance had already developed during the 1940s. This resistance was mediated by the production of a beta-lactamase enzyme that inactivates drugs such as penicillin, ampicillin and amoxicillin. Consequently, beta-lactamase-stable drugs (e.g. methicillin and cloxacillin) as well as beta-lactamase inhibitors (e.g. clavulanic acid and sulbactam) that could be combined with the antibacterial drugs were developed. Strains of *S. aureus* resistant to these penicillinase-stable antibacterial drugs have acquired a novel gene (mecA) that codes for a novel penicillin-binding protein; these strains are termed methicillin-resistant *Staphylococcus aureus* (MRSA).

The first strains of MRSA emerged during the 1960s. Initially, MRSA was mainly a problem in hospital-acquired infections. Over the past decade, community-acquired MRSA has increased significantly in a number of countries. Fortunately, many of these community-acquired MRSA strains have so far retained susceptibility to a number of non-beta-lactam antimicrobials, whereas most health-care associated MRSA infections are caused by difficult-to-treat multiresistant strains. For the latter, the treatment of last resort has been glycopeptides such as vancomycin (since the 1950s) and teicoplanin, which can only be given by injection and also needs careful monitoring to avoid adverse side-effects. New treatment options for MRSA (but also associated with problematic side-effects) have been developed more recently: linezolid (1970s) and daptomycin (1980s) are the most recently licensed antibacterial drug classes.

Section 2

Methicillin resistance in *Staphylococcus aureus*

Figure 7 shows the sources of resistance data in each country according to the methods in Annex 1, and the major knowledge gaps for MRSA proportions in *S. aureus*, based on the data available for this report.

Figure 7 **Sources of data on *Staphylococcus aureus*: Resistance to beta-lactam antibacterial drugs (i.e. methicillin-resistant *S. aureus*, MRSA)**

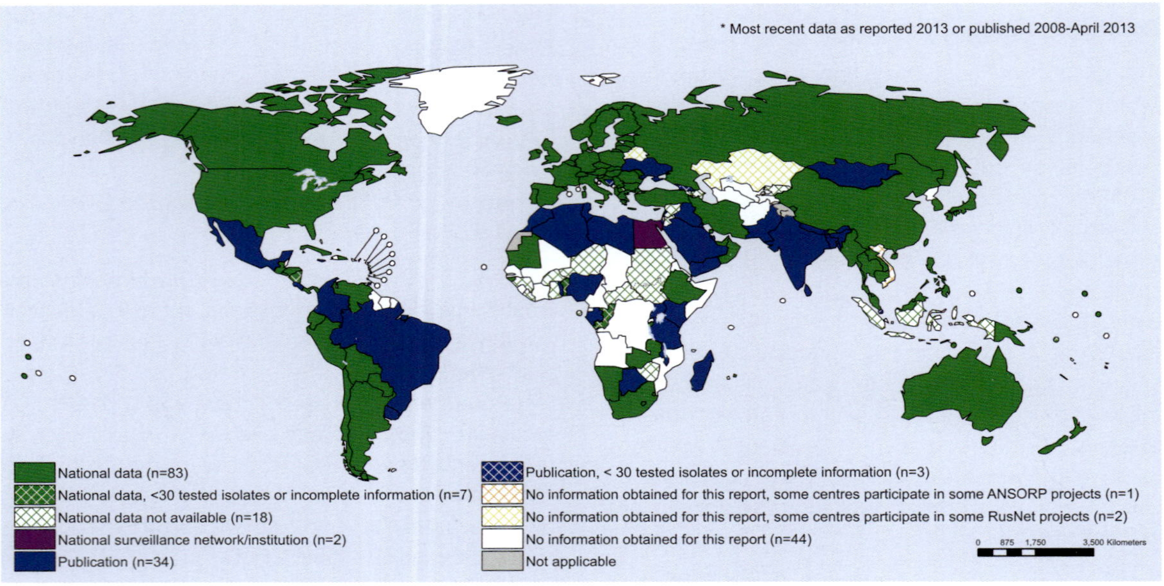

National data refers to requested data returned as described in the methods. The definition does not imply that the data collected are representative for that country as a whole because information gaps are likely. (For details on data see Tables A2.25–A2.30, Annex 2).

Data obtained from Member States are summarized by WHO region in Table 7. Details at the country level are in Annex 2, Tables A2.25–A2.30.

Table 7 *Staphylococcus aureus:* Resistance to beta-lactam antibacterial drugs (i.e. methicillin-resistant *S. aureus*, MRSA)

Data sources based on at least 30 tested isolates[a]	Overall reported range of resistant proportion (%)	Reported range of resistant proportion (%) in invasive isolates[b] (no. of reports)
African Region – National data (n=9 countries) – Publications (n=27) from 10 additional countries	 12–80 0–100	 52 (n=1) 33–95 (n=3)
Region of the Americas – National data or report to ReLAVRA (n=15 countries) – National networks (n=2) no additional country – Publications (n=17) from 7 additional countries	 21–90 21–84 2.4–90	 43–45 (n=2)
Eastern Mediterranean Region – National data (n=4 countries) – Hospital network[c] (n=1) from 1 additional country – Publications (n=31) from 10 additional countries	 10–53 46 0–92	 53 (n=1) 13–18 (n=3)
European Region – National data or report to EARS-Net n=36 countries) – Publications (n=5) from 2 additional countries	 0.3–60 27–80	 0.3–6 (n=32) 27–50 (n=3)
South-East Asia Region – National reports (n=3 countries) – Publications (n=25) from 4 additional countries	 10–26 2–81	 37 (n=1)
Western Pacific Region – National data (n=16 countries) – Institute surveillance (n=2 from one additional country) – Publications (n=1) from one additional country	 4–84 1–4 60	

EARS-Net; European Antimicrobial Resistance Surveillance Network; ReLAVRA, Latin American Antimicrobial Resistance Surveillance Network.
a. Some countries report data from more than one surveillance system.
b. Invasive isolates are deep infections, mostly bloodstream infections and meningitis.
c. US Naval Medical Research Unit No 3, Global Disease Detection Program, Egypt.

Public health implications

The implication of high reported proportions of MRSA is that treatment for suspected or verified *S. aureus* infections in many countries may require second-line antibacterials. This may also be the case for prophylaxis in orthopaedic and many other surgical procedures. Second-line drugs needed to treat or prevent MRSA infections are more expensive and, because of their side-effects, monitoring during treatment is advisable. As for the other bacteria, however, there is a risk that empiric treatment recommendations based on small and skewed patient samples may lead to an unnecessary overuse of more expensive second-line drugs.

The systematic reviews summarized in Section 3 address the impact on health and economic burden from infections caused by MRSA. The available evidence discloses a clear increase in mortality and use of health-care resources, and therefore additional costs, associated with MRSA.

Key messages

- Data on MRSA proportions among *S. aureus* were obtained from 85 (44%) of the Member States.

- Most reported MRSA proportions exceed 20% in all WHO regions, and even exceed 80% in some reports.

- High MRSA proportions imply increased risk for patients and a need for second-line more toxic drug treatment. This will increase costs and side-effects, and may drive resistance further in staphylococci or other species (or both).

2.2.4 *Streptococcus pneumoniae* – resistance (non-susceptibility) to penicillin

S. pneumoniae (the bacteria are also known as pneumococcl) is the leading cause worldwide of community-acquired pneumonia, which is among the main killers of children under 5 years of age. Other diseases caused by *S. pneumoniae* include common mild, self-limiting infections such as acute otitis media, but also extend to cases of invasive disease with high mortality such as meningitis. Among the bacterial causes of meningitis, *S. pneumoniae* is associated with the highest case–fatality rate and is the most likely to leave survivors with permanent residual symptoms.

The clinical burden of pneumococcal infection is concentrated among the eldest and youngest sections of the population. According to one estimate, *S. pneumoniae* caused about 826 000 deaths (582 000—926 000) in children aged 1—59 months. For HIV-negative children pneumococcal infection corresponds to 11% of all deaths in this age group (4). Pneumococci are commonly found in asymptomatic nasopharyngeal carriage, where the prevalence varies by age and region. The asymptomatic carriage state is responsible for much of the transmission within populations, such as day-care centres.

Evolution of antibacterial resistance in *Streptococcus pneumoniae*

Resistance to beta-lactam antibacterial drugs in clinical isolates of *S. pneumoniae* occurs through the acquisition of mutations in the genes coding for the penicillin-binding proteins (PBPs), essential components of the bacterial cell wall. The successive acquisition of multiple mutations in the different PBPs results in increasing minimum inhibitory concentrations (MICs) for penicillin and the other beta-lactam drugs. The methodology needed to detect this gradual increased resistance and characterize as "non-susceptible" (NS) or "resistant" (R) is different; thus, it is reported differently from different sources, depending on the capacity the sources have.

As for the other bacteria considered in this report, some particularly successful strains have emerged and rapidly spread worldwide.

Resistance and reduced susceptibility to penicillin in *Streptococcus pneumoniae*

Figure 8 shows the sources of collected data on non-susceptibility or resistance to penicillin in *S. pneumoniae* in each country, and that there were larger gaps in the available resistance data for this typically community-acquired pathogen, compared to the bacteria–antibacterial drug combinations described previously.

Figure 8 **Sources of data on *Streptococcus pneumoniae*: Resistance or non-susceptibility to penicillin**

National data refers to requested data returned as described in the methods. The definition does not imply that the data collected are representative for that country as a whole because information gaps are likely. (For details on data see Tables A2.31–A2.36, Annex 2).

Data obtained from Member States are summarized by WHO region in Table 8. Details at the country level are in Annex 2, Tables A2.31–A2.36.

Table 8 ***Streptococcus pneumoniae*: Resistance or non-susceptibility to penicillin**

Data sources based on at least 30 tested isolates	Overall reported range of proportion resistant (R) and/or non-susceptible (NS)	Reported range of proportion resistant or non-susceptible in invasive isolates[a] (no. of reports)
African Region – National data (n=5 countries) – Publications (n=16) from 14 additional countries	3–16 (R) or 57–60 (NS) 1–100 (R) or 9–69 NS or 0–79 [b]	3 (R) (n=1) 9–18 (NS) or 24–79 [b] (n=5)
Region of the Americas – National data or report to ReLAVRA or SIREVA (n=15 countries) – Publications (n=1) from 1 additional country	0–48 [b] 53 (non-meningitis) (NS)	0–48 [b] (n=14) 64 (meningitis) (NS)
Eastern Mediterranean Region – National data (n=3 countries) – Publications (n=17) from 9 additional countries	13–34 (R) or 5 (NS) 0.3–64 (R) or 17–48 (NS) or 0–93 [b]	34 (R) (n=1) 2–14 (R) or 17–40 (NS) (n=10)
European Region – National data or report to EARS-Net (n=31 countries) – Publications (n=1) from 1 additional country	0–61 (R) or 0.9–73 (NS) 13–68 (NS)	0.9–61 (NS) or 32–45 [b] (n=27) 13 (NS) (n=1)
South-East Asia Region – National data (n=2 countries) – Publications (n=2) from 2 additional countries	47–48 [b] 0–6 (R)	 0 (R) (n=1)
Western Pacific Region – National data (n=10 countries) – Hospital data (two hospitals in 1 country) – Publications (n=4) from 2 additional countries	17–64 (NS) or 0–47 [b] 0–2 44–96 (R) or 0–69 (NS)	 44 (R) or 0 (NS) (n=2)

EARS-Net, European Antimicrobial Resistance Surveillance Network; NS, non-susceptible; R, resistant; ReLAVRA, Latin American Antimicrobial Resistance Surveillance Network; SIREVA, Sistema de Redes de Vigilancia de los Agentes Responsables de Neumonías y Meningitis Bacterianas (System of Networks for Surveillance of the Bacterial Agents Responsible for Pneumonia and Meningitis).
(for details see Annex 2, Table A2.31–A2.36)

a. Invasive isolates are deep infections, mostly bloodstream infections and meningitis.

b. Not specified whether R or NS.

Of the countries providing data sets on at least 30 tested isolates, 57 came from three WHO regions – Region of the Americas, the European Region and the Western Pacific Region – leaving major gaps in data from the other regions.

Compilation of data was complicated by differences in the terminology and microbiological methods used in the different data sources. Results may be presented in different categories: resistant (R); non-susceptible (NS), which includes resistant plus reduced susceptibility; or susceptible (S), which refers to those that are not NS. It is likely that this classification may not be interpreted or applied identically by all laboratories. Despite discrepancies, non-susceptibility to penicillin is detected in all WHO regions, and exceeds 50% in reports based on some types of samples.

Public health implications

When penicillin was introduced, it dramatically changed the outcome for patients with pneumococcal pneumonia and concomitant bloodstream infection (which is common) from a case–fatality rate of about 90% to a survival rate of about 90% (Figure 9).

Figure 9 **Survival after pneumococcal pneumonia with bloodstream infection before and after penicillin treatment became available.**

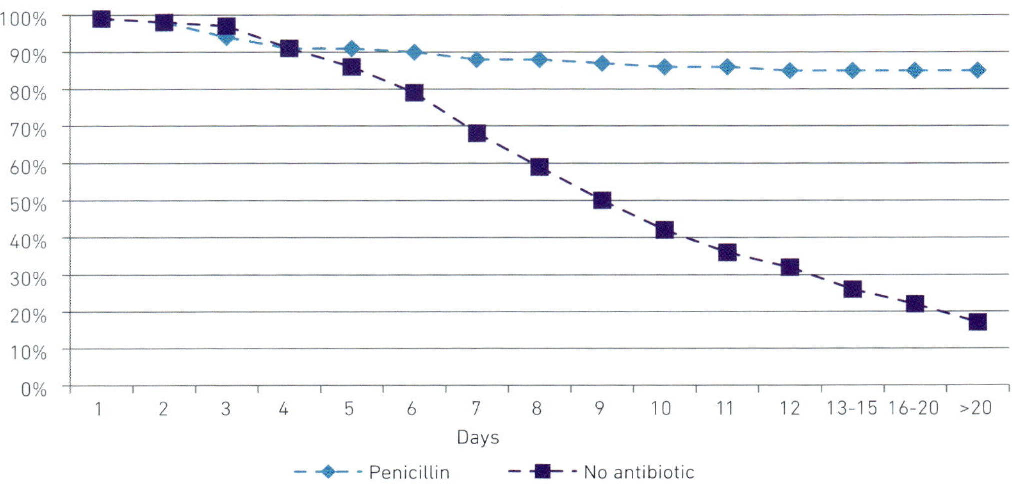

Adapted from Austrian et al. (5).

Resistance has been linked to worse clinical outcomes in patients with pneumococcal meningitis, but the clinical implications for patients with bloodstream infections caused by *S. pneumoniae* strains with reduced susceptibility to penicillin are less clear (6-9). Nevertheless, resistance data may influence treatment guidelines for bloodstream infections, entailing increased health-care costs that may not always be justified. Thus, more data on resistance would be valuable. However, and as mentioned previously, to distinguish R from NS requires different methodologies and would need increased laboratory capacity for conducting AST.

Key messages

- Data were obtained from only 67 (35%) of the Member States. The major gaps in surveillance of this important, typically community-acquired pathogen, according to the data compiled for this report, were in three WHO regions: the African Region, the Eastern Mediterranean Region and the South-East Asia Region.

- Non-susceptibility to penicillin has been detected in all WHO regions.

- Differences between microbiological methods and in terminology for reporting resistance add to difficulties in assessing the magnitude of the impact of resistance on disease burden and clinical outcomes.

2.2.5 Nontyphoidal *Salmonella* – resistance to fluoroquinolones

Bacteria of the genus *Salmonella* are a major cause of foodborne illness throughout the world. As a zoonotic pathogen, *Salmonella* can be found in the intestines of many food-producing animals such as poultry and pigs. Infection is usually acquired by consumption of contaminated water or food of animal origin: mainly undercooked meat, poultry, eggs and milk. Human or animal faeces can also contaminate the surface of fruits and vegetables, which can lead to foodborne outbreaks.

Most *Salmonella* strains cause gastroenteritis, while some strains, particularly *Salmonella enterica* serotypes Typhi and Paratyphi, are more invasive and typically cause enteric fever. Enteric fever is a more serious infection that poses problems for treatment due to ABR in many parts of the world.

This report focuses on nontyphoidal *Salmonella* (NTS), because these are main diarrhoeal pathogens transmitted via the food chain. In many countries, The incidence of NTS infections has increased markedly in recent years, for reasons that are unclear. One estimate suggests that there are around 94 million cases, resulting in 155 000 deaths, of NTS gastroenteritis each year. The majority of the disease burden, according to this study, is in the South-East Asian Region and the Western Pacific Region (*10*).

Evolution of antibacterial resistance in nontyphoidal *Salmonella*

ABR varies between different serotypes of NTS, and is significant in some of them. During the late 1990s and early 2000s, several clones of multidrug-resistant *Salmonella* emerged, and since then they have expanded worldwide. For instance, in *Salmonella enterica* serotype Typhimurium, the genomic element that carries resistance to five antimicrobials (ampicillin, chloramphenicol, streptomycin, sulfonamides and tetracycline) may spread horizontally among other serotypes and acquire additional resistance determinants.

Resistance to fluoroquinolones in nontyphoidal *Salmonella*

Figure 10 shows the sources of collected resistance data in each country according to the methods in Annex 1, and notes where there are major knowledge gaps for resistance to fluoroquinolones in NTS, based on the data available for this report. Comparatively little information was available on this community-acquired pathogen from African and Asian countries.

Figure 10   Sources of data on nontyphoidal *Salmonella*: Resistance to fluoroquinolones[a]

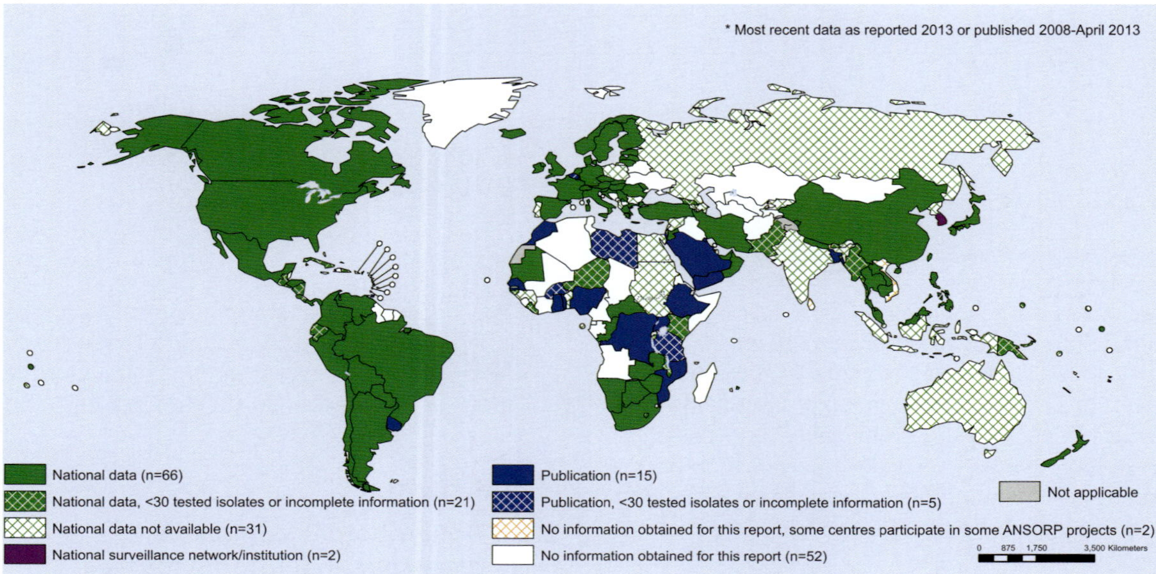

National data refers to requested data returned as described in the methods. The definition does not imply that the data collected are representative for that country as a whole because information gaps are likely. (For details on data see Tables A2.37–A2.42, Annex 2).
a.   ciprofloxacin, norfloxacin.

Data obtained from Member States are summarized by WHO region in Table 9, and details at country level are given in Tables A2.37–A2.42, Annex 2.

Table 9   Nontyphoidal *Salmonella*: Resistance to fluoroquinolones[a] (summary of reported or published proportions of resistance, by WHO region)

Data sources based on at least 30 tested isolates	Overall reported range of resistant proportion (%)	Reported range of resistant proportion (%) in blood isolates (no. of reports)
African Region – National data (n=9 countries) – Publications (n=11) from 8 additional countries	0–35 0–30	 0–30 (n=4)
Region of the Americas – National data (n=13 countries) – Publications (n=1) from 1 additional country	0–96 0	
Eastern Mediterranean Region – National data (n=4 countries) – Publications (n=4) from 4 additional countries	2–49 0–46	6 (n=1)
European Region – National data or report to FWD-Net, (n=29 countries) – Publications (n=1) from1 additional country	2–3 13	
South-East Asia Region – National data (n=2 countries) – Publication (n=1) from 1 additional country	0.2–4 1.4	
Western Pacific Region – National data (n=9 countries) – Network/institution data (n=4 from 2 countries) – Publications from remaining countries (n=0)	0–14 0–0.3	

FWD-Net, Foodborne and Waterborne Diseases and Zoonoses Network.
a.   ciprofloxacin, norfloxacin.

Some of the information gaps were in the South-East Asian and Western Pacific Regions, where the disease burden has been estimated to be highest (*10*). The resistance in NTS to fluoroquinolones was less than 5% in a majority of national data, although there were some from the African Region and the Eastern Mediterranean Region of 35%–49% and one from Region of the Americas of 96%. A possible imprecision in the definition of the term NTS (and therefore of which results should be included), and the inclusion of only a subset of *Salmonella* types in some reports, probably contributed to this observed variation in resistance proportions.

Public health implications

Infections caused by NTS are common and usually self-limiting. In severe cases antibacterial treatment may be warranted. Multidrug-resistant *Salmonella enterica* serotype Typhimurium has been associated with a higher risk of invasive infection, higher frequency and duration of hospitalization, longer illness, and increased risk of death as compared to infections caused by susceptible strains (*11*). Reduced susceptibility to oral drugs such as ciprofloxacin, and increasing numbers of treatment failures, are of concern.

Key messages

• Data on resistance in NTS to fluoroquinolones were obtained from 68 (35%) of the Member States. Some of the major information gaps were in regions where the disease burden is highest, such as in South-East Asia.

• Reported resistance was less than 5% in most of the reporting countries: a low proportion that may be partly attributable to differing interpretation of the definition of the *Salmonella* serotypes to be included. Thus, the data should be interpreted with caution.

2.2.6 *Shigella* species – resistance to fluoroquinolones

Shigella species are a major cause of diarrhoea and dysentery throughout the world. These bacteria are transmitted by ingestion of contaminated food or water, or through person-to-person contact. Shigellosis is primarily a disease of resource-poor crowded communities that do not have adequate sanitation or safe water. *Shigella* is never considered to be part of the normal intestinal flora. Ingestion of just a few of these organisms is enough to result in development of symptoms. Most patients recover without complications within 7 days, but shigellosis can be a life-threatening or fatal disease, particularly in children. The annual number of *Shigella* episodes worldwide is estimated to be 165 million, of which more than 100 million occur in the developing world, causing more than 1 million deaths. The highest rate of *Shigella* infection (69% of cases) and the highest death rate (61% of deaths) occur in those younger than 5 years (*12-14*).

Evolution of antibacterial resistance in *Shigella*

Formerly, *Shigella* strains were susceptible to co-trimoxazole. However, as resistance has emerged to this antimicrobial, treatment recommendations have shifted to ciprofloxacin or azithromycin. Mobile genetic units (including plasmids, gene cassettes in integrons and transposons) are important in the spread of resistance determinants among *Shigella* isolates, as well as in other enterobacteria such as *Klebsiella* and *E. coli*.

Resistance to fluoroquinolones in *Shigella* species

Figure 11 shows the sources of collected resistance data in each country according to the methods in Annex 1.

Figure 11 Sources of data on *Shigella* species, resistance to fluoroquinolones[a]

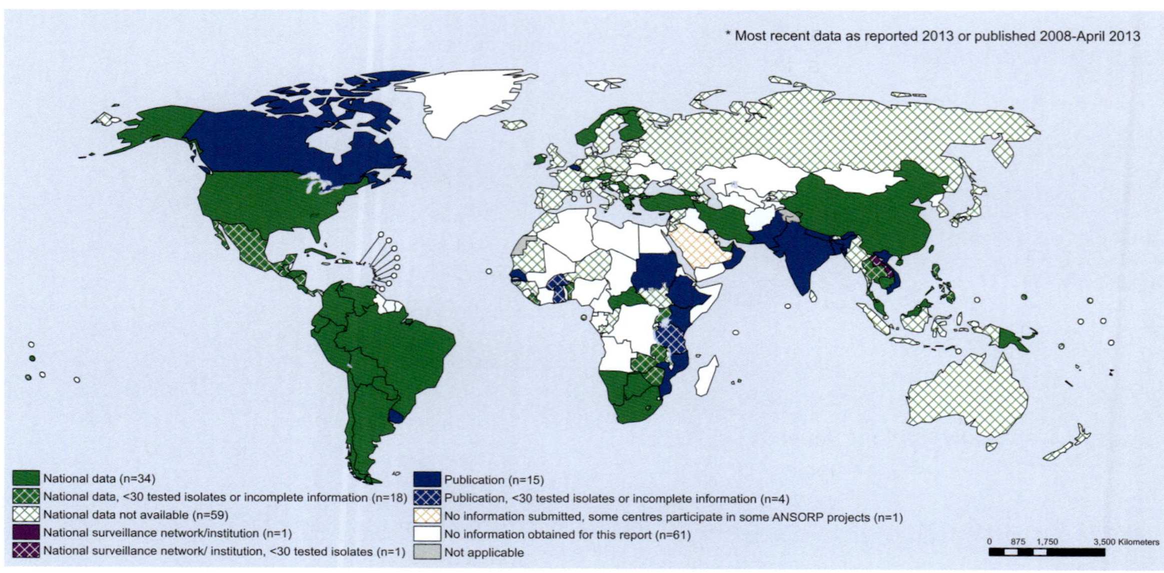

National data refers to requested data returned as described in the methods. The definition does not imply that the data collected are representative for that country as a whole because information gaps are likely. (For details on data see Tables A2.43–A2.48, Annex 2).

a. ciprofloxacin, norfloxacin.

Data obtained from Member States are summarized by WHO region in Table 10, see Tables A2.43–A2.48, Annex 2 for details.

Table 10 *Shigella* species: Resistance to fluoroquinolones[a]

Data sources based on at least 30 tested isolates	Overall reported range of resistant proportion (%)
African Region – National data (n=4 countries) – Publications (n=8) from 4 additional countries	0–3 0–9
Region of the Americas – National data (n=14 countries) – Publications (n=2) from 2 additional countries	0–8 0–20
Eastern Mediterranean Region – National data (n=2 countries) – Publications (n=7) from 5 additional countries	3–10 0–41.3
European Region – National data or reports to FWD-Net (n=10 countries) – Publications (n=2) from 1 additional country	0–47 0
South-East Asia Region – National data (n=0 countries) – Publications (n=11) from 3 additional countries	0–82
Western Pacific Region – National data (n=4 countries) – Network/ institution data (two hospitals in 1 country) – Publications (n=1) from 1 additional country	3–28 0 2

FWD-Net, Foodborne and Waterborne Diseases and Zoonoses Network (coordinated by the ECDC).

a. ciprofloxacin, norfloxacin.

Except in AMRO, national data were generally scarce, especially from countries where shigellosis is a significant public health problem, particularly in children (*12-14*). Most reporting countries reported resistance proportions below 10%, although a proportion of 82% was reported by one country. More information on the situation is needed.

Public health implications

Antibacterial drugs have a proven effect in the management of *Shigella* infections and may be life-saving. Emerging resistance has been reported as a concern from some countries. For this reason, the gaps in surveillance data at national level are of concern and raise the question as to whether or not representative local data are available to also inform treatment guidelines.

Key messages

- Data were obtained from only 35 (18%) of the Member States, with gaps in knowledge about resistance in *Shigella* species in countries where the major disease burden is.

- Better understanding of the frequency and patterns of resistance in *Shigella* species could inform treatment policy-making for reduction of disease burden and mortality.

2.2.7 *Neisseria gonorrhoeae* – decreased susceptibility to third-generation cephalosporins

N. gonorrhoeae is the bacterium that causes gonorrhoea (the bacteria are also known as gonococci). Gonorrhoea is a sexually transmitted, acute infection of the reproductive tract that may be symptomatic or asymptomatic. If untreated, or inappropriately treated, this infection can result in severe complications, including genital and reproductive tract inflammation and damage, and infertility. *N. gonorrhoeae* can also be transmitted sexually to infect other anatomic sites such as the pharynx and the rectum. Infection in pregnant women can result in infections in the newborn, including eye infections that may lead to blindness. The most recent WHO estimates from 2008 suggested that there were 106 million new cases of gonorrhoea in adults aged 15–49 years globally (*15*).

Evolution of antibacterial resistance in *Neisseria gonorrhoeae*

The history of emergence of ABR in gonococci has followed the same general pattern for many decades; the release of each new class of antibacterial drugs for the treatment of gonorrhoea has been followed by the development of resistance to it. This acquired resistance has expanded globally and been sustained over time, persisting even after the specific antibacterial drug has been withdrawn from the market.

The emergence of gonococcal resistance to penicillin and tetracycline was identified in Asia during the 1970s, and became widespread in multiple regions in the early 1980s. In the early to mid-1990s, high levels of resistance to fluoroquinolones also emerged in Asia and started to spread internationally. The third-generation cephalosporins, which are the last remaining options for empiric monotherapy, are now recommended as the first-line treatment regimen for gonococcal infections (in the USA and Europe in a dual antimicrobial regimen, generally combined with azithromycin) (*16, 17*). There is no ideal alternative to the third-generation cephalosporins, and there are very few new treatment options in the drug development pipeline.

In this context, alarmingly, several countries have reported treatment failures with oral cephalosporin (cefixime), and there are now some verified reports of treatment failure with the parenteral cephalosporin (ceftriaxone) in patients with pharyngeal gonorrhoea (*18*). The gonococcal strains causing those clinical failures were resistant to most other antibacterial drugs relevant for treatment, and have been classified as multidrug-resistant gonococci or even extensively drug-resistant gonococci.

Surveillance of decreased susceptibility to third-generation cephalosporins in *N. gonorrhoeae*

The WHO Gonococcal Antimicrobial Surveillance Programme (GASP) was established in 1992 in the Western Pacific Region, and since then a global laboratory network has been developed to coordinate gonococcal antimicrobial resistance surveillance, monitor longitudinal trends in antimicrobial resistance and provide data to inform treatment guidelines. In each WHO region there is a GASP coordinating laboratory that works in partnership with the corresponding WHO regional office. The regional coordinating laboratory provides technical support to countries to strengthen laboratory capacity, and an external quality assessment programme including maintenance and distribution of the WHO panels of *N. gonorrhoeae* reference strains for quality assurance (*19*). In high-income countries, the widespread adoption of molecular methods for detecting *N. gonorrhoeae* has reduced the number of specimens being cultured, therefore decreasing the number of isolates undergoing AST.

When considering and interpreting data it must be noted that the GASP reporting laboratories use a number of different methods of AMR testing and there are important differences in these methods, in particular for the reporting of ceftriaxone. Although the issue of comparability remains unresolved, the use of WHO *N. gonorrhoeae* control strains in testing, and the WHO Global Action Plan (*20*), which in 2012 suggested the level for decreased susceptibility for ceftriaxone, have somewhat improved the situation.

Figure 12 shows the sources of collected resistance data in each country according to the methods in Annex 1. In situations where data were obtained from more than one national data source (n=3 for which data on >30 isolates were obtained and n=1 providing data on < 30 isolates), the priority was given to illustrating country participation in the WHO GASP/Gonococcal Isolate Surveillance Project (GISP)/Gonococcal Resistance to Antimicrobials Surveillance Programme (GRASP) network in the map. The number of countries participating in GASP varies by region, as does the extent to which those countries perform gonococcal resistance surveillance.

Figure 12 **Sources of data on *Neisseria gonorrhoeae*: Decreased susceptibility to third-generation cephalosporins[a]**

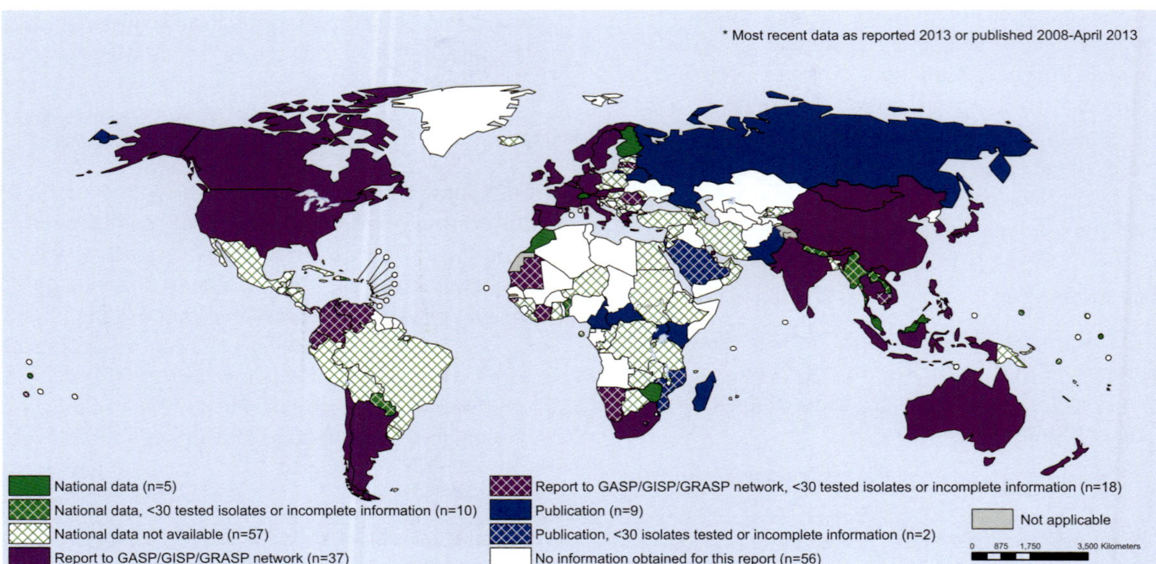

National data refers to requested data returned as described in the methods. The definition does not imply that the data collected are representative for that country as a whole because information gaps are likely. (For details on data see Tables A2.31–A2.36, Annex 2).
a. ceftriaxone, cefixim.

Data obtained from Member States reporting data via the GASP/GISP/GRASP network, or via the questionnaire, are summarized by WHO region in Table 11. (See Table A2.49–A2.54, Annex 2 for details).

Table 11 *Neisseria gonorrhoeae*: decreased susceptibility to third-generation cephalosporins[a]

Data sources based on at least 30 tested isolates	Overall reported range of proportion with decreased susceptibility (%)
African Region – National data and/or GASP data (n=2 countries) – Publications (n=5) from 5 additional countries	0–12 0
Region of the Americas – National data and/or GASP/ GISP data (n=4 countries) – Publications from remaining countries (n=0)	0–31
Eastern Mediterranean Region – National data and/or GASP data (n=2 countries) – Publications (n=1) from 1 additional country	0–12 0
European Region – National data and/or EURO-GASP/GRASP data (n=17) – Publications (n=3) from 3 additional countries	0–36 0
South-East Asia Region – National data and/or GASP data (n=5 countries) – Publications from remaining countries (n=0)	0–5
Western Pacific Region – National data and/or GASP data (n=12 countries) – Publications from remaining countries (n=0)	0–31

EURO, European; GASP, Gonococcal Antimicrobial Surveillance Programme; GISP, Gonococcal Isolate Surveillance Project; Gonococcal Resistance to Antimicrobials Surveillance Programme (GRASP) network.
a. Based on antibacterial susceptibility testing with ceftriaxone or cefixime.

In countries where quality assured gonococcal antimicrobial susceptibility surveillance is taking place, there are rising trends in decreased susceptibility and resistance in *N. gonorrhoeae* to cefixime and ceftriaxone. There are 36 countries that report decreased susceptibility to third-generation cephalosporins (*21-24*) (Figure 13).

Figure 13 **Detection of decreased susceptibility to third-generation cephalosporins in *Neisseria gonorrhoeae*[a] (*20-23*) and treatment failure (*24-34*) up to 2010**

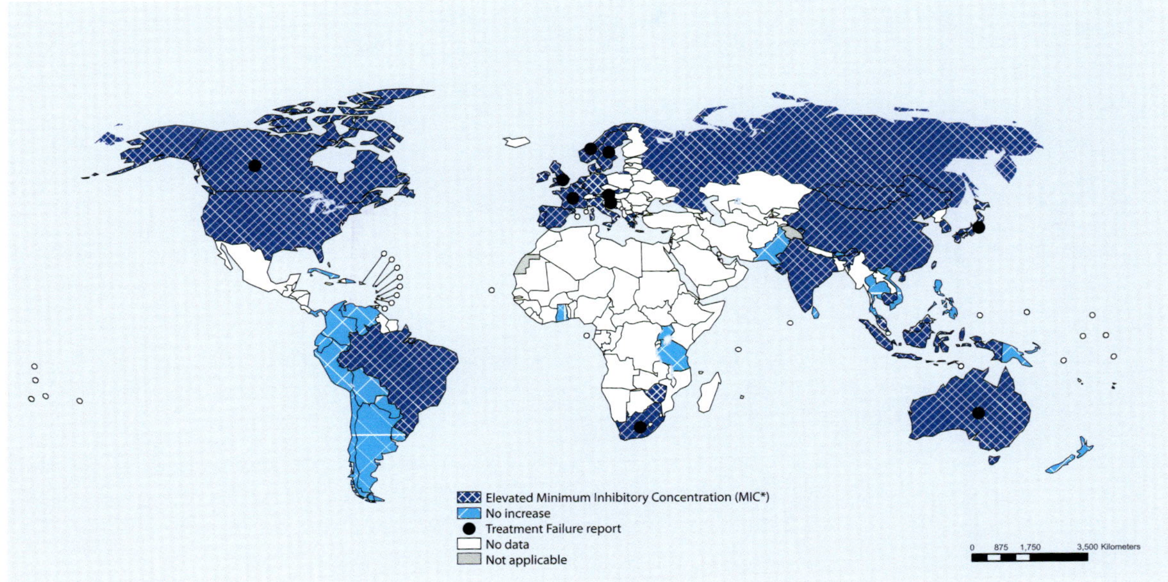

** Note: cefixime >0.25µg/L or ceftriaxone >0.125µg/L. The definition of decreased susceptibility to third-generation cephalosporins differs across AMR testing methods. Countries are shaded where there has been any report of decreased susceptibility within their jurisdiction.*

Public health implications

Emerging resistance has created important barriers for the treatment and control of gonorrhoea, in both resource-constrained and higher income countries. Because of widespread resistance, older and cheaper antibacterial drugs are no longer of use in treatment regimens.

Treatment failures with a third-generation cephalosporin (cefixime) were first reported in Japan in 2007 (*25*), and during subsequent years verified treatment failures have also been reported in Australia, Canada, France, Norway, South Africa and the United Kingdom of Great Britain and Northern Ireland (UK) (*26, 27, 31, 32, 34, 35*). Furthermore, reports of treatment failure of pharyngeal gonorrhoea with ceftriaxone have been verified in Australia (*29*), Japan, Slovenia and Sweden (*28, 30, 33, 36*).

Most of the reports on treatment failure with third-generation cephalosporins are from developed countries, but most gonococcal disease occurs in less well-resourced countries and settings. Accordingly, the reports of treatment failures are under-reported because surveillance data on antibacterial susceptibility, and particularly treatment failures, from resource-constrained settings are scarce.

It is anticipated to be only a matter of time before gonococci with full resistance to the third-generation extended spectrum cephalosporins emerge and spread internationally. Consequently, gonorrhoea may become untreatable unless new drugs become available. This is of global concern because there will be a major impact on disease control efforts due to increased prevalence of serious complications, and separate gonococcal entities such as neonatal infections and disseminated gonococcal infections will become much more common, as in the era before antibacterial treatment was available. In addition, untreated gonococcal infection is associated with an increased risk of acquisition and transmission of HIV infection.

Based on the 2008 global estimates of incident gonococcal infections, the estimate for global disability-adjusted life years (DALYs) generated by gonorrhoea is approximately 440 000. AMR in gonorrhoea will further increase this burden and cost for society, due to prolonged infections and greater numbers of patients with complications such as infertility, with potentially serious developmental implications. Financial costs for health services and individual patients will certainly increase due to the higher cost of treating resistant gonorrhoea (*37*).

To facilitate effective actions against the spread of multidrug-resistant *N. gonorrhoeae*, in 2012 WHO launched the *Global Action Plan to Control the Spread and Impact of Antimicrobial Resistance in Neisseria gonorrhoeae* (*20*). This action plan has to be implemented in the context of enhanced surveillance of sexually transmitted infection to facilitate early detection of emerging resistant strains, combined with a public health response to prevent and treat gonococcal infections and mitigate the impact of cephalosporin-resistant *N. gonorrhoeae* on sexual and reproductive health morbidity.

Key messages

- Data were obtained from only 42 of 194 (22%) of the Member States.

- The emergence of resistance to the last-resort drugs, the third-generation cephalosporins, is fast outpacing the development of alternative treatment, and will influence disease burden with potential developmental impact.

- ABR surveillance is often lacking in countries with high disease rates. Thus, there is widespread absence of reliable resistance data for gonorrhoea where most needed, and consequently there is inadequate knowledge of the extent of the spread of resistant gonococci.

2.3 References

1. Downie L, Armiento R, Subhi R, Kelly J, Clifford V, Duke T. Community-acquired neonatal and infant sepsis in developing countries: Efficacy of WHO's currently recommended antibiotics – systematic review and meta-analysis. *Arch Dis Child*, 2013, 98(2):146-154. doi:10.1136/archdischild-2012-302033.

2. Munoz-Price LS, Poirel L, Bonomo RA, Schwaber MJ, Daikos GL, Cormican M et al. Clinical epidemiology of the global expansion of *Klebsiella pneumoniae* carbapenemases. *Lancet Infect Dis*, 2013, 13(9):785-796. doi:10.1016/S1473-3099(13)70190-7.

3. Knothe H, Shah P, Krcmery V, Antal M, Mitsuhashi S. Transferable resistance to cefotaxime, cefoxitin, cefamandole and cefuroxime in clinical isolates of *Klebsiella pneumoniae* and Serratia marcescens. *Infection*, 1983, 11(6):315-317. (http://www.ncbi.nlm.nih.gov/pubmed/6321357, accessed 5 February 2014).

4. O'Brien KL, Wolfson LJ, Watt JP, Henkle E, Deloria-Knoll M, McCall N et al. Burden of disease caused by Streptococcus pneumoniae in children younger than 5 years: global estimates. *Lancet*, 2009, 374(9693):893-902. doi:10.1016/S0140-6736(09)61204-6.

5. Austrian R, Gold J. Pneumococcal bacteremia with especial reference to bacteremic pneumococcal pneumonia. *Ann Intern Med*, 1964, 60(5):759-776.

6. Choi SH, Chung JW, Sung H, Kim MN, Kim SH, Lee SO et al. Impact of penicillin nonsusceptibility on clinical outcomes of patients with nonmeningeal Streptococcus pneumoniae bacteremia in the era of the 2008 clinical and laboratory standards institute penicillin breakpoints. *Antimicrob Agents Chemother*, 2012, 56(9):4650-4655. doi:10.1128/AAC.00239-12.

7. Klugman K, Yu V. No impact of penicillin resistance on mortality (author reply). *Clin Infect Dis*, 2006, 43(2):261-262.

8. Klugman KP, Walsh AL, Phiri A, Molyneux EM. Mortality in penicillin-resistant pneumococcal meningitis. *Pediatr Infect Dis J*, 2008, 27(7):671-672. doi:10.1097/INF.0b013e31817709cf.

9. Yu VL, Chiou CC, Feldman C, Ortqvist A, Rello J, Morris AJ et al. An international prospective study of pneumococcal bacteremia: correlation with in vitro resistance, antibiotics administered, and clinical outcome. *Clin Infect Dis*, 2003, 37(2):230-237. (http://www.ncbi.nlm.nih.gov/pubmed/12856216, accessed 5 February 2014).

10. Majowicz SE, Musto J, Scallan E, Angulo FJ, Kirk M, O'Brien SJ et al. The global burden of nontyphoidal Salmonella gastroenteritis. *Clin Infect Dis*, 2010, 50(6):882-889. doi:10.1086/650733 .

11. European Centre for Disease Prevention and Control (ECDC), European Food Safety Authority (EFSA), European Drugs Agency (EMEA), Scientific Committee on Emerging and Newly Identified Health Risks (SCENIHR). Joint opinion on antimicrobial resistance (AMR) focused on zoonotic infections. *EFSA Journal*, 2009, 7(11):1372. (http://www.ema.europa.eu/docs/en_GB/document_library/Other/2009/11/WC500015452.pdf, accessed 27 December 2013).

12. Agtini MD, Soeharno R, Lesmana M, Punjabi NH, Simanjuntak C, Wangsasaputra F et al. The burden of diarrhoea, shigellosis, and cholera in North Jakarta, Indonesia: findings from 24 months surveillance. *BMC Infect Dis*, 2005, 5:89. doi:10.1186/1471-2334-5-89.

13. Kotloff KL, Winickoff JP, Ivanoff B, Clemens JD, Swerdlow DL, Sansonetti PJ et al. Global burden of Shigella infections: implications for vaccine development and implementation of control strategies. *Bull World Health Organ*, 1999, 77(8):651-666. (http://www.ncbi.nlm.nih.gov/pubmed/10516787, accessed 5 February 2014).

14. Lee H, Kotloff K, Chukaserm P, Samosornsuk S, Chompook P, Deen JL et al. Shigellosis remains an important problem in children less than 5 years of age in Thailand. *Epidemiol Infect*, 2005, 133(3):469-474. (http://www.ncbi.nlm.nih.gov/pubmed/15962553, accessed 5 February 2014).

15. *Global HIV/AIDS response: Edpidemic update and health sector progress towards universal access.* 2011. (http://whqlibdoc.who.int/publications/2011/9789241502986_eng.pdf, accessed 27 January 2014).

16. Bignell C, Fitzgerald M. United Kingdom national guideline for the management of gonorrhoea in adults, 2011. *Int J STD AIDS*, 2011, 22(10):541-547. (http://www.ncbi.nlm.nih.gov/pubmed/21998172, accessed 8 April 2014).

17. Bignell C, Unemo M. 2012 European guideline on the diagnosis and treatment of gonorrhoea in adults. *Int J STD AIDS*, 2013, 24(2):85-92. (http://www.ncbi.nlm.nih.gov/pubmed/24400344, accessed 5 February 2014).

18. Unemo M, Nicholas RA. Emergence of multidrug-resistant, extensively drug-resistant and untreatable gonorrhea. *Future Microbiol*, 2012, 7(12):1401-1422. doi:10.2217/fmb.12.117.

19. Unemo M, Fasth O, Fredlund H, Limnios A, Tapsall J. Phenotypic and genetic characterization of the 2008 WHO *Neisseria gonorrhoeae* reference strain panel intended for global quality assurance and quality control of gonococcal antimicrobial resistance surveillance for public health purposes. *J Antimicrob Chemother*, 2009, 63(6):1142-1151. doi:10.1093/jac/dkp098.

20. *Global action plan to control the spread and impact of antimicrobial resistance in Neisseria gonorrhoeae.* Geneva, World Health Organization, 2012. (http://whqlibdoc.who.int/publications/2012/9789241503501_eng.pdf, accessed 14 March 2014).

21. *Sexually transmitted diseases surveillance 2010.* Atlanta, Centers for Disease Control and Prevention, 2011. (http://www.cdc.gov/std/stats10/default.htm, accessed 29 December 2013).

22. Cole MJ, Unemo M, Hoffmann S, Chisholm SA, Ison CA, van de Laar MJ. The European gonococcal antimicrobial surveillance programme, 2009. *Eur Surveill*, 2011, 16(42)(http://www.eurosurveillance.org/ViewArticle.aspx?ArticleId=19995, accessed 29 December 2013).

23. Lahra MM. Surveillance of antibiotic resistance in Neisseria gonorrhoeae in the WHO Western Pacific and South East Asian Regions, 2010. *Commun Dis Intell Q Rep*, 2012, 36(1):95-100. (http://www.ncbi.nlm.nih.gov/pubmed/23153085, accessed 29 December 2013).

24. Starnino S, Group G-LW, Galarza P, Carvallo M, Benzaken A, Ballesteros A et al. Retrospective analysis of antimircrobial susceptibility trends (2000-2009) in Neisseria gonorrhoeae isolates from countries in Latin America and the Caribean shows evolving resistance to ciprofloxacin, azithromycin and decreased susceptibility to ceftriaxone. *Sex Transm Dis*, 2012, 39(10):813-821.

25. Yokoi S, Deguchi T, Ozawa T, Yasuda M, Ito S, Kubota Y et al. Threat to cefixime treatment for gonorrhea. *Emerg Infect Dis*, 2007, 13(8):1275-1277. doi:10.3201/eid1308.060948.

26. Unemo M, Golparian D, Syversen G, Vestrheim DF, Moi H. Two cases of verified clinical failures using internationally recommended first-line cefixime for gonorrhoea treatment, Norway, 2010. *Eur Surveill*, 2010, 15(47):19721. (http://www.eurosurveillance.org/ViewArticle.aspx?ArticleId=19721, accessed 6 April 2014).

27. Unemo M, Golparian D, Nicholas R, Ohnishi M, Gallay A, Sednaoui P. High-level cefixime- and ceftriaxone-resistant Neisseria gonorrhoeae in France: novel penA mosaic allele in a successful international clone causes treatment failure. *Antimicrob Agents Chemother*, 2012, 56(3):1273-1280. doi:10.1128/AAC.05760-11.

28. Unemo M, Golparian D, Hestner A. Ceftriaxone treatment failure of pharyngeal gonorrhoea verified by international recommendations, Sweden, July 2010. *Eur Surveill*, 2011, 16(6). (http://www.ncbi.nlm.nih.gov/pubmed/21329645, accessed 5 February 2014).

29. Read PJ, Limnios EA, McNulty A, Whiley D, Lahra MM. Pharyngeal gonorrhoea treatment failure following 500mg Ceftriaxone in Sydney, Australia. *Sexual Health*, 2013, 10(5):460-462. doi:10.1071/SH13077.

30. Ohnishi M, Golparian D, Shimuta K, Saika T, Hoshina S, Iwasaku K et al. Is *Neisseria gonorrhoeae* initiating a future era of untreatable gonorrhea?: detailed characterization of the first strain with high-level resistance to ceftriaxone. *Antimicrob Agents Chemother*, 2011, 55(7):3538-3545. doi:10.1128/AAC.00325-11.

31. Lewis DA, Sriruttan C, Muller EE, Golparian D, Gumede L, Fick D et al. Phenotypic and genetic characterization of the first two cases of extended-spectrum-cephalosporin-resistant *Neisseria gonorrhoeae* infection in South Africa and association with cefixime treatment failure. *J Antimicrob Chemother*, 2013, 68(6):1267-1270. doi:10.1093/jac/dkt034.

32. Ison CA, Hussey J, Sankar KN, Evans J, Alexander S. Gonorrhoea treatment failures to cefixime and azithromycin in England, 2010. *Eur Surveill: Euro Comm Dis Bull*, 2011, 16(14):19833.

33. Chen YM, Stevens K, Tideman R, Zaia A, Tomita T, Fairley CK et al. Failure of 500 mg of ceftriaxone to eradicate pharyngeal gonorrhoea, Australia. *J Antimicrob Chemother*, 2013, 68(6):1445-1447. doi:10.1093/jac/dkt017.

34. Allen VG, Mitterni L, Seah C, Rebbapragada A, Martin IE, Lee C et al. *Neisseria gonorrhoeae* treatment failure and susceptibility to cefixime in Toronto, Canada. *Journal of the American Medical Association*, 2013, 309(2):163-170. doi:10.1001/jama.2012.176575.

35. Unemo M, Golparian D, Stary A, Eigentler A. First Neisseria gonorrhoeae strain with resistance to cefixime causing gonorrhoea treatment failure in Austria, 2011. *Eur Surveill*, 2011, 16(43). pii: 19998. (http://www.ncbi.nlm.nih.gov/pubmed/22085601, accessed 5 February 2014).

36. Unemo M, Golparian D, Potocnik M, Jeverica S. Treatment failure of pharyngeal gonorrhoea with internationally recommended first-line ceftriaxone verified in Slovenia, September 2011. *Eur Surveill*, 2012, 17(25). pii: 20200. (http://www.ncbi.nlm.nih.gov/pubmed/22748003, accessed 5 February 2014).

37. Ndowa F, Lusti-Narasimhan M. The threat of untreatable gonorrhoea: implications and consequences for reproductive and sexual morbidity. *Reproductive Health Matters*, 2012, 20(40):76-82. doi:10.1016/S0968-8080(12)40653-X.

SECTION

03

The health and economic burden due to antibacterial resistance

Whether antibiotic resistance poses a significant health and economic burden for patients and health-care systems is a key question (*1*). Previous studies to review the health and economic burden are limited (*2-5*). To address this knowledge gap, systematic reviews were carried out for this report, in order to systematically examine the current evidence relating to the health and economic burden of ABR in the following set of bacteria of major public health importance:

- *Escherichia coli;* resistance to third-generation cephalosporins and fluoroquinolones;

- *Klebsiella pneumoniae;* resistance to third-generation cephalosporins and carbapenems; and

- *Staphylococcus aureus;* resistance to methicillin (MRSA).

The burden due to each bacteria–antibacterial resistance combination was examined separately, based on the following questions:

- Are clinical outcomes different in patients who are treated for infections caused by bacteria with a specific resistance compared to those who are treated for infections without this resistance?

- Are economic outcomes and costs different for patients who are treated for infections caused by bacteria with a specific resistance compared to those who are treated for infections without this resistance?

3.1 Methods

A detailed description of the procedures is provided in Annex 3. The strategy for assembling and analysing the evidence from published studies (1946 to 26 March 2013) comprised three fundamental steps based on a predefined protocol with parameters of interest for the study questions:

1. A systematic review of the available published studies related to the study questions. Although the yield of articles from the literature search was high (>13 000 for each bacterium), only a limited number of publications addressed the questions adequately and were therefore included.

2. A meta-analysis to compare the patient health and health care-associated outcomes for infections caused by resistant and susceptible bacteria. All of the included studies reported at least one health or economic outcome of interest. Not all studies reported all outcomes, which is why the number of studies analysed varied by outcome considered.

3. Use of the Grading of Recommendations Assessment, Development and Evaluation (GRADE) approach for the grading of the quality of evidence into four categories: very low, low, moderate and high (*6*).

Ultimately, 25 studies met the inclusion criteria for third generation cephalosporin, and 12 for fluoroquinolone resistance in *E. coli*. Twenty-four studies were included for third-generation cephalosporin-resistant *K. pneumoniae*, and 13 for carbapenem-resistant *K. pneumoniae*. A total of 147 studies met the inclusion criteria for *S. aureus*. A full reference list with citations is provided in the detailed report in Annex 3. Among the included studies, all but nine (all of which were on *S. aureus*) were based on data collected during the 1990s and 2000s, and none included data before the 1970s.

3.2 Findings

All included studies on *E. coli* and *K. pneumoniae* were conducted in high- or upper-middle-income countries (Table 12) (*7*). Studies included for *S .aureus* were also predominantly focused on populations in high- or upper-middle-income settings (95% of included studies).

Table 12 **Overview of studies included in the systematic review that addressed the health or economic impact of infections caused by the selected types of resistant bacteria**

	Antibacterial resistance	Studies included in SR (n)	Country income status[a]				
			Low income (n)	Lower-middle income (n)	Upper-middle income (n)	High income (n)	Mixed upper-middle and high income (n)
Escherichia coli	3rd generation cephalosporin-resistant	25	0	0	7	17	1[a]
	Fluoroquinolone-resistant	12	0	0	0	12	0
Klebsiella pneumoniae	3rd generation cephalosporin-resistant	24	0	0	13	10	1
	Carbapenem-resistant	13	0	0	3	10	0
Staphylococcus aureus	Methicillin-resistant	147	0	2	23	117	5[b]

n, evaluated number of studies; SR, systematic review.

a. All countries included in the studies were high income except for one study that was in an upper-middle-income country.

b. One study of 75 different countries. In 2 studies, country of origin was unclear.

The GRADE tables summarizing the quality of the evidence concerning the health and economic burden for the investigated bacteria–antibacterial combinations (discussed below in Sections 3.2.1 and 3.2.2) are provided in Annex 3.

3.2.1 Health burden

The main findings on the difference in outcomes for infections caused by bacteria that were resistant or sensitive to the studied antibacterial drugs are summarized in Table 13. Detailed findings for the complete list of outcomes are provided in Annex 3, Table A3.2.

Table 13 **Overview of the findings addressing the question: Does the published scientific literature support that there is a difference in outcome for patients with infections caused by the selected bacteria if they are resistant or sensitive to the relevant specific antibacterial drugs?**

	Escherichia coli		*Klebsiella pneumoniae*		*Staphylococcus aureus*
Antibacterial resistance					
	3rd generation cephalosporins	Fluoroquinolones	3rd generation cephalosporins	Carbapenems	MRSA
Outcome parameter					
Bacterium-attributable mortality	Yes (n=4)	No (n=1)	Yes (n=4)	No (n=1)	Yes (n=46)
30-day mortality	Yes (n=11)	Yes (n=5)	Yes (n=7)	Yes (n=3)	Yes (n=16)
Hospital LOS	No (n=3)	No (n=3)	No (n=9)	Unclear (n=3)[a]	Yes (n=50)
Admission to ICU	No (n=1)	Yes (n=1)	Yes (n=3)	ND	No (n=17)
Post-infection LOS	No (n=3)	ND	Yes (n=4)	No (n=1)	Yes (n=27)

ICU, intensive care unit; LOS, length of stay; MRSA, methicillin-resistant Staphylococcus aureus; n, evaluated number of studies; ND, no data.

a. Data in two studies were inconsistent, and a third study could not be included in the analysis.

b. A small study found that there was not a significant increase in the risk of health-care facility transfer for patients with carbapenem-resistant *K. pneumoniae* infections; however, patients enrolled in this study may have come from long-term care facilities at the time of study enrolment, so this result may not be directly attributable to *K. pneumoniae*.

A sufficient number of publications were identified in the systematic review to provide an overall evaluation of the impact of resistance for several of the health outcomes of interest. A summary of the health outcomes identified in the systematic review are listed below, with the details provided in Annex 3.

For patients with third-generation cephalosporin-resistant (including ESBL) *E. coli* infections there was:

• a significant twofold increase in all-cause mortality, bacterium-attributable mortality and in 30-day mortality;

• no significant increase in length of stay (LOS), ICU admission (based on only one study) and post-infection LOS.

For patients with fluoroquinolone-resistant *E. coli* infections there was:

• a significant twofold increase in both all-cause mortality and 30-day mortality for patients with fluoroquinolone-resistant *E. coli* infections;

• no increase in bacterium-attributable mortality (based on only one study), and no significant increase in LOS (but results were inconsistent in the two studies contributing to this result); and

• a significant twofold risk increase in infection-attributable ICU admission (based on only one study), and a significant increase in septic shock (but the result was imprecise and based on only one study).

For patients with third-generation cephalosporin-resistant *K. pneumoniae* infections there was:

• a significant increase in all-cause mortality, bacterium-attributable mortality and 30-day mortality, and in the risk of ICU admission;

• no significant increase in total LOS (but the results, which all indicated an increase in LOS, were too inconsistent across studies to pool into a single estimate), and no relationship found with progression to septic shock; and

• an increase in post-infection LOS found in four studies (but results were too inconsistent to allow a single estimate).

For patients with carbapenem-resistant *K. pneumoniae* infections there was:

• a significant increase in both all-cause mortality and 30-day mortality;

• no significant increase in attributable mortality or ICU mortality (based only on one small study), or in LOS (but results from the two studies that contributed to this estimate were inconsistent);

• an increase in ICU LOS (but based on only one study and its significance could not be ascertained), but no significant increase in post-infection LOS (but based on only one small study);

• no significant increase in the risk of health-care facility transfer for patients (but based only on one small study), but a significant increase in the risk of discharge for long-term care (but patients enrolled in this study may have come from long-term care facilities at the time of study enrolment, so this result may not be directly attributable to *K. pneumoniae*).

For patients with methicillin-resistant *S. aureus* infections there was:

• a significant increase in:

  – all-cause mortality, bacterium-attributable mortality and ICU mortality;

  – post-infection LOS and ICU LOS;

  – septic shock;

  – discharge to long-term care for MRSA compared to methicillin-susceptible *S. aureus* (MSSA), and more than twofold risk increase for discharge to long-term care for MRSA compared to MSSA;

• no significant increase in:

  – 30-day mortality (but results were inconsistent across the studies);

  – LOS (but results across studies were somewhat inconsistent);

  – admission to ICU (but data from the studies that contributed to this estimate were inconsistent);

  – attributable readmission in patients with MRSA when compared to those with MSSA; and

• no significant risk of requiring mechanical ventilation with MRSA (but data from the studies that contributed to this estimate were inconsistent).

3.2.2 Economic burden

Few economic evaluations, or studies collecting health-care resource use alongside the clinical study, or retrospective data collection studies, were identified in the published scientific literature for *E. coli*, and none for *K. pneumoniae*. Some studies located in the literature search reported resource-use outcomes and were selected for inclusion in the health burden review. Although some published studies have evaluated the economic burden of ABR, few presented data that were sufficiently specific to be included in this review (*3, 5, 8, 9*). These results are consistent with the conclusion that the cost impact of ABR to health services, patients and society has not been adequately measured.

The main findings on the possible excess costs for infections caused by bacteria resistant to selected antibacterial drugs are summarized in Table 14. Detailed findings on costs are provided in Annex 3, Table C2. The costs summarized in these tables are the costs provided in the studies that were included in the systematic review of the clinical outcomes.

Table 14 Overview of the findings addressing the question: Does the published scientific literature indicate that there is an excess cost due to infections caused by the selected bacteria if they are resistant to the relevant specific antibacterials?

	Antibacterial resistance	Studies included in SR (n)	Studies reporting cost data (n)	Excess cost (n=studies reporting costs)			
				Hospitalization[a]	Antibacterial therapy[b]	Medical care[c]	Additional cost variables[d]
Escherichia coli	3rd generation cephalosporin-resistant	25	2	Yes (n=2)	Yes (n=1)	Yes (n=1)	Yes (n=1)
	Fluoroquinolone-resistant	12	0	–	–	–	–
Klebsiella pneumoniae	3rd generation cephalosporin-resistant	24	0	–	–	–	–
	Carbapenem-resistant	13	0	–	–	–	–
Staphylococcus aureus	Methicillin-resistant	147	19	Yes (n=17)	Yes (n=6)	Yes (n=6)	Yes (n=9)

SR, systematic review.

a. Definitions vary by study, and were not consistently reported. Costs generally represent billing charges for all services provided between hospital admission and discharge, and may or may not include readmissions.

b. Some studies reported actual cost of antimicrobial drugs dispensed, while others may have reported the total cost of pharmaceutical management, including medication, determination of drug levels, dispensing by pharmacist, monitoring and adverse event management, and nursing costs related to administration.

c. Similar to hospitalization, and also not consistently reported. Numbers generally exclude costs related to hospital administration and focus more directly on costs related to direct medical treatment.

d. Additional cost variables available include: costs specifically related to the type of infection reported, daily hospital or patient costs; costs before or after infection; costs for specific allied health care; costs broken down into very specific categories; costs related to inpatient or outpatient treatment; costs reported by a specific time period (vs. entire stay), or adjusted or modelled cost variables produced in a study.

All costs for infections caused by resistant strains were consistently greater than those for infections caused by susceptible strains, with few exceptions (in very specific categories where small numbers of patients were assessed).

Studies on health-care resource use for *E. coli* were generally limited to the capture of hospital LOS data in upper-middle or high-income countries and the proportion of patients requiring treatment in ICU. The LOS for patients with fluoroquinolone or cephalosporin resistance was similar to that for patients with non-resistant infections, although the proportion of patients requiring ICU admission was higher (numerically for third-generation cephalosporin resistance, and statistically significant for fluoroquinolone resistance), suggesting that the intensity of care needed while in hospital differs in patients with infections caused by resistant bacteria compared to those caused by sensitive bacteria. Further, two studies (*10, 11*) found that the proportion of patients experiencing septic shock was statistically greater in patients with fluoroquinolone-resistant infections, which would involve more health-care resources than are required to treat patients with fluoroquinolone-sensitive infections.

Studies on *K. pneumoniae* related to economic burden were also generally limited to the capture of hospital LOS in upper-middle or high-income countries, and the proportion of patients requiring ICU admission.

There were numerically longer LOS in hospital and ICUs for patients with resistant infections, although the differences did not reach statistical significance. The proportion of patients requiring ICU admission was not reported in any of the studies. In one study (*12*) a higher proportion of patients with resistant infections were transferred to long-term care facilities, and this difference was statistically significant. However, many of these patients originally came from a long-term care facility to the hospital, and this factor must be taken into account in assessing whether patients with resistant infections may require more health-care resources in hospital and following discharge.

Regarding any increased cost associated with resistant *E. coli* and *K. pneumoniae* infections, few studies reported data, and the studies that were identified during the search have been included in previous reviews (*2, 3, 5*). For example, it was reported in one study from the United Kingdom that the additional costs for urinary tract infections caused by resistant (six drugs tested, included cephalosporins and fluoroquinolones) *E. coli* managed in general practice was £3.62 (*13*), and in another study from Thailand that the hospitalization costs increased to a median US$ 528 from US$ 108, respectively, in patients with ESBL-producing *E. coli* infections (*14*). A study in the USA in which *Klebsiella spp* and *E. coli* were included among other Gram-negative bacteria, reported that "patients infected with resistant bacteria had a median total hospital cost US$ 38 121 higher than that for patients infected with susceptible bacteria (US$ 144,414 and 106,293 respectively)" (*15*).

The clinical trials for MRSA captured a number of resource-use outcomes (LOS, rates of readmissions, need for mechanical ventilation and discharge to secondary-care facility). Based on these trials, there was a longer duration of both hospital (mean difference of 4.65 days) and ICU LOS (mean difference of 4.0 days) for patients with MRSA compared to those with MSSA. In addition, a higher proportion of patients with MRSA tended to be discharged from hospital to other care facilities (long-term care facility or other health-care facilities). The information on resource use while in hospital is limited; few trials collected these data and the number of patients was often small. Based on the data on LOS, and the fact that a higher proportion of patients with MRSA were discharged to secondary-care facilities, the findings suggest that MRSA cases tended to require higher levels of care and resource use for both acute treatment and possible longer term complications.

The results of the present review are generally consistent with those of a recent review of data in the USA (*5*), which had a similar focus but was broader in its data gathering by including, for example, societal costs and impact of control programmes. In reviewing LOS and mortality, and patient costs attributable to AMR in the USA, cost appears to have been judged against uninfected controls, or against infected or susceptible controls, whereas this review considered only infected controls. Both reviews found that costs were generally higher and that cost estimates were dependent on many methodological factors including whether studies were done at single or multiple institutions; the type of comparison (resistant vs. susceptible, or resistant vs. no infection), different methods used to estimate or collect costs, single or multiple diseases, and whether preventive measures were included in the cost estimates (this review did not include preventive measures). Both reviews also found that there was a wide range in the cost amounts across the studies; that the studies were heavily reliant on hospital-based data, and limited to middle-high and high-income settings; and that, because costs of resistance are mainly measured in inpatients, the overall burden may be underestimated.

A recent study (*3*) published since this review came to similar conclusions, and emphasized the need for research to estimate the impact of widespread resistance for the health system overall, including on care of patients with chronic noncommunicable diseases, and the need to bring together the relevant expertise to address knowledge gaps and provide robust estimates. For the time being, the limited information available should nevertheless be used to inform the development of improved models that can be applied to the assessment of the economic impact of resistance on health systems and society.

3.3 Knowledge gaps

A challenge for the systematic reviews was the lack of economic studies comparing the resource use associated with resistant versus non-resistant pathogens, because most economic evaluations tend to focus on the assessment of interventions. Available economic studies in this area tended to consider the costs due to resistant pathogens without comparing to non-resistant pathogens, or reported costs without describing the associated resource use, which made it difficult to determine the general applicability of the results. Ideally, comparative studies that directly capture resource use, with study duration sufficient to capture any long-term effect on health-care resource use, are needed. Such studies would allow for a better assessment of the economic consequences associated with resistant pathogens.

The findings in this report confirm those published previously – that there is a paucity of definitive cost-evidence available to allow for a comprehensive study of the economic burden of AMR. This is especially true with regard to data to assess the global and regional impact of specific bacteria–antibacterial resistance combinations. Data are currently limited to hospital systems of upper-middle and high-income countries, and this further complicates the task of attempting to estimate the burden in developing countries, where potentially the burden could be most detrimental.

For the purposes of modelling cost–effectiveness, a "minimum data set" has been proposed with the following categories: epidemiological or clinical factors relating to resistance; cost factors relating to resistance; pattern of antimicrobial usage; impact on AMR in humans from non-human consumption of antimicrobials; and information concerning the costs and effectiveness of the policy evaluated (*9*).

Based on the current findings, the following gaps need to be addressed:

- standardization and implementation of a minimum data set;

- evaluation of both clinical outcomes and resource use in high-quality studies;

- evaluation of health and economic burden in a broader array of settings – including low- and low–middle-income countries; and

- need for improved models to assess economic impact on health-care systems and society.

3.4 Key messages

- A systematic review of published studies supports the hypothesis that infection with strains of the chosen bacteria carrying the investigated resistance mechanisms is associated with worse clinical outcomes for the patients.

- A number of comparative studies are available for making a general determination of the health burden of the investigated resistance mechanisms in the chosen bacteria in high-income settings, but there is a paucity of data concerning the health burden in low- and low–middle-income countries.

- There is a lack of properly designed and conducted economic studies to compare the resource use associated with resistant versus non-resistant pathogens.

3.5 References

1. *Antibiotic resistance threats in the United States.* US Centers for Disease Control and Prevention, 2013. (http://www.cdc.gov/drugresistance/threat-report-2013/, accessed 2 December 2013).

2. Cosgrove SE, Sakoulas G, Perencevich EN, Schwaber MJ, Karchmer AW, Carmeli Y. Comparison of mortality associated with methicillin-resistant and methicillin-susceptible *Staphylococcus aureus* bacteremia: a meta-analysis. *Clin Infect Dis*, 2003, 36(1):53-59.

3. Smith RD, Coast J. *The economic burden of antimicrobial resistance: Why it is more serious than current studies suggest.* London, London School of Hygiene & Tropical Drug, 2013. (http://www.lshtm.ac.uk/php/intrafacultyinitiatives/economics/assets/dhamr2012appendix.pdf, accessed 27 December 2013).

4. Roberts RR, Hota B, Ahmad I, Scott RD, Foster SD, Abbasi F et al. Hospital and societal costs of antimicrobial-resistant infections in a Chicago teaching hospital: implications for antibiotic stewardship. *Clin Infect Dis*, 2009, 49(8):1175-1184. doi:10.1086/605630.

5. Smith R, Coast J. The true cost of antimicrobial resistance. *BMJ (Clinical Research Ed.)*, 2013, 346:f1493. doi:10.1136/bmj.f1493.

6. Guyatt G, Oxman AD, Akl EA, Kunz R, Vist G, Brozek J et al. GRADE guidelines: 1. Introduction-GRADE evidence profiles and summary of findings tables. *J Clin Epidemiol*, 2011, 64(4):383-394. doi:10.1016/j.jclinepi.2010.04.026.

7. *World Bank list of economies.* World Bank, 2013. (http://data.worldbank.org/about/country-classifications/country-and-lending-groups, accessed 2 December 2013).

8. Cosgrove SE, Kaye KS, Eliopoulous GM, Carmeli Y. Health and economic outcomes of the emergence of third-generation cephalosporin resistance in Enterobacter species. *Arch Intern Med*, 2002, 162(2):185-190.

9. Smith R, Coast J, Millar M, Wilton P, Karcher AM. *Interventions against antimicrobial resistance: a review of the literature and exploration of modelling cost-effectiveness.* The Global Forum for Health Research, Norwich, United Kingdom, World Health Organization, 2001.

10. Jeon JH, Kim K, Han WD, Song SH, Park KU, Rhee JE et al. Empirical use of ciprofloxacin for acute uncomplicated pyelonephritis caused by *Escherichia coli* in communities where the prevalence of fluoroquinolone resistance is high. *Antimicrob Agents Chemother*, 2012, 56(6):3043-3046. doi:10.1128/AAC.06212-11.

11. Pepin J, Plamondon M, Lacroix C, Alarie I. Emergence of and risk factors for ciprofloxacin-gentamicin-resistant *Escherichia coli* urinary tract infections in a region of Quebec. *Can J Infect Dis Med Microbiol*, 2009, 20(4):e163-168. (http://www.ncbi.nlm.nih.gov/pubmed/21119795, accessed 29 January 2014).

12. Carbapenem-resistant *Klebsiella pneumoniae* associated with a long-term--care facility --- West Virginia, 2009-2011. *Morb Mortal Wkly Rep*, 2011, 60(41):1418-1420. (http://www.ncbi.nlm.nih.gov/pubmed/22012114, accessed 27 January 2014).

13. Alam MF, Cohen D, Butler C, Dunstan F, Roberts Z, Hillier S et al. The additional costs of antibiotics and re-consultations for antibiotic-resistant *Escherichia coli* urinary tract infections managed in general practice. *Int J Antimicrob Agents*, 2009, 33(3):255-257. doi:10.1016/j.ijantimicag.2008.08.027.

14. Apisarnthanarak A, Kiratisin P, Saifon P, Kitphati R, Dejsirilert S, Mundy LM. Clinical and molecular epidemiology of community-onset, extended-spectrum beta-lactamase-producing *Escherichia coli* infections in Thailand: a case-control study. *Am J Infect Control*, 2007, 35(9):606-612. (http://www.ncbi.nlm.nih.gov/pubmed/17980240, accessed 5 February 2014).

15. Mauldin PD, Salgado CD, Hansen IS, Durup DT, Bosso JA. Attributable hospital cost and length of stay associated with health care-associated infections caused by antibiotic-resistant gram-negative bacteria. *Antimicrob Agents Chemother*, 2010, 54(1):109-115. doi:10.1128/AAC.01041-09.

Section 3

SECTION
04

Surveillance of antimicrobial drug resistance in disease-specific programmes

4.1 Tuberculosis

Tuberculosis (TB) is caused by the bacterium *Mycobacterium tuberculosis,* which differs in several ways from the other bacteria considered in this report. Mycobacteria grow only slowly; consequently, culture in the laboratory, which is necessary to study resistance to anti-TB drugs, is difficult. Also, mycobacteria can survive inside the body's immune defence cells, which is one of the reasons for the long duration of TB treatment.

Despite the progress in prevention and treatment of TB in recent years, 8.7 million people developed TB in 2012, and 1.3 million died as a result of the disease.

Drug-resistant tuberculosis (DR-TB) threatens global TB control and is a major public health concern in several countries. In 2012, an estimated 450 000 cases of multidrug-resistant TB (MDR-TB)[a] emerged globally confidence interval, (CI: 300 000–600 000) which corresponds to around 3.6% of all new cases and 20.2% of all previously treated cases of TB (Table 15). Over 50% of the estimated MDR-TB cases emerging in the world in 2012 were in China, India and the Russian Federation. An estimated 170 000 deaths (CI: 100 000–240 000) were caused by MDR-TB globally in 2012, including patients with concomitant HIV infection.

Table 15 Estimated proportions of multidrug-resistant cases among new and previously treated TB cases, 2012, by WHO region

	New			Previously treated		
WHO region	% MDR	95% confidence intervals		% MDR	95% confidence intervals	
AFR	2.3	0.2	4.4	10.7	4.4	17
AMR	2.2	1.4	3.0	13.5	4.7	22.3
EMR	3.5	0.1	11.3	32.5	11.5	53.5
EUR	15.7	9.5	21.9	45.3	39.2	51.5
SEA	2.2	1.6	2.8	16.1	11.1	21
WPR	4.7	3.3	6.1	22.1	17.6	26.5
Global	3.6	2.1	5.1	20.2	13.3	27.2

AFR, African Region; AMR, Region of the Americas; EMR, Eastern Mediterranean Region; EUR, European Region; MDR, multidrug resistance; SEA, South-East Asia Region; WPR, Western Pacific Region.

Section 4

---

[a] MDR-TB is defined as resistance to at least rifampicin and isoniazid, the two most powerful first-line anti-TB medicines.

4.1.1 Evolution of drug resistance in tuberculosis

The development of resistance to anti-TB drugs began shortly after the initial introduction of antibacterial drugs for the treatment of TB. Already, during the first randomized clinical trial (RCT) in the 1940s, resistance to streptomycin was detected in a large majority of patients treated with that drug. The spread of drug-resistant strains was soon recognized and, despite the introduction of combination drug regimens throughout the world many years ago, the presence of drug resistance has been documented with increasing frequency from an ever wider geographic area. Drug-susceptible TB is treated for 6 months with a combination of four drugs – rifampicin, isoniazid, ethambutol and pyrazinamide. However, most treatment courses for MDR-TB last 20 months or longer, and require daily administration of drugs that are less effective and have more side-effects than those used to treat drug-susceptible forms of TB. Extensively drug-resistant TB is the most resistant variant.[a]

4.1.2 Surveillance of drug-resistant tuberculosis

Coverage of drug-resistance surveillance

Data on drug resistance have been systematically collected and analysed from 136 countries worldwide (70% of the WHO 194 Member States) since 1994, when the WHO Global Project on Anti-tuberculosis Drug Resistance Surveillance was launched. Of these countries, 71 have continuous surveillance systems based on routine diagnostic drug susceptibility testing (DST) of all TB patients, and 65 rely on special epidemiological surveys of representative samples of patients. The progress towards obtaining worldwide drug resistance data is shown in Figure 14.

Figure 14 **Progress in global coverage of surveillance data on anti-TB drug resistance, 1994–2012**

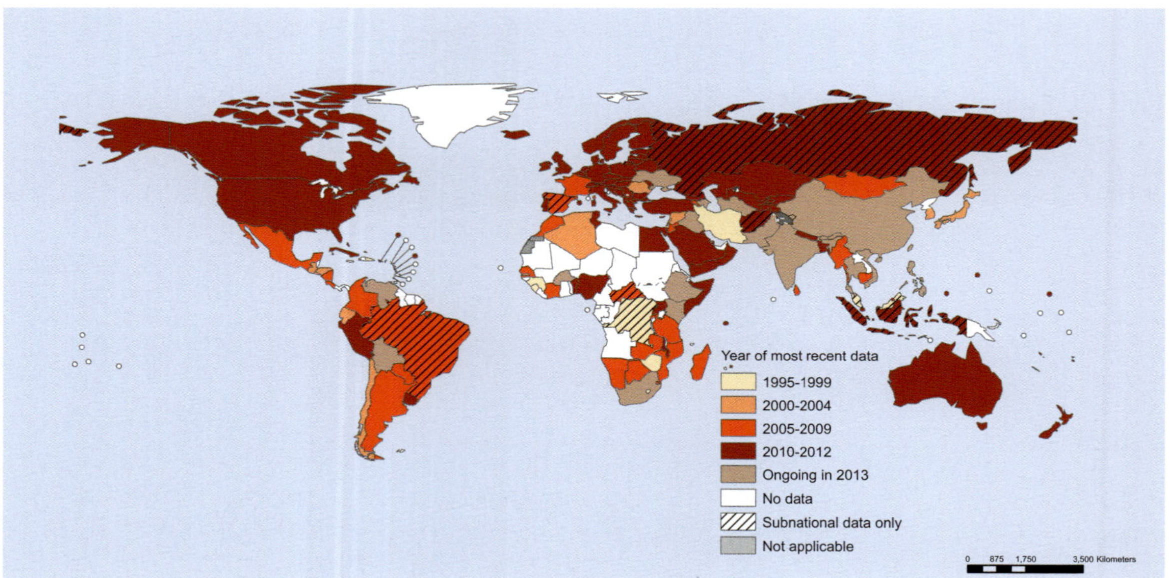

Continuous surveillance based on routine DST of TB patients – with systematic collection, collation and analysis of data – is the most effective way to monitor trends in drug resistance over time. Additionally, surveillance systems can detect outbreaks that might otherwise go undetected, even if the original outbreak site had not been selected for inclusion in a survey. The number of countries that can rely on data generated by continuous surveillance systems is progressively increasing, due to the increasing availability of laboratory facilities for culture and DST services.

Special surveys of a representative sample of notified TB cases are still the most common method of investigating the burden of drug resistance in settings where routine DST is not available for all TB patients due to lack of laboratory capacity or adequate resources (1). On average, every year national surveys are carried out in 20 countries worldwide, and 20 more are in preparation. Data generated by

[a] XDR-TB is defined as MDR-TB plus resistance to at least a fluoroquinolone and one second-line injectable agent (amikacin, kanamycin or capreomycin).

molecular technologies are now being incorporated into drug-resistance surveys, to simplify logistics and reduce laboratory workloads. In particular, in countries that do not yet have facilities for conventional culture and DST methods, or where laboratories cannot cope with the large workload generated by a survey, the new rapid test – Xpert® MTB/RIF – can play an important role. Xpert® MTB/RIF is an automated assay for the simultaneous detection of TB and rifampicin resistance directly from sputum in less than 2 hours. This method can be used to screen specimens for rifampicin resistance, and identify those requiring further testing at the NRL or supranational TB reference laboratory (SRL).

Drug-resistance surveys should be conducted regularly, approximately every five years, so that time trends in drug resistance can be monitored. Drug-resistance data are most lacking from central and francophone African countries, largely because of weakness of the laboratory infrastructure.

Anti-TB drug-resistance surveillance in countries is supported by an SRL Network, presently comprising 29 laboratories covering all six WHO regions.[a] The SRL Network is expanding its membership to include Centres of Excellence, a new category of laboratory specifically recognizing well-performing laboratories in large low- and middle-income countries that are also working specifically to build in-country laboratory capacity.

Multidrug-resistant tuberculosis

The proportions of new TB cases with MDR-TB most recently reported by countries are shown in Figure 15.

Figure 15 Proportion of new TB cases with multidrug resistance (MDR-TB) worldwide[a]

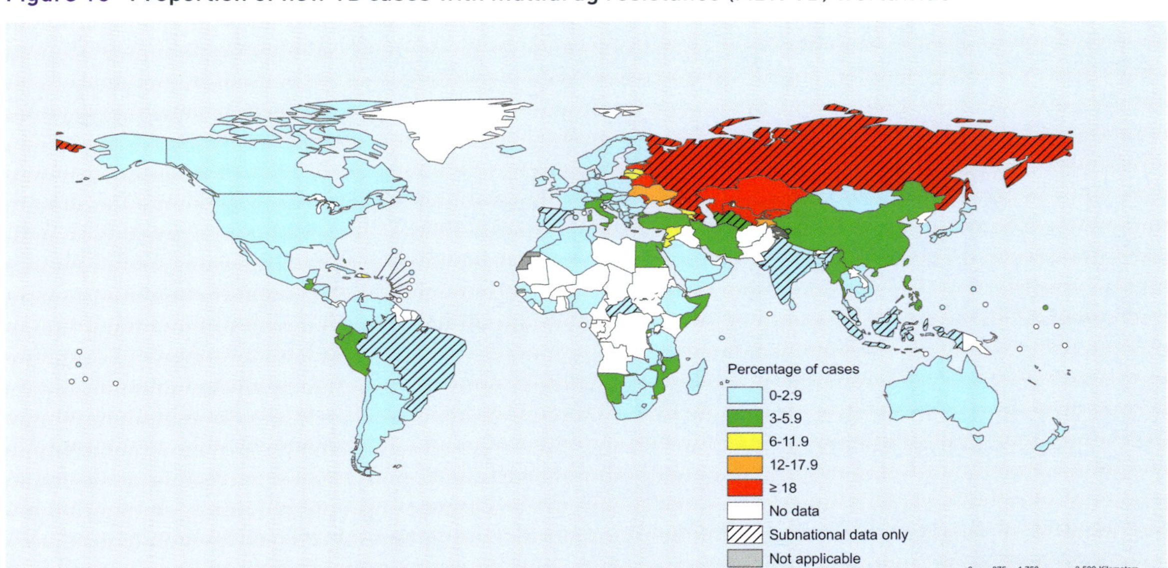

Numbers are based on the most recent year for which data have been reported, which varies among countries.

Proportions ranged from 0% to 34.8% and were highest in Azerbaijan (22.3% in 2007), Belarus (34.8% in 2012), Estonia (19.7% in 2012), Kazakhstan (22.9% in 2012), Kyrgyzstan (26.4% in 2012), the Republic of Moldova (23.7% in 2012), the Russian Federation (average: 23.1% in 2011) and Uzbekistan (23.2% in 2011). The proportion of previously treated TB cases with MDR-TB ranged from 0% to 68.6% for those countries reporting more than 10 previously treated cases in 2012.

Countries or subnational areas with the highest reported proportions of MDR-TB patients who had been previously treated were Azerbaijan (Baku city: 55.8% in 2007), Belarus (68.6% in 2012), Estonia (50.0% in 2012), Kazakhstan (55.0% in 2012), Kyrgyzstan (68.4% in 2012), the Republic of Moldova (62.3% in 2012), Tajikistan (56.0 in 2012) and Uzbekistan (62.0% in 2011). In the Russian Federation, although the national average proportion of cases with MDR-TB is less than 50% (average: 48.6% in 2011), it is well above 50% in several oblasts.

These data confirm that Eastern European and central Asian countries continue to be the regions with the highest levels of MDR-TB, with MDR-TB accounting for nearly one third of new TB cases and two thirds of previously treated TB cases in some settings.

---

[a]   For the global SRL Network, see: www.stoptb.org/wg/gli/srln.asp

Extensively drug-resistant tuberculosis

Extensively drug-resistant TB (XDR-TB) had been reported by 92 countries by the end of 2012 (Figure 16).

Figure 16 **Countries that notified at least one case of extensively drug-resistant TB (XDR-TB) by the end of 2012**

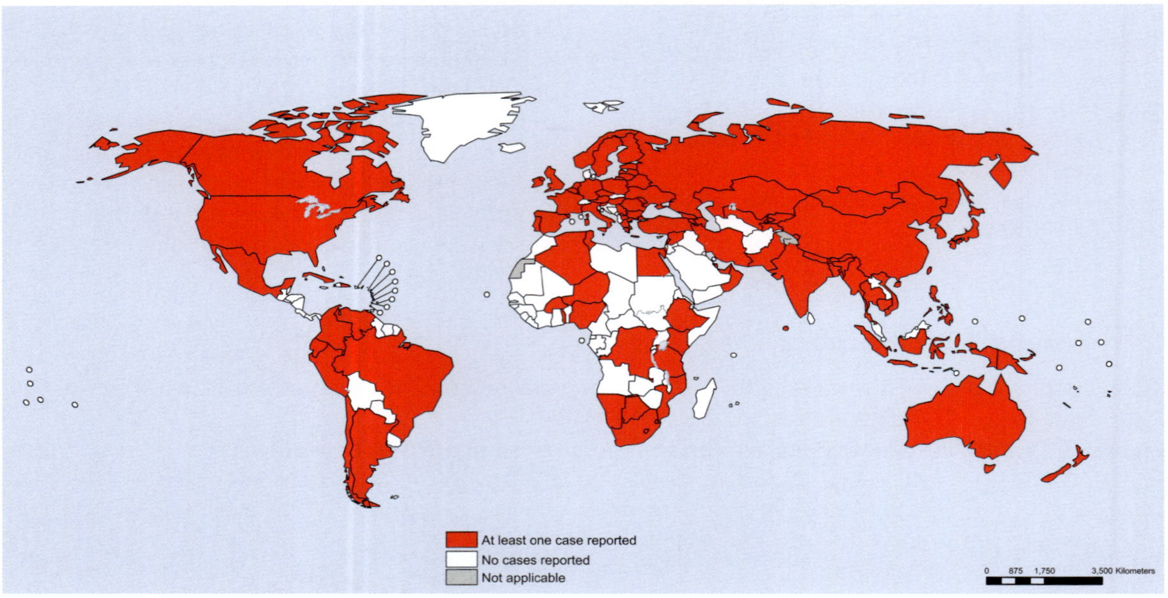

A total of 75 countries and 4 territories reported representative data from continuous surveillance or special surveys on the proportion of XDR-TB among MDR-TB cases. Combining their data, the proportion of MDR-TB cases with XDR-TB was 9.6% (95% CI: 8.1%–11%). Of these countries, 13 reported more than 10 XDR-TB cases. Proportions of MDR-TB cases with XDR-TB are highest in Azerbaijan (Baku city: 12.8%), Belarus (11.9%), Latvia (16.0%), Lithuania (24.8%) and Tajikistan (Dushanbe city and Rudaki district: 21.0%).

4.1.3 Global public health response to drug-resistant tuberculosis

Coverage of drug susceptibility testing

Targets included in the Global Plan to Stop TB 2011–2015 (*2*) stipulate that by 2015 all new cases of TB considered at high risk of MDR-TB (about 20% of all new confirmed cases), as well as all previously treated cases, should receive DST for at least the first-line drugs rifampicin and isoniazid, and that all patients with confirmed MDR-TB should also be tested for XDR-TB.

Globally, 5% of new bacteriologically confirmed TB cases and 9% of those previously treated were tested for MDR-TB in 2012. The proportions have increased slightly in recent years but remain below the target set for 2012 by the Global Plan. Among TB cases which were notified and confirmed as MDR-TB in 2012, 23% were reported to have had DST carried out for both fluoroquinolones and second-line injectable drugs, to test for XDR-TB. Much more widespread use of routine DST is urgently needed to improve the detection of MDR-TB and XDR-TB. Expansion of DST will require strengthening of laboratory capacity, the introduction of new rapid diagnostics, and improved reporting from diagnostic centres. The increasing recognition of XDR-TB in the world (Figure 16) reflects the increased risk of acquisition of additional drug resistance or the increased transmissibility of resistant strains of TB when care and prevention are inadequate.

4.1.4 Notification of MDR-TB cases and enrolment on treatment

The very limited use of DST in many countries is one of the main reasons why the number of patients with diagnosed MDR-TB remains low. In total, approximately 84 000 cases of MDR-TB were notified to WHO in 2012, with India, the Russian Federation and South Africa reporting more than a half of these cases. For 27 high burden countries, the estimated MDR-TB cases among notified pulmonary cases in 2012, notified cases of MDR-TB and enrolments on MDR-TB treatment in 2009–2012, and treatment outcomes reported for the cohort starting treatment in 2010 are shown in Table 16.

Table 16 Recent estimated and notified MDR-TB cases, treatment enrolments and outcomes, in 27 high MDR-TB burden countries, by WHO region

	Estimated MDR-TB among notified pulmonary TB cases, 2012			Notified cases					Cases enrolled on MDR-TB treatment				MDR-TB cases reported with treatment outcome data, 2010 cohort[b,c]	
	Best estimate	Range											x	
		Low	High	2009	2010	2011	2012	2012 notified/ estimated (%)[a]	2009	2010	2011	2012	N	%
AFR	38 000	14 000	62 000	10 741	9340	12 384	18 129	48	5994	7209	7467	9303	6166	66
AMR	7100	4500	9600	2884	2661	3474	2967	42	3153	3249	3087	3102	2374	89
EMR	18 000	0	42 000	496	873	841	2236	12	707	967	756	1602	676	77
EUR	74 000	60 000	88 000	28 157	33 776	34 199	36 708	51	17 169	28 336	36 313	42 399	19 496	58
SEAR	90 000	71 000	110 000	2560	3942	6615	19 202	21	2040	3901	4597	15 845	3113	79
WPR	74 000	57 000	91 000	2059	4295	4394	4473	6	1429	2210	4946	5070	2456	57
	300 000	220 000	380 000	46 897	54 887	61 907	83 715	28	30 492	45 872	57 166	77 321	34 281	62

a. Notified cases of MDR-TB in 2012 as a percentage of the estimated MDR-TB cases among all cases of pulmonary TB in the same year: the percentage may exceed 100% if estimates of the number of MDR-TB cases are too conservative and in the absence of linkage between the clinical and laboratory registers.
b. The percentage of MDR-TB cases originally notified in 2010 with outcomes reported: the percentage may exceed 100% due to inclusion of updated information on MDR-TB cases in 2010, absence of linkage between notification systems for TB and MDR-TB, and the inclusion in the treatment cohort of cases of MDR-TB from a year prior to 2010.
c. Treatment outcome reporting for 2010 cohort, in 27 high MDR-TB burden countriesc and WHO regions . These countries account for about 85% of estimated MDR-TB cases globally, and are defined by overall number of cases or the level of MDR-TB among previously untreated cases.

The reported MDR-TB cases represent only about 21% of the estimated 450 000 (range 300 000–600 000) cases of MDR-TB likely to have emerged globally in 2012. Nonetheless, there has been an increase in the total number of MDR-TB cases detected and notified by countries between 2011 and 2012 in all WHO regions, except in the Region of the Americas. Although the total number of TB cases receiving second-line treatment for MDR-TB remains low compared with the Global Plan's targets, enrolment of MDR-TB patients worldwide increased by more than 150% between 2009 and 2012.

The proportion of MDR-TB patients starting second-line treatment in 2012 was 92% of all notified cases globally, but lower in the African (51%) and South-East Asian (83%) regions, reflecting a widespread shortfall in the capacity to provide treatment for diagnosed MDR-TB cases, particularly in those regions. Common constraints include the lack of trained staff, inadequate availability of second-line medication, insufficient treatment or monitoring facilities, incomplete reporting, and other weaknesses in the coordinated functions required for effective programmatic management of DR-TB.

To reach the targets set out in the Global Plan and advance towards universal access to treatment, a strong concerted effort is still needed on many aspects of TB care, particularly in the countries where the burden is highest.

4.1.5 Public health implications: treatment outcomes for multidrug-resistant and extensively drug-resistant tuberculosis

Standardized monitoring methods and indicators have enabled countries to report MDR-TB treatment outcomes in a comparable manner in recent years (*3*). The number of cases reported in annual MDR-TB treatment outcome cohorts tripled between 2007 and 2010, reflecting a steady increase in the extent of monitoring in all regions during this period (Figure 17).

Figure 17 Treatment outcomes for patients diagnosed with MDR-TB, by WHO region, 2007–2010 cohorts

The total number of cases with outcome data is shown below each bar following the year of start of treatment.

Overall, the proportion of MDR-TB patients in the 2010 cohort who were successfully treated was 48%, while 28% of these patients were reported as lost to follow-up or had no outcome information. Treatment success was highest in the Eastern Mediterranean Region (56%), as well as in the Region of the Americas (54%) where this proportion has increased steadily since 2007 together with a reduction in the proportion of cases that were not evaluated. In the 2010 cohort, mortality was highest in the African Region (17%) and the proportion of patients whose treatment failed was highest in the European Region (11%). Among a subset of 795 XDR-TB patients in 26 countries, treatment success was 20% overall, with 44% deaths.

Further progress towards the global target for treatment success will require the scale-up of treatment programmes, enhancement of drug regimen effectiveness, supporting patients to encourage completion of treatment, and improved data collection and reporting. Positive recent developments include the introduction of short treatment regimens as WHO policy, and the introduction of bedaquiline for the treatment of MDR-TB in 2012, important steps towards better treatment outcomes for more TB patients.

4.1.6 Key messages

- Drug-resistant TB threatens global TB control and is a major public health concern in several countries.

- In 2012 it was estimated that, on a global level, 3.6% of new tuberculosis cases and 20.2% of previously treated cases had multidrug-resistant TB (MDR-TB). Frequencies of MDR-TB are much higher in Eastern Europe and central Asia than elsewhere in the world.

- There were an estimated 450 000 new MDR-TB cases in 2012, about half of which were in India, China and the Russian Federation.

- Extensively drug-resistant TB (XDR-TB) has been reported by 92 countries. The average proportion of MDR-TB cases which have XDR-TB is estimated to be 9.6%.

- There has been steady progress in the detection and treatment of MDR-TB since 2010. However, the approximate 84 000 cases of MDR-TB and 10 000 additional rifampicin-resistant TB cases notified to WHO globally in 2012 represented only 21% of the MDR-TB cases estimated to have emerged worldwide in that year.

- Of the MDR-TB patients who started treatment in 2010, only 48% (range 46%–56% in the WHO regions) were cured after completion of treatment. The treatment success rate was lower among XDR-TB cases.

4.2 Malaria

Malaria is caused by the protozoan parasite *Plasmodium* which is transmitted via the bite of female *Anopheles* mosquitoes. In the human body, parasites travel in the bloodstream to the liver, where they multiply and subsequently infect red blood cells. Among the five species of *Plasmodium* parasites that infect humans (*P. falciparum, P. vivax, P. ovale, P. malariae* and *P. knowlesi*), *P. falciparum* and *P. vivax* are the most common. The most dangerous form of malaria, with the highest rates of complications and mortality, is caused by *P. falciparum*.

Early and effective treatment of malaria is a cornerstone of malaria control programmes. Malaria can quickly become life-threatening as the vital organs are deprived of oxygen and nutrients due to disruptions in the blood supply. WHO estimated that in 2010, 219 million cases of malaria occurred worldwide (CI 54 million to 289 million) and 660 000 people died from the disease (CI 490 000 to 836 000) (4).

4.2.1 Evolution of antimalarial drug resistance

There is no simple laboratory test to identify drug resistance in malaria. Instead, WHO defines antimalarial drug resistance as the ability of a parasite strain to survive and/or multiply despite administration and absorption of a drug given in doses equal to or higher than those usually recommended, but within tolerance of the patient (5). Cross-resistance can occur to drugs belonging to the same chemical family, or those that share the same modes of action.

Resistance develops in two phases. First, an initial genetic event produces a resistant parasite (de novo mutation). Such genetic events are spontaneous and rare. In some instances, a single genetic event may be all that is required to confer drug resistance; in others, multiple independent events may be necessary before a resistant strain of the parasite emerges (6). In the second phase, resistant parasites are selected for and begin to multiply, eventually resulting in a parasite population that is no longer susceptible to treatment. Non-immune patients who are heavily infected and who receive inadequate amounts of an antimalarial drug are at high risk for de novo resistance. This can be prevented by provision of effective treatment and ensuring that patients follow exactly the prescribed drug regimens (7). The spread of resistance is further driven by the use of drugs which are eliminated only slowly from the body, such as chloroquine, mefloquine or piperaquine, thereby preventing infection by susceptible parasites but allowing infection by resistant parasites (8).

Resistance to antimalarial drugs has threatened global malaria control since the emergence of resistance to chloroquine in the 1970s. Studies have demonstrated that *P. falciparum* resistance to chloroquine and pyrimethamine both originated in South-East Asia and subsequently spread to Africa (9). Similarly, in the 1980s, resistance to mefloquine emerged rapidly on the western border of Cambodia and on the northwest border of Thailand only a few years after its introduction (10). In the 1990s, resistance of *P. falciparum* to amodiaquine and sulfadoxine-pyrimethamine was observed; these drugs are now among those used as partner drugs in artemisinin-based combination therapy (ACT).

4.2.2 Surveillance of antimalarial therapeutic efficacy and resistance

P. falciparum resistance to artemisinin is suspected when ≥ 10% of patients who received treatment with an ACT have parasites detectable on the third day after the start of treatment. This resistance is confirmed when failure occurs after treatment with an oral artemisinin-based monotherapy with adequate concentration of the drug in the patient's blood, as evidenced by the persistence of parasites for 7 days, or the presence of parasites at day 3 and recrudescence within 28 or 42 days. Since 2006, when the first two cases of artemisinin resistance were confirmed in Cambodia, foci of either suspected or confirmed artemisinin resistance have been identified in Cambodia, Myanmar, Thailand and Viet Nam.

Antimalarial therapeutic efficacy can only be assessed by conducting clinical studies which estimate the failure rate following supervised administration of treatment, and which follow patients over a set follow-up period. For this purpose, and in response to the emergence of chloroquine resistance, WHO developed a standardized therapeutic efficacy study (TES) protocol. The protocol has evolved and been updated over time, most recently in 2009 (*11*). The WHO protocol provides study teams with standardized methods for making repeated assessments of clinical and parasitological outcomes in patients who received supervised administration of treatment, over a follow-up of 28 or 42 days.

Therapeutic efficacy studies

Sentinel sites for TESs are selected based on population density, accessibility, and feasibility of supervision, malaria epidemiology, population mobility and migration; 4–8 sites generally provide adequate coverage of the variations in malaria transmission and prevalence that can occur within a given country. However, it is critical that the national malaria control programme (NMCP) has the capacity and resources to manage the studies: fewer studies of high quality are preferable to numerous studies of substandard quality. When a TES is conducted at the same sentinel site once every 24 months at the same time of the year, study findings provide a fundamental data source for the early detection of changes to antimalarial drug sensitivity, enabling timely changes to national treatment policy.

NMCPs are supported by regional networks for monitoring antimalarial drug resistance. Over the last 10 years, WHO has supported the creation of 10 networks, of which 6 are currently active (Figure 18).

Figure 18 **Regional and subregional therapeutic efficacy study networks for monitoring antimalarial drug efficacy**

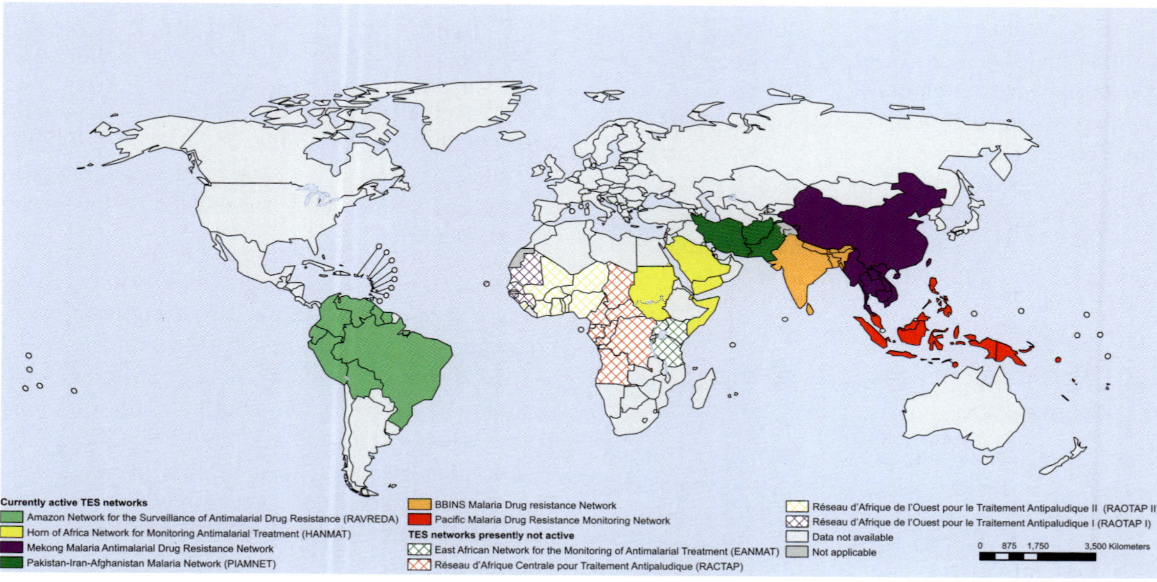

The networks help to strengthen national capacity for monitoring antimalarial drug efficacy. During the network meetings, held every year or every second year, NMCPs have the opportunity to present their most recent data, to share common challenges and collectively find solutions, plan subsequent studies, and discuss the status of antimalarial drug efficacy and treatment policies in areas close to common borders. Network meetings provide an important venue for programme staff to stay informed about the evolving picture of antimalarial drug resistance in their region and globally. Stronger networks are likely to have played a role in increasing the number of countries conducting TES, from 31 countries in 2008–2009, to 47 in 2010–2011, and 49 countries in 2012–2013 (*4*). The results of TESs are published by WHO every five years (*5*).

An effective global surveillance system for drug efficacy involves support and coordination at the global, regional, subregional, and national levels. WHO regional offices support the NMCPs in maintaining continuity and momentum over time. WHO Headquarters provides regularly updated and simplified tools such as the WHO standardized protocol, and assists with protocol review, facilitating ethical clearance for studies, conducting clinical monitoring, procuring antimalarial drugs and providing financial support. An important factor in successful monitoring has been attribution of full credit and ownership of the studies to the NMCPs who are responsible for study design and implementation.

4.2.3 Global public health implications of antimalarial drug resistance

Antimalarial drug resistance is a major threat to malaria control, and has important implications for global public health. The emergence of chloroquine resistance in Africa in the 1980s was associated with increases in both hospital admissions and mortality at the community level (12, 13), increased risk of anaemia in pregnancy and low birth weight (14), and increased transmission (15).

Resistance to antimalarial drugs has had a significant impact on the cost of global malaria control, as new drugs have had to be developed to replace those that have become ineffective. In addition, patients whose treatment fails due to infection with a resistant strain require repeated consultations at health facilities for further diagnosis and treatment, resulting in lost work-days, absences from school, and increased health-care costs (16).

In the event that parasite sensitivity to artemisinin may become reduced, ACTs will continue to cure patients, provided the partner drug remains efficacious. In the short-term, the emergence of resistance to one component of the combination will not initially lead to high mortality rates, as patients will still be protected by the partner drug. However, the emergence of resistance to artemisinin increases the risk that resistance to the partner drug will also develop. Without an effective alternative treatment, widespread resistance to both components of ACTs would be disastrous. To date, treatment failures following treatment with an ACT have only been observed in South-East Asia. Specifically, treatment failures occurred following administration of artesunate-mefloquine in Cambodia (17) and Thailand (18), and dihydroartemisinin-piperaquine in Cambodia (19). Without an alternative ACT, patients in western Cambodia now have to be treated with atovaquone-proguanil. However, this treatment is also vulnerable to resistance.

Because of the potential consequences if resistance to artemisinin were to become widespread, intensive efforts are under way to limit the emergence and spread of resistant parasites, notably in the Greater Mekong subregion (20, 21).

4.2.4 Key messages

- The estimated annual cost of containment operations in areas of artemisinin resistance is US$ 10 – 20 per person at risk (21-22);

- Surveillance of antimalarial drug efficacy and resistance depends on clinical detection of treatment failures;

- An effective global surveillance system for antimalarial drug efficacy requires coordination at the global, regional, subregional, and national levels;

- Foci of either suspected or confirmed artemisinin resistance have been identified in Cambodia, Myanmar, Thailand and Viet Nam: further spread of resistant strains of malaria parasites, or the independent emergence of artemisinin resistance in other regions, could jeopardize all recent gains in malaria control and have major implications for public health.

4.3 HIV

Human immunodeficiency virus (HIV) infects cells of the immune system, destroying or impairing their function. If untreated, infection with the virus results in the progressive deterioration of the immune system, eventually leading to the development of acquired immunodeficiency syndrome (AIDS).

According to estimates by WHO and UNAIDS, 34 million people were living with HIV infection at the end of 2011. That same year, some 2.5 million people were newly infected, and 1.7 million (including 230 000 children) died of AIDS-related causes.

Antiretroviral therapy (ART) can slow progression of the disease by preventing the virus from replicating and thus decreasing the amount of virus (i.e. the viral load) in an infected person's blood. HIV drug resistance refers to the ability of HIV to replicate in the presence of drugs that usually suppress its replication. Such resistance is caused by mutations in the genetic structure of the virus. Mutations are common in HIV because the virus replicates rapidly and does not contain the proteins needed to correct any mistakes made during this process. Therefore, some degree of HIV drug resistance is expected to occur, even when appropriate regimens are provided and adherence to treatment is optimal.

Transmitted HIV drug resistance refers to previously uninfected individuals being infected with drug-resistant virus, and *acquired HIV drug resistance* refers to mutations being selected during viral replication in patients receiving ART. Pretreatment HIV drug resistance measures the level of resistance in patients at the start of ART; such resistance can be both transmitted and acquired, depending on whether there was exposure to antiretroviral (ARV) drugs before the start of ART. This might have happened unknowingly (as part of pre- or post-exposure prophylactic use of ARV drugs), during pregnancy (as part of efforts to curtail mother to child transmission of HIV) or as a result of unsuccessful attempts to start ART in the past.

4.3.1 Surveillance of anti-HIV drug resistance

Understanding the emergence and transmission of HIV drug resistance at population level, and the interaction between its various determinants, requires routine monitoring of the performance of health services in delivering ART, and surveillance of HIV drug resistance in selected populations. The WHO Global HIV Drug

Resistance Surveillance and Monitoring Strategy includes the following elements (*22*):

- monitoring of early warning indicators of HIV drug resistance, which assess the performance of health services in delivering ART;

- surveillance of HIV drug resistance among:

   - adults initiating ART;

   - adults taking ART;

   - adults recently infected with HIV who are treatment naive; and

   - children under 18 months of age.

To ensure that high-quality assessment of HIV drug resistance is available to support country decision-making, WHO has developed a comprehensive HIV drug resistance laboratory strategy, and has accredited laboratories that implement rigorous quality assurance of genotyping data. As of 2012, WHO had accredited 29 testing laboratories for HIV drug resistance in 21 countries (Figure 19).

Figure 19 Countries having implemented one or more elements of the WHO Global HIV Drug Resistance Surveillance and Monitoring Strategy (blue), and location of WHO-accredited genotyping laboratories for HIV drug resistance (as at end of 2012)

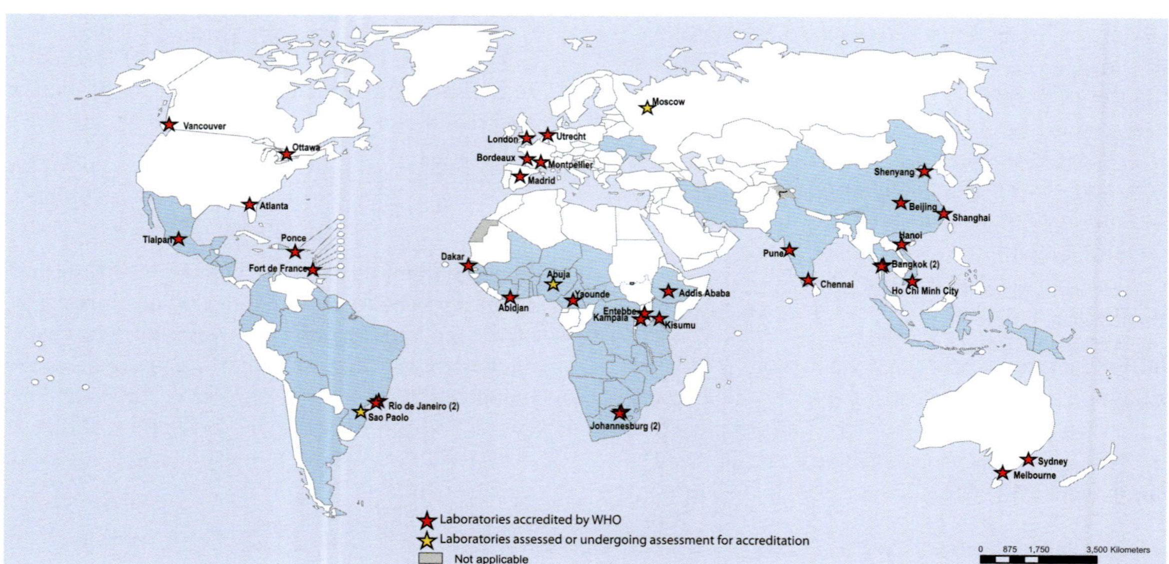

WHO and its collaborators in the HIVResNet have been monitoring the emergence of HIV drug resistance since 2004.

Data from 82 surveys found evidence of increasing levels of transmitted drug resistance to non-nucleoside reverse transcriptase inhibitors (NNRTIs) among recently infected and previously untreated patients. This was particularly the case in the areas surveyed in Africa, where the prevalence of NNRTI resistance reached 3.4% (CI: 1.8%–5.2%) in 2009. More widespread use of ART was associated with a higher prevalence

of NNRTI resistance, although this effect remained modest in most of the areas surveyed (*23*).

Among patients initiating ART, data from 36 WHO surveys in 12 low- and middle-income countries found that the overall prevalence of HIV drug resistance to any ARV drug ranged from 4.8% (CI: 3.8%–6.0%) in 2007 to 6.8% (CI: 4.8%–9.0%) in 2010.

In about 90% of patients still alive and on therapy at 12 months, the viral load was suppressed. Among those for whom viral load suppression was not achieved, resistance was present in 72%, mostly to nucleoside reverse transcriptase inhibitors (NRTIs) and NNRTIs. In the remaining 28%, no resistance mutations were found; therefore, these patients experienced treatment failure for other reasons, such as poor adherence to treatment or extended interruptions of treatment, and may have been switched to costlier second-line regimens unnecessarily.

The resistance patterns among patients for whom first-line treatment failed after 12 months suggest that switching to standard second-line therapies (comprising two nucleoside class drugs and a boosted protease inhibitor) soon thereafter would be effective in suppressing the viral load in most cases.

Results from 50 countries monitoring early warning indicators for HIV drug resistance have found important gaps in service delivery and programme performance. This is particularly the case with respect to drug procurement and supply systems, adherence to treatment and the ability of treatment programmes to retain people in care.

4.3.2 Global public health implications of anti-HIV drug resistance

Evidence of HIV drug resistance before the start of treatment is strongly associated with treatment failure (i.e. virological confirmation that treatment has not suppressed the patient's viral load) (24, 25). Minimizing the emergence of drug resistance is therefore critical to maintain the long-term effectiveness of ART. Such therapy must be taken for life, and although the number of alternative drug combinations is increasing, it remains limited. In addition, the cost of alternative regimens is considerably greater than that of standard first-line combinations. Protecting the efficacy of the limited therapeutic options is essential for the sustainability of HIV programmes.

4.4 Influenza

Influenza imposes a global public health and economic burden for all populations, due to recurrent annual seasonal epidemics of acute respiratory illness caused by highly transmissible influenza A and B viruses. The threat of a pandemic event arises when a novel influenza A virus emerges to which humans have little or no immunity, and which has the potential to spread easily from person to person. Although annual epidemics result in about 250 000–500 000 deaths worldwide (26), pandemics may result in much higher mortality rates, as occurred in the 1918–1919 'Spanish Flu' pandemic, which resulted in as many as 50 million deaths (27).

Routine surveillance of HIV drug resistance has not kept pace with the scale-up of treatment in many countries, limiting the ability to reliably identify levels and patterns of HIV drug resistance and to assess trends over time. As ART continues to be rolled out, increased rates of drug resistance may occur. Hence, robust systems to assess levels of HIV drug resistance and monitor the factors associated with its emergence need to be in place to detect these patterns in a timely manner. National programmes are encouraged to carry out routine surveillance of HIV drug resistance in order to enhance programme planning and management, and to inform treatment policies.

4.3.3 Key messages

- HIV drug resistance causes ART failure. Therefore, minimizing the emergence of HIV drug resistance and its transmission is critical to ensure the continued effectiveness of ART, in view of the need for lifelong treatment, the limited treatment options available, and the fact that second-line and salvage treatment regimens are considerably more expensive, less patient-friendly and have more side-effects than WHO-recommended first-line regimens.

- With the expanded availability and use of ART, resistance to ARV drugs is slowly increasing.

- To limit the impact of HIV drug resistance on the effectiveness of ART, it is essential to ensure high-quality treatment and care services. The performance of treatment programmes can be monitored and improved using the early warning indicators for HIV drug resistance proposed by WHO. In addition, levels of HIV drug resistance should be monitored using WHO-recommended surveillance methods. Member States are encouraged to report their findings to WHO because they can play a critical role in the development of its ART guidelines.

4.4.1 Evolution of resistance in influenza viruses

Influenza A viruses that affect humans may originate from a variety of animal hosts, but primarily birds and swine. They are subtyped according to the combination of their haemagglutinin (17 H subtypes) and neuraminidase (10 N subtypes) surface proteins. The A(H1N1) and A(H3N2) subtypes are currently in general circulation in human populations. These viruses evolve continuously, and the resultant new circulating viruses of the same subtype cause annual seasonal epidemics.

WHO has been continuously monitoring the evolution of influenza viruses for more than 60 years. The WHO Global Influenza Surveillance and Response System (GISRS), through its worldwide network (Figure 20) provides a solid scientific basis for global risk assessment and recommendations in areas such as laboratory diagnostics, composition of influenza vaccines and antiviral drugs. In addition, GISRS provides a global alert mechanism for the emergence of influenza viruses with pandemic potential.

Figure 20 WHO Global Influenza Surveillance and Response System

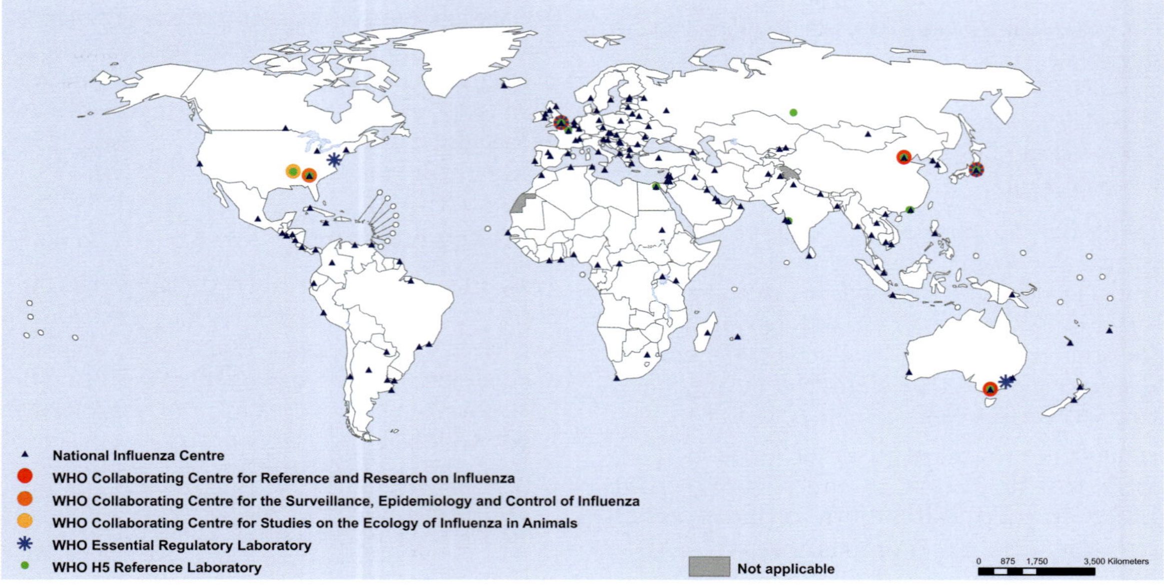

4.4.2 Anti-influenza drug resistance

Although vaccines remain the primary tool for influenza prevention and control, over the past 10 years, antiviral drugs have been increasingly used for the treatment of epidemic and pandemic influenza. WHO has published guidance on their use in clinical management (*28*).

Currently, two classes of antiviral drugs are available for the treatment of influenza: adamantanes and neuraminidase inhibitors. However, due to widespread resistance to the adamantanes, these antiviral drugs are currently not recommended for use against circulating seasonal influenza A and influenza B viruses (*26, 29*). Adamantane resistance became fixed in A(H3N2) viruses after a rapid increase in prevalence during 2004–2005. For the 2009 pandemic influenza A(H1N1)pdm09 virus, the adamantane resistance M gene was acquired from its parental Eurasian swine virus.

The neuraminidase inhibitors oseltamivir and zanamivir, developed in the 1990s, are effective against both influenza A and B viruses, and are widely available. Oseltamivir has also been the principal choice for antiviral stockpiles, an important component of pandemic preparedness. The frequency of oseltamivir resistance in currently circulating A(H1N1)pdm09 viruses is low (1%–2%) (*30*). However, the emergence and rapid global spread in 2007–2008 of oseltamivir resistance in the former seasonal A(H1N1) viruses has shown that viruses resistant to neuraminidase inhibitors could pose a serious threat to public health, and has raised the priority given to antiviral susceptibility surveillance in the WHO GISRS (*31*).

4.4.3 Surveillance of anti-influenza drug resistance

Resistance and decreased susceptibility to anti-influenza drugs are detected by laboratory testing of virus isolates from patients with and without exposure to antiviral drugs. There are two sets of laboratory methods for the detection of resistance or decreased susceptibility: genotypic assays and phenotypic assays. The capacity in GISRS for antiviral susceptibility testing was developed only recently, mainly in countries where antiviral drugs are in use. Although all WHO regions currently have the capacity to carry out this testing, the laboratories use a wide range of protocols, and standards for interpreting and reporting test results are lacking.

Antiviral susceptibility testing is carried out by the GISRS WHO Collaborating Centres (WHO CCs) and some national influenza centres (NICs), providing broad baseline susceptibility data during each influenza season. However, NICs are in a position to generate more timely antiviral susceptibility data than the

WHO CCs, and this rapidity is critical for the early detection of resistant strains in the community and in clinical management.

The WHO Expert Working Group on Surveillance of Influenza Antiviral Susceptibility (AVWG) was formed in 2011 to develop practical approaches for GISRS NICs by advising on: appropriate surveillance strategy, laboratory methodologies, interpretation of laboratory surveillance data, classification criteria for reporting results, reference materials, quality and capacity-building. The AVWG also reviews the uptake of existing antiviral drugs, the status of development of new antiviral drugs, progress of new antiviral drugs through clinical trials into licensure and use, and current gaps in the methodologies of GISRS NICs to better incorporate these drugs for effective antiviral susceptibility surveillance (32).

4.4.4 Public health implications of anti-influenza drug resistance

Influenza antivirals have several public health applications, including prevention of disease in exposed individuals at high risk for severe disease, therapy to reduce morbidity and mortality in patients with severe illness or at higher risk of developing severe disease, therapy among a broader population for disease mitigation, and reduction of secondary transmission. Specifically, influenza antiviral drugs, if taken properly, can reduce the risk of infection by 70% to 90% and duration of illness by 1–2 days; it can also reduce complications from secondary bacterial infections (28).

However, should anti-influenza drug resistance emerge undetected, the public health applications of influenza antivirals could be undermined, increasing the threat of pandemics and severity of illness. For example, A(H5N1) influenza virus with high-level resistance to oseltamivir was discovered in two Vietnamese patients receiving treatment in January 2005 (33). Both patients died of the infection, despite early initiation (within 48 hours of the onset of symptoms) of high-dose treatment in one patient. Furthermore, antiviral drug resistance may complicate clinical treatment approaches in several ways, including limiting the options for combination therapy. Thus, during the 2005–2006 influenza season, the US CDC recommended against amantadine and rimantadine, because of widespread resistance among currently circulating seasonal A(H3N2) and A(H1N1) viruses (34).

4.4.5 Key messages

- Influenza causes annual epidemics and periodic pandemics that have claimed millions of lives, imposing a major global public health and economic burden.

- Over the past 10 years, influenza antiviral drugs have become essential for treatment of epidemic and pandemic influenza infection; WHO has published guidance on the use of these drugs (29), and many countries have established stockpiles for pandemic preparedness.

- Widespread resistance to adamantanes currently circulating A(H1N1) and A(H3N2) viruses have left neuraminidase inhibitors as the primary antiviral agents recommended for influenza prevention and treatment, but resistance to these drugs is a growing concern.

4.5 References

1. *Guidelines for surveillance of drug resistance in tuberculosis.* Geneva, World Health Organization, 2009. (http://whqlibdoc.who.int/publications/2009/9789241598675_eng.pdf, accessed 27 December 2013).

2. *The Global Plan to Stop TB 2011–2015.* Geneva, Stop TB Partnership and World Health Organization, 2010. (http://whqlibdoc.who.int/hq/2006/WHO_HTM_STB_2006.368_eng.pdf, accessed 5 February 2014).

3. *Multidrug-resistant tuberculosis (MDR-TB) indicators. A minimum set of indicators for the programmatic management of MDR-TB in national tuberculosis control programmes.* Geneva, World Health Organization, 2010. (http://whqlibdoc.who.int/hq/2010/WHO_HTM_TB_2010.11_eng.pdf, accessed 27 December 2013).

4. *World malaria report 2012.* Geneva, World Health Organization, 2012. (http://www.who.int/malaria/publications/world_malaria_report_2012/en/, accessed 29 December 2013).

5. *Global report on antimalarial efficacy and drug resistance: 2000-2010.* Geneva, World Health Organization, 2010. (http://www.who.int/malaria/publications/atoz/9789241500470/en/, accessed 29 December 2013).

6. Valderramos SG, Valderramos JC, Musset L, Purcell LA, Mercereau-Puijalon O, Legrand E et al. Identification of a mutant PfCRT-mediated chloroquine tolerance phenotype in *Plasmodium falciparum. PLoS Pathog*, 2010, 6(5):e1000887. doi:10.1371/journal.ppat.1000887.

7. White NJ, Pongtavornpinyo W, Maude RJ, Saralamba S, Aguas R, Stepniewska K et al. Hyperparasitaemia and low dosing are an important source of anti-malarial drug resistance. *Malar J*, 2009, 8:253. doi:10.1186/1475-2875-8-253.

8.   Yeung S, Pongtavornpinyo W, Hastings IM, Mills AJ, White NJ. Antimalarial drug resistance, artemisinin-based combination therapy, and the contribution of modeling to elucidating policy choices. *Am J Trop Med Hyg*, 2004, 71(2):179-186. (http://www.ncbi.nlm.nih.gov/pubmed/15331836, accessed 8 April 2014).

9.   Roper C, Pearce R, Nair S, Sharp B, Nosten F, Anderson T. Intercontinental spread of pyrimethamine-resistant malaria. *Science*, 2004, 305(5687):1124. (http://www.ncbi.nlm.nih.gov/pubmed/15326348, accessed 8 April 2014).

10. Wongsrichanalai C, Sirichaisinthop J, Karwacki JJ, Congpuong K, Miller RS, Pang L et al. Drug resistant malaria on the Thai-Myanmar and Thai-Cambodian borders. *Southeast Asian J Trop Med Public Health*, 2001, 32(1):41-49. (http://www.ncbi.nlm.nih.gov/pubmed/11485094, accessed 8 April 2014).

11. *Methods for surveillance of antimalarial drug efficacy*. Geneva, World Health Organization, 2009. (http://www.who.int/malaria/publications/atoz/9789241597531/en/index.html, accessed 29 December 2013).

12. Zucker JR, Lackritz EM, Ruebush TK, Hightower AW, Adungosi JE, Were JB et al. Childhood mortality during and after hospitalization in western Kenya: effect of malaria treatment regimens. *Am J Trop Med Hyg*, 1996, 55(6):655-660. (http://www.ncbi.nlm.nih.gov/pubmed/9025694, accessed 8 April 2014).

13. Trape JF, Pison G, Preziosi MP, Enel C, Desgrées du Loû A, Delaunay V et al. Impact of chloroquine resistance on malaria mortality. *C R Acad Sci III*, 1998, 321(8):689-697. (http://www.ncbi.nlm.nih.gov/pubmed/9769862, accessed 8 April 2014).

14. Bjorkman A. Malaria associated anaemia, drug resistance and antimalarial combination therapy. *Int J Parasitol*, 2002, 32(13):1637-1643. (http://www.ncbi.nlm.nih.gov/pubmed/12435448, accessed 8 April 2014).

15. Price RN, Nosten F. Drug resistant falciparum malaria: clinical consequences and strategies for prevention. *Drug Resist Updat*, 2001, 4(3):187-196. (http://www.ncbi.nlm.nih.gov/pubmed/11768332, accessed 8 April 2014).

16. Talisuna AO, Bloland P, D'Alessandro U. History, dynamics, and public health importance of malaria parasite resistance. *Clin Microbiol Rev*, 2004, 17(1):235-254. (http://www.ncbi.nlm.nih.gov/pubmed/14726463, accessed 8 April 2014).

17. Denis MB, Tsuyuoka R, Poravuth Y, Narann TS, Seila S, Lim C et al. Surveillance of the efficacy of artesunate and mefloquine combination for the treatment of uncomplicated falciparum malaria in Cambodia. *Trop Med Int Health*, 2006, 11(9):1360-1366. (http://www.ncbi.nlm.nih.gov/pubmed/16930257, accessed 8 April 2014).

18. Vijaykadga S, Rojanawatsirivej C, Cholpol S, Phoungmanee D, Nakavej A, Wongsrichanalai C. In vivo sensitivity monitoring of mefloquine monotherapy and artesunate-mefloquine combinations for the treatment of uncomplicated falciparum malaria in Thailand in 2003. 2006, 11(2):211-219. (http://www.ncbi.nlm.nih.gov/pubmed/16451346, accessed 8 April 2014).

19. Leang R, Barrette A, Bouth DM, Menard D, Abdur R, Duong S et al. Efficacy of dihydroartemisinin-piperaquine for treatment of uncomplicated *Plasmodium falciparum* and *Plasmodium vivax* in Cambodia, 2008 to 2010. *Antimicrob Agents Chemother*, 2013, 57(2):818-826. doi:10.1128/AAC.00686-12.

20. *Global plan for artemisinin resistance containment (GPARC)*. Geneva, World Health Organization, 2011 (http://www.who.int/entity/malaria/publications/atoz/artemisinin_resistance_containment_2011.pdf, accessed 27 December 2013).

21. *Emergency response to artemisinin resistance in the greater Mekong subregion*. Geneva, World Health Organization, 2013. (http://apps.who.int/iris/bitstream/10665/79940/1/9789241505321_eng.pdf, accessed 7 December 2013).

22. *WHO Gobal Strategy for the Surveillance and Monitoring of HIV Drug Resistance*. Geneva, World Health Organization (WHO), 2012. (http://apps.who.int/iris/bitstream/10665/77349/1/9789241504768_eng.pdf, accessed 8 August 2013).

23. *WHO HIV drug resistance report*. Geneva, World Health Organization (WHO), 2012. (http://apps.who.int/iris/bitstream/10665/75183/1/9789241503938_eng.pdf, accessed 29 August 2013).

24. Wittkop L, Gunthard HF, de Wolf F, Dunn D, Cozzi-Lepri A, de Luca A et al. Effect of transmitted drug resistance on virological and immunological response to initial combination antiretroviral therapy for HIV (EuroCoord-CHAIN joint project): a European multicohort study. *Lancet Infect Dis*, 2011, 11(5):363 371. doi:10.1016/S1473-3099(11)70032-9.

25. Hamers RL, Schuurman R, Sigaloff KC, Wallis CL, Kityo C, Siwale M et al. PharmAccess African Studies to Evaluate Resistance (PASER) Investigators. Effect of pretreatment HIV-1 drug resistance on immunological, virological, and drug-resistance outcomes of first-line antiretroviral treatment in sub-Saharan Africa: a multicentre cohort study. *Lancet Infect Dis*, 2012, 12(4):307-17. doi:10.1016/S1473-3099(11)70255-9.

26. *Fact sheet N°211, Influenza.* Geneva, World Health Organization, 2003. (http://www.who.int/mediacentre/factsheets/2003/fs211/en/, accessed 9 December 2013).

27. Neumann G, Noda T, Kawaoka Y. Emergence and pandemic potential of swine-origin H1N1 influenza virus. *Nature*, 2009, 459(7249):931-939. doi:10.1038/nature08157.

28. *WHO guidelines for pharmacological management of pandemic influenza A(H1N1) 2009 and other influenza viruses.* Geneva, World Health Organization, 2010. (http://www.who.int/csr/resources/publications/swineflu/h1n1_guidelines_pharmaceutical_mngt.pdf?ua=1, accessed 13 February 2014).

29. Bright RA, Medina MJ, Xu X, Perez-Oronoz G, Wallis TR, Davis XM et al. Incidence of adamantane resistance among influenza A (H3N2) viruses isolated worldwide from 1994 to 2005: a cause for concern. *Lancet*, 2005, 366(9492):1175-1181. (http://www.ncbi.nlm.nih.gov/pubmed/16198766, accessed 8 April 2014).

30. Meetings of the WHO working group on surveillance of influenza antiviral susceptibility - Geneva, November 2011 and June 2012. *Wkly Epidemiol Rec*, 2012, 87(39):369-374.

31. *Influenza A(H1N1) virus resistance to oseltamivir.* Geneva, World Health Organization, 2008. (http://www.who.int/influenza/patient_care/antivirals/oseltamivir_summary/en/, accessed 9 December 2013).

32. *Laboratory methodologies for testing the antiviral susceptibility of influenza viruses.* Geneva, World Health Organization, 2012. (http://www.who.int/influenza/gisrs_laboratory/antiviral_susceptibility/en/, accessed 9 December 2013).

33. Gupta RK, Nguyen-Van-Tam JS. Oseltamivir resistance in influenza A (H5N1) infection. *N Engl J Med*, 2006, 354(13):1423-1424, author reply 1423-1424. (http://www.ncbi.nlm.nih.gov/pubmed/16571890, accessed 8 April 2014).

34. High levels of adamantane resistance among influenza A (H3N2) viruses and interim guidelines for use of antiviral agents – United States, 2005–06 influenza season. *Morb Mortal Wkly Rep*, 2006, 55(2):44-46. (http://www.cdc.gov/mmwr/preview/mmwrhtml/mm5502a7.htm, accessed 29 December 2013).

Section 4

SECTION
05

5.2.1 Antifungal drug resistance in *Candida* species

Currently, there are only three classes of antifungal agents available to treat serious *Candida* infections: the azoles, the echinocandins and the polyenes (e.g. amphotericin B).

Azoles are used most frequently to treat *Candida* infections, but some *Candida* species are inherently less susceptible to the azoles, and some species develop resistance during prolonged therapy (*37, 38*). Echinocandins, when available, are the empiric treatment of choice. Formulations of amphotericin B are available in many countries, but this agent has higher toxicity than azoles and echinocandins. A few *Candida* species, such as *C. lusitaniae*, can develop resistance during amphotericin B therapy. Although many azole-resistant *Candida* infections can be treated with drugs of a different class, significant cost, toxicity and absence of an oral formulation can present barriers to their use. In some developing countries only a single class of antifungal drug is available and, if resistance develops, there are no other treatment options. Given the limitations of available antifungal drugs, the following resistance profiles are of particular concern:

- resistance to azoles, especially fluconazole, because this is the standard (or only available) antifungal therapy in many countries;

- resistance to the newer class of antifungals, the echinocandins, which have replaced fluconazole as empiric therapy in developed countries; and

- multidrug-resistant bloodstream infections for which there may not be any available treatment options.

5.2.2 Antifungal drug resistance surveillance

Resources allocated for monitoring and reducing antifungal drug resistance are limited, and few countries carry out surveillance. There are significant gaps in information from most of Asia, Africa, the Middle East and parts of South America. Also, many of the existing data are limited to single-centre reports, which may bias results towards certain patient populations.

Antifungal susceptibility testing methods have changed over time, making trend comparisons difficult. Antifungal susceptibility testing is not performed in most resource-limited countries, and resistance in these settings is unknown. Little is known about developing resistance among the echinocandins.

There are also only limited available data on how antifungal drug laboratory values correspond to how patients respond to the drug, especially among different populations. Moreover, the standard design of surveillance programmes is to collect the first isolate from each episode of infection, and generally before antifungal treatment. This method would not capture isolates that developed resistance after exposure to antifungal drugs. For these reasons, resistance might be greater than is currently being detected or reported.

More standardized data are needed to understand the full impact that resistant *Candida* species have on patient treatment and clinical outcomes.

Section 5

5.2.3 Magnitude of resistance at a global level

Figure 21 shows resistance rates against fluconazole for *Candida albicans,* non-*C. albicans*, and all *Candida* isolates combined in selected countries from which data are available.

Figure 21 Fluconazole drug resistance, by *Candida*, species and country (*12, 37, 39-45*)

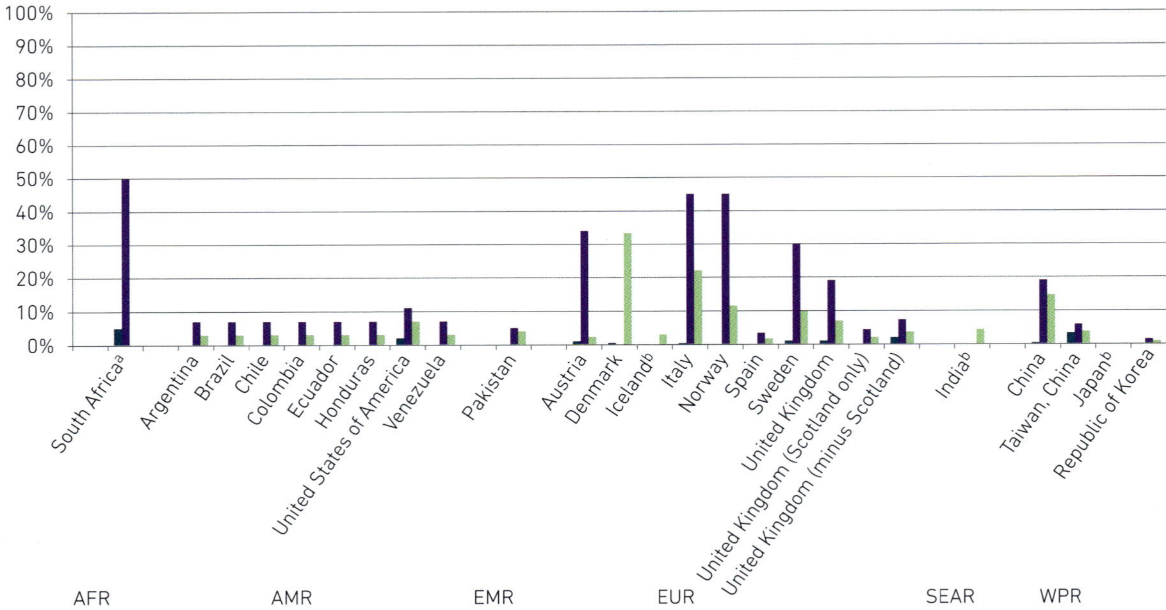

AFR, African Region; AMR/PAHO, Region of the Americas/Pan American Health Organization; EMR, Eastern Mediterranean Region; EUR, European Region; SEAR, South-East Asia Region; WPR; Western Pacific Region.

a. No data on overall resistance to fluconazole.
b. No data on per cent resistant by species.

Data are compiled from prior published reports of candidaemia in hospitalized patients among state or national surveillance projects, and prospective laboratory surveillance projects. In most countries where data are available, drug resistance appears to be higher among non-*C. albicans* species than among *C. albicans* species. Resistance varies greatly by location and species, and overall reported resistance is highest in Denmark (33%) and lowest in the Republic of Korea (0.9%).

5.2.4 Public health importance

Health impact

In some locations, candidaemia is the most common cause of all bloodstream infections related to vascular catheters. Inappropriate antifungal therapy is associated with increased mortality, increased attributable costs, and increased burden of fluconazole non-susceptible *Candida* species (*46*).

Economic impact

Invasive *Candida* infections have been reported to be associated with high morbidity and mortality (mortality of approximately 35%), as well as higher health-care costs and prolonged length of hospitalization (*46, 47*). Patients with resistant infections may experience delay in receiving appropriate therapy, which can increase costs, LOS, and morbidity and mortality (*48, 49*). In 2005, CDC estimated that each case of *Candida* infection results in 3–13 days of additional hospitalization, and incurs a total of US$ 6000 to US$ 29 000 in direct health-care costs (*46*). Based on current data and projections, these infections add a total of US$ 8 billion to US health-care expenditures every year (*44, 46, 49, 50*). Although it is suspected that resistant infections greatly increase these costs, few data exist on the economic impact of resistant *Candida* infections.

Public health impact

Candida infections are a persistent and increasingly important public health problem, particularly for vulnerable populations such as cancer patients, transplant recipients, and in neonates and other patients in intensive care units. Geographic variability exists among patients with candidiasis in incidence, resistance, antifungal use and antifungal availability. In some locations, half of all infections are resistant to first-line therapy. Resistance to azoles is probably increasing, and resistance to the echinocandins is emerging. It is likely that the global burden will increase with increasing populations of immunocompromized patients as economies develop and health care improves. Given these changes, it is critically important to have active surveillance activities for resistance trends in *Candida* infections, to determine the burden of infections due to antifungal-resistant *Candida*, its economic impact, and possible areas where prevention and control strategies can be focused.

5.2.5 Key messages

- Candidiasis is the most common fungal infection worldwide, and invasive *Candida* infections have high morbidity and mortality rates.

- Antifungal drug resistance to candidiasis contributes to a burden for patients and the health-care system.

- Resistance to fluconazole, a common antifungal drug, varies widely by country and species.

- Resistance to the newest class of antifungal agents, the echinocandins, is emerging in some countries.

- There are large gaps in information on antifungal resistance and the global burden of antifungal-resistant *Candida*.

5.3 References

1. *Joint FAO/WHO/OIE Expert Meeting on Critically Important Antimicrobials* Rome, Italy, Food and Agriculture Organization of the United Nations / World Organisation for Animal Health / World Health Organization / 2007. (http://www.who.int/foodborne_disease/resources/Report%20joint%20CIA%20Meeting.pdf, accessed 16 October 2013).

2. European Centre for Disease Prevention and Control (ECDC), European Food Safety Authority (EFSA), European Drugs Agency (EMEA), Scientific Committee on Emerging and Newly Identified Health Risks (SCENIHR). Joint opinion on antimicrobial resistance (AMR) focused on zoonotic infections. *EFSA Journal*, 2009, 7(11):1372. (http://www.ema.europa.eu/docs/en_GB/document_library/Other/2009/11/WC500015452.pdf, accessed 27 December 2013).

3. *Reports of Joint Committee on the Use of Antibiotics in Animal Husbandry and Veterinary Drug (Swann Committee)*. London, Her Majesty's Stationary Office, 1969.

4. Nisi R, Brink N, Diaz F, Moulin G. *Antimicrobial use in animals: Analysis of the OIE survey on monitoring of the quantities of antimicrobial agents used in animals*. Paris, France, World Organisation for Animal Health. (http://www.oie.int/eng/A_AMR2013/Presentations/S2_4_Fran%C3%A7oisDiaz.pdf, accessed 27 December 2013).

5. *Antimicrobials sold or distributed for use in food-producing animals*. Food and Drug Administration Department of Health and Human Services 2011. (http://www.fda.gov/downloads/ForIndustry/UserFees/AnimalDrugUserFeeActADUFA/UCM338170.pdf, accessed 27 December 2013).

6. *Sales of veterinary antimicrobial agents in 19 EU/EEA countries in 2010*. European Drugs Agency, 2012. (http://www.ema.europa.eu/docs/en_GB/document_library/Report/2012/10/WC500133532.pdf, accessed 27 December 2013).

7. *Canadian Integrated Program for Antimicrobial Resistance Surveillance (CIPARS), annual reports*. Public Health Agency of Canada, 2008. (http://www.phac-aspc.gc.ca/cipars-picra/pubs-eng.php#ar, accessed 23 December 2013).

8. *The Danish Integrated Antimicrobial Resistance Monitoring and Research Programme, DANMAP, annual reports*. DANMAP. (http://www.danmap.org/Downloads/Reports.aspx, accessed 23 December 2013).

9. *FINRES-Vet Resistance Monitoring Programme*. The Finnish Food Safety Authority, EVIRA, 2012. (http://www.evira.fi/portal/en/animals/animal+health+and+diseases/animal+medication/monitoring+of+antibiotic+resistance, accessed 23 December 2013).

10. *The French National Observatory for Epidemiology of Bacterial Resistance to Antimicrobials, ONERBA, annual reports*. France, Onerba. (http://www.onerba.org/spip.php?rubrique19, accessed 23 December 2013).

11. *The Japanese Veterinary Antimicrobial Resistance Monitoring System, JVARM*. (http://www.maff.go.jp/nval/tyosa_kenkyu/taiseiki/monitor/e_index.html, accessed 27 January 2014).

12. NORM/NORM-VET. *Norwegian veterinary institute. Norm Norm-Vet Report: A report on usage of antimicrobial agents and occurence of antimicrobial resistance in Norway in animals and humans.* Tromsø/Oslo, 2011. (http://www.vetinst.no/eng/Publications/Norm-Norm-Vet-Report, accessed 29 December 2013).

13. *Consumption of antimicrobial agents and antimicrobial resistance among medically important bacteria in the Netherlands and Monitoring of antimicrobial resistance and antibiotic usage in animals in the Netherlands in 2012.* NETHMAP/MARAN, 2013. (http://www.wageningenur.nl/upload_mm/7/8/9/52388c6c-858c-483c-b57d-227029fe778a_005738_Nethmap_2013%20def_web.pdf, accessed 27 December 2013).

14. *The USA Animal and Veterinary National Antimicrobial Resistance Monitoring System, NARMS.* 2013. (http://www.fda.gov/AnimalVeterinary/SafetyHealth/AntimicrobialResistance/NationalAntimicrobial ResistanceMonitoringSystem/default.htm, accessed 23 December 2013).

15. *The Swedish Antibiotic Utilisation and Resistance in Human Medicine/Swedish Veterinary Antimicrobial Resistance Monitoring, SWEDRES/SVARM.* Solna, Sweden, Swedish Institute for Communicable Disease Control and National Veterinary Institute, 2012. (http://www.smittskyddsinstitutet.se/upload/publikationer/ Swedres-Svarm_2013-101-1-mini.pdf, accessed 27 December 2013).

16. The European Union Summary Report on antimicrobial resistance in zoonotic and indicator bacteria from humans, animals and food in 2011. *EFSA Journal*, 2013, 11(5):3196. (http://www.efsa.europa.eu/ en/efsajournal/doc/3196.pdf, accessed 29 December 2013).

17. *World Health Day policy briefs.* Geneva, World Health Organization, 2011. (http://www.who.int/world-health-day/2011/policybriefs/en/index.html, accessed 27 December 2013).

18. *Integrated surveillance of antimicrobial resistance. Guidance from a WHO advisory group.* Geneva, World Health Organization (WHO), 2013. (http://www.who.int/iris/bitstream/10665/91778/1/9789241506311_eng.pdf, accessed 18 December 2013).

19. *Global principles for the containment of antimicrobial resistance in animals intended for food.* Geneva, World Health Organization, 2000. (http://whqlibdoc.who.int/hq/2000/WHO_CDS_CSR_APH_2000.4.pdf, accessed 16 October 2013).

20. *Terrestrial animal health code.* Paris, World Organisation for Animal Health, 2012. (http://www.oie.int/en/ international-standard-setting/terrestrial-code/, accessed 16 October 2013).

21. *Aquatic animal health code.* Paris, World Organisation for Animal Health, 2012. (http://www.oie.int/en/ international-standard-setting/aquatic-code/, accessed 16 October 2013).

22. *Guidelines for risk analysis of foodborne antimicrobial resistance.* Codex Alimentarius: International food standards (CAC/GL 77-2011), World Health Organization and Food and Agriculture Organization of the United Nations, 2011. (http://www.codexalimentarius.org/download/standards/11776/CXG_077e.pdf, accessed 27 December 2013).

23. The WHO Advisory Group on Integrated Surveillance of Antimicrobial Resistance (WHO-AGISAR). World Health Organization (WHO), 2013. (http://www.who.int/foodborne_disease/resistance/agisar/en/, accessed 9 December 2013).

24. *Critically important antimicrobials for human drug.* Geneva, World Health Organization, 2011. (http://apps. who.int/iris/bitstream/10665/77376/1/9789241504485_eng.pdf, accessed 13 February 2014).

25. Vaarten J. Clinical impact of antimicrobial resistance in animals. *Rev Sci Tech*, 2012, 31(1):221-229. (http://www.ncbi.nlm.nih.gov/pubmed/22849278, accessed 8 April 2014).

26. *Reflection paper on meticillin-resistant Staphylococcus pseudintermedius.* London, Committee for Veterinary Medicinal Products, 2011. (http://www.ema.europa.eu/docs/en_GB/document_library/Scientific_ guideline/2011/02/WC500102017.pdf, accessed 27 December 2013).

27. *OIE list of antimicrobial agents of veterinary importance.* World Organisation for Animal Health (OIE), 2013. (http://www.oie.int/fileadmin/Home/eng/Our_scientific_expertise/docs/pdf/OIE_list_antimicrobials.pdf, accessed 29 December 2013).

28. Streit JM, Jones RN, Toleman MA, Stratchounski LS, Fritsche TR. Prevalence and antimicrobial susceptibility patterns among gastroenteritis-causing pathogens recovered in Europe and Latin America and Salmonella isolates recovered from bloodstream infections in North America and Latin America: report from the SENTRY Antimicrobial Surveillance Program (2003). *Int J Androl*, 2006, 27(5):367-375. (http://www.ncbi.nlm.nih.gov/pubmed/16647842, accessed 8 April 2014).

29. Guerrant RL, Van Gilder T, Steiner TS, Thielman NM, Slutsker L, Tauxe RV et al. Practice guidelines for the management of infectious diarrhea. *Clin Infect Dis*, 2001, 32(3):331-351. (http://www.ncbi.nlm.nih.gov/pubmed/11170940, accessed 8 April 2014).

30. Murray CJ, Lopez AD. Global mortality, disability, and the contribution of risk factors: Global Burden of Disease Study. *Lancet*, 1997, 349(9063):1436-1442. (http://www.ncbi.nlm.nih.gov/pubmed/9164317, accessed 8 April 2014).

31. Smith R, Coast J. The true cost of antimicrobial resistance. *BMJ*, 2013, 346:f1493. doi:10.1136/bmj.f1493.

32. *Antibiotic resistance threats in the United States*. US Centers for Disease Control and Prevention, 2013. (http://www.cdc.gov/drugresistance/threat-report-2013/, accessed 2 December 2013).

33. Casey JA, Curriero FC, Cosgrove SE, Nachman KE, Schwartz BS. High-density livestock operations, crop field application of manure, and risk of community-associated methicillin-resistant *Staphylococcus aureus* infection in Pennsylvania. *JAMA Internal Drug*, 2013, 173(21):1980-1990. doi:10.1001/jamainternmed.2013.10408.

34. *High-level technical meeting to address health risks at the human-animal-ecosystems interfaces*. Mexico City, Food and Agriculture Organization of the United Nations/World Organisation for Animal Health/World Health Organization, 2011. (http://www.who.int/iris/bitstream/10665/78100/1/9789241504676_eng.pdf, accessed 16 October 2013).

35. Wisplinghoff H, Bischoff T, Tallent SM, Seifert H, Wenzel RP, Edmond MB. Nosocomial bloodstream infections in US hospitals: analysis of 24,179 cases from a prospective nationwide surveillance study. *Clin Infect Dis*, 2004, 39(3):309-317. (http://www.ncbi.nlm.nih.gov/pubmed/15306996, accessed 8 April 2014).

36. Pfaller MA, Diekema DJ. Epidemiology of invasive candidiasis: a persistent public health problem. *Clin Microbiol Rev*, 2007, 20(1):133-163. (http://www.ncbi.nlm.nih.gov/pubmed/17223626, accessed 8 April 2014).

37. Morgan J. Global trends in candidemia: review of reports from 1995-2005. *Curr Infect Dis Rep*, 2005, 7(6):429-439. (http://www.ncbi.nlm.nih.gov/pubmed/16225780, accessed 8 April 2014).

38. Cuenca-Estrella M, Gomez-Lopez A, Cuesta I, Zaragoza O, Mellado E, Rodriguez-Tudela JL et al. Frequency of voriconazole resistance in vitro among Spanish clinical isolates of Candida spp. According to breakpoints established by the Antifungal Subcommittee of the European Committee on Antimicrobial Susceptibility Testing. *Antimicrob Agents Chemother*, 2011, 55(4):1794-1797. doi:10.1128/AAC.01757-10.

39. Asmundsdottir LR, Erlendsdottir H, Gottfredsson M. Increasing incidence of candidemia: results from a 20-year nationwide study in Iceland. *J Clin Microbiol*, 2002, 40(9):3489-3492. (http://www.ncbi.nlm.nih.gov/pubmed/12202600, accessed 8 April 2014).

40. Asmundsdottir LR, Erlendsdottir H, Gottfredsson M. Nationwide study of candidemia, antifungal use, and antifungal drug resistance in Iceland, 2000 to 2011. *J Clin Microbiol*, 2013, 51(3):841-848. doi:10.1128/JCM.02566-12.

41. Ericsson J, Chryssanthou E, Klingspor L, Johansson AG, Ljungman P, Svensson E et al. Candidaemia in Sweden: a nationwide prospective observational survey. *Clin Microbiol Infect*, 2013, 19(4):E218-E221. doi:10.1111/1469-0691.12111.

42. Nucci M, Queiroz-Telles F, Alvarado-Matute T, Tiraboschi IN, Cortes J, Zurita J et al. Epidemiology of candidemia in Latin America: a laboratory-based survey. *PLoS ONE*, 2013, 8(3):e59373. doi:10.1371/journal.pone.0059373.

43. Odds FC, Hanson MF, Davidson AD, Jacobsen MD, Wright P, Whyte JA et al. One year prospective survey of Candida bloodstream infections in Scotland. *J Med Microbiol*, 2007, 56(Pt 8):1066-1075. (http://www.ncbi.nlm.nih.gov/pubmed/17644714, accessed 8 April 2014).

44. Tortorano AM, Kibbler C, Peman J, Bernhardt H, Klingspor L, Grillot R. Candidaemia in Europe: epidemiology and resistance. *Int J Antimicrob Agents*, 2006, 27(5):359-366. (http://www.ncbi.nlm.nih.gov/pubmed/16647248, accessed 5 February 2014).

45. Tortorano AM, Prigitano A, Lazzarini C, Passera M, Deiana ML, Cavinato S et al. A 1-year prospective survey of candidemia in Italy and changing epidemiology over one decade. *Infection*, 2013, 41(3):655-662. doi:10.1007/s15010-013-0455-6.

46. Morgan J, Meltzer MI, Plikaytis BD, Sofair AN, Huie-White S, Wilcox S et al. Excess mortality, hospital stay, and cost due to candidemia: a case-control study using data from population-based candidemia surveillance. *Infect Control Hosp Epidemiol*, 2005, 26(6):540-547. (http://www.ncbi.nlm.nih.gov/pubmed/16018429, accessed 8 April 2014).

47. Fridkin SK. Candidemia is costly--plain and simple. *Clin Infect Dis*, 2005, 41(9):1240-1241. (http://www.ncbi.nlm.nih.gov/pubmed/16206096, accessed 8 April 2014).

48. Zilberberg MD, Kollef MH, Arnold H, Labelle A, Micek ST, Kothari S et al. Inappropriate empiric antifungal therapy for candidemia in the ICU and hospital resource utilization: a retrospective cohort study. *BMC Infect Dis*, 2010, 10:150. doi:10.1186/1471-2334-10-150.

49. Arnold HM, Micek ST, Shorr AF, Zilberberg MD, Labelle AJ, Kothari S et al. Hospital resource utilization and costs of inappropriate treatment of candidemia. *Pharmacotherapy*, 2010, 30(4):361-368. doi:10.1592/phco.30.4.361.

50. Cleveland AA, Farley MM, Harrison LH, Stein B, Hollick R, Lockhart SR et al. Changes in incidence and antifungal drug resistance in candidemia: results from population-based laboratory surveillance in Atlanta and Baltimore, 2008-2011. *Clin Infect Dis*, 2012, 55(10):1352-1361. doi:10.1093/cid/cis697.

SECTION
06

Conclusions

6.1 Main findings

6.1.1 Current status of resistance to antibacterial drugs

Whether plentiful or scarce, data on the resistance patterns for the bacteria of public health importance examined for this report were available in all WHO regions. National data obtained for *E. coli*, *K. pneumoniae* and *S. aureus* showed that the proportion resistant to commonly used specified antibacterial drugs exceeded 50% in many settings.

The reported and published data sets indicate that there are limitations in effective oral treatment options for some common community-acquired infections in several countries, and that there remain few, if any, treatment options for some common severe and health-care associated infections in many places. Of particular concern is the fact that *K. pneumoniae* resistant to carbapenems, usually the last line of available treatment, is reported in all WHO regions. Treatment failure due to resistance to available drugs is a reality in both gonorrhoea and TB.

However, with uncertainty about representativeness and considerable gaps in coverage, the magnitude of the problem at both population and global levels is unclear and needs to be clarified. It is also unclear to what extent differences in reported data for some bacteria–antibacterial drug combinations reflect real differences in resistance patterns, or are attributable to differences in sampling of patients, laboratory performance and methodology. Surveillance standards and international collaboration have been established for two types of bacterial infection –TB and gonorrhoea – but not for other common bacteria. To improve the quality and comparability of data, international collaboration based on standardized methodology is needed.

6.1.2 Burden of resistance to antibacterial drugs

The evidence obtained shows that ABR has a significant adverse impact on clinical outcomes and leads to higher costs due to consumption of health-care resources. However, the overall health and economic burden resulting from acquired ABR cannot be fully assessed with the presently available data; new methodologies are needed to more precisely assess the total impact of resistance, to better inform health policies and to prioritize the deployment of resources. The scarcity of new classes of antibacterial drugs for Gram-negative bacteria adds additional urgency. It is essential to take appropriate measures to preserve the efficacy of the existing drugs so that common and life-threatening infections can be cured.

6.1.3 Surveillance of antibacterial resistance

Coordination and coverage

The data collected for this report reveal the lack of structures for coordination and information sharing that could provide an up-to-date overview of the present situation of ABR. Major gaps exist in national data from many countries. The most complete information was obtained from countries in the EU and the Americas, where long-standing regional surveillance and collaboration exist. Reports with a high proportion of limited data sets were obtained from countries in other regions, which may reflect other priorities or shortage of capacity in the health systems, or both.

Many of the submitted data sets were collected in 2011 or earlier. More recent data are needed at all levels to systematically monitor trends, to inform patient treatment guidelines and to inform and evaluate containment efforts. It is likely that patients in many places are treated for suspected bacterial infections in the absence of any information about the resistance situation in the local area.

There is no common coordinated widely agreed strategy or public health goal among identified surveillance efforts. The tables in Annex 2 illustrate the variety of sources for the data available for this report. There is agreement within EARS-Net and CAESAR (European Region) and ReLAVRA (Latin America) on the type of samples from which to compile data, but the methodology differs between these systems. WHO has provided standards and guidance for surveillance in several documents, as listed in Appendix 2. However, there is still no agreed methodology to be consistently implemented for global surveillance of ABR in common bacteria, and no agreed standard set of epidemiological information that should be collected to provide information on morbidity, mortality and costs for treatment and heath-care systems.

Limitations of available data

Most data compiled for this report present proportions of resistant bacteria among tested isolates of clinical samples compiled from routine testing at laboratories (i.e. laboratory-based routine surveillance), predominantly in hospital settings. This entails major pitfalls, such as lack of representativeness and ability to measure impact in the population.

When most samples come from patients with severe infections (particularly health-care associated infections and those for which first-line treatment failed), community-acquired and uncomplicated infections are underrepresented. This imbalance is likely to result in higher reported resistance rates than would be found for the same bacteria in community or population-based samples, as was shown in some reports with data submitted separately for these patient groups. In addition, lack of information on the source (patient) may lead to overrepresentation of a limited group of patients (e.g. patients with repeated hospitalizations or multiple sample collection, and outbreak settings), further biasing the results. Non-representativeness and biased sampling are major pitfalls for the interpretation and comparison of results. Treatment guided by limited and biased information may increase the risk of unnecessary use of broad-spectrum antibacterial drugs. This will increase the economic impact and accelerate the emergence of resistance to last-resort antibacterial drugs.

Laboratory-based routine surveillance can be valuable to inform treatment guidelines, and to provide information on trends and alerts to emerging ABR problems. However, this type of surveillance does not provide the information needed to measure the impact of ABR, including the consequences of ABR for patients as a result of failure of treatment that results in prolonged illness and excessive mortality, or how much of the population or which patient groups are affected, and so on. For this purpose, targeted surveillance based on defined populations and epidemiological samples would be necessary to provide the information needed to estimate ABR impact, as has been done in a few surveillance programmes and in the disease-specific programmes for TB, malaria and HIV. Lessons can be learnt from these programmes, and there may be opportunities for synergies from collaboration, although such solutions are not entirely transferable to surveillance of common bacteria. As exemplified by these other programmes, a long-term commitment, effort and considerable resources are needed to collect adequate data to determine the magnitude of the ABR problem and guide interventions. Population-based surveillance of ABR would therefore be challenging, but is urgently needed to adequately guide policies and interventions.

Timely information sharing

Surveillance systems need to be flexible and adaptable to emerging resistance, so that they are not restricted to monitoring what is already known. Surveillance systems should also be able to deliver information promptly to avoid any delay in public health actions at the local, national, regional and global level. WHONET, a widely used and freely available software supporting laboratory-based surveillance, can be useful for this purpose in stand-alone laboratories in resource-limited settings where commercial information technology systems are not accessible. WHONET also provides a platform for management and sharing of data. Increased collaboration between networks and surveillance centres will make it increasingly important to share experiences; shared experience will form the basis of coordinated collaboration on global surveillance of ABR.

6.1.4 Surveillance and present status of antimicrobial drug resistance in disease-specific programmes

Resistance to antimicrobial drugs is a problem that has been addressed for many years by programmes dedicated to the control of TB and malaria, and more recently to the control of HIV and influenza. In these disease-specific programmes, unlike the situation for ABR, methodologically solid surveillance systems have been developed, with somewhat different approaches in each. The programmes are supported through broad stakeholder engagement, including by governments, public health institutes, reference laboratories and donor agencies. After years of sustained effort, the programmes have been able to deliver surveillance data to inform strategic planning and further actions. Despite some disease-specific considerations, there is scope for exploring potential opportunities for an integrated AMR surveillance approach, sharing lessons learnt, and collaborating to strengthen capacity for AMR surveillance. The emergence of AMR threatens the control of these diseases and is also a major public health concern.

6.1.5 Antibacterial resistance in food-producing animals and the food chain

There are major gaps in surveillance and sharing of data on resistant bacteria that are transmitted through the food chain. Surveillance in food-producing animals, as for surveillance in humans, is hampered by lack of harmonized global standards and platforms for data sharing. A multisectoral approach is needed to contain ABR in food-producing animals and the food chain. The tripartite collaboration between WHO, FAO and OIE, in the spirit of the 'One Health' approach, provides a coordinating platform for work in this area.

6.1.6 Resistance in systemic candidiasis

Although it is known in industrialized countries that antifungal resistance contributes a substantial burden to the health-care system, there are large gaps in knowledge of the global burden of antifungal-resistant *Candida*. The AST methods differ for fungi and bacteria; however, as diagnosis and treatment are frequently under the same health-care structures, there may be opportunities for collaborative efforts to strengthen surveillance capacities.

6.2 Gaps

The information compiled for this report on global AMR surveillance revealed the following main gaps:

- lack of coordinated global ABR surveillance – with a defined goal and agreed epidemiological and microbiological methods and standards – to provide a comprehensive situation analysis;

- a general lack of population-based ABR surveillance to provide information on the overall morbidity and mortality, and the economic burden and societal impact of ABR;

- gaps in methodology and integrated surveillance of resistance in human and foodborne pathogens; and

- lack of coordination among existing surveillance networks and surveillance centres to support opportunities for collaboration and data sharing.

6.3 The way forward

As this first WHO report on AMR surveillance shows, there is a need for an improved and coordinated global effort, including wider sharing of surveillance data, for public health actions, particularly for ABR. As outlined in the 2001 global strategy for containment of AMR (*1*), World Health Assembly resolution WHA58.27 and the 2011 World Health Day policy package (*2*), commitment is needed from Member States and partners. WHO can support and collaborate with Member States, existing surveillance networks, OIE and FAO and other relevant stakeholders to promote:

- development of tools and standards for harmonized surveillance of ABR and its consequences in humans, and continued support for integrated surveillance of ABR in food-producing animals and the food chain;

- collaboration between existing surveillance networks and surveillance centres towards coordinated regional and global surveillance;

- elaboration of strategies for population-based surveillance of AMR to provide more extensive information on health and economic impact.

6.4 References

1. *WHO Global Strategy for Containment of Antimicrobial Resistance*. Geneva, World Health Organization (WHO), 2001. (http://www.who.int/drugresistance/WHO_Global_Strategy.htm/en/, accessed 23 January 2014).

2. *World Health Day policy briefs*. Geneva, World Health Organization, 2011. (http://www.who.int/world-health-day/2011/policybriefs/en/index.html, accessed 27 December 2013).

Section 6

ANNEXES

Annex 1
Methods for collecting data on surveillance and antibacterial resistance

The aim was to describe the status of surveillance and data on antibacterial resistance (ABR) in Member States. Data were sought from the following sources:

- national official sources, such as reports or other compilations at the national level at ministries of health, national reference laboratories, public health institutes or other sources identified by WHO;

- national and international networks for ABR surveillance; and

- scientific literature published from 2008.

Presentation of data in maps and tables:

- Because the focus of this report is to describe the status of national surveillance, priority was given to presentation of data collected from national official

sources, and information from other sources was not sought when the country information was based on a denominator of at least 30 tested isolates.

- In cases where data were not available from national official sources, available data included fewer than 30 tested isolates or collected data were incomplete, national surveillance networks or institutions were asked for additional information whenever possible.

- When data based on testing of at least 30 tested isolates were not available from the above sources, information was sought from publications (A1.3).

However, the tables in Annex 2 present all data obtained from national sources, surveillance networks or sites, and data that were received in parallel.

A1.1 Definitions

- **Data set** is the data on a returned questionnaire or data on requested resistance proportions returned in any other compilation.

A1.1.1 Data sources

- **National data** refers to data returned on the questionnaire obtained from:

  - national official sources such as reports or other compilations at the national level from ministries of health, national reference laboratories, public health institutes or similar;

  - international official networks collecting national data, such as European Antimicrobial Resistance Surveillance Network (EARS-Net), Foodborne and Waterborne Diseases and Zoonoses Network (FWD-Net), Gonococcal Antimicrobial Surveillance Programme/Gonococcal Isolate Surveillance Project/Gonococcal Resistance to Antimicrobials Surveillance Programme (GASP/GISP/GRASP), Latin American Antimicrobial Resistance Surveillance Network (ReLAVRA) and Sistema de Redes de Vigilancia de los Agentes Responsables de Neumonías y Meningitis Bacterianas (SIREVA); and

  - other country sources identified by WHO.

This definition does not imply that the data collected are representative for that country as a whole, because information gaps are likely.

- **National data not available or incomplete** (either no data at all, or no data for a certain bacteria–antibacterial drug resistance) refers to the following situations:

  - a response from the national official source that no national data are available on the questionnaire, via email or telephone contact, or from a WHO country situation analysis of antimicrobial resistance (AMR) activities; or

  - the returned questionnaires from the national official source contain blanks; or state N/A (not applicable), NT (not tested) or 0 tested isolates for the requested bacteria–antibacterial drug resistance combinations.

- **National surveillance network/institution** refers to networks (a group of hospitals or laboratories) doing surveillance within a country, or institutions such as single hospitals, laboratories or similar that provide data directly or through national institutions.

- **Publication** refers to original studies published in peer-reviewed scientific publications.

- **Information obtained from Asian Network for Surveillance of Resistant Pathogens (ANSORP)** refers to the response to the surveillance network questionnaire (Appendix 1) obtained from the ANSORP coordinator.

- **Information obtained from RusNet** refers to the response to the surveillance network questionnaire (Appendix 1) obtained from the RusNet coordinator.

- **No information obtained for this report** refers to the fact that no information could be gathered for the purpose of this report during the project time.

A1.1.2 Type of surveillance, population or samples

- Whenever available, information on the type of surveillance, investigated population or samples was presented in the tables in Annex 2.

- **Comprehensive surveillance** refers to surveillance based on inclusion of all bacterial isolates.

- **Targeted surveillance** refers to surveillance that includes only a subset of tested bacterial isolates (e.g. blood isolates or urinary isolates).

- **Type of population** (applies only to data extracted from literature review). The aim with the literature review was to see whether it could add any information on resistance rates where such information was not obtained from Member States. Whenever possible, a sense of the population studied is provided, to give some information on the variety of settings.

- **Samples** refers to anatomic site for sampling.

A1.2 Data collection from Member States and networks

A standard questionnaire (Appendix 1) addressing existing national ABR reports or other types of national data compilations and recorded proportions of resistance in the selected set of nine bacteria–antibacterial resistance combinations was distributed to Member States.

The method for data collection varied somewhat by WHO region. To avoid duplication of work, resistance data already collected through the existing networks EARS-Net and FWD-Net were entered in the questionnaire by the European Centre for Disease Prevention and Control (ECDC). The questionnaires were then passed on for completion by the designated national AMR focal points, ministries of health, or public health institutes (as appropriate) in the participating countries. Some countries added data at this stage. Similarly, the WHO Regional Office for the Americas (AMRO) entered the information for the countries participating in ReLAVRA and SIREVA. In the other WHO regions, the questionnaires were distributed

by the WHO regional offices via country offices (as appropriate), usually to the ministry of health, a national reference laboratory or a public health institute.

The questionnaires were translated and distributed in English, French , Russian and Spanish, as considered appropriate by the WHO regional offices. In the WHO Regional Office for the Eastern Mediterranean (EMRO), the questions were transferred to a WHO web-based data entry interface (DataCol).

A similar protocol (Appendix 1) to that sent to Member States, with additional questions on methodological and technical points, was sent to a few national and international surveillance networks. The identification of networks was informed by the WHO technical consultation 2012 (1).

Data collection from Member States and international networks started in April 2013, and from national networks in June 2013. All information provided by the end of 2013 has been included in the report.

A1.3 Literature search for data in scientific publications

The literature search for data was designed and carried out in collaboration with a medical information specialist, who assisted with selection of search terms for bacteria, resistance to listed antibacterial drugs, publications related to prevalence in humans and geographical location for study. Scientific journal articles on resistance rates in human isolates of the selected bacteria–antibacterial drug combinations published between 2008 and March 23 2013 were sought in the databases EMBASE and the WHO regional databases AIM (WHO Regional Office for Africa [AFRO]),

LILACS (AMRO), IMEMR (EMRO), IMSEAR (Regional Office for South-East Asia [SEARO]), WPRIM (WHO Regional Office for the Western Pacific Region [WPRO]).

The final yield (after removal of duplicates) was 6155 papers from EMBASE plus 411 from the regional databases, giving a total of 6566 papers, which were stored in two databases. These databases were searched as needed for the nine bacteria–antibacterial resistance combinations in cases where information on resistance-based on testing of at least 30 isolates had not been obtained from countries.

Studies with the following information were considered for inclusion:

- publications addressing resistance proportions based on defined patient populations, samples of individuals from the community or medical facilities (with or without symptoms), healthy carriers and populations subject to screening (e.g. health-care staff, day-care children), and, finally, results from antibacterial susceptibility testing (AST) on clinical samples collected in microbiology laboratories; and

- publications on proportions, prevalence or rates of ABR that included the name of any one of the requested bacteria (or "*enterobacteriaceae*" or "*Klebsiella*"); if resistance rates were not stated in the abstract, it was requested that it should be clearly indicated in the title or in the abstract that the paper included information on AST.

Published reports that were excluded were those that:

- did not fulfil the inclusion criteria;

- were posters, conference abstracts or similar;

- did not include original data, such as reviews, policy or position papers, treatment guidelines and similar;

- were based on a preselection (bias) of bacterial strains (e.g. outbreaks, case-reports, subspecies, serotypes and genotypes) or patient groups that had received prophylaxis with antibacterial drugs;

- evaluated interventions (e.g. infection control or antibacterial stewardship measures);

- focused on risk-factor analysis for carriage, infection or outcome after intervention;

- dealt specifically with enteric fever (*Salmonella enterica* serotypes Typhi and Paratyphi);

- focused on evaluation of microbiological or laboratory methods and pharmacodynamics;

- were related to evaluation (or marketing) of one specific antibacterial drug;

- reported clinical trials on treatment;

- were articles or abstracts from journals that could not be obtained from WHO library Internet services, if additional papers with sufficient information from the country in question was already available;

- did not report susceptibility (S), non-susceptibility (NS) or resistance (R) data from AST; and

- were based on fewer than 30 tested isolates, when larger series were available.

The retrieved abstracts were reviewed by one person. The minimal information considered necessary was the proportion of resistance, number of tested isolates, and information that either data collection or year of publication was 2008 or later. If any of this information was missing from the abstract, the full paper was evaluated.

Results on R, NS, and S were used as reported by the authors.

Data from the most recent time period were presented when:

- a single publication compared data over different time periods; and

- a single surveillance network published data for different years in different reports.

A1.4 Reference

1. *Strategies for global surveillance of antimicrobial resistance: Report of a technical consultation* (WHO/HSE/PED/2013.10358), Geneva, World Health Organization, 2013. (http://www.who.int/drugresistance/publications/surveillance-meeting2012/en/index.html, accessed 6 January 2014).

Annex 2
Reported or published resistance rates in common bacterial pathogens, by WHO region

Table A2.1 *Escherichia coli*: Resistance to third-generation cephalosporins[a]
African Region

Countries, territories and other areas or groupings	Data source[b, c, d]	Resistance (%)	No. tested isolates	Type of surveillance, population or samples[c]	Period for data collection	Year of publication or report
Algeria	National data from international publication (1)	17	236	Invasive isolates	(2003)–2005	2008
Angola	No information obtained for this report					
Benin	National data	34	44	Invasive isolates	2012	2013
Botswana	National data	28.4	67	Invasive isolates	2012	2013
Burkina Faso	National data	36	220	Invasive isolates	2008–2009	2013
Burundi	National data	7.2	1645	Targeted	2012	2013
Cameroon	No information obtained for this report					
Cabo Verde	No information obtained for this report					
Central African Republic	National data	30	183	Comprehensive	2012	2013
Chad	No information obtained for this report					
Comoros	No information obtained for this report					
Congo	National data	31	71	Invasive isolates	2012	2013
Côte d'Ivoire	No information obtained for this report					
Democratic Republic of the Congo	No information obtained for this report					
Equatorial Guinea	No information obtained for this report					
Eritrea	No information obtained for this report					
Ethiopia	National data	53 (caz); 70 (cro)	138 (caz); 154 (cro)	Comprehensive	2011–2012	2013
Gabon	No information obtained for this report					
Gambia	National data not available					2013
Ghana	National data	23.5 (cro); 41 (ctx)	88 (cro); 32 (ctx)	Comprehensive	2013	2008
Guinea	National data	100	1	Comprehensive	2012	2013
Guinea-Bissau	National data	25 (ctx); 33.3 (cro)	35	Comprehensive	2013	2013
Kenya	National data, incomplete	60		Targeted	2012	2013
Kenya	National network[e]	20	15	Targeted	2013	2013
Kenya	Publication (2)	87.2	109	Private hospital	2007–2009	2012
Lesotho	National data	2	107	Comprehensive	2012	2013
Liberia	National data not available					2010
Madagascar	Publication (3)	18.2	88	Hospital isolates	(2006)–2008[f]	2010
Malawi	National data	0	1	Comprehensive	2013	
Mali	No information obtained for this report					
Mauritania	National data	10	10	Comprehensive	2013	
Mauritius	National data	43.5	184	Hospital samples	2012	2013
Mozambique	No information obtained for this report					
Namibia	National data	12	2345	Comprehensive	2012	2013
Niger	National data not available					2013
Nigeria	Publication (4)	10	310	Blood isolates (children)	2006–2008	2010
Nigeria	Publication (5)	20	80	Carriers	(2003)–2007	2008
Nigeria	Publication (6)	37.5 (cro); 34.4 (caz); 28.1 (ctx);	32	Clinical samples	2007	2009
Nigeria	Publication (7)	11.4	128	Hospital samples	2007	2009
Nigeria	Publication (8)	2.3	364	Hospital acquired urinary tract infections	2007–2008	2009
Nigeria	Publication (9)	0	31	Blood isolates	2004–2009	2010
Nigeria	Publication (10)	64.3	42	Urinary isolates		2010
Nigeria	Publication (11)	28.9[e]	66	Urine and stool samples (HIV/AIDS-patients)	2009–2010	2011
Nigeria	Publication (12)	3	32	Blood isolates (HIV-infected children)		2010

Countries, territories and other areas or groupings	Data source[b, c, d]	Resistance (%)	No. tested isolates	Type of surveillance, population or samples[c]	Period for data collection	Year of publication or report
Rwanda	Publication (13)	38.3 (hospital patients); 5.9 (outpatients)	94 (hospital patients); 102 (outpatients)	Urinary isolates	2009	2011
Sao Tome and Principe	National data not available					2013
Senegal	No information obtained for this report					
Seychelles	No information obtained for this report					
Sierra Leone	No information obtained for this report					
South Africa	National data not available					2013
South Africa	Publication (14)	7	503	Blood isolates	2007	2008
South Africa	Publication (15)	7.6	473	Intra-abdominal infections	(2004)–2009	2013
South Africa	Publication (16)	10.2	431	Urinary isolates	2005–2006	2009
South Sudan	National data not available					
Swaziland	National data, incomplete		11	Comprehensive	2013	2013
Togo	No information obtained for this report					
Uganda	National data	0	9	Comprehensive	2012	2013
United Republic of Tanzania	National data not available					2013
United Republic of Tanzania	Publication (17)	4.7	64	Children with diarrhoea	2004	2011
Zambia	National data	37.4	107	Targeted	2012	2013
Zimbabwe	National data not available					2013

a. caz, ceftazidim; ctx, cefotaxim; cro, ceftriaxone
b. National data refers to data returned on the questionnaires as defined in Annex 1. This definition does not imply that the data collected is representative for that country as a whole because information gaps are likely.
c. See Annex 1 for definitions.
d. "National data not available" means that there was information that no data were available; "No information obtained for this report" means that no information was obtained from authorities, networks or publications.
e. Data only on proportion producing ESBL (extended spectrum beta-lactamases).

Table A2.2 *Escherichia coli*: Resistance to third-generation cephalosporins[a]
Region of the Americas

Countries, territories and other areas or groupings	Data source[b, c, d]	Resistance (%)	No. tested isolates	Type of surveillance, population or samples[c]	Period for data collection	Year of publication or report
Antigua and Barbuda	No information obtained for this report					
Argentina	National data	5.1	30 484	Uncomplicated urinary tract infection	2010	2012
Bahamas	No information obtained for this report					
Barbados	No information obtained for this report					
Belize	No information obtained for this report					
Bolivia (Plurinational State of)	National data not available					2013
Brazil	National data	0	247	Uncomplicated urinary tract infection	2010	2013
Canada	National data	6.5 (caz); 9.4 (cro)	646	Sentinel hospitals	2011	2013
Chile	National data not available					2013
Chile	National data from international publication (18)	36.8[e]	76	Clinical isolates	2004–2007	2008
Chile	National data from international publication (19)	23.8[e]	496	Hospitalized patients	2008–2010	2012
Colombia	National data not available					2013
Colombia	Publication (20)	4.7(cro); 11.8 (ctx); 18.5 (caz)	254	Urinary isolates	(2005)–2008[f]	2010
Colombia	National data from international publication (18)	20.2[e]	89	Clinical isolates	2004–2007	2008
Costa Rica	National data not available					2013
Cuba	National data	42.9	179	Uncomplicated urinary tract infection	2009	2013
Dominica	No information obtained for this report					
Dominican Republic	National data	33	2812	Hospital samples	2009	2013
Ecuador	National data	15.1	9259	Uncomplicated urinary tract infection	2010	2013
El Salvador	National data, incomplete		486	Uncomplicated urinary tract infection	2010	2013
Grenada	No information obtained for this report					
Guatemala	National data	39.8	1607	Uncomplicated urinary tract infection	2010	2013
Guyana	No information obtained for this report					
Haiti	No information obtained for this report					
Honduras	National data	36.7	3010	Uncomplicated urinary tract infection	2010	2013
Jamaica	National data from international publication (18)	8[e]	25	Clinical isolates	2004–2007	2008
Mexico	National data not available					2013
Mexico	Publication (21)	55.7 (caz); 68.3 (cro)	165 (caz); 136 (cro)	Hospital laboratory	2004–2007	2012
Mexico	National data from international publication (19)	48.4[e]	316	Hospitalized patients	2008–2010	2012
Mexico	National data from international publication (18)	34[e]	238	Clinical isolates	2004–2007	2008
Mexico	Publication (22)	32.2 (caz); 41.7 (cro);	563	Clinical isolates (hospital)	2005–2010	2012
Nicaragua	National data	48.1	271	Uncomplicated urinary tract infection	2010	2013
Panama	National data	9.7	2318	Uncomplicated urinary tract infection	2010	2010
Panama	National network	9	4321	Comprehensive	2011–2012	2013
Paraguay	National data	1.4	1601	Uncomplicated urinary tract infection	2010	2013
Peru	National data	24.8	1009	Uncomplicated urinary tract infection	2010	2013
Peru	National network	50	3298	Comprehensive	2012	2013
Saint Kitts and Nevis	No information obtained for this report					
Saint Lucia	No information obtained for this report					
Saint Vicent and the Grenadines	No information obtained for this report					
Suriname	No information obtained for this report					
Trinidad and Tobago	Publication (23)	9.4	716	Clinical isolates	(2004)–2007	2008
United States of America	National data	14.6	9443	Health care associated infections	2009–2010	
Uruguay	National data not available					2013

Countries, territories and other areas or groupings	Data source[b, c, d]	Resistance (%)	No. tested isolates	Type of surveillance, population or samples[c]	Period for data collection	Year of publication or report
Uruguay	Publication (24)	0	253	Urinary isolates	2007–2008	2010
Venezuela (Bolivarian Republic of)	National data	12.5	4114	Uncomplicated urinary tract infection	2010	2013
International	Publication (25)	26.8	504	Intra-abdominal infections	2008	2011
International	Publication (19)	9 (caz); 23.9 (cro)	1517	Hospitalized patients	2008–2010	2012

a. caz, ceftazidim; ctx, cefotaxim; cro, ceftriaxone

b. National data refers to data returned on the questionnaires as defined in Annex 1. This definition does not imply that the data collected is representative for that country as a whole because information gaps are likely.

c. See Annex 1 for definitions.

d. "National data not available" means that there was information that no data were available; "No information obtained for this report" means that no information was obtained from authorities, networks or publications.

e. Data only on proportion producing ESBL (extended spectrum beta-lactamases).

f. For data from time periods of several years, or where data from a subset of year(s) were available, the format (2001)–2011, indicates the first year of data collection within parenthesis, and the most recent year with separate data outside the parenthesis.

Table A2.3 *Escherichia coli*: Resistance to third-generation cephalosporins[a]
Eastern Mediterranean Region

Countries, territories and other areas or groupings	Data source[b, c, d]	Resistance (%)	No. tested isolates	Type of surveillance, population or samples[c]	Period for data collection	Year of publication or report
Afghanistan	No information obtained for this report					
Bahrain	National data	55	3795		2012	2013
Djibouti	No information obtained for this report					
Egypt	National data not available					2013
Egypt	National surveillance (Hospital network[e])	38.7 (caz); 50.1 (cro)	315	Hospital samples	(2002)–2010[f]	2013
Iran (Islamic Republic of)	National data	41	885	Invasive isolates	2012	2013
Iraq	Publication (26)	9.6	73	Hospital samples	2005	2013
Iraq	Publication (27)	32.7	49	Urinary isolates (outpatients)		2012
Jordan	National data not available					2013
Jordan	Publication (28)	22.5 (caz)	113	Urinary isolates (children)	2008	2011
Jordan	National data from international publication (1)	31	84	Invasive isolates	(2003)–2005	2008
Kuwait	Publication (29)	28	54	Invasive isolates (children)	2005–2009	2012
Kuwait	Publication (30)	17 (community); 27 (hospital)[g]	1745 (community); 770 (hospital)	Urinary tract infections: Community acquired and hospital acquired	2005–2007	2010
Lebanon	National data not available					2013
Lebanon	Publication (31)	18.6	628	Comprehensive, (hospital laboratory)	2000–2009	2011
Lebanon	Publication (32)	33 (ctx); 24 (caz)	3811	Clinical isolates	2010–2011	2012
Lebanon	National data from international publication (1)	25	36	Invasive isolates	(2003)–2005	2008
Libya	No information obtained for this report					
Morocco	National data	78	17	Comprehensive (hospital samples)	2012	2013
Morocco	Publication (33)	21.7 (caz); 31.9 (cro)	32	Intensive care unit	(2004)–2008	2009
Morocco	National data from international publication (1)	33	52	Invasive isolates	(2003)–2005	2008
Morocco	Publication (34)	8.8	80	Urinary isolates (children)	(2005)–2009	2010
Morocco	Publication (35)	15	221	Urinary isolates	2005–2007	2010
Morocco	Publication (36)	2	192	Urinary isolates	2001–2005	2010
Morocco	Publication (37)	1.3	767	Urinary isolates	2004–2009	2011
Oman	National data	63	1360	Comprehensive	2012	2013
Pakistan	National data, incomplete	10		Targeted		2013
Pakistan	Publication (38)	12.6[h]	670	Clinical isolates children	2011–2012	2012
Pakistan	Publication (39)	94	110	Intensive care unit	2007	2010
Pakistan	Publication (40)	42	50	Laboratory isolates	2006	2009
Pakistan	Publication (41)	62.3 (ctx); 71.7 (caz); 71.7 (cro)	53	Medical intensive care	2007–2008	2010
Pakistan	Publication (42)	46.3	296	Urinary isolates	(2002)–2005	2010
Pakistan	Publication (43)	62.8	38	Urinary isolates	(2004)–2006	2008
Pakistan	Publication (44)	84.2	101	Urinary isolates (hospitalized patients)	2006–2007	2011
Pakistan	Publication (45)	30	180	Urinary isolates		2010
Pakistan	Publication (46)	88	100	Urinary isolates (hospitalized patients)		2011
Pakistan	Publication (47)	26.1 (ctx); 29.6 (caz)	144	Vaginal swabs	(2004)–2006	2008
Pakistan	Publication (48)	51	59	Urinary isolates		2011
Qatar	Publication (49)	27.8	97	Blood isolates	2007–2008	2010
Saudi Arabia	Publication (50)	18.3[g]	20 268	Clinical isolates	(2007)–2011	2012
Saudi Arabia	Publication (51)	33.3	339	Urinary isolates (hospital)	2009–2011	2013
Saudi Arabia	Publication (52)	Community 8.1; Hospital; 7.4[g]	Community 2508; Hospital; 71.4	Urinary isolates(community and hospital patients)		2009
Saudi Arabia	Publication (53)	61	392 (entire period)	Laboratory collection of gram-negatives	(2004)–2009	2010
Saudi Arabia	Publication (54)	5.2	166	Urine samples (non-hospitalized children)	2003–2009	2012

Countries, territories and other areas or groupings	Data source[b, c, d]	Resistance (%)	No. tested isolates	Type of surveillance, population or samples[c]	Period for data collection	Year of publication or report
Saudi Arabia	Publication (55)	15.7 Hospitalized patients; 4.8 (outpatients)[h]	690 Hospitalized patients; 4813 (outpatients)	Laboratory	2004–2005	2009
Saudi Arabia	Publication (56)	19.5 (caz); 23.8 (cro)	308 (caz); 294 (cro)	Isolates from different hospitals	2010–2011	2012
Saudi Arabia	Publication (57)	49	39	Laboratory records	2009	2010
Saudi Arabia	Publication (58)	10.4 (cro); 15 (caz)	173	Urine samples (paediatric)	2003–2006	2008
Somalia	No information obtained for this report					
Sudan	National data not available					2013
Sudan	Publication (59)	64 (cro); 35 (caz)	232	Hospital samples	2011	2012
Syrian Arab Republic	National data not available					2013
Syrian Arab Republic	Publication (60)	48 (cro); 49 (ctx); 52.3 (caz)	107	Urinary isolates	2011	2012
Tunisia	Publication (61)	21	15 175	Hospital samples	(1999)–2005	2008
Tunisia	National data from international publication (1)	11	194	Invasive isolates	(2003)–2005	2008
Tunisia	Publication (36)	2	192	Urinary isolates	2001–2005	2010
Tunisia	Publication (62)	5	43	Urinary isolates (children)	2009	2011
United Arab Emirates	National data[i]	22	5276	Comprehensive	2012	2013
United Arab Emirates	Publication (63)	26.7[j]	1355	Clinical isolates	(1994 and) 2005	2009
United Arab Emirates	Publication (64)	39	83	Hospitalized patients	2005–2006	
Yemen	No information obtained for this report					
International network	ANSORP[k]	Blood isolates: 17.9 (caz); 28.3 (ctx); Urinary isolates: 18.5 (caz); 30.3 (ctx)	374 Blood isolates; 621 Urinary isolates	Blood isolates and urinary isolates	2012	2013

a. caz, ceftazidim; ctx, cefotaxim; cro, ceftriaxone
b. National data refers to data returned on the questionnaires as defined in Annex 1. This definition does not imply that the data collected is representative for that country as a whole because information gaps are likely.
c. See Annex 1 for definitions.
d. "National data not available" means that there was information that no data were available; "No information obtained for this report" means that no information was obtained from authorities, networks or publications.
e. US Naval Medical Research Unit No 3, Global Disease Detection Program, Egypt.
f. For data from time periods of several years, or where data from a subset of year(s) were available, the format (2001)–2011, indicates the first year of data collection within parenthesis, and the most recent year with separate data outside the parenthesis.
g. Data only on proportion producing ESBL (extended spectrum beta-lactamases).
h. Data only on resistance caused by AmpC beta-lactamase.
i. Data from United Arab Emirates originate from Abu Dhabi only.
j. Aggregated from three hospitals that reported 15.8%, 18% and 62%, respectively.
k. Some centres from the following countries, territories and areas participate in some ANSORP (Asian Network for Surveillance of Resistant Pathogens) projects: India, Indonesia, Japan, Malaysia, Philippines, Republic of Korea, Singapore, Sri Lanka, Saudi Arabia, Thailand, Viet Nam, in addition to China, Hong Kong SAR (Special Administrative Region) and Taiwan, China.

Table A2.4 *Escherichia coli*: Resistance to third-generation cephalosporins[a]
European Region

Countries, territories and other areas or groupings	Data source[b,c,d]	Resistance (%)	No. tested isolates	Type of surveillance, population or samples[c]	Period for data collection	Year of publication or report
Albania	National data not available					2013
Andorra	No information obtained for this report					
Armenia	National data not available					2013
Austria	National data	9.1	3160	Invasive isolates	2011	2013
Azerbaijan	National data not available					2013
Belarus	No information obtained for this report[e]					
Belgium	National data	6	3985	Invasive isolates	2011	2013
Bosnia and Herzegovina	Publication (65)	1.5	21 918	Urinary isolates (outpatients)	(2001)–2003[f]	2010
Bosnia and Herzegovina	Publication (66)	1.1	1618	Urinary tract infections (community)	2004	2010
Bulgaria	National data	22.9	179	Invasive isolates	2011	2013
Croatia	National data	6	19 274	Comprehensive	2012	2013
Cyprus	National data	36.2	138	Invasive isolates	2011	2013
Czech Republic	National data	11.4	2684	Invasive isolates	2011	2013
Denmark	National data	8.5	2532	Invasive isolates	2011	2013
Estonia	National data	12.2	90	Invasive isolates	2011	2013
Finland	National data	5.1	2419	Invasive isolates	2011	2013
France	National data	8.2	8479	Invasive isolates	2011	2009
Georgia	National data not available					2013
Georgia	Publication (67)	9	11	Blood isolates (neonates)	2003–2004	2009
Germany	National data	8	3642	Invasive isolates	2011	2013
Greece	National data	14.9	1435	Invasive isolates	2011	2013
Hungary	National data	15.1	1224	Invasive isolates	2011	2013
Iceland	National data	6.2	130	Invasive isolates	2011	2013
Ireland	National data	9	2166	Invasive isolates	2011	2013
Israel	Publication (68)	4.6 (community); 7.7 (hospital); 0 (long-term care facility, LTCF)[g]	174 (community); 56 (hospital); 13 (LTCF)	Bacteremia (community, hospital, LTCF)	2001–2006	2009
Israel	Publication (69)	2.2	1560 (all years)	Blood isolates	(1997)–2004	2008
Israel	Publication (70)	0	94	Intra-abdominal infections	1995–2004	2009
Italy	National data	19.8	1870	Invasive isolates	2011	2013
Kazakhstan	No information obtained for this report[e]					
Kyrgyzstan	National data not available					2013
Latvia	National data	15.9	132	Invasive isolates	2011	2013
Lithuania	National data	7	385	Invasive isolates	2011	2013
Luxembourg	National data	8.2	353	Invasive isolates	2011	2013
Malta	National data	12.8	219	Invasive isolates	2011	2013
Monaco	No information obtained for this report					
Montenegro	National data not available					2013
Netherlands	National data	5.7	4408	Invasive isolates	2011	2011
Norway	National data	3.6	2523	Invasive isolates	2011	2013
Poland	National data	11.7	938	Invasive isolates	2011	2013
Portugal	National data	11.3	1901	Invasive isolates	2011	2013
Republic of Moldova	National data	28	4788		2012	2013
Romania	National data	22	91	Invasive isolates	2011	2013
Russian Federation	National data	13.1 (caz); 22.9 (ctx)[h]	761	Hospital samples, community urinary isolates	2011–2012	2013
San Marino	No information obtained for this report					
Serbia	National data	21.3	145	Invasive isolates	2012	2013
Slovakia	National data	31	738	Invasive isolates	2011	2013
Slovenia	National data	8.8	1002	Invasive isolates	2011	2013
Spain	National data	12	5600	Invasive isolates	2011	2013
Sweden	National data	3	3939	Invasive isolates	2011	2013
Switzerland	National data	8.2	68 965	Comprehensive	2012	2013
Tajikistan	No information obtained for this report					
The former Yugoslav Republic of Macedonia	National data	47.4	19	Invasive isolates		2013
Turkey	National data	43.3	1306	Invasive isolates	2011	2013
Turkmenistan	No information obtained for this report					

Countries, territories and other areas or groupings	Data source[b,c,d]	Resistance (%)	No. tested isolates	Type of surveillance, population or samples[c]	Period for data collection	Year of publication or report
Ukraine	No information obtained for this report[e]					
United Kingdom	National data	9.6	5182	Invasive isolates	2011	2013
Uzbekistan	No information obtained for this report					
International	Publication (71)	14 (ctx); 14 (cro); 14.7 (caz)	1491	Intra-abdominal infections	2008	2011

a. caz, ceftazidim; ctx, cefotaxim; cro, ceftriaxone
b. National data refers to data returned on the questionnaires as defined in Annex 1. This definition does not imply that the data collected is representative for that country as a whole because information gaps are likely.
c. See Annex 1 for definitions.
d. "National data not available" means that there was information that no data were available; "No information obtained for this report" means that no information was obtained from authorities, networks or publications.
e. Some centres participate in some RusNet projects.
f. For data from time periods of several years, or where data from a subset of year(s) were available, the format (2001)–2011, indicates the first year of data collection within parenthesis, and the most recent year with separate data outside the parenthesis.
g. Data only on proportion producing ESBL (extended spectrum beta-lactamases).
h. Hospital isolates: 66.4 (caz); 82.1 (ctx); Community urinary isolates: 6.5 (caz); 10.2 (ctx).

Table A2.5 *Escherichia coli*: Resistance to third-generation cephalosporins[a]
South East Asian Region

Countries, territories and other areas or groupings	Data source[b, c, d]	Resistance (%)	No. tested isolates	Type of surveillance, population or samples[c]	Period for data collection	Year of publication or report
Bangladesh	National data not available					2013
Bangladesh	Publication (72)	53.5[e]	114	Urinary isolates	2010–2011	2013
Bangladesh	Publication (73)	59	475	Clinical isolates (national network)	2011–2012	2013
Bangladesh	Publication (74)	50.2 (caz); 63.1 (ctx)	203	Urinary isolates (children)	2009–2011	2012
Bangladesh	Publication (75)	16.2 (caz); 12.5 (cro)	80	Private facility / referred patients		2010
Bhutan	National data	16 (caz); 20.4 (cro);	410 (caz); 1405 (cro)	Comprehensive	2011–2012	2012
Democratic People's Republic of Korea	No information obtained for this report					
India	National data not available[f]					2013
India	Publication (76)	61	1103	Blood samples	2000- 2009	2012
India	Publication (77)	25 (ctx); 37.3 (caz)	180	Urinary samples (pregnant women with bacteriuria)		2011
India	Publication (78)	27.8	54	Diabetic foot infections	2005	2008
India	Publication (79)	28.7	181	Hospital isolates	2006	2008
India	Publication (80)	40.4	171	Urinary isolates		2012
India	Publication (81)	64.8	250	Clinical samples	2006–2007	2008
India	Publication (82)	95	239	Healthy carriers	2011	2012
India	Publication (83)	74.1	46	Lower resp. tract infections (hospital patients)	2011–2012	2013
India	Publication (84)	60.5	1817	Intra-abdominal infections (hospital patients)	2009	2011
India	Publication (85)	20	120	Urinary samples (hospital patients)	2008	2011
India	Publication (86)	87.5	56	Ventilator-associated pneumonia	2004–2009	2011
India	Publication (87)	33.5	340	Intra-abdominal infections (hospital patients)	2008	2010
India	Publication (88)	84.9	106	Cancer patients (hospital patients)		2010
India	Publication (89)	60.5	2671	Urinary samples (hospital patients)	2008–2009	2012
India	Publication (90)	42 (caz); 63 (ctx); 64 (cro)	307 (caz); 229 (ctx); 234 (cro)	Hospital patients	2012	2013
India	Publication (91)	73	149	Hospital patients	2007–2009	2012
India	Publication (92)	74.8 (cro); 68.1 (ctx); 50 (caz); 78.6 (cfp); 86.8 (cpd)	210	Clinical samples	(2004)-2005[g]	2009
India	Publication (93)	56	527	Mixed hospital and outpatients	2010	2011
India	Publication (94)	20.3	103	Hospital samples, blood isolates	2009–2010	2010
India	Publication (95)	50[e]	62	Clinical isolates (hospitalized patients)		2012
India	Publication (96)	19 (inpatients); 16 (outpatients)	1054 (total)	Urinary isolates (hospitalized and outpatients)	2007	2012
India	Publication (97)	40	38	burn unit		2011
Indonesia	National data not available					2013
Indonesia	Publication (98)	10 (ctx); 13.8 (cro)	29	Blood isolates	2002–2008	2009
Maldives	No information obtained for this report					
Myanmar	National data	68	1444	Comprehensive	2012	2013
Nepal	National data	37.9	140	Targeted. Urinary isolates	2012	2013
Sri Lanka	National data	58.9	117	Targeted	2009	2013
Thailand	National data	30.5 (caz); 41.4 (cro); 42.7 (ctx)	36 545 (caz); 22 236 (cro); 39 949 (ctx)	Comprehensive	2012	2013
Timor-Leste	National data not available					2013

Countries, territories and other areas or groupings	Data source[b, c, d]	Resistance (%)	No. tested isolates	Type of surveillance, population or samples[c]	Period for data collection	Year of publication or report
Timor-Leste	National data, incomplete, from national laboratory[h]	2			2010–2012	2013
International network	ANSORP[f]	Blood isolates: 17.9 (caz); 28.3 (ctx); 18.5 Urinary isolates: (caz); 30.3 (ctx)	Blood isolates 374; Urinary isolates 621	Blood isolates Urinary isolates	2012	2013

a. caz, ceftazidim; cfp, cefoperazone; cpd, cefpodoxime; ctx, cefotaxim; cro, ceftriaxone
b. National data refers to data returned on the questionnaires as defined in Annex 1. This definition does not imply that the data collected is representative for that country as a whole because information gaps are likely.
c. See Annex 1 for definitions.
d. "National data not available" means that there was information that no data were available; "No information obtained for this report" means that no information was obtained from authorities, networks or publications.
e. Data only on proportion producing ESBL (extended spectrum beta-lactamases).
f. Some centres from the following countries, territories and areas participate in some ANSORP (Asian Network for Surveillance of Resistant Pathogens) projects: India, Indonesia, Japan, Malaysia, Philippines, Republic of Korea, Singapore, Sri Lanka, Saudi Arabia, Thailand, Viet Nam, in addition to China, Hong Kong SAR (Special Administrative Region) and Taiwan, China.
g. For data from time periods of several years, or where data from a subset of year(s) were available, the format (2001)–2011, indicates the first year of data collection within parenthesis, and the most recent year with separate data outside the parenthesis.
h. Data were provided, but no formal national data compilation was available.

Table A2.6 *Escherichia coli*: Resistance to third-generation cephalosporins[a]
Western Pacific Region

Countries, territories and other areas or groupings	Data source[b, c, d]	Resistance (%)	No. tested isolates	Type of surveillance, population or samples[c]	Period for data collection	Year of publication or report
Australia	National data	5.8 (caz); 9.6 (cro)	1827	Comprehensive	2011	2013
Brunei Darussalam	National data from hospital laboratory	6.1 (cro); 6.8 (caz)	1345	Comprehensive	2012	2013
Cambodia	National data[e] collected from several sources by public health institute (NIPH). Pasteur Institute (PI)	49 (NIPH); 43 (PI)	63 (NIPH); 122 (PI)	Clinical samples (NIPH); Laboratory data (mixed patients) (PI)	2013 2013	2013 2013
China	National data	31.3 (caz); 65.6 (cro); 70 (ctx)	146 497 (caz); 113 892 (cro); 79 906 (ctx)	Comprehensive	2012	2013
Cook Islands	No information obtained for this report					
Fiji	National data not available					2013
Fiji	Institute surveillance[e, f]	12.2	2895	Mixed samples	2012	2013
Japan	National data	16.6	113 383	Comprehensive	2012	2013
Kiribati	National data	0	72	Comprehensive	2013	2013
Lao People's Democratic Republic	National data	40.7	27		2012–2013	2013
Lao People's Democratic Republic	Institute surveillance	38	21	Comprehensive (Laboratory)	2011–2012	2013
Malaysia	National data	14.9 (caz); 18 (cro); 20 (ctx)	28 418 (caz); 13 448 (cro); 24 880 (ctx)	Comprehensive	2012	2013
Marshall Islands	National data not available					
Micronesia	National data	77	158	Comprehensive	2011	2013
Mongolia	Publication (99)	57.5 (ctx); 70.6 (caz)	153	Urinary infections (community)		2013
Nauru	No information obtained for this report					
New Zealand	National data	4.7 (Blood isolates); 2.9 (Urinary isolates)	1661 (Blood isolates) 55 888 (Urinary isolates)	Blood isolates, urinary isolates	2011	2013
Niue	No information obtained for this report					
Palau	No information obtained for this report					
Papua New Guinea	National data	24.1[g]	174	Blood, stool, urine, "pus bench"	2012	2013
Philippines	National data	26.7	3614	Comprehensive	2012	2013
Republic of Korea	National data	23.9 (caz); 24 (ctx)[h]	18 484	Comprehensive	2011	2013
Republic of Korea	National network	28	4628	Comprehensive	2012	2013
Samoa	National data	12.9	43	Comprehensive	2011	2013
Singapore	National data, incomplete[i]		3940 All clinical isolates 510 Bacteraemia	(i) All clinical isolates (ii) Bacteraemia	2012	2013
Singapore	Publication (100)	27	189	Hospital laboratories	2006–2007	2008
Singapore	Publication (101)	20 (all); 21.7 (blood)	6629 (all); 854 (blood)	Hospital network	2006–2008	2010
Singapore	Publication (102)	8.1	248	Urinary isolates	2009	2011
Solomon Islands	National data not available					2013
Tonga	National data, incomplete	0				2013
Tuvalu	No information obtained for this report					
Vanuatu	No information obtained for this report					
Viet Nam	No information obtained for this report[j]					
International network	ANSORP[j]	Blood isolates. 17.9 (caz); 28.3 (ctx); Urinary isolates: 18.5 (caz); 30.3 (ctx)	374 (Blood isolates) 621 (Urinary isolates)	Blood isolates Urinary isolates	2012	2013

a. caz, ceftazidim; ctx, cefotaxim; cro, ceftriaxone
b. National data refers to data returned on the questionnaires as defined in Annex 1. This definition does not imply that the data collected is representative for that country as a whole because information gaps are likely.
c. See Annex 1 for definitions.
d. "National data not available" means that there was information that no data were available; "No information obtained for this report" means that no information was obtained from authorities, networks or publications.
e. Data were provided, but no formal national data compilation was available.
f. Data from three hospitals aggregated. Mixed samples – urine or "other" in one hospital, and comprehensive in two hospitals.
g. National data from different types of samples (blood, urinary, stool and «pus bench») aggregated.
h. Data aggregated from several sources: "Hospitals"; 31.4 (ctx); 31.6 caz; «Clinics»; 12.9 (ctx); 13 (caz); «General hospitals»; 23.6 (ctx); 24 (caz).
i. No data on proportions obtained. Incidence in hospitals (i) 20.4 per 10,000 inpatient days, (ii) 2.6 per 10,000 inpatient days.
j. Some centres from the following countries, territories and areas participate in some ANSORP (Asian Network for Surveillance of Resistant Pathogens) projects: India, Indonesia, Japan, Malaysia, Philippines, Republic of Korea, Singapore, Sri Lanka, Saudi Arabia, Thailand, Viet Nam, in addition to China, Hong Kong SAR (Special Administrative Region) and Taiwan, China.

Table A2.7 *Escherichia coli*: Resistance to fluoroquinolones[a]
African Region

Countries, territories and other areas or groupings	Data source[b, c, d]	Resistance (%)	No. tested isolates	Type of surveillance, population or samples[c]	Period for data collection	Year of publication or report
Algeria	Publication (*1*)	2	131	Invasive isolates	(2003)–2005[e]	2008
Angola	No information obtained for this report					
Benin	National data	34	44	Invasive isolates	2012	2013
Botswana	National data not available					2013
Botswana	Publication (*103*)	25	173	Urinary infections (hospital patients)	2007–2009	2013
Burkina Faso	National data	52.8	213	Invasive isolates	2008–2009	2013
Burundi	National data	16	1645	Targeted	2012	2013
Cameroon	No information obtained for this report					
Cabo Verde	No information obtained for this report					
Central African Republic	National data	53	183	Comprehensive	2012	2013
Chad	No information obtained for this report					
Comoros	No information obtained for this report					
Congo	National data	30	71	Comprehensive	2013	2013
Côte d'Ivoire	No information obtained for this report					
Democratic Republic of the Congo	No information obtained for this report					
Equatorial Guinea	No information obtained for this report					
Eritrea	No information obtained for this report					
Ethiopia	National data	71	152	Comprehensive	2011–2012	2013
Gabon	No information obtained for this report					
Gambia	National data not available					2013
Ghana	National data	36 (lvx); 47.6 (cip)	87 (lvx); 160 (cip)	Comprehensive	2013	2013
Guinea	National data	38	13	Comprehensive	2012	2013
Guinea-Bissau	National data	40	35	Comprehensive	2012	2013
Kenya	National data, incomplete	2		Targeted	2012	2013
Kenya	National network[f]	26.7	15	Targeted	2013	2013
Kenya	Publication (*2*)	92.7 (cip); 90.0 (lvx)	109	Private hospital	2007–2009	2012
Lesotho	National data	14	107	Comprehensive	2011	2013
Liberia	National data	15	13	Targeted	2011	2013
Madagascar	Publication (*3*)	52.3	88	Hospital isolates	2006–2008	2010
Malawi	National data	0	1	Comprehensive	2013	2013
Mali	No information obtained for this report					
Mauritania	National data	20	116	Comprehensive	2013	2013
Mauritius	National data	57.6	184	Hospital samples	2012	2013
Mozambique	No information obtained for this report					
Namibia	National data	16	3176	Comprehensive	2011	2013
Niger	National data not available					2013
Nigeria	Publication (*104*)	31.4	35	Carriers	2011	2012
Nigeria	Publication (*4*)	10	310	Blood isolates (children)	2006–2008	2010
Nigeria	Publication (*105*)	43.4 (cip); 49.7 (lvx)	1909	Urinary isolates	2005–2009	2012
Nigeria	Publication (*106*)	36.3 (pfl); 41.2 (ofx); 71.3 (spx); 79 (cip)	80	Urinary isolates (asymptomatic students)		2012
Nigeria	Publication (*5*)	29 (ofx)	80	Healthy carriers	(2003–2007	2008
Nigeria	Publication (*10*)	24.2 (cip); 23.8 (ofl)	42	Urinary isolates		2010
Nigeria	Publication (*107*)	0 (cip); 0 (ref); 4.8 (ofx); 9.6 (spx)	84	Asymptomatic bacteriuria (HIV-infected)	2007–2008	2009
Nigeria	Publication (*108*)	9.5	85	Urinary isolates	2007–2009	2011
Nigeria	Publication (*109*)	7.1 (lvx); 14 (cip); 14.4 (mox); 28.6 (ofl); 35.7 (pef)	62 (lvx); 122 (cip); 125 (mox); 249 (ofl); 311 (pef)	Urinary samples (mixed patients)	2001–2004	2009
Nigeria	Publication (*110*)	9.1	33	Carriers	2008–2009	2012
Nigeria	Publication (*8*)	1.5	364	Hospital acquired urinary tract infections	2007–2008	2009
Nigeria	Publication (*111*)	0 (ofx); 0 (cip)	31	Blood isolates	2004–2009	2010
Nigeria	Publication (*112*)	11 (AIDS patients); 9 (non-AIDS patients)	135 (AIDS patients); 154 (non-AIDS patients)	Urinary infections (AIDS and non-AIDS patients)	2003–2009	2010

Countries, territories and other areas or groupings	Data source[b, c, d]	Resistance (%)	No. tested isolates	Type of surveillance, population or samples[c]	Period for data collection	Year of publication or report
Nigeria	Publication (*113*)	2.7	37	Urinary infections (antenatal clinic)	2007–2009	2012
Nigeria	Publication (*12*)	3	32	Blood isolates (HIV-infected children)		2010
Rwanda	Publication (*13*)	31.9 (Outpatients); 57.4 (Intpatients)	72 (Outpatients); 47 (Intpatients)	Outpatients and hospital patients	2009	2011
Sao Tome and Principe	National data not available					2013
Senegal	No information obtained for this report					
Seychelles	No information obtained for this report					
Sierra Leone	No information obtained for this report					
South Africa	National data not available					2013
South Africa	Publication (*114*)	25.6	43	Urinary tract infection (outpatients)	2008	2011
South Africa	Publication (*16*)	16.1	453	Urinary isolates	2005–2006	2009
South Sudan	National data not available					2013
Swaziland	National data	37.5	32	Clinical samples	2013	2013
Togo	No information obtained for this report					
Uganda	National data	0	9		2011	2013
United Republic of Tanzania	National data not available					2013
United Republic of Tanzania	Publication (*17*)	0	64	Children with diarrhoea	2004	2011
Zambia	National data	50.5	190	Targeted	2012	2013
Zimbabwe	National data not available					2013

a. cip, ciprofloxacin; gat, gatifloxacin; lvx, levofloxacin; mox, moxifloxacin; nor, norfloxacin; ofx, ofloxacin; pfl, pefloxacin; ref, refloxacin; spx, sparfloxacin. Ciprofloxacin mostly used where not specified (a few reported on norfloxacin).

b. National data refers to data returned on the questionnaires as defined in Annex 1. This definition does not imply that the data collected is representative for that country as a whole because information gaps are likely.

c. See Annex 1 for definitions.

d. "National data not available" means that there was information that no data were available; "No information obtained for this report" means that no information was obtained from authorities, networks or publications.

e. For data from time periods of several years, or where data from a subset of year(s) were available, the format (2001)–2011, indicates the first year of data collection within parenthesis, and the most recent year with separate data outside the parenthesis.

f. Global Disease Detection Center, Kenya/Division of Global Health Protection/Center for Global Health/ CDC (US Centers for Disease Control and Prevention).

Annex 2

Table A2.8 *Escherichia coli*: Resistance to fluoroquinolones[a]
Region of the Americas

Countries, territories and other areas or groupings	Data source[b, c, d]	Resistance (%)	No. tested isolates	Type of surveillance, population or samples[c]	Period for data collection	Year of publication or report
Antigua and Barbuda	No information obtained for this report					
Argentina	National data	7.8	13 102	Uncomplicated urinary tract infection	2010	2013
Bahamas	No information obtained for this report					
Barbados	No information obtained for this report					
Belize	No information obtained for this report					
Bolivia (Plurinational State of)	National data	47	8259	Uncomplicated urinary tract infection	2010	2013
Brazil	National data	8	247	Uncomplicated urinary tract infection	2010	2013
Canada	National data	26.9	646	Sentinel hospitals	2011	2013
Chile	National data not available					2013
Colombia	National data not available					2013
Colombia	Publication (20)	58 (cip); 60 (nor)	254	Urinary isolates	2005–2008	2010
Costa Rica	National data not available					2013
Cuba	National data	56	179	Uncomplicated urinary tract infection	2009	2013
Dominica	No information obtained for this report					
Dominican Republic	National data	49	2812	Hospital samples	2009	2013
Ecuador	National data	43.8	9259	Uncomplicated urinary tract infection	2010	2013
El Salvador	National data	16.7	486	Uncomplicated urinary tract infection	2010	2013
Grenada	No information obtained for this report					
Guatemala	National data	41.8	1607	Uncomplicated urinary tract infection	2010	2013
Guyana	No information obtained for this report					
Haiti	No information obtained for this report					
Honduras	National data	43.1	3010	Uncomplicated urinary tract infection	2010	2013
Jamaica	No information obtained for this report					
Mexico	National data not available					2013
Mexico	Publication (115)	32.6	907	Urinary isolates		2008
Mexico	Publication (22)	57.9 (cip); 56.7 (lvx)	563	Clinical isolates (hospital)	2005–2011	2012
Nicaragua	National data	42.9	271	Uncomplicated urinary tract infection	2010	2013
Panama	National data	40.2	2318	Uncomplicated urinary tract infection	2010	2013
Panama	National network	18	7422	Comprehensive	2011–2012	2013
Paraguay	National data	22.1	1601	Uncomplicated urinary tract infection	2010	
Peru	National data	58.5	2563	Uncomplicated urinary tract infection	2010	2013
Peru	National network	66	3523	Comprehensive	2012	2013
Saint Kitts and Nevis	No information obtained for this report					
Saint Lucia	No information obtained for this report					
Saint Vicent and the Grenadines	No information obtained for this report					
Suriname	No information obtained for this report					
Trinidad and Tobago	Publication (116)	1.6	64	Hospitalized children	2007	2010
United States of America	National data	33.3	8992	Health-care associated infections	2009–2010	2013
Uruguay	National data not available					2013
Uruguay	Publication (24)	15	253	Urinary isolates	2007–2008	2010
Venezuela (Bolivarian Republic of)	National data	37.2	4114	Uncomplicated urinary tract infection	2010	2013

a. cip, ciprofloxacin; gat, gatifloxacin; lvx, levofloxacin; mox, moxifloxacin; nor, norfloxacin; ofx, ofloxacin; pfl, pefloxacin; ref, refloxacin; spx, sparfloxacin. Ciprofloxacin mostly used where not specified (a few reported on norfloxacin).

b. National data refers to data returned on the questionnaires as defined in Annex 1. This definition does not imply that the data collected is representative for that country as a whole because information gaps are likely.

c. See Annex 1 for definitions.

d. "National data not available" means that there was information that no data were available; "No information obtained for this report" means that no information was obtained from authorities, networks or publications.

Table A2.9 *Escherichia coli*: Resistance to fluoroquinolones[a]
Eastern Mediterranean Region

Countries, territories and other areas or groupings	Data source[b, c, d]	Resistance (%)	No. tested isolates	Type of surveillance, population or samples[c]	Period for data collection
Afghanistan	No information obtained for this report				
Bahrain	National data	62	3759		2012
Djibouti	No information obtained for this report				
Egypt	National data not available				
Egypt	National surveillance (Hospital network)[e]	34.9	315	Comprehensive (hospital samples)	2002–2010
Iran (Islamic Republic of)	National data	54	885	Invasive isolates	2012
Iraq	No information obtained for this report				
Jordan	National data not available				
Jordan	National data from international publication (1)	31	52	Invasive isolates	(2003)–2005[f]
Jordan	Publication (28)	14.5	435	Hospital samples (children)	2008
Kuwait	No information obtained for this report				
Lebanon	National data not available				
Lebanon	National data from international publication (1)	53	36	Invasive isolates	(2003)–2005
Lebanon	Publication (32)	47	3811	Clinical isolates	2010–2011
Libya	Publication (117)	7.1–17.1[g]	119	Clinical isolates	
Morocco	National data	75	17	Comprehensive (hospital infections)	2012
Morocco	Publication (118)	31	229	Clinical isolates	2011–2012
Morocco	Publication (35)	27	221	Clinical isolates	2005–2007
Morocco	National data from international publication (1)	24	62	Invasive isolates	(2003)–2005
Morocco	Publication (36)	10	192	Urinary isolates	2001–2005
Oman	National data	21	1360	Comprehensive	2012
Pakistan	National data, incomplete	9		Targeted	
Pakistan	Publication (47)	21 (cip)	144	Vaginal swabs	2004–2006
Pakistan	Publication (119)	15.5 (gat); 0 (lfx)	45	Laboratory isolates	
Pakistan	Publication (39)	91	119	Intensive care unit (ICU)	2007
Pakistan	Publication (41)	75.5	53	Medical ICU patients	2007–2008
Pakistan	Publication (40)	64	50	Laboratory isolates	2006
Pakistan	Publication (42)	46.3	296	Urinary isolates	(2002–)2005
Pakistan	Publication (120)	38.5	270	Hospital samples	
Pakistan	Publication (44)	34.6	101	Urinary isolates (hospitalized patients)	2006–2007
Pakistan	Publication (120)	33.1	3953	Hospital samples	2002–2005
Qatar	Publication (49)	40.2	97	Blood isolates	2007–2008
Saudi Arabia	No information obtained for this report				
Saudi Arabia	Publication (51)	33.3	339	Urinary isolates	2009–2011
Saudi Arabia	Publication (120)	31.6	7906	Clinical isolates	2005
Saudi Arabia	Publication (52)	74.1	2530	Urinary isolates	
Saudi Arabia	Publication (56)	25	304	Isolates from different hospitals	2010–2011
Saudi Arabia	Publication (57)	51	39	Laboratory records	2009
Saudi Arabia	Publication (58)	22.8	173	Urine samples (paediatric)	2003–2006
Somalia	No information obtained for this report				
Sudan	National data not available				2013
Sudan	Publication (59)	58.4 (cip); 55.1 (ofl)	214	Hospital samples	2011
Syrian Arab Republic	National data not available				
Tunisia	No information obtained for this report				
Tunisia	Publication (59)	10	192	Urinary isolates	2001–2005
Tunisia	Publication (121)	7.1	436	Urinary isolates (community)	1999–2009
Tunisia	Publication (122)	0	13	Materno-fetal infections	1993–2003
Tunisia	National data from international publication (1)	15	164	Invasive isolates	(2003)–2005
United Arab Emirates	National data[h]	33.3	6770	Comprehensive	2012
United Arab Emirates	Publication (63)	27[i]	1037	Clinical isolates	(1994)–2005

Countries, territories and other areas or groupings	Data source[b, c, d]		Resistance (%)	No. tested isolates	Type of surveillance, population or samples[c]	Period for data collection
Yemen	Publication (123)		84.6	52	Urinary isolates	2003–2006
International network	ANSORP[j]		36.6 (Blood isolates); 40.9 (Urinary isolates)	374 (Blood isolates); 621 (Urinary solates)	Blood isolates Urinary isolates	2012
International	Publication (1)		21	5091	Invasive isolates	2003–2005

a. cip, ciprofloxacin; gat, gatifloxacin; lvx, levofloxacin; mox, moxifloxacin; nor, norfloxacin; ofx, ofloxacin; pfl, pefloxacin; ref, refloxacin; spx, sparfloxacin. Ciprofloxacin mostly used where not specified (a few reported on norfloxacin).
b. National data refers to data returned on the questionnaires as defined in Annex 1. This definition does not imply that the data collected is representative for that country as a whole because information gaps are likely.
c. See Annex 1 for definitions.
d. "National data not available" means that there was information that no data were available; "No information obtained for this report" means that no information was obtained from authorities, networks or publications.
e. US Naval Medical Research Unit No 3, Global Disease Detection Program, Egypt.
f. For data from time periods of several years, or where data from a subset of year(s) were available, the format (2001)–2011, indicates the first year of data collection within parenthesis, and the most recent year with separate data outside the parenthesis.
g. Variation during study period, no further details given.
h. Data from United Arab Emirates originate from Abu Dhabi only.
i. Data aggregated from three hospitals.
j. Some centres from the following countries, territories and areas participate in some ANSORP (Asian Network for Surveillance of Resistant Pathogens) projects: India, Indonesia, Japan, Malaysia, Philippines, Republic of Korea, Singapore, Sri Lanka, Saudi Arabia, Thailand, Viet Nam, in addition to China, Hong Kong SAR (Special Administrative Region) and Taiwan, China.

Table A2.10 *Escherichia coli*: Resistance to fluoroquinolones[a]
European Region

Countries, territories and other areas or groupings	Data source[b, c, d]	Resistance (%)	No. tested isolates	Type of surveillance, population or samples[c]	Period for data collection	Year of publication or report
Albania	National data not available					2013
Andorra	No information obtained for this report					
Armenia	National data not available					2013
Austria	National data	22.3	3162	Invasive isolates	2011	2013
Azerbaijan	National data not available					2013
Belarus	No information obtained for this report[e]					
Belgium	National data	21.5	3549	Invasive isolates	2011	2013
Bosnia and Herzegovina	Publication (66)	7.8	1618	Community-acquired urinary tract infection	2004	2010
Bulgaria	National data	30.2	179	Invasive isolates	2011	2013
Croatia	National data	14	20 227	Comprehensive	2012	2013
Cyprus	National data	47.4	137	Invasive isolates	2011	2013
Czech Republic	National data	23.5	2682	Invasive isolates	2011	2013
Denmark	National data	14.1	3583	Invasive isolates	2011	2013
Estonia	National data	9.9	312	Invasive isolates	2011	2013
Finland	National data	10.8	2420	Invasive isolates	2011	2013
France	National data	17.9	8694	Invasive isolates	2011	2013
Georgia	National data not available					2013
Georgia	Publication (67)	1/11	11	Blood isolates, neonates	2003–2004	2009
Germany	National data	23.7	3636	Invasive isolates	2011	2013
Greece	National data	26.6	1433	Invasive isolates	2011	2013
Hungary	National data	31.2	1213	Invasive isolates	2011	2013
Iceland	National data	14	121	Invasive isolates	2011	2013
Ireland	National data	22.9	2153	Invasive isolates	2011	2013
Israel	Publication (69)	17.9	719 (entire period)	Blood isolates	(1997)–2004[f]	2008
Israel	Publication (70)	0	94	Intra-abdominal infections	1995–2004	2009
Italy	National data	40.5	1899	Invasive isolates	2011	2013
Kazakhstan	No information obtained for this report[e]					
Kyrgyzstan	National data not available					2013
Latvia	National data	16.8	131	Invasive isolates	2011	2013
Lithuania	National data	12.9	381	Invasive isolates	2011	2013
Luxembourg	National data	24.1	353	Invasive isolates	2011	2013
Malta	National data	32	219	Invasive isolates	2011	2013
Monaco	No information obtained for this report					
Montenegro	National data not available					2013
Netherlands	National data	14.3	4427	Invasive isolates	2011	2013
Norway	National data	9	2505	Invasive isolates	2011	2013
Poland	National data	27.3	1141	Invasive isolates	2011	2013
Portugal	National data	27.2	1917	Invasive isolates	2011	2013
Republic of Moldova	National data	15.3	4839		2012	2013
Romania	National data	30.4	46	Invasive isolates	2011	2013
Russian Federation	National data	71.7 (Hospital isolates); 15.9 (Community urinary)	134 (Hospital isolates), 627 (Community urinary)	Hospital isolates and community urinary isolates	2011–2012	2013
San Marino	No information obtained for this report					
Serbia	National data	16	145	Invasive isolates	2012	2013
Slovakia	National data	41.9	737	Invasive isolates	2011	2013
Slovenia	National data	20.7	1002	Invasive isolates	2011	2013
Spain	National data	34.5	5597	Invasive isolates	2011	2013
Sweden	National data	7.9	3295	Invasive isolates	2011	2013
Switzerland	National data	20.2	69 940	Comprehensive	2012	2013
Tajikistan	No information obtained for this report					
The former Yugoslav Republic of Macedonia	National data not available					2013
Turkey	National data	46.3	1249	Invasive isolates	2011	2013
Turkmenistan	No information obtained for this report					
Ukraine	No information obtained for this report[e]					
United Kingdom	National data	17.5	5564	Invasive isolates	2011	2013

Countries, territories and other areas or groupings	Data source[b, c, d]	Resistance (%)	No. tested isolates	Type of surveillance, population or samples[c]	Period for data collection	Year of publication or report
Uzbekistan	No information obtained for this report					
International	Publication (71)	24.1 (lvx); 25.5 (cip)	1495	Intra-abdominal infections	2008	2011

a. cip, ciprofloxacin; gat, gatifloxacin; lvx, levofloxacin; mox, moxifloxacin; nor, norfloxacin; ofx, ofloxacin; pfl, pefloxacin; ref, refloxacin; spx, sparfloxacin. Ciprofloxacin mostly used where not specified (a few reported on norfloxacin).

b. National data refers to data returned on the questionnaires as defined in Annex 1. This definition does not imply that the data collected is representative for that country as a whole because information gaps are likely.

c. See Annex 1 for definitions.

d. "National data not available" means that there was information that no data were available; "No information obtained for this report" means that no information was obtained from authorities, networks or publications.

e. Some centres participate in some RusNet projects.

f. For data from time periods of several years, or where data from a subset of year(s) were available, the format (2001)–2011, indicates the first year of data collection within parenthesis, and the most recent year with separate data outside the parenthesis.

Table A2.11 *Escherichia coli*: Resistance to fluoroquinolones[a]
South East Asian Region

Countries, territories and other areas or groupings	Data source[b, c, d]	Resistance (%)	No. tested isolates	Type of surveillance, population or samples[c]	Period for data collection	Year of publication or report
Bangladesh	National data not available					2013
Bangladesh	Publication (72)	65.2	114	Urinary isolates	2010–2011	2013
Bangladesh	Publication (73)	89	475	Clinical isolates	2011–2012	2013
Bangladesh	Publication (75)	7.5	80	Private facility (referred patients, clinical samples)		2010
Bhutan	National data	52.3 (cip); 36.2 (nor); 32.4 (ofl)	132 (cip); 1414 (nor); 1023 (ofl)	Comprehensive	2011–2012	2013
Democratic People's Republic of Korea	No information obtained for this report					
India	National data not available					2013
India	Publication (77)	35	180	Urinary samples (pregnant women with bacteriuria)		2011
India	Publication (94)	86.4	103	Hospital samples	2009–2010	2010
India	Publication (124)	81.8	46	Lower respiratory tract infection (hospitalized patients)	2011–2012	2013
India	Publication (84)	49.6	1817	Intra-abdominal infections (hospitalized patients)	2009	2011
India	Publication (86)	71.4	56	Ventilator-associated pneumonia	2004–2009	2011
India	Publication (87)	16.5	340	Intra-abdominal infections (hospitalized patients)	2008	2010
India	Publication (88)	77.4	106	Hospitalized cancer patients		2010
India	Publication (89)	73	2671	Urinary tract infections (hospitalized patients)	2008–2009	2012
India	Publication (90)	65	461	Hospitalized patients	2012	2013
India	Publication (125)	4	1095	Healthy carriers (community)	2003–2004	2008
India	Publication (91)	85	149	Hospitalized patients	2007–2009	2012
India	Publication (93)	62	527	Hospitalized patients and outpatients	2010	2011
India	Publication (126)	80	669	Hospitalized patients	2001–2006	2008
India	Publication (127)	22.7	181	Hospitalized patients	2003	2008
India	Publication (128)	32	205	Hospitalized patients	2011	2012
India	Publication (96)	46 (hospitalized); 34 (outpatients)	1054 (total)	Urinary isolates (hospitalized and outpatients)	2007	2012
Indonesia	National data not available					2013
Indonesia	Publication (98)	17.3	29	Blood isolates	2002–2008	2009
Maldives	No information obtained for this report					
Myanmar	National data	55	1348	Comprehensive	2012	2013
Nepal	National data	64.3	140	Targeted	2012	2013
Sri Lanka	National data	58.8	102	Targeted	2009	2013
Thailand	National data	50.9 (cip); 51 (lvx); 52.9 (ofl); 55.3 (nor); 67.2 (mox)	31 761 (cip); 14 566 (lvx); 2904 (ofl); 16 335 (nor); 1670 (mox)	Comprehensive	2012	2013
Timor-Leste	National data not available					2013
International network	ANSORP[e]	36.6 (Blood isolates); 40.9 (Urinary isolates)	374 (Blood isolates); 621 (Urinary isolates)	Blood isolates, urinary isolates	2012	2013

a. cip, ciprofloxacin; gat, gatifloxacin; lvx, levofloxacin; mox, moxifloxacin; nor, norfloxacin; ofx, ofloxacin; pfl, pefloxacin; ref, refloxacin; spx, sparfloxacin. Ciprofloxacin mostly used where not specified (a few reported on norfloxacin).

b. National data refers to data returned on the questionnaires as defined in Annex 1. This definition does not imply that the data collected is representative for that country as a whole because information gaps are likely.

c. See Annex 1 for definitions.

d. "National data not available" means that there was information that no data were available; "No information obtained for this report" means that no information was obtained from authorities, networks or publications.

e. Some centres from the following countries, territories and areas participate in some ANSORP (Asian Network for Surveillance of Resistant Pathogens) projects: India, Indonesia, Japan, Malaysia, Philippines, Republic of Korea, Singapore, Sri Lanka, Saudi Arabia, Thailand, Viet Nam, in addition to China, Hong Kong SAR (Special Administrative Region) and Taiwan, China.

Table A2.12 *Escherichia coli*: Resistance to fluoroquinolones[a]
Western Pacific Region

Countries, territories and other areas or groupings	Data source[b, c, d]	Resistance (%)	No. tested isolates	Type of surveillance, population or samples[c]	Period for data collection	Year of publication or report
Australia	National data	10.6	1827	Comprehensive	2011	2013
Brunei Darussalam	National data from hospital laboratory	12	1358	Comprehensive	2012	2013
Cambodia	National data[e] collected from several sources by public health institute (NIPH) Pasteur Institute (PI)	52 (NIPH); 82 (PI)	63 (NIPH); 122 (PI)	Clinical samples and surveillance of respiratory infections (NIPH) Laboratory data (mixed patients, PI)	2013 2013	2013 2013
China	National data	53.2 (lvx); 56.9 (cip)	129 240 (lvx), 135 736 (cip)	Comprehensive	2012	2013
Cook Islands	No information obtained for this report					
Fiji	National information not available					2013
Fiji	Institute surveillance[e,f]	11.9	2566	Mixed samples	2012	2013
Japan	National data	34.3	136 288	Comprehensive	2012	2013
Kiribati	National data	3	72	Comprehensive	2013	2013
Lao People's Democratic Republic	National data	53.7	41		2012–2013	2013
Malaysia	National data	23	27 168	Comprehensive	2012	2013
Marshall Islands	National data	13	202		2011–2012	2013
Micronesia	National data	16	158	Comprehensive	2011	2013
Mongolia	Publication (*99*)	64.7	153	Community-acquired infections	2011	2013
Nauru	No information obtained for this report					
New Zealand	National data	7.5 (Blood isolates); 6.5 (Urinary isolates)	1711 (Blood); 84 301 (Urine)	Blood isolates; Urinary isolates	2011	2013
Niue	No information obtained for this report					
Palau	No information obtained for this report					
Papua New Guinea	National data[g]	13.3	526	Blood, stool, urine, "pus bench"	2012	2013
Philippines	National data	40.9	3687	Comprehensive	2012	2013
Republic of Korea	National datas[h]	40.4	18 480	Comprehensive	2011	2013
Republic of Korea	National network	43	4628	Comprehensive (Nosocomial infections)	2012	2013
Samoa	National data	13.9	43	Comprehensive	2011	2013
Singapore	National data, incomplete[i]		(i) 6442 (ii) 773	(i) All clinical isolates (ii) Bacteraemia	2011	2013
Singapore	Publication (*100*)	41.8	189	Hospital laboratories	2006–2007	2008
Singapore	Publication (*102*)	24.4	248	Urinary isolates	2009	2011
Singapore	Publication (*101*)	38.7 (all); 31 (blood)	12 081 (all); 1285 (blood)	Hospital network	2006–2008	2010
Solomon Islands	National data	95.6	115		2012	2013
Tonga	National data, incomplete	21			2012	2013
Tuvalu	No information obtained for this report					
Vanuatu	No information obtained for this report					
Viet Nam	Publication (*129*)	0.2	818	Carriers (healthy children)	2007	2012
International network	ANSORP[j]	36.6 (blood isolates); 40.9 (Urinary isolates)	374 (blood isolates), 621 (urinary solates	Blood isolates, Urinary isolates	2012	2013

a. cip, ciprofloxacin; gat, gatifloxacin; lvx, levofloxacin; mox, moxifloxacin; nor, norfloxacin; ofx, ofloxacin; pfl, pefloxacin; ref, refloxacin; spx, sparfloxacin. Ciprofloxacin mostly used where not specified (a few reported on norfloxacin).
b. National data refers to data returned on the questionnaires as defined in Annex 1. This definition does not imply that the data collected is representative for that country as a whole because information gaps are likely.
c. See Annex 1 for definitions.
d. "National data not available" means that there was information that no data were available; "No information obtained for this report" means that no information was obtained from authorities, networks or publications.
e. Data were provided, but no formal national data compilation was available.
f. Data from three hospitals aggreated.
g. National data from different types of samples (blood, stool, urine and «pus bench») aggregated.
h. Data aggregated from several sources: "Hospitals» 47.5%; «Clinics»; 30%; «General hospitals» 39.5%).
i. No data on proportions obtained. Incidence in hospitals (i) 36.3 per 10,000 inpatient-days (ii) 4.5 per 10,000 inpatient-days.
j. Some centres from the following countries, territories and areas participate in some ANSORP (Asian Network for Surveillance of Resistant Pathogens) projects: India, Indonesia, Japan, Malaysia, Philippines, Republic of Korea, Singapore, Sri Lanka, Saudi Arabia, Thailand, Viet Nam, in addition to China, Hong Kong SAR (Special Administrative Region) and Taiwan, China.

Table A2.13 *Klebsiella pneumoniae*: Resistance to third-generation cephalosporins[a]
African Region

Countries, territories and other areas or groupings	Data source[b, c, d]	Resistance (%)	No. tested isolates	Type of surveillance, population or samples[c]	Period for data collection	Year of publication or report
Algeria	No information obtained for this report					
Angola	No information obtained for this report					
Benin	National data	41	54	Invasive isolates	2012	2013
Botswana	National data	62.2 (ctx); 78.6 (caz)	37 (ctx); 14 (caz)	Invasive isolates	2012	2013
Burkina Faso	National data	55.2	116	Invasive isolates	2008–2009	2013
Burundi	National data	12	50	Targeted	2012	2013
Cameroon	No information obtained for this report					
Cabo Verde	No information obtained for this report					
Central African Republic	National data	65	43	Comprehensive	2012	2013
Chad	No information obtained for this report					
Comoros	No information obtained for this report					
Congo	National data	67.4	43	Comprehensive	2012	2013
Côte d'Ivoire	No information obtained for this report					
Democratic Republic of the Congo	No information obtained for this report					
Equatorial Guinea	No information obtained for this report					
Eritrea	No information obtained for this report					
Ethiopia	National data	14 (caz); 20 (cro)	48	Comprehensive	2011–2012	2013
Gabon	No information obtained for this report					
Gambia	National data not available					2013
Ghana	National data	32.1 (ctx); 34.7 (cro)	53 (ctx); 44 (cro)	Comprehensive	2013	2013
Guinea	National data	25	4	Comprehensive	2013	2013
Guinea-Bissau	National data	55 (ctx); 100 (cro)	17	Comprehensive	2013	2013
Kenya	National data not available					2013
Lesotho	National data	10	39		2011	2013
Liberia	National data not available					2013
Madagascar	No information obtained for this report					
Malawi	National data not available	0	0	Comprehensive		2013
Mali	No information obtained for this report					
Mauritania	National data not available					2013
Mauritius	National data	54.8	104	Hospital isolates	2012	2013
Mozambique	No information obtained for this report					
Namibia	National data	8	996	Comprehensive	2012	2013
Niger	National data not available					
Nigeria	Publication (6)	51.6 (cro); 45.2 (caz); 69.3 (ctx)	62	Clinical samples	2007	2009
Nigeria	Publication (130)	51 (cro); 39 (caz)	81	Hospital infections	2007–2010	2012
Nigeria	Publication (5)	17	70	Healthy carriers	(2003)–2007[e]	2008
Nigeria	Publication (11)	9[f]	60	Urine and stool samples (HIV/AIDS–paients)	2009–2010	2011
Rwanda	No information obtained for this report					
Sao Tome & Principe	National data not available					2013
Senegal	No information obtained for this report					
Seychelles	No information obtained for this report					
Sierra Leone	No information obtained for this report					
South Africa	National data	77	923	Blood cultures	2012	2013
South Sudan	National data not available					2013
Swaziland	National data not available					2013
Togo	No information obtained for this report					
Uganda	National data	50	4	Comprehensive	2012	2013
United Republic of Tanzania	National data not available					2013
United Republic of Tanzania	Publication (131)	8	10	Surgical site infections	2009–2010	2011
Zambia	National data	50	36		2012	2013
Zimbabwe	National data not available					2013

a. caz, ceftazidim; ctx, cefotaxim; cro, ceftriaxone

b. National data refers to data returned on the questionnaires as defined in Annex 1. This definition does not imply that the data collected is representative for that country as a whole because information gaps are likely.

c. See Annex 1 for definitions.

d. "National data not available" means that there was information that no data were available; "No information obtained for this report" means that no information was obtained from authorities, networks or publications.

e. For data from time periods of several years, or where data from a subset of year(s) were available, the format (2001)–2011, indicates the first year of data collection within parenthesis, and the most recent year with separate data outside the parenthesis.

f. Data only on proportion producing ESBL (extended spectrum beta-lactamases).

Table A2.14 *Klebsiella pneumoniae*: Resistance to third-generation cephalosporins[a]
Region of the Americas

Countries, territories and other areas or groupings	Data source[b, c, d]	Resistance (%)	No. tested isolates	Type of surveillance, population or samples[c]	Period for data collection	Year of publication or report
Antigua and Barbuda	No information obtained for this report					
Argentina	National data	65	1622	Hospital isolates	2010	2013
Bahamas	No information obtained for this report					
Barbados	No information obtained for this report					
Belize	No information obtained for this report					
Bolivia (Plurinational State of)	National data	49	1176	Hospital isolates	2010	2013
Brazil	National data not available					2013
Brazil	Publication (*132*)	55.6	81	Blood isolates	2004–2006	2009
Canada	National data	4	226	Sentinel hospitals	2011	
Chile	National data not available					2013
Colombia	National data	30 (caz); 32 (ctx)	4561	Hospital isolates	2010	2013
Costa Rica	National data not available					2013
Cuba	National data	8 (ctx); 9 (caz)	39	Hospital isolates	2009	2013
Dominica	No information obtained for this report					
Dominican Republic	National data	40	2021	Hospital isolates	2009	2009
Ecuador	National data	60 (caz); 62 (ctx)	933	Hospital isolates	2010	2013
El Salvador	National data	67 (ctx); 71 (caz)	490	Hospital isolates	2010	2013
Grenada	No information obtained for this report					
Guatemala	National data	30 (caz); 31 (ctx)	2884	Hospital isolates	2010	2013
Guyana	No information obtained for this report					
Haiti	No information obtained for this report					
Honduras	National data	60 (ctx); 70 (caz)	920	Hospital isolates	2010	2013
Jamaica	No information obtained for this report					
Mexico	National data not available					
Mexico	Publication (*133*)	37 (cro); 38 (caz)	150	Clinical isolates	2006–2009	2010
Nicaragua	National data	66	234	Hospital isolates	2010	2013
Panama	National data	14 (ctx); 26 (caz)	2260	Hospital isolates	2010	2013
Panama	National network	19	1205	Comprehensive	2011–2012	2013
Paraguay	National data	61	341	Hospital isolates	2010	2013
Peru	National data	71	498	Hospital isolates	2010	2013
Peru	National network	75	930	Comprehensive	2012	2013
Saint Kitts and Nevis	No information obtained for this report					
Saint Lucia	No information obtained for this report					
Saint Vicent and the Grenadines	No information obtained for this report					
Suriname	No information obtained for this report					
Trinidad and Tobago	No information obtained for this report					
Trinidad and Tobago	Publication (*23*)	15,2	402	Clinical isolates	2004–2007	2008
United States of America	National data	23	16 597	Health care associated infections	2009–2010	2013
Uruguay	National data	49 (ctx); 58 (caz)	108 (ctx); 274 (caz)	Hospital isolates	2010	2013
Venezuela (Bolivarian Republic of)	National data	22 (ctx); 36 (caz)	1069	Hospital isolates	2010	2013
International	Publication (*25*)	37.7	151	Intra-abdominal infections	2008	2011

a. caz, ceftazidim; ctx, cefotaxim; cro, ceftriaxone

b. National data refers to data returned on the questionnaires as defined in Annex 1. This definition does not imply that the data collected is representative for that country as a whole because information gaps are likely.

c. See Annex 1 for definitions.

d. "National data not available" means that there was information that no data were available; "No information obtained for this report" means that no information was obtained from authorities, networks or publications.

Table A2.15 *Klebsiella pneumoniae*: Resistance to third-generation cephalosporins[a]
Eastern Mediterranean Region

Countries, territories and other areas or groupings	Data source[b, c, d]	Resistance (%)	No. tested isolates	Type of surveillance, population or samples[c]	Period for data collection	Year of publication or report
Afghanistan	No information obtained for this report					
Bahrain	National data	50	1166	Comprehensive	2012	2013
Djibouti	No information obtained for this report					
Egypt	National data not available					2013
Egypt	National surveillance (Hospital network)[e]	72.2 (caz), 82.5 (cro)	594	Comprehensive	2002–2010	2013
Iran (Islamic Republic of)	National data	48	110	Invasive isolates	2012	2013
Iraq	Publication (*27*)	32.3 (all cephalosporins)	31	Urinary isolates (outpatients)		2012
Iraq	Publication (*134*)	17 (ctx); 43 (caz); 50 (cro)	30	Blood isolates (neonate intensive care unit [ICU])		2013
Jordan	National data not available					2013
Kuwait	No information obtained for this report					
Kuwait	Publication (*30*)	20 (community); 33 (hospital)	353 (community); 217 (hospital)	Urinary infections: (Community and hospital acquired)	2005–2007	2010
Lebanon	National data not available					2013
Lebanon	Publication (*32*)	29 (ctx); 21 (caz)	947	Hospital samples	2010–2011	2012
Libya	No information obtained for this report					
Morocco	National data	93	10	Hospital infections	2013	2013
Morocco	Publication (*33*)	69.5 (caz); 75 (cro)	39	ICU	2004–2008	2009
Morocco	Publication (*36*)	20	40	Urinary isolates	2001–2005	2010
Morocco	Publication (*37*)	5.6	36	Urinary isolates	2004–2009	2011
Oman	National data	22	425	Comprehensive	2012	2013
Pakistan	National data, incomplete	12		Targeted		2013
Pakistan	Publication (*41*)	47.2 (caz); 59.7 (ctx); 62.5 (cro)	72	Medical ICU patients	2007–2008	2010
Pakistan	Publication (*47*)	20.9 (ctx); 28.6 (caz)	77	Vaginal swabs	2004–2006	2008
Pakistan	Publication (*43*)	71.4	56	Urinary pathogens	2004–2006	2008
Pakistan	Publication (*135*)	31.2	15 914	Hospital samples	2002–2007	2010
Qatar	No information obtained for this report					
Saudi Arabia	Publication (*53*)	19.9[f]	9126	Clinical isolates	2007–2011	2012
Saudi Arabia	Publication (*55*)[f]	13.7 Hospitalized patients; 3.1 (outpatients)	225 (Hospitalized patients); 955 (outpatients)	Laboratory	2004–2005	2009
Saudi Arabia	Publication (*57*)	58 (caz); 59 (cro)	96	Laboratory records	2009	2010
Somalia	No information obtained for this report					
Sudan	National data not available					2013
Syrian Arab Republic	National data not available					2013
Tunisia	Publication (*61*)	46	4776	Hospital samples	1999–2005	2008
United Arab Emirates[f]	National data	17.4	3075	Comprehensive	2012	2013
United Arab Emirates	Publication (*64*)	42	45	Hospitalized patients	2005–2006	2008
Yemen	No information obtained for this report					
International network	ANSORP[g]	Urine isolates: 16.6 (caz); 20.2 (ctx). Blood isolates: 29.5 (caz); 36.4 (ctx)	213 (Urine isolates); 88 (Blood isolates)	Blood isolates and urinary infections	2012	2013

a. caz, ceftazidim; ctx, cefotaxim; cro, ceftriaxone

b. National data refers to data returned on the questionnaires as defined in Annex 1. This definition does not imply that the data collected is representative for that country as a whole because information gaps are likely.

c. See Annex 1 for definitions.

d. "National data not available" means that there was information that no data were available; "No information obtained for this report" means that no information was obtained from authorities, networks or publications.

e. US Naval Medical Research Unit No 3, Global Disease Detection Program, Egypt.

f. Data only on proportion producing ESBL (extended spectrum beta-lactamases).

g. Data from United Arab Emirates originate from Abu Dhabi only.

h. Some centres from the following countries, territories and areas participate in some ANSORP (Asian Network for Surveillance of Resistant Pathogens) projects: India, Indonesia, Japan, Malaysia, Philippines, Republic of Korea, Singapore, Sri Lanka, Saudi Arabia, Thailand, Viet Nam, in addition to China, Hong Kong SAR (Special Administrative Region) and Taiwan, China.

Table A2.16 *Klebsiella pneumoniae*: Resistance to third-generation cephalosporins[a]
European Region

Countries, territories and other areas or groupings	Data source[b, c, d]	Resistance (%)	No. tested isolates	Type of surveillance, population or samples[c]	Period for data collection	Year of publication or report
Albania	National data not available					2013
Andorra	No information obtained for this report					
Armenia	National data not available					2013
Austria	National data	13.3	795	Invasive isolates	2011	2013
Azerbaijan	National data not available					2013
Belarus	No information obtained for this report[e]					
Belgium	National data	13.6	668	Invasive isolates	2011	2013
Bosnia and Herzegovina	Publication (65)	4.1	1553	Urinary isolates (outpatients)	2001–2003	2010
Bosnia and Herzegovina	Publication, incomplete (136)	50 (ctx); 60 (cro); 61.5 (caz)		Gynaecology department	2006	2009
Bulgaria	National data	81	121	Invasive isolates	2011	2013
Croatia	National data	34	5021	Comprehensive	2012	2013
Cyprus	National data	41	83	Invasive isolates	2011	2013
Czech Republic	National data	48.3	1287	Invasive isolates	2011	2013
Denmark	National data	11.1	637	Invasive isolates	2011	2013
Estonia	National data	39.5	43	Invasive isolates	2011	2013
Finland	National data	3.4	319	Invasive isolates	2011	2013
France	National data	25.3	1654	Invasive isolates	2011	2013
Georgia	National data	85.7	7	Comprehensive	2012	2013
Germany	National data	12,5	519	Invasive isolates	2011	2013
Greece	National data	75.8	1665	Invasive isolates	2011	2013
Hungary	National data	53,1	431	Invasive isolates	2011	2013
Iceland	National data	7.7	26	Invasive isolates	2011	2013
Ireland	National data	7.6	304	Invasive isolates	2011	2013
Israel	No information obtained for this report					
Italy	National data	45.9	627	Invasive isolates	2011	2013
Kazakhstan	No information obtained for this report[e]					
Kyrgyzstan	National data not available					2013
Latvia	National data	38.5	65	Invasive isolates	2011	2013
Lithuania	National data	60.6	137	Invasive isolates	2011	2013
Luxembourg	National data	35.4	48	Invasive isolates	2011	2013
Malta	National data	13.5	52	Invasive isolates	2011	2013
Monaco	No information obtained for this report					
Montenegro	National data not available					2013
Netherlands	National data	8.1	720	Invasive isolates	2011	2013
Norway	National data	2.9	421	Invasive isolates	2011	2013
Poland	National data	59.7	278	Invasive isolates	2011	2013
Portugal	National data	35.4	616	Invasive isolates	2011	2013
Republic of Moldova	National data	30.7	2489		2012	2013
Romania	National data	44	25	Invasive isolates	2011	2013
Russian federation	National data	Hospital isolates: 87.8 (caz); 90.2 (ctx); Community urinary: 35.2 (caz); 38.5 (ctx)	287 (hospital isolates), 91 (Community urinary isolates)	Hospital isolates and community urinary isolates	2011–2012 (Hospital isolates); 2010–2011 (Urinary isolates)	2013
San Marino	No information obtained for this report					
Serbia	National data	82.1	100	Invasive isolates	2012–2013	2013
Slovakia	National data	68	463	Invasive isolates	2011	2013
Slovenia	National data	30.2	232	Invasive isolates	2011	2013
Spain	National data	13.4	1145	Invasive isolates	2011	2013
Sweden	National data	2.3	736	Invasive isolates	2011	2013
Switzerland	National data	6.8	10 951	Comprehensive	2012	2013
Tajikistan	No information obtained for this report					
The former Yugoslav Republic of Macedonia	National data	91	22			2013
Turkey	National data	52.4	794	Invasive isolates	2011	2013
Turkmenistan	No information obtained for this report					
Ukraine	No information obtained for this report[e]					
United Kingdom	National data	5.3	935	Invasive isolates	2011	2013
Uzbekistan	No information obtained for this report					
International	Publication (71)	21.4 (ctx); 23 (caz, cro)	318	Intra-abdominal infections	2008	2011

a. caz, ceftazidim; ctx, cefotaxim; cro, ceftriaxone

b. National data refers to data returned on the questionnaires as defined in Annex 1. This definition does not imply that the data collected is representative for that country as a whole because information gaps are likely.

c. See Annex 1 for definitions.

d. "National data not available" means that there was information that no data were available; "No information obtained for this report" means that no information was obtained from authorities, networks or publications.

e. Some centres participate in some RusNet projects.

Table A2.17 *Klebsiella pneumoniae*: Resistance to third-generation cephalosporins[a]
South East Asian Region

Countries, territories and other areas or groupings	Data source[b, c, d]	Resistance (%)	No. tested isolates	Type of surveillance, population or samples[c]	Period for data collection	Year of publication or report
Bangladesh	National data not available					2013
Bangladesh	Publication (*137*)	97.8 (ctx, cro); 82.2 (caz)	45	Blood isolates (neonates)	2007–2010	2010
Bhutan	National data	33.3 (caz); 50.8 (cro)	36 (caz); 120 (cro)	Comprehensive	2011–2012	2013
Democratic People's Republic of Korea	No information obtained for this report					
India	National data not available					2013
India	Publication (*138*)	100	62	Blood isolates	2006–2008	2010
India	Publication (*80*)	44.9	58	Urinary tract infections		2012
India	Publication (*78*)	20	80	Diabetic foot infections	2005	2008
India	Publication (*79*)	15.9	176	Hospital isolates	2006	2008
India	Publication (*139*)	12.5	144	Laboratory surveillance	2005–2007	2009
India	Publication (*82*)	5	239	Healthy carriers	2011	2012
India	Publication (*140*)	58 (ctx); 77 (caz); 100 (cro)	173	Blood isolates (children)	1994–2003	2008
India	Publication (*83*)	76.5 (cro) 84.1 (caz)	125	Lower respiratory tract infection (hospitalized patients)	2011–2012	2013
India	Publication (*84*)	35	689	Intra-abdominal infections (hospitalized patients)	2009	2011
India	Publication (*85*)	60.3	73	Urinary tract infections (hospitalized patients)	2008	2011
India	Publication (*86*)	91.4	104	Ventilator-associated pneumonia	2004–2009	2011
India	Publication (*141*)	23.7	65	COPD[e] patients	2002	2011
India	Publication (*87*)	47.8	90	Intra-abdominal infections (hospitalized patients)	2008	2010
India	Publication (*88*)	75.8	99	Cancer patients (hospitalized)		2010
India	Publication (*89*)	59.3	327	Urinary tract infections (hospitalized patients)	2008–2009	2012
India	Publication (*90*)	44.7	177	Hospitalized patients	2012	2013
India	Publication (*91*)	82	107	Hospitalized patients	2007–2009	2012
India	Publication (*127*)	16.4	61	Hospitalized patients	2003	2008
India	Publication (*95*)	50[f]	62	Clinical isolates (hospitalized patients)		2012
India	Publication (*96*)	25 (Hospitalized); 21 (Outpatients)	239 (Hospitalized); 140 (Outpatients)	Urinary isolates (hospitalized and outpatients)	2007	2012
Indonesia	National data not available					2013
Indonesia	Publication (*98*)	53.3 (ctx); 67.2 (cro)	67	Blood isolates	2002–2008	2011
Maldives	No information obtained for this report					
Myanmar	National data	60	268	Comprehensive	2012	2013
Nepal	National data	0	19	Targeted	2012	2013
Nepal	Publication (*142*)	48.3	145	Urinary isolates	2011–2012	2013
Sri Lanka	National data	80.9	105	Targeted	2009	2013
Thailand	National data	37.4 (caz); 40.3 (cro); 41.1 (ctx)	25 421 (caz); 16 502 (cro); 22 546 (ctx)	Comprehensive	2012	2013
Timor-Leste	National data not available					2013
International network	ANSORP[g]	Urine isolates: 16.6 (caz); 20.2 (ctx). Blood isolates: 29.5 (caz); 36.4 (ctx)	213 (Urine isolates); 88 (Blood isolates)	Blood isolates and urinary infections	2012	2013

a. caz, ceftazidim; ctx, cefotaxim; cro, ceftriaxone

b. National data refers to data returned on the questionnaires as defined in Annex 1. This definition does not imply that the data collected is representative for that country as a whole because information gaps are likely.

c. See Annex 1 for definitions.

d. "National data not available" means that there was information that no data were available; "No information obtained for this report" means that no information was obtained from authorities, networks or publications.

e. Chronic obstructive pulmonary disease.

f. Based on detection of extended-spectrum betalactamases (ESBL) only.

g. Some centres from the following countries, territories and areas participate in some ANSORP (Asian Network for Surveillance of Resistant Pathogens) projects: India, Indonesia, Japan, Malaysia, Philippines, Republic of Korea, Singapore, Sri Lanka, Saudi Arabia, Thailand, Viet Nam, in addition to China, Hong Kong SAR (Special Administrative Region) and Taiwan, China.

Table A2.18 *Klebsiella pneumoniae*: Resistance to third-generation cephalosporins[a]
Western Pacific Region

Countries, territories and other areas or groupings	Data source[b, c, d]	Resistance (%)	No. tested isolates	Type of surveillance, population or samples[c]	Period for data collection	Year of publication or report
Australia	National data	9.8 (caz); 12.1(cro)	396	Comprehensive	2011	2013
Brunei Darussalam	National data from hospital laboratory	6.2 (cro); 6.8 (caz)	1038	Comprehensive	2012	2013
Cambodia	National data[e] collected from several sources by public health institute (NIPH); Pasteur Institute (PI)	32 (NIPH); 31 (PI)	63 (NIPH); 30 (PI)	Clinical samples and surveillance of respiratory infections (NIPH); Laboratory data (mixed patients) (PI)	2013	2013
China	National data	25.1 (caz); 44.4 (cro); 52.5 (ctx)	102 420(caz); 81 541 (cro); 55 433 (ctx)	Comprehensive	2012	2013
Cook Islands	No information obtained for this report					
Fiji	National data not available					2013
Fiji	Institute surveillance[e,f]	25	2900	Mixed samples	2012	2013
Japan	National data	5.4	62 242	Comprehensive	2012	
Kiribati	National data	1	111	Comprehensive	2012	2013
Lao People's Democratic Republic	National data	0	3		2013	2013
Lao People's Democratic Republic	Institute surveillance	25	4	Comprehensive (Laboratory)	2011–2012	2013
Malaysia	National data	21.1 (cro); 20.8 (caz); 24 (ctx)	23 963 (caz); 14 200 (cro); 20 030 (ctx)	Comprehensive	2012	2013
Marshall Islands	National data not available					2013
Micronesia	National data	71	87	Comprehensive	2011	2013
Mongolia	No information obtained for this report					
Mongolia	Publication (99)	33.7 (ctx); 34.8 (caz)	92	Community infections	2011	2013
Nauru	No information obtained for this report					
New Zealand	National data	12.7	416	Blood isolates	2011	2013
Niue	No information obtained for this report					
Palau	No information obtained for this report					
Papua New Guinea	National data	63.5[g]	252	Blood, urine, "pus bench"	2012	2013
Philippines	National data	30	1451	Comprehensive	2012	2013
Republic of Korea[h]	National data	44 (caz); 41.7 (ctx)[i]	7130[h]	Comprehensive	2011	
Republic of Korea	National network	47	2421	Hospital infections	2012	2013
Samoa	National data	7.7 (cro); 19.8 (ctx)	116	Comprehensive	2011	2013
Singapore	National data, incomplete[j]		(i) 2806 (ii) 395	(i) All clinical isolates (ii) Bacteraemia	2011	2013
Singapore	Publication (100)	30.8	198	Hospital laboratories	2006–2007	2008
Singapore	Publication (101)	32.3 (All); 27.4 (Blood isolates)	685 (Blood isolates); 6321 (All isolates)	Hospital network	2006–2008	2010
Solomon Islands	National data	27	30		2012	2013
Tonga	National data, incomplete	0			2012	2013
Tuvalu	No information obtained for this report					
Vanuatu	No information obtained for this report					
Vietnam	No information obtained for this report[k]					
International network	ANSORP[l]	Urine isolates: 16.6 (caz); 20.2 (ctx). Blood isolates: 29.5 (caz); 36.4 (ctx)	213 (Urine isolates); 88 (Blood isolates)	Blood isolates and urinary infections	2012	2013

a. caz, ceftazidim; ctx, cefotaxim; cro, ceftriaxone
b. National data refers to data returned on the questionnaires as defined in Annex 1. This definition does not imply that the data collected is representative for that country as a whole because information gaps are likely.
c. See Annex 1 for definitions.
d. "National data not available" means that there was information that no data were available; "No information obtained for this report" means that no information was obtained from authorities, networks or publications.
e. Data were provided, but no formal national data compilation was available.
f. Data from three hospitals aggregated.
g. National data from different types of samples (Blood, «pus bench» and urine) aggregated.
h. Data from more than one surveillance source.
i. Information aggregated from more than one surveillance system: «Hospitals»; 45.5 (ctx); 47.9 caz); «Clinics»; 22 (ctx); 23.1 (caz); «General hospitals»; 37.9 (ctx); 39 (caz).
j. No information on proportions obtained. Incidence in hospitals: (i) 15.4 per 10,000 inpatient-days (ii) 2.1 per 10,000 inpatient-days.
k. Some centres participate in some ANSORP (Asian Network for Surveillance of Resistant Pathogens) projects.
l. Some centres from the following countries, territories and areas participate in some ANSORP projects: India, Indonesia, Japan, Malaysia, Philippines, Republic of Korea, Singapore, Sri Lanka, Saudi Arabia, Thailand, Viet Nam, in addition to China, Hong Kong SAR (Special Administrative Region) and Taiwan, China.

Table A2.19   *Klebsiella pneumoniae*: Resistance to carbapenems[a]
African Region

Countries, territories and other areas or groupings	Data source[b, c, d]	Resistance (%)	No. tested isolates	Type of surveillance, population or samples[c]	Period for data collection	Year of publication or report
Algeria	No information obtained for this report					
Angola	No information obtained for this report					
Benin	National data not available					2013
Botswana	National data not available					2013
Burkina Faso	National data	0	20	Invasive isolates	2008–2009	2013
Burundi	National data not available					2013
Cameroon	No information obtained for this report					
Cabo Verde	No information obtained for this report					
Central African Republic	National data	0	43	Comprehensive		2013
Chad	No information obtained for this report					
Comoros	No information obtained for this report					
Congo	National data not available					2013
Côte d'Ivoire	No information obtained for this report					
Democratic Republic of the Congo	No information obtained for this report					
Equatorial Guinea	No information obtained for this report					
Eritrea	No information obtained for this report					
Ethiopia	National data not available					2013
Gabon	No information obtained for this report					
Gambia	National data not available					2013
Ghana	National data not available					2013
Guinea	National data not available					2013
Guinea-Bissau	National data not available					2013
Kenya	National data not available					2013
Lesotho	National data not available					2013
Liberia	National data not available					2013
Madagascar	No information obtained for this report					
Malawi	National data not available					2013
Mali	No information obtained for this report					
Mauritania	National data not available					2013
Mauritius	National data	1.9	104	Hospital isolates	2012	2013
Mozambique	No information obtained for this report					
Namibia	National data	1	280		2012	2013
Niger	National data not available					2013
Nigeria	No information obtained for this report					
Rwanda	No information obtained for this report					
Sao Tome and Principe	National data not available					2013
Senegal	No information obtained for this report					
Seychelles	No information obtained for this report					
Sierra Leone	No information obtained for this report					
South Africa	National data	1 (mem); 3.8 (etp)	923	Blood cultures	2012	2013
South Sudan	National data not available					2013
Swaziland	National data not available					2013
Togo	No information obtained for this report					
Uganda	National data, incomplete		4	Comprehensive	2012	2013
United Republic of Tanzania	National data not available					2013
Zambia	National data	0	9	Targeted		2013
Zimbabwe	National data not available					2013

a. dor, doripenem; etp, ertapenem; imi, imipenem; mem, meropenem

b. National data refers to data returned on the questionnaires as defined in Annex 1. This definition does not imply that the data collected is representative for that country as a whole because information gaps are likely.

c. See Annex 1 for definitions.

d. "National data not available" means that there was information that no data were available; "No information obtained for this report" means that no information was obtained from authorities, networks or publications.

Table A2.20 *Klebsiella pneumoniae*: Resistance to carbapenems[a]
Region of the Americas

Countries, territories and other areas or groupings	Data source[b, c, d]	Resistance (%)	No. tested isolates	Type of surveillance, population or samples[c]	Period for data collection	Year of publication or report
Antigua and Barbuda	No information obtained for this report					
Argentina	National data	6 (imi); 8 (mem)	1622	Hospital isolates	2010	2013
Bahamas	No information obtained for this report					
Barbados	No information obtained for this report					
Belize	No information obtained for this report					
Bolivia (Plurinational State of)	National data	4 (imi); 5 (mem)	1176	Hospital isolates	2010	2013
Brazil	National data not available					2013
Brazil	Publication (*143*)	0 (imi); 1.6 (etp)	63	Clinical isolates	2009	2011
Canada	National data	0	226	Sentinel hospitals	2011	2013
Chile	National data not available					2013
Colombia	National data	6 (imi); 7 (mem)	4561	Hospital isolates	2010	2013
Costa Rica	National data not available					2013
Cuba	National data	5 (imi); 6 (mem)	39	Hospital isolates	2009	2013
Dominica	No information obtained for this report					
Dominican Republic	National data	0	2021	Hospital isolates	2009	2013
Ecuador	National data	2	933	Hospital isolates	2010	2013
El Salvador	National data	2	490	Hospital isolates	2010	2013
Grenada	No information obtained for this report					
Guatemala	National data	0 (imi); 3 (mem)	2884	Hospital isolates	2010	2013
Guyana	No information obtained for this report					
Haiti	No information obtained for this report					
Honduras	National data	2	920	Hospital isolates	2010	2013
Jamaica	No information obtained for this report					
Mexico	National data not available					2013
Nicaragua	National data	6 (imi); 9 (mem)	234	Hospital isolates	2010	2013
Panama	National data	0 (imi); 1 (mem)	2260	Hospital isolates	2010	2013
Panama	National network	3	4199	Comprehensive	2011–2012	2013
Paraguay	National data	1 (imi); 3 (mem)	315 (imi); 577 (mem)	Hospital isolates	2010	2013
Peru	National data	0.3	319 (imi); 365 (mem)	Hospital isolates	2010	2013
Peru	National network	0.4	926	Comprehensive	2012	2013
Saint Kitts and Nevis	No information obtained for this report					
Saint Lucia	No information obtained for this report					
Saint Vincent and the Grenadines	No information obtained for this report					
Suriname	No information obtained for this report					
Trinidad and Tobago	No information obtained for this report					
Trinidad and Tobago	Publication (*116*)	0	92	Hospitalized children	2007	2010
United States of America	National data	11	7932	Health-care associated infections	2009–2010	2013
Uruguay	National data	0.7 (mem); 1.2 (imi)	263 (mem); 249 (imi)	Hospital isolates	2010	2013
Venezuela (Bolivarian Republic of)	National data	3 (imi); 4 (mem)	1069	Hospital isolates	2010	2013
International	Publication (*25*)	1.3	151	Intra-abdominal infections	2008	2011

a. dor, doripenem; etp, ertapenem; imi, imipenem; mem, meropenem

b. National data refers to data returned on the questionnaires as defined in Annex 1. This definition does not imply that the data collected is representative for that country as a whole because information gaps are likely.

c. See Annex 1 for definitions.

d. "National data not available" means that there was information that no data were available; "No information obtained for this report" means that no information was obtained from authorities, networks or publications.

Table A2.21 *Klebsiella pneumoniae*: Resistance to carbapenems[a]
Eastern Mediterranean Region

Countries, territories and other areas or groupings	Data source[b, c, d]	Resistance (%)	No. tested isolates	Type of surveillance, population or samples[c]	Period for data collection	Year of publication or report
Afghanistan	No information obtained for this report					
Bahrain	National data	40	495		2012	2013
Djibouti	No information obtained for this report					
Egypt	National surveillance (Hospital network)[e]	5.6	594	Comprehensive,	2002–2010	
Iran (Islamic Republic of)	National data	54	35	Invasive isolates	2013	2013
Iraq	Publication (*134*)	0	30	Blood isolates (neonate intensive care unit [ICU])		2013
Jordan	National data not available					2013
Kuwait	No information obtained for this report					
Lebanon	National data not available					2013
Lebanon	Publication (*32*)	0.7	947	Hospital samples	2010–2011	2012
Lebanon	Publication (*144*)	1.8 (dor); 8.8 (imi)	57	Hospital samples		2012
Libya	Publication (*117*)	0	50	Urinary isolates		2010
Morocco	National data	0	10	Hospital infections	2012	2013
Oman	National data	0	425	Comprehensive	2012	2013
Pakistan	National data, incomplete	3		Targeted		2013
Pakistan	Publication (*41*)	20.8	72	Medical ICU patients	2007–2008	2010
Pakistan	Publication (*135*)	0.4	5016	Hospital samples	2002–2007	2010
Pakistan	Publication (*47*)	0	77	Vaginal swabs	2004–2006	2008
Qatar	No information obtained for this report					
Saudi Arabia	Publication (*53*)	0.4	285	ICUs	2004–2009	2010
Saudi Arabia	Publication (*56*)	7.8	128	Hospital isolates	2010–2011	2012
Somalia	No information obtained for this report					
Sudan	National data not available					2013
Syrian Arab Republic	National data not available					2013
Tunisia	No information obtained for this report					
United Arab Emirates	National data[f]	1.5	3084	Comprehensive	2012	2013
Yemen	No information obtained for this report					
International network	ANSORP[g]	Blod isolates: 0.9 (etp), 1.4 (imi) Urinary isolates: 5.7 (imi), 10.2 (etp)	213 (blood isolates), 88 (urinary isolates)	Blood isolates, urinary isolates	2012	2013

a. dor, doripenem; etp, ertapenem; imi, imipenem; mem, meropenem

b. National data refers to data returned on the questionnaires as defined in Annex 1. This definition does not imply that the data collected is representative for that country as a whole because information gaps are likely.

c. See Annex 1 for definitions.

d. "National data not available" means that there was information that no data were available; "No information obtained for this report" means that no information was obtained from authorities, networks or publications.

e. US Naval Medical Research Unit No 3, Global Disease Detection Program, Egypt.

f. Data from United Arab Emirates originate from Abu Dhabi only.

g. Some centres from the following countries, territories and areas participate in some ANSORP (Asian Network for Surveillance of Resistant Pathogens) projects: India, Indonesia, Japan, Malaysia, Philippines, Republic of Korea, Singapore, Sri Lanka, Saudi Arabia, Thailand, Viet Nam, in addition to China, Hong Kong SAR (Special Administrative Region) and Taiwan, China.

Table A2.22 *Klebsiella pneumoniae*: Resistance to carbapenems[a]
European Region

Countries, territories and other areas or groupings	Data source[b, c, d]	Resistance (%)	No. tested isolates	Type of surveillance, population or samples[c]	Period for data collection	Year of publication or report
Albania	National data not available					2013
Andorra	No information obtained for this report					
Armenia	National data not available					2013
Austria	National data	0.2	610	Invasive isolates	2011	2013
Azerbaijan	National data not available					2013
Belarus	No information obtained for this report[e]					
Belgium	National data	0.3	646	Invasive isolates	2011	2013
Bulgaria	National data	0	116	Invasive isolates	2011	2013
Croatia	National data	0	4945	Comprehensive	2012	2013
Cyprus	National data	15.7	83	Invasive isolates	2011	2013
Czech Republic	National data	0.1	1193	Invasive isolates	2011	2013
Denmark	National data	0	589	Invasive isolates	2011	2013
Estonia	National data	0	73	Invasive isolates	2011	2013
Finland	National data	0	318	Invasive isolates	2011	2013
France	National data	0	1640	Invasive isolates	2011	2013
Georgia	National data	57.1	7	Comprehensive	2012	2013
Georgia	Publication (67)	2	45	Blood isolates (neonates)	2003–2004	2009
Germany	National data	0	512	Invasive isolates	2011	2013
Greece	National data	68.2	1636	Invasive isolates	2011	2013
Hungary	National data	1.9	413	Invasive isolates	2011	2013
Iceland	National data not available					2013
Ireland	National data	0.3	302	Invasive isolates	2011	2013
Israel	Publication (145)	7	299	Patient screening	2007–2008	2012
Israel	Publication (146)	5.4	298	Carrier screening		2010
Italy	National data	26.7	615	Invasive isolates	2011	2013
Kazakhstan	No information obtained for this report[e]					
Kyrgyzstan	National data not available					2013
Latvia	National data	0	65	Invasive isolates	2011	2013
Lithuania	National data	0	19	Invasive isolates	2011	2013
Luxembourg	National data	0	48	Invasive isolates	2011	2013
Malta	National data	3.8	52	Invasive isolates	2011	2013
Monaco	No information obtained for this report					
Montenegro	National data not available					
Netherlands	National data	0.3	722	Invasive isolates	2011	2013
Norway	National data	0	443	Invasive isolates	2011	2013
Poland	National data	0.5	376	Invasive isolates	2011	2013
Portugal	National data	0.3	580	Invasive isolates	2011	2013
Republic of Moldova	National data	20.3	483		2012	2013
Romania	National data	0	10	Invasive isolates	2011	2013
Russian Federation	National data	Hospital isolates: 3.1 (mem); 5.2 (imi); 18.5 (etp) Community urinary: 0 (mem); 1.1 (imi); 4.4 (etp)	287 (Hospital isolates; 91 (Community urinary)	Hospital isolates; community urinary isolates	Hospital isolates 2011–2012; urinary isolates 2010–2011	2013
San Marino	No information obtained for this report					
Serbia	National data	11.2	100	Invasive isolates	2012	2013
Slovakia	National data	0.7	432	Invasive isolates	2011	2013
Slovenia	National data	0	232	Invasive isolates	2011	2013
Spain	National data	0.3	1144	Invasive isolates	2011	2013
Sweden	National data	0	900	Invasive isolates	2011	2013
Switzerland	National data	1	9433	Comprehensive	2012	2013
Tajikistan	No information obtained for this report					
The former Yugoslav Republic of Macedonia	National data	0	22	Invasive isolates	Invasive isolates	2013
Turkey	National data not available					2013
Turkey	Publication (147)	0/18	18	Burn patients		2013
Turkmenistan	No information obtained for this report					
Ukraine	No information obtained for this report[e]					
United Kingdom	National data	0.4	825	Invasive isolates	2011	2013
Uzbekistan	No information obtained for this report					
International	Publication (71)	4.7 (imi); 6.6 (etp)	1495	Intra-abdominal infections	2008	2011

a. dor, doripenem; etp, ertapenem; imi, imipenem; mem, meropenem

b. National data refers to data returned on the questionnaires as defined in Annex 1. This definition does not imply that the data collected is representative for that country as a whole because information gaps are likely.

c. See Annex 1 for definitions.

d. "National data not available" means that there was information that no data were available; "No information obtained for this report" means that no information was obtained from authorities, networks or publications.

e. Some centres participate in some RusNet projects.

Table A2.23 *Klebsiella pneumoniae*: Resistance to carbapenems[a]
South East Asian Region

Countries, territories and other areas or groupings	Data source[b, c, d]	Resistance (%)	No. tested isolates	Type of surveillance, population or samples[c]	Period for data collection	Year of publication or report
Bangladesh	National data not available					2013
Bangladesh	Publication (137)	0	45	Blood isolates (neonates)	2007–2010	2010
Bhutan	National data	0	40	Comprehensive	2011–2012	2013
Democratic People's Republic of Korea	No information obtained for this report					
India	National data not available					2013
India	Publication (148)	1.4	144	Laboratory surveillance	2005–2007	2009
India	Publication (76)	52	256	Blood isolates	2000- 2009	2012
India	Publication (94)	39.4 (imi); 36.5 (mem)	104	Blood isolates	(2007)–2010	2010
India	Publication (82)	0	239	Screening (healthy carriers)	2011	2012
India	Publication (138)	29.6	27 (last study year)	Neuro intensive care unit	(2006)–2008	2010
India	Publication (83)	7.8	125	Lower respiratory tract infection (hospital patients)	2011–2012	2013
India	Publication (84)	7.6	689	Intra-abdominal infections (hospital patients)	2009	2011
India	Publication (86)	55	104	Ventilator-associated pneumonia	2004–2009	2011
India	Publication (87)	14.4	90	Intra-abdominal infections (hospital patients)	2008	2010
India	Publication (88)	0	99	Cancer patients (hospitalized)		2010
India	Publication (89)	18.6	327	Urinary tract infections (hospital patients)	2008–2009	2012
India	Publication (90)	2	177	Hospital patients	2012	2013
India	Publication (91)	2	107	Hospital patients)	2007–2009	2012
India	Publication (78)	0	80	Diabetic foot infections	2005	2008
Indonesia	National data not available[e]					2013
Maldives	No information obtained for this report					
Myanmar	National data	8	58	Comprehensive	2012	2013
Nepal	National data	0	19	Urinary isolates		2013
Sri Lanka	National data	0	90	Targeted	2009	2013
Thailand	National data	0.5 (dor); 1.3 (imi); 1.3 (mem); 2.1 (etp)	577 (dor); 21 110 (imi); 20 021 (mem); 3435 (etp);	Comprehensive	2012	2013
Timor-Leste	National data not available					2013
International network	ANSORP[f]	Blood isolates: 0.9 (etp); 1.4 (imi) Urinary isolates: 5.7 (imi); 10.2 (etp)	213 (Blood isolates), 88 (Urinary isolates)	Blood isolates, urinary isolates	2012	2013

a. dor, doripenem; etp, ertapenem; imi, imipenem; mem, meropenem
b. National data refers to data returned on the questionnaires as defined in Annex 1. This definition does not imply that the data collected is representative for that country as a whole because information gaps are likely.
c. See Annex 1 for definitions.
d. "National data not available" means that there was information that no data were available; "No information obtained for this report" means that no information was obtained from authorities, networks or publications.
e. Some centres participate in some ANSORP (Asian Network for Surveillance of Resistant Pathogens) projects.
f. Some centres from the following countries, territories and areas participate in some ANSORP projects: India, Indonesia, Japan, Malaysia, Philippines, Republic of Korea, Singapore, Sri Lanka, Saudi Arabia, Thailand, Viet Nam, in addition to China, Hong Kong SAR (Special Administrative Region) and Taiwan, China.

Table A2.24 *Klebsiella pneumoniae*: Resistance to carbapenems[a]
Western Pacific Region

Countries, territories and other areas or groupings	Data source[b, c, d]	Resistance (%)	No. tested isolates	Type of surveillance, population or samples[c]	Period for data collection	Year of publication or report
Australia	National data	0.5 (mem); 1 (etp)	396		2011	2013
Brunei Darussalam	National data from hospital laboratory	0.3 (mem); 0.8 (imi)	1038	Comprehensive	2012	2013
Cambodia	National data[e] collected from several sources by public health institute (NIPH). Pasteur Institute (PI)	3 (NIPH); 2.1 (PI)	34 (NIPH); 41 (PI)	Clinical samples and surveillance of respiratory infections (NIPH); Laboratory data (mixed patients, PI)	2012 (NIPH); 2007–2010 (PI)	2013
China	National data	7.1 (mem); 7.7 (imi)	54 671 (mem); 100 805 (imi)	Comprehensive	2012	2013
Cook Islands	No information obtained for this report					
Fiji	National data not available					
Fiji	Institute surveillance[e,f]	0.7	2175	Comprehensive in one of the hospitals	2012	2013
Japan	National data	0.2	70 330	Comprehensive	2012	2013
Kiribati	National data not available					2013
Lao People's Democratic Republic	National data not available					2013
Lao People's Democratic Republic	Institute surveillance	0	4	Comprehensive (laboratory)	2011–2012	2013
Malaysia	National data	0.5 (imi), 0.7 (mem)	23 333 (imi), 22 965 (mem)	Comprehensive	2012	2013
Marshall Islands	National data not available					2013
Micronesia	National data, incomplete	"Nc"	≤ 30	Comprehensive	2011	2013
Mongolia	Publication (*99*)	10.9	92	Community infections	2011	2013
Nauru	No information obtained for this report					
Niue	No information obtained for this report					
New Zealand	National data	0	366	Comprehensive		2013
Palau	No information obtained for this report					
Papua New Guinea	National data not available					2013
Philippines	National data	3.8	3696	Comprehensive	2012	2013
Republic of Korea*	National data	0.3[g]	7131 ("Hospitals" + "Clinics"); NI[i] (General hospitals)	Comprehensive	2011	2013
Republic of Korea	National network/ institute surveillance	3	2421	Comprehensive	2012	2013
Samoa	National data not available					2013
Singapore	National data, incomplete[h]		73	Comprehensive	2011	2013
Singapore	Publication (*100*)	0	198	Hospital laboratories	2006–2007	2008
Solomon Islands	National data not available					2013
Tonga	National data not available					2013
Tuvalu	No information obtained for this report					
Vanuatu	No information obtained for this report					
Viet Nam[i]	No information obtained for this report					
International network	ANSORP[j]	Blod isolates: 0.9 (etp); 1.4 (imi); Urinary isolates: 5.7 (imi); 10.2 (etp)	213 (blood isolates); 88 (urinary isolates)	Blood isolates, urinary isolates	2012	2013

a. dor, doripenem; etp, ertapenem; imi, imipenem; mem, meropenem
b. National data refers to data returned on the questionnaires as defined in Annex 1. This definition does not imply that the data collected is representative for that country as a whole because information gaps are likely.
c. See Annex 1 for definitions.
d. "National data not available" means that there was information that no data were available; "No information obtained for this report" means that no information was obtained from authorities, networks or publications.
e. Data were provided, but no formal national data compilation was available.
f. Data from three hospitals aggregated.
g. Information aggregated from more than one surveillance system: «Hospitals»; 0.3%; «Clinics»; 0.3% and "General hospitals" 0.6%.
h. No proportions given. Incidence in hospitals: 0.38 per 10 000 inpatient–days.
i. Some centres participate in some ANSORP (Asian Network for Surveillance of Resistant Pathogens) projects.
j. Some centres from the following countries, territories and areas participate in some ANSORP projects: India, Indonesia, Japan, Malaysia, Philippines, Republic of Korea, Singapore, Sri Lanka, Saudi Arabia, Thailand, Viet Nam, in addition to China, Hong Kong SAR (Special Administrative Region) and Taiwan, China.

Table A2.25 *Staphylococcus aureus*: **Resistance to methicillin[a] (MRSA)**
African Region

Countries, territories and other areas or groupings	Data source[b, c, d]	Resistance (%)	No. tested isolates	Type of surveillance, population or samples[c]	Period for data collection	Year of publication or report
Algeria	Publication (149)	40.5 (Community); 47.4 (Hospital)	84 (Community); 137 (Hospital)	S. aureus infections	2006–2007	2011
Angola	No information obtained for this report					
Benin	National data, incomplete					2013
Botswana	National data, incomplete		26	Invasive isolates	2012	2013
Botswana	Publication (150)	23	857	Skin and soft tissue infections	2000–2007	2011
Burkina Faso	National data not available					2013
Burundi	National data	13	265	Targeted	2012	2013
Cameroon	No information obtained for this report					
Cabo Verde	No information obtained for this report					
Central African Republic	National data not available					2013
Chad	No information obtained for this report					
Comoros	No information obtained for this report					
Congo	National data	Not tested	26	Invasive isolates	2012	2013
Côte d'Ivoire	No information obtained for this report					
Democratic Republic of the Congo	No information obtained for this report					
Equatorial Guinea	No information obtained for this report					
Eritrea	No information obtained for this report					
Ethiopia	National data	31.6	175	Comprehensive	2011–2012	2013
Gabon	Publication (151)	1.6	34	Carriage (children with sickle-cell anemia)	2009–2010	2013
Gabon	Publication (152)	3.7	163	Infections and carriers	2008–2010	2011
Gambia	National data not available					2013
Ghana	National data not available					2013
Guinea	National data not available					2013
Guinea-Bissau	National data	100	31	Comprehensive	2013	2013
Kenya	National data not available					2013
Kenya	Publication (153)	20	207	Surgical site infections		2012
Lesotho	National data	12	75		2012	2013
Liberia	National data not available					2013
Madagascar	Publication (3)	13.6	103	Hospital acquired infections	2006–2008	2010
Malawi	National data	0	13	Comprehensive	2013	2013
Malawi	Publication (154)	31.3	147	Clinical isolates	2006–2007	2012
Mali	No information obtained for this report					
Mauritania	National data	80	41	Comprehensive	2013	2013
Mauritius	National data	51.5	171	Hospital isolates	2012	2013
Mozambique	No information obtained for this report					
Namibia	National data	15	1843		2012	2013
Nigeria	Publication (4)	70	200	Blood isolates (children)	2006–2008	2009
Nigeria	Publication (155)	14	293	Intestinal carriage, children	2006	2012
Nigeria	Publication (104)	60.8	156	Healthy carriers	2011	2012
Nigeria	Publication (5)	70 (clox)	180	Healthy carriers	(2003)–2007	2008
Nigeria	Publication (110)	87.9 (clox)	124	Healthy carriers	2008–2009	2012
Nigeria	Publication(156)	16.3	98	Ear discharge in otitis media	2009–2010	2011
Nigeria	Publication (157)	88	100	Clinical samples (hospitalized patients)		2011
Nigeria	Publication (158)	100	46	Urinary isolates	2010	2012
Nigeria	Publication (112)	11 (AIDS pts); 0 (non-AIDS pts)	54 (AIDS pts); 0 (non-AIDS pts)	Urinary infections (AIDS and non-AIDS patients)	2003–2009	2010
Nigeria	Publication (104)	60.8	188	Healthy carriers	2011	2012
Nigeria	Publication (159)	27.5	40	Healthy carriers	2009	2011
Nigeria	Publication (160)	64.2	150	Clinical isolates	2009	2011
Nigeria	Publication (161)	33.3	33	Blood isolates newborns	2006–2007	2011
Nigeria	Publication (162)	64.2	150	Clinical isoalates	2009	2011
Nigeria	Publication (163)	12.5	96	Consecutive hospital isolates	2007	2011
Nigeria	Publication (164)	40	2511	Clinical samples	1987–2000	2011
Nigeria	Publication (12)	94.8	58	Blood isolates (HIV-infected children)		2010
Rwanda	No information obtained for this report					

Countries, territories and other areas or groupings	Data source[b, c, d]	Resistance (%)	No. tested isolates	Type of surveillance, population or samples[c]	Period for data collection	Year of publication or report
Sao Tome and Principe	National data not available					2013
Senegal	No information obtained for this report					
Seychelles	No information obtained for this report					
Sierra Leone	No information obtained for this report					
South Africa	National data	52	1177	Invasive isolates	2012	2013
South Sudan	National data not available					2013
Swaziland	National data	0	25	Comprehensive	2013	2013
Togo	Publication (165)	35.7	84	Infected dermatology patients	2003–2005	2011
Uganda	National data, incomplete		9	Comprehensive	2012	2013
Uganda	Publication (166)	0	54	Surgical site infections	2007	2009
United Republic of Tanzania	National data not available					2013
United Republic of Tanzania	Publication (167)	15	160	Skin and soft tissue infections	2008	2012
Zambia	National data	32	424	Targeted	2012	2013
Zimbabwe	National data not available					2013

a. cef, cefoxitin; clox, cloxacillin; oxa, oxacilin. Data on cefoxitin used when not specified.

b. National data refers to data returned on the questionnaires as defined in Annex 1. This definition does not imply that the data collected is representative for that country as a whole because information gaps are likely.

c. See Annex 1 for definitions.

d. "National data not available" means that there was information that no data were available; "No information obtained for this report" means that no information was obtained from authorities, networks or publications.

Table A2.26 *Staphylococcus aureus*: Resistance to methicillin[a] (MRSA) Region of the Americas

Countries, territories and other areas or groupings	Data source[b, c, d]	Resistance (%)	No. tested isolates	Type of surveillance, population or samples[c]	Period for data collection	Year of publication or report
Antigua and Barbuda	No information obtained for this report					
Argentina	National data	54	2177	Community isolates	2010	2013
Bahamas	No information obtained for this report					
Barbados	No information obtained for this report					
Belize	No information obtained for this report					
Bolivia (Plurinational State of)	National data	49	1805		2010	2013
Brazil	National data, incomplete		5		2010	2013
Brazil	Publication (*168*)	16	388	Carriers (health care staff)	2006–2008	2011
Brazil	Publication (*169*)	43.4	53	Blood isolates (dialysis patients)		2010
Brazil	Publication (*170*)	2.4	102	Carriers (students)	2007	2010
Brazil	Publication (*171*)	44.5 (CF patients); 35 (non-CF– patients)	164 (CF patients); 200 non-CF patients	Cystic fibrosis (CF) patients and "non-CF" patients		2010
Brazil	Publication (*172*)	5.8	52	Carriers (health care staff)	2007	2008
Brazil	Publication (*173*)	31	2218	Consecutive laboratory isolates	2005–2008	2009
Brazil	Publication (*174*)	41.5	105	Maternity hospital	2002–2003	2009
Canada	National data	21	1052	Sentinel hospitals	2010	2013
Chile	National data	90	135		2010	2013
Colombia	National data not available					2013
Colombia	Publication (*175*)	25	36	Healthy children	2008	2010
Colombia	Publication (*176*)	7.2	182	Screening intensive care unit (ICU) patients	2007–2008	2010
Colombia	Publication (*177*)	60	39	Children with *S. aureus* infections	2008–2009	2010
Costa Rica	National data not available					2013
Costa Rica	Publication (*168*)	20.9	296	Health-care workers	2006	2011
Cuba	National data	60	79	Community isolates	2009	2013
Dominica	No information obtained for this report					
Dominican Republic	National data	30	1210	Community isolates	2009	2013
Ecuador	National data	29	1111	Community isolates	2010	2013
El Salvador	National data	29	198	Community isolates	2010	2013
Grenada	No information obtained for this report					
Guatemala	National data	52	666	Community isolates	2010	2013
Guyana	No information obtained for this report					
Haiti	No information obtained for this report					
Honduras	National data	30	975	Community isolates	2010	2013
Jamaica	Publication (*178*)	2.9	35	Patients with breast abscesses		2012
Mexico	National data not available					2013
Mexico	Publication (*179*)	29.9	1008	Clinical samples	2000–2007	2009
Nicaragua	National data	0	7	Community isolates	2010	2013
Panama	National data	22	403	Community isolates	2010	2013
Panama	National network	21	3865	Comprehensive	2012	2013
Paraguay	National data	27	264	Community isolates	2010	2013
Peru	National data	36	230	Community isolates	2010	2013
Peru	National network	84	380	Comprehensive	2012	2013
Saint Kitts and Nevis	No information obtained for this report					
Saint Lucia	No information obtained for this report					
Saint Vincent and the Grenadines	No information obtained for this report					
Suriname	No information obtained for this report					
Trinidad and Tobago	Publication (*116*)	12.5	32	Hospitalized children	2007	2010
United States of America	National data	51.3	12 327	Health-care associated infections	2009–2010	2013
Uruguay	National data not available					2013
Uruguay	Publication (*180*)	40	1253	Paediatric holspital	(2001)–2006	2009
Uruguay	Publication (*181*)	76.4	89	Clinical isolates community (children)	2003–2006	2013
Venezuela (Bolivarian Republic of)	National data	31	913	Community isolates	2010	2013

a. cef, cefoxitin; oxa, oxacilin. Data on cefoxitin used when not specified.

b. National data refers to data returned on the questionnaires as defined in Annex 1. This definition does not imply that the data collected is representative for that country as a whole because information gaps are likely.

c. See Annex 1 for definitions.

d. "National data not available" means that there was information that no data were available; "No information obtained for this report" means that no information was obtained from authorities, networks or publications.

Table A2.27 *Staphylococcus aureus*: **Resistance to methicillin[a] (MRSA)**
Eastern Mediterranean Region

Countries, territories and other areas or groupings	Data source[b, c, d]	Resistance (%)	No. tested isolates	Type of surveillance, population or samples[c]	Period for data collection	Year of publication or report
Afghanistan	No information obtained for this report					
Bahrain	National data	10	109			2012	2013
Djibouti	No information obtained for this report					
Egypt	National data not available					2013
Egypt	National surveillance (Hospital network)[e]	46	122	Health-care associated infections	2002–2010	2013
Iran (Islamic Republic of)	National data	53	2690	Invasive isolates	2012	2013
Iraq	Publication (*182*)	46.1	657	Clinical samples	2005–2009	2011
Iraq	Publication (*134*)	84	79	Blood isolates (neonate intensive care unit)		2013
Jordan	National data not available					2013
Kuwait	Publication (*183*)	32	1846	13 hospital (hospitalized patients and outpatients)	2005	2008
Lebanon	National data not available					2013
Lebanon	Publication (*32*)	20	479	Clinical isolates	2010–2011	2012
Libya	Publication (*184*)	31	200	Clinical isolates	2007	2011
Morocco	National data	6.2	16	Hospital isolates	2012	2013
Morocco	Publication (*185*)	52.9	31	Intensive care unit	2002–2005	2008
Morocco	Publication (*186*)	19	461	Hospital samples	2006–2008	2009
Oman	National data	50	751	Comprehensive	2012	2013
Pakistan	National data, incomplete	12				2013
Pakistan	Publication (*187*)	28	1102	Clinical isolates	2006–2008	2011
Pakistan	Publication (*188*)	72.2	346	Clinical isolates	2004–2006	2008
Pakistan	Publication (*39*)	38.4	52	Intensive care unit	2007	2010
Pakistan	Publication (*47*)	30.7	289	Vaginal swabs	2004–2006	2008
Pakistan	Publication (*189*)	1.5	85	MRSA carriage among health-care workers	2007–2008	2010
Pakistan	Publication (*187*)	38.1	1102	Hospital isolates	2006–2008	2011
Pakistan	Publication (*190*)	52.6	38	MRSA carriage among hospital patients	2007	2009
Qatar	Publication (*49*)	13.2	53	Blood isolates	2007–2008	2012
Qatar	Publication (*191*)	0.2	514	Student carriers		2010
Saudi Arabia	Publication (*192*)	92	112	Health-care staff	2007	2010
Saudi Arabia	Publication (*148*)	22.3	166	Hospital isolates	2004–2007	2009
Saudi Arabia	Publication (*193*)	39.5	186	Hospital patients	2009–2010	2012
Saudi Arabia	Publication (*194*)	0	41	Childhood osteomyelitis	1997–2006	2008
Saudi Arabia	Publication (*195*)	39.4	688	Clinical isolates	2008–2009	2011
Saudi Arabia	Publication (*56*)	10.7	56	Hospital isolates	2010–2011	2012
Saudi Arabia	Publication (*57*)	65.7	67	Laboratory records	2009	2010
Somalia	No information obtained for this report					
Sudan	National data not available					2013
Syrian Arab Republic	National data not available					2013
Tunisia	Publication (*196*)	46.4	375	Hospital patients	2005–2006	2008
Tunisia	Publication (*197*)	15.7	70	Children with osteomyelitis	2007–2009	2012
Tunisia	Publication (*198*)	68.1	251	Burn patients	2005–2006	2009
Tunisia	Publication (*199*)	56.3	744	Burn patients	2008–2011	2013
United Arab Emirates	National data[f]	27.5	3547	Comprehensive	2012	2013
United Arab Emirates	Publication (*63*)	39.5[g]	34349[g]	Clinical isolates	(1994 and) 2005	2009
Yemen	Publication (*200*)	48.3	60	Health-care staff		2011
International network	ANSORP[h]	64	161	Blood isolates	2012	2013

a. cef, cefoxitin; oxa, oxacilin. Data on cefoxitin used when not specified.
b. National data refers to data returned on the questionnaires as defined in Annex 1. This definition does not imply that the data collected is representative for that country as a whole because information gaps are likely.
c. See Annex 1 for definitions.
d. "National data not available" means that there was information that no data were available; "No information obtained for this report" means that no information was obtained from authorities, networks or publications.
e. US Naval Medical Research Unit No 3, Global Disease Detection Program, Egypt.
f. Data from United Arab Emirates originate from Abu Dhabi only.
g. Data aggregated from three hospitals.
h. Some centres from the following countries, territories and areas participate in some ANSORP (Asian Network for Surveillance of Resistant Pathogens) projects: India, Indonesia, Japan, Malaysia, Philippines, Republic of Korea, Singapore, Sri Lanka, Saudi Arabia, Thailand, Viet Nam, in addition to China, Hong Kong SAR (Special Administrative Region) and Taiwan, China.

Table A2.28 *Staphylococcus aureus*: Resistance to methicillin[a] (MRSA) European Region

Countries, territories and other areas or groupings	Data source[b, c, d]	Resistance (%)	No. tested isolates	Type of surveillance, population or samples[c]	Period for data collection	Year of publication or report
Albania	National data	21	736	Clinical isolates	2011–2012	2013
Andorra	No information obtained for this report					
Armenia	National data not available					2013
Austria	National data	7.4	1967	Invasive isolates	2011	2013
Azerbaijan	National data not available					2013
Belarus	No information obtained for this report[e]					
Belgium	National data	17.4	1744	Invasive isolates	2011	2013
Bosnia and Herzegovina	Publication (*136*)	80	5	Clinic for gynaecology and obstetrics	2006	2009
Bulgaria	National data	22.4	214	Invasive isolates	2011	2013
Croatia	National data	13	702	Comprehensive	2012	2013
Cyprus	National data	41.6	113	Invasive isolates	2011	2013
Czech Republic	National data	14.5	1554	Invasive isolates	2011	2013
Denmark	National data	1.2	1452	Invasive isolates	2011	2013
Estonia	National data	1.7	116	Invasive isolates	2011	2013
Finland	National data	2.8	1487	Invasive isolates	2011	2013
France	National data	20.1	4716	Invasive isolates	2011	2013
Georgia	National data not available					2013
Georgia	Publication (*67*)	6/15	15	Blood isolates, neonates	2003–2004	2009
Germany	National data	16.2	2374	Invasive isolates	2011	2013
Greece	National data	39.2	784	Invasive isolates	2011	2013
Hungary	National data	26.2	1156	Invasive isolates	2011	2013
Iceland	National data	2.8	71	Invasive isolates	2011	2013
Ireland	National data	23.7	1057	Invasive isolates	2011	2013
Israel	Publication (*69*)	48.3	834 (entire period)	Blood isolates	(1997–)2004	2008
Israel	Publication (*201*)	48.2 (Hospital acquired); 42.2 (Health-care associated); 27.3 (community);	735 (Hospital acquired); 526 (Health-care associated);	Blood isolates	1988–1994 and 1999–2007	2012
Israel	Publication (*68*)	32.3 Hospital); 50 (Long-term care facility [LTCF])	22 (Community); 45 (Hospital); 4 (LTCF)	Bacteraemia (community, hospital, LTCF)	2001–2006	2009
Italy	National data	38.2	1261	Invasive isolates	2011	2013
Kazakhstan	No information obtained for this report[e]					
Kyrgyzstan	National data not available					2013
Latvia	National data	9.9	192	Invasive isolates	2011	2013
Lithuania	National data	5.8	278	Invasive isolates	2011	2013
Luxembourg	National data	20.5	127	Invasive isolates	2011	2013
Malta	National data	49.2	130	Invasive isolates	2011	2013
Monaco	No information obtained for this report					
Montenegro	National data not available					2013
Netherlands	National data	1.4	1801	Invasive isolates	2011	2013
Norway	National data	0.3	1223	Invasive isolates	2011	2013
Poland	National data	24.3	860	Invasive isolates	2011	2013
Portugal	National data	54.6	1307	Invasive isolates	2011	2013
Republic of Moldova	National data	50.3	2064		2012	2013
Romania	National data	50.5	107	Invasive isolates	2011	2013
Russian Federation	National data	Hospital isolates: 66.8; Community: 3.8	Hospiptal: 284; Community: 417	Comprehensive (hospital and community, respectively)	Hospital: 2011–2012 Community: 2006	2013
San Marino	No information obtained for this report					
Serbia	National data	44.5	172	Invasive isolates	2012	2013
Slovakia	National data	25.9	560	Invasive isolates	2011	2013
Slovenia	National data	7.1	464	Invasive isolates	2011	2013
Spain	National data	22.5	1950	Invasive isolates	2011	2013
Sweden	National data	0.8	3099	Invasive isolates	2011	2013
Switzerland	National data	10.2	18 527	Comprehensive	2012	2013
Tajikistan	No information obtained for this report					

Countries, territories and other areas or groupings	Data source[b, c, d]	Resistance (%)	No. tested isolates	Type of surveillance, population or samples[c]	Period for data collection	Year of publication or report
The former Yugoslav Republic of Macedonia	National data	36	25			2013
Turkey	National data	31.5	887	Invasive isolates	2011	2013
Turkmenistan	No information obtained for this report					
Ukraine	Publication (*202*)	53.8	23 292	Hospital samples		2010
United Kingdom	National data	13.6	3408	Invasive isolates	2011	2013
Uzbekistan	No information obtained for this report					

a. cef, cefoxitin; oxa, oxacilin. Data on cefoxitin used when not specified.

b. National data refers to data returned on the questionnaires as defined in Annex 1. This definition does not imply that the data collected is representative for that country as a whole because information gaps are likely.

c. See Annex 1 for definitions.

d. "National data not available" means that there was information that no data were available; "No information obtained for this report" means that no information was obtained from authorities, networks or publications.

e. Some centres participate in some RusNet projects.

Table A2.29 *Staphylococcus aureus*: Resistance to methicillin[a] (MRSA) South East Asian Region

Countries, territories and other areas or groupings	Data source[b, c, d]	Resistance (%)	No. tested isolates	Type of surveillance, population or samples[c]	Period for data collection	Year of publication or report
Bangladesh	National data not available					2013
Bangladesh	Publication (73)	46	103	Clinical isolates	2011–2012	2013
Bhutan	National data	10	130	Comprehensive	2011–2012	2013
Democratic peoples republic of Korea	No information obtained for this report					
India	National data not available					2013
India	Publication (140)	37	38	Blood isolates (children)	(1994)–2002–2003	2008
India	Publication (97)	40	38	Burn unit		2011
India	Publication (203)	5.5	109	Dental outpatient clinic	2011–2012	2012
India	Publication (204)	4.2	96	Carriage (urban community)		2009
India	Publication (205)	80.4 (Community); 80.6 (Hospital)	485 (Community); 1022 (Hospital)	Community and hospital isolates	2009–2012	2013
India	Publication (206)	43	100	Burn unit	2010	2012
India	Publication (207)	41	26 310	Hospital patients (in- and out patients)	2008–2009	2013
India	Publication (208)	55	74	Community–acquired bone/joint infections	2004–2008	2013
India	Publication (209)	20.8	284	Hospital		2012
India	Publication (210)	63	38	Hospital (orthopaedic surgical unit)	2007–2009	2013
India	Publication (211)	19	63	Carriage (community)		2009
India	Publication (212)	11.4	70	Carriage (health-care workers)	2009–2010	2013
India	Publication (91)	30	221	Clinical samples	2007–2009	2012
India	Publication (213)	11.1	43	Neonatal septicemia isolates	2003–2007	2010
India	Publication (214)	54	70	Hospital		2012
Indonesia	National data not available[e]					2013
Maldives	No information obtained for this report					
Myanmar	National data	26	2650	Comprehensive	2012	2013
Nepal	National data not available					2013
Nepal	Publication (215)	68	600	Skin and soft tissue infections	68	2010
Nepal	Publication (216)	63	38	Orthopaedic surgery	2001–2009	2010
Nepal	Publication (217)	26.1	750	Clinical isolates	2003–2004	2008
Nepal	Publication (218)	69.1	162	Clinical isolates	2005–2007	2009
Nepal	Publication (219)	56.1	57	Carriers (children <15)	2007	2008
Nepal	Publication (220)	31.1	264	Clinical isolates		2010
Nepal	Publication (221)	45	149	Clinical isolates (hospital infections)	2007–2008	2009
Nepal	Publication (222)	2.3	35	Carriers (hospital staff)	2008	2009
Sri Lanka	National data not available					2013
Sri Lanka	Publication (223)	13.6	59	Carriers (patients with atopic dermatitis)		2010
Thailand	National data	21.6 (cef); 24.2 (oxa)	14 722 (cef); 6574 (oxa)	Comprehensive	2012	2013
Timor-Leste	Naitional data, incomplete, from national laboratory[f]	25			2010–2012	2013
International network	ANSORP[g]	64	161	Blood isolates	2012	2013

a. cef, cefoxitin; oxa, oxacilin. Data on cefoxitin used when not specified.
b. National data refers to data returned on the questionnaires as defined in Annex 1. This definition does not imply that the data collected is representative for that country as a whole because information gaps are likely.
c. See Annex 1 for definitions.
d. "National data not available" means that there was information that no data were available; "No information obtained for this report" means that no information was obtained from authorities, networks or publications.
e. Some centres participate in some ANSORP (Asian Network for Surveillance of Resistant Pathogens) projects.
f. Data were provided, but no formal national data compilation was available.
g. Some centres from the following countries, territories and areas participate in some ANSORP projects: India, Indonesia, Japan, Malaysia, Philippines, Republic of Korea, Singapore, Sri Lanka, Saudi Arabia, Thailand, Viet Nam, in addition to China, Hong Kong SAR (Special Administrative Region) and Taiwan, China.

Table A2.30 *Staphylococcus aureus*: Resistance to methicillin[a] (MRSA)
Western Pacific Region

Countries, territories and other areas or groupings	Data source[b, c, d]	Resistance (%)	No. tested isolates	Type of surveillance, population or samples[c]	Period for data collection	Year of publication or report
Australia	National data	30	703	Comprehensive	2011	2013
Brunei Darussalam	National data from hospital laboratory	8.2	911	Comprehensive	2012	2013
Cambodia	National data not available					2013
Cambodia	National data[e] collected from several sources by public health institute (NIPH). Pasteur Institute (PI)	55.6 (NIPH); 37.8 (PI)	36 (NIPH); 45 (PI	Blood, sputum, and wound (NIPH); Laboratory data (PI)	2013	2013
China	National data	37.1 (oxa), 41.1 (cef)	57 294 (oxa), 25 636 (cef)	Comprehensive	2012	2013
Cook Islands	No information obtained for this report					
Fiji	National data not available					2013
Fiji	Institute surveillance[e,f]	2.4	2502	Comprehensive (2 hospitals); NI[g] (one hospital)	2012	2013
Japan	National data	53	221 239	Comprehensive	2012	2013
Kiribati	National data	31	36	Comprehensive	2012	2013
Lao People's Democratic Republic	National data	8.8	34		2012–2013	2013
Lao People's Democratic Republic	Institute surveillance	21.6	37	Comprehensive (laboratory)	2011–2012	2013
Malaysia	National data	17.3	30 766	Comprehensive	2012	2013
Marshall Islands	National data, incomplete				2011–2012	2013
Micronesia	National data	4	113	Comprehensive	2011	2013
Mongolia	Publication (99)	60.1	92	Community-acquired infections	2011	2013
Nauru	No information obtained for this report					2013
New Zealand	National data	10.4	108 786	Comprehensive	2011	2013
Niue	No information obtained for this report					
Palau	No information obtained for this report					
Papua New Guinea	National data[h]	43.9	164	Blood, urine, wounds	2012	2013
Philippines	National data	54.9	1958	Comprehensive	2012	2013
Republic of Korea*	National data	57.7;[i] 70.6 "General hospitals"	12 579 ("Hospitals" + "Clinics"); NI[g] ("General hospitals")	Comprehensive	(2007)-2011	2013
Republic of Korea	National network/ institute surveillance	73	3673	Comprehensive (hospital samples)	2012	2013
Samoa	National data	24	389	Comprehensive	2011	2013
Singapore	National data, incomplete[j]		3409	(i) Comprehensive and (ii) Bacteraemia, respectively	2011	2013
Singapore	Publication (224)	82	28	Cirrhotic patients	2007–2008	2011
Solomon Islands	National data, incomplete		50		2012	2013
Tonga	National data	17.2	430		2012	2013
Tuvalu	No information obtained for this report					2013
Vanuatu	No information obtained for this report					2013
Viet Nam	No information obtained for this report[k]					
International network	ANSORP[l]	64	161	Blood isolates	2012	2013

a. cef, cefoxitin; oxa, oxacilin. Data on cefoxitin used when not specified.
b. National data refers to data returned on the questionnaires as defined in Annex 1. This definition does not imply that the data collected is representative for that country as a whole because information gaps are likely.
c. See Annex 1 for definitions.
d. "National data not available" means that there was information that no data were available; "No information obtained for this report" means that no information was obtained from authorities, networks or publications.
e. Data were provided, but no formal national data compilation was available.
f. Data from three hospitals aggregated.
g. NI – No information obtained, or incomplete.
h. National data from different types of samples (blood, urinary and wounds) aggregated.
i. Data aggregated from two surveillance systems «Hospitals» and «Clinics».
j. No proportions obtained. Incidence in hospitals: (i) 16.3 per 10,000 inpatient-days (ii) 1.0 per 10,000 inpatient-days.
k. Some centres participate in some ANSORP (Asian Network for Surveillance of Resistant Pathogens) projects.
l. Some centres from the following countries, territories and areas participate in some ANSORP projects: India, Indonesia, Japan, Malaysia, Philippines, Republic of Korea, Singapore, Sri Lanka, Saudi Arabia, Thailand, Viet Nam, in addition to China, Hong Kong SAR (Special Administrative Region) and Taiwan, China.

Table A2.31 *Streptococcus pneumoniae*: Resistance, or non-susceptibility, to penicillin
African Region

Countries, territories and other areas or groupings	Data source[a, b, c]	Not specified whether resistant or non-susceptible (%)	Resistant (%)	Non-susceptible (%)	No. tested isolates	Type of surveillance, population or samples[b]	Period for data collection	Year of publication or report
Algeria	Publication (*225*)		23.5 (Meningitis); 1 (Other)		111 (Meningitis); 183 (Other)		2001–2010	2012
Algeria	National data from international publication (*226*)			44	71	Invasive isolates	(2003)–2005	2009
Angola	No information obtained for this report							
Benin	National data, incomplete							2013
Botswana	National data not available							2013
Botswana	Publication (*227*)		36		125	Patients with meningitis	2000–2008	2011
Burkina Faso	National data not available							
Burkina Faso	Publication (*228*)		3.8		235	Infected children	2000–2001	2009
Burundi	National data	20			5		2012	2013
Cameroon	Publication (*229*)		100		30	Upper respiratory tract (children)	2004–2005	2012
Cabo Verde	No information obtained for this report							
Central African Republic	National data	50			4		2012	2013
Central African Republic	Publication (*230*)	6			62	Paediatric patients	2004–2005	2008
Chad	No information obtained for this report							
Comoros	No information obtained for this report							
Congo	National data not available							2013
Côte d'Ivoire	No information obtained for this report							
Democratic Republic of the Congo	No information obtained for this report							
Equatorial Guinea	No information obtained for this report							
Eritrea	No information obtained for this report							
Ethiopia	National data	14			8	Comprehensive	2011–2012	2013
Ethiopia	Publication (*231*)			69	49	Hospital patients	2001–2005	2008
Gabon	Publication (*151*)			9	30	Carriage (children with sickle-cell anemia)		2013
Gambia	National data not available							2013
Ghana	National data	58.1			50	Comprehensive	2013	2013
Guinea	National data not available							2013
Guinea-Bissau	National data	33.3			3	Comprehensive		2013
Kenya	National data not available							2013
Kenya	Publication (*232*)	24			33	Invasive infections in neonates and infants	2001–2009	2010
Lesotho	National data	0			4		2012	2013

Countries, territories and other areas or groupings	Data source[a, b, c]	Not specified whether resistant or non-susceptible (%)	Resistant (%)	Non-susceptible (%)	No. tested isolates	Type of surveillance, population or samples[b]	Period for data collection	Year of publication or report
Liberia	National data not available							2013
Madagascar	No information obtained for this report							
Malawi	National data not available							2013
Malawi	Publication (233)		9–18 (during study period)[d]		4445	Invasive isolates	2000–2009	2011
Mali	No information obtained for this report							
Mauritania	National data not available							2013
Mauritius	National data	60			45	Comprehensive	2012	2013
Mozambique	Publication (234)			11	326	Meningitis in children	2001–2006	2010
Namibia	National data	57			150		2012	2013
Niger	National data not available							
Nigeria	Publication (235)			29.7	37	Carriers (children)		2009
Rwanda	No information obtained for this report							
Sao Tome and Principe	National data not available							2013
Senegal	Publication (236)	33.3			105	Respiratory samples	2007–2008	2009
Seychelles	No information obtained for this report							
Sierra Leone	No information obtained for this report							
South Africa	National data	3			129	Invasive isolates	2012	2013
South Sudan	National data not available							2013
Swaziland	National data not available							2013
Togo	No information obtained for this report							
Uganda	National data	24			4	Comprehensive	2012	2013
Uganda	Publication (237)	79			38	Invasive isolates	2006–2007	2009
Uganda	Publication (238)	32			68	Invasive (HIV patients)	1996–2007	2010
United Republic of Tanzania	National data not available							2013
United Republic of Tanzania	Publication (239)	67.8			115	Carriers (children)		2012
Zambia	National data	16.2			37		2012	2013
Zimbabwe	National data	20			5	Targeted	2012	2013
International[e]	Publication (240)			47	236	Clinical isolates	2006–2007	2009
International	Publication (241)	0			442	Invasive isolates	2003–2007	2009

a. National data refers to data returned on the questionnaires as defined in Annex 1. This definition does not imply that the data collected is representative for that country as a whole because information gaps are likely.

b. See Annex 1 for definitions.

c. "National data not available" means that there was information that no data were available; "No information obtained for this report" means that no information was obtained from authorities, networks or publications.

d. No further details on denominator given.

e. Kenya, Uganda, United Republic of Tanzania and Ethiopia.

Table A2.32   *Streptococcus pneumoniae*: Resistance, or non-susceptibility, to penicillin
Region of the Americas

Countries, territories and other areas or groupings	Data source[a, b, c]	Not specified whether resistant or non-susceptible (%)	Resistant (%)	Non-susceptible (%)	No. tested isolates	Type of surveillance, population or samples[b]	Period for data collection	Year of publication or report
Antigua and Barbuda	No information obtained for this report							
Argentina	National data	27.5			754	Invasive isolates	2010	2013
Bahamas	No information obtained for this report							
Barbados	No information obtained for this report							
Belize	No information obtained for this report							
Bolivia (Plurinational State of)	National data	65			11	Invasive isolates	2010	2013
Brazil	National data	20.1			807	Invasive isolates	2010	2013
Canada	National data	4.3			185	Sentinel hospitals	2011	2013
Chile	National data	42.1			815	Invasive isolates	2010	2013
Colombia	National data	34.5			369	Invasive isolates	2010	2013
Costa Rica	National data	24.9			64	Invasive isolates	2010	2013
Cuba	National data	28.6			63	Invasive isolates	2010	2013
Dominica	No information obtained for this report							
Dominican Republic	National data	46.5			43	Invasive isolates	2010	2013
Ecuador	National data	4.4			44	Invasive isolates	2010	2013
El Salvador	National data	29.8			47	Invasive isolates	2010	2013
Grenada	No information obtained for this report							
Guatemala	National data	33			8	Invasive isolates	2010	2013
Guyana	No information obtained for this report							
Haiti	No information obtained for this report							
Honduras	National data	66			3	Community isolates	2010	2013
Jamaica	No information obtained for this report							
Mexico	National data	57.8			19	Community isolates	2010	2013
Mexico	Publication (*242*)			64 (Meningitis); 53 (Non-meningitis)	58 (Meningitis); 47 (Non-meningitis)	Invasive infections	2000–2005	2008
Nicaragua	National data	0.4			12	Community isolates	2010	2013
Panama	National data	0			63	Invasive isolates	2010	2013
Panama	National network	11			140	Comprehensive	2011–2012	2013
Paraguay	National data	47.7			109	Invasive isolates	2010	2013
Peru	National data	58.8			17	Community isolates	2010	2013
Peru	National network	47			17	Comprehensive	2012	2013
Saint Kitts and Nevis	No information obtained for this report							
Saint Lucia	No information obtained for this report							

Countries, territories and other areas or groupings	Data source[a, b, c]	Not specified whether resistant or non-susceptible (%)	Resistant (%)	Non-susceptible (%)	No. tested isolates	Type of surveillance, population or samples[b]	Period for data collection	Year of publication or report
Saint Vicent and the Grenadines	No information obtained for this report							
Suriname	No information obtained for this report							
Trinidad and Tobago	No information obtained for this report							
United States of America	National data	4.2			3197	Invasive isolates	2011	2013
Uruguay	National data	1.1			176	Invasive isolates	2010	2013
Venezuela (Bolivarian Republic of)	National data			0	145	Invasive isolates	2010	2013

a. National data refers to data returned on the questionnaires as defined in Annex 1. This definition does not imply that the data collected is representative for that country as a whole because information gaps are likely.

b. See Annex 1 for definitions.

c. "National data not available" means that there was information that no data were available; "No information obtained for this report" means that no information was obtained from authorities, networks or publications.

Table A2.33 *Streptococcus pneumoniae*: Resistance, or non-susceptibility, to penicillin
Eastern Mediterranean Region

Countries, territories and other areas or groupings	Data source[a, b, c]	Not specified whether resistant or non-susceptible (%)	Resistant (%)	Non-susceptible (%)	No. tested isolates	Type of surveillance, population or samples[b]	Period for data collection	Year of publication or report
Afghanistan	No information obtained for this report							
Bahrain	National data not available							2013
Djibouti	No information obtained for this report							
Egypt	National data not available							2013
Egypt	National data from international publication (226)			17	123	Invasive isolates	2003–2005	2009
Iran (Islamic Republic of)	National data	33.9			115	Invasive	2007	2013
Iraq	No information obtained for this report							
Jordan	National data not available							2013
Jordan	National data from international publication (226)			46	57	Invasive isolates	2003–2005	2009
Kuwait	Publication (243)	56			1353	Hospital patients	1997–2007	2010
Kuwait	Publication (244)		15.4 (Meningitis); 0.3 (Other)		13 (Meningitis); 382 (Other)	Clinical isolates	2006–2011	2012
Kuwait	Publication (245)		64		397	Consecutive clinical isolates	2004–2005	2008
Lebanon	National data not available							2013
Lebanon	Publication (246)			17.4	257	Invasive isolates		2012
Libya	No information obtained for this report							
Morocco	National data	25			3	Sentinel sites	2013	2013
Morocco	Publication (247)			34.7	302	Carriers, children	2008–2009	2011
Morocco	Publication (248)			24.8	955	Comprehensive	1998–2008	2012
Morocco	National data from international publication (226)			17	42	Invasive isolates	2003–2005	2009
Oman	National data			5	131	Comprehensive	2012	2013
Pakistan	National data, incomplete		14.0			Targeted		2013
Pakistan	Publication (249)		3		100	Community-acquired infections	2006	2008
Pakistan	Publication (250)			41	37	Children	2009–2010	2011
Qatar	No information obtained for this report							
Saudi Arabia	Publication (251)		2.4	48.5	41	Invasive	2001–2007	2009
Saudi Arabia	Publication (252)		13.9	40.7	311	Invasive (children)	2005–2010	2012
Somalia	No information obtained for this report							
Sudan	National data not available							2013
Syrian Arab Republic	National data not available							2013
Tunisia	Publication (225)	0			34	Severe pneumonia	1999–2008	2012

Countries, territories and other areas or groupings	Data source[a, b, c]	Not specified whether resistant or non-susceptible (%)	Resistant (%)	Non-susceptible (%)	No. tested isolates	Type of surveillance, population or samples[b]	Period for data collection	Year of publication or report
Tunisia	Publication (*253*)	52.8			210	Children	1998–2004	2009
Tunisia	National data from international publication (*226*)			27	33	Invasive isolates	(2003)–2005	2009
United Arab Emirates[d]	National data		12.9		139	Comprehensive	2012	2013
Yemen	Publication (*254*)	93.3			32	Carriers, children	2006	2008
International network[e]	ANSORP			4.6	2144	Non-meningitis infections	2008–2009	2012
International	Publication (*240*)			47	236	Clinical isolates	2006–2008	2009
International	Publication (*255*)			65	702	Invasive	1990–2007	2009
International	Publication (*226*)			26	1298	Invasive isolates	2003–2005	2009

a. National data refers to data returned on the questionnaires as defined in Annex 1. This definition does not imply that the data collected is representative for that country as a whole because information gaps are likely.

b. See Annex 1 for definitions.

c. "National data not available" means that there was information that no data were available; "No information obtained for this report" means that no information was obtained from authorities, networks or publications.

d. Data from United Arab Emirates originate from Abu Dhabi only.

e. Some centres from the following countries, territories and areas participate in some ANSORP (Asian Network for Surveillance of Resistant Pathogens) projects: India, Indonesia, Japan, Malaysia, Philippines, Republic of Korea, Singapore, Sri Lanka, Saudi Arabia, Thailand, Viet Nam, in addition to China, Hong Kong SAR (Special Administrative Region) and Taiwan, China.

Table A2.34 *Streptococcus pneumoniae*: Resistance, or non-susceptibility, to penicillin
European Region

Countries, territories and other areas or groupings	Data source[a, b, c]	Not specified whether resistant or non-susceptible (%)	Resistant (%)	Non-susceptible (%)	No. tested isolates	Type of surveillance, population or samples[b]	Period for data collection	Year of publication or report
Albania	National data not available							2013
Andorra	No information obtained for this report							
Armenia	National data not available							2013
Austria	National data		1.7	2.9	405	Invasive isolates	2011	2013
Azerbaijan	National data not available							2013
Belarus	No information obtained for this report[d]							
Belgium	National data		0.8	0.9	1829	Invasive isolates	2011	2013
Bosnia and Herzegovina	No information obtained for this report							
Bulgaria	National data		21.2	21.2	33	Invasive isolates	2011	2013
Croatia	National data			30	2950	Comprehensive	2012	2013
Cyprus	National data		25	25	12	Invasive isolates	2011	2013
Cyprus	National data from international publication (226)			15	26	Invasive isolates	2003–2005	2009
Czech Republic	National data		0	3.8	316	Invasive isolates	2011	2013
Denmark	National data		0.2	4.8	896	Invasive isolates	2011	2013
Estonia	National data		2	2	51	Invasive isolates	2011	2013
Finland	National data		0.9	27.7	754	Invasive isolates	2012	2013
France	National data		0.1		23.8	Invasive isolates	2011	2013
Georgia	National data not available							2013
Germany	National data		0.3	1.7	347	Invasive isolates	2011	2013
Greece	National data not available							2013
Hungary	National data		5.8	11.6	139	Invasive isolates	2011	2013
Iceland	National data		6.3	9.4	32	Invasive isolates	2011	2013
Ireland	National data		6.2	19.5	324	Invasive isolates	2011	2013
Israel	No information obtained for this report							
Italy	National data		6.3	6.9	174	Invasive isolates	2011	2013
Kazakhstan	No information obtained for this report[d]							
Kyrgyzstan	National data not available							2013
Latvia	National data		10.0	12.5	40	Invasive isolates	2011	2013
Lithuania	National data		2.1	18.8	48	Invasive isolates	2011	2013
Luxembourg	National data		2	8	50	Invasive isolates	2011	2013
Malta	National data		10	50	10	Invasive isolates	2011	2013
Malta	National data from international publication (226)			13	40	Invasive isolates	2003–2005	2009
Monaco	No information obtained for this report							
Montenegro	National data not available							2013
Netherlands	National data		0.3	1.1	1067	Invasive isolates	2011	2013
Norway	National data		0.0	3.4	619	Invasive isolates	2011	2013
Poland	National data		4.2	18.1	165	Invasive isolates	2011	2013
Portugal	National data		8.4	10.5	439	Invasive isolates	2011	2013
Republic of Moldova	National data			72.7	1361		2012	2013
Romania	National data		61.1	61.1	36	Invasive isolates	2011	2013
Russian Federation	National data		0.6	10.8	788		2008–2009	2013
San Marino	No information obtained for this report							

Countries, territories and other areas or groupings	Data source[a, b, c]	Not specified whether resistant or non-susceptible (%)	Resistant (%)	Non-susceptible (%)	No. tested isolates	Type of surveillance, population or samples[b]	Period for data collection	Year of publication or report
Serbia	National data	32.3			31	Invasive isolates	2012	2013
Slovakia	National data		3.8	7.6	26	Invasive isolates	2011	2013
Slovenia	National data		0.8	12.3	252	Invasive isolates	2011	2013
Spain	National data		9.8	30.2	736	Invasive isolates	2011	2013
Sweden	National data		3.2	3.5	1013	Invasive isolates	2011	2013
Switzerland	National data		3.1		1713	Comprehensive	2012	2013
Tajikistan	No information obtained for this report							
The former Yugoslav Republic of Macedonia	National data	0			3	Invasive isolates	Invasive isolates	2013
Turkey	National data	44.8			58	Meningitis	2011	2013
Turkmenistan	No information obtained for this report							
Ukraine	No information obtained for this report[d]							
United Kingdom	National data		0.8	5.5	1324	Invasive isolates	2011	2013
Uzbekistan	No information obtained for this report							

a. National data refers to data returned on the questionnaires as defined in Annex 1. This definition does not imply that the data collected is representative for that country as a whole because information gaps are likely.
b. See Annex 1 for definitions.
c. "National data not available" means that there was information that no data were available; "No information obtained for this report" means that no information was obtained from authorities, networks or publications.
d. Some centres participate in some RusNet projects.

Table A2.35 *Streptococcus pneumoniae*: Resistance, or non-susceptibility, to penicillin
South East Asian Region

Countries, territories and other areas or groupings	Data source[a, b, c]	Not specified whether resistant or non-susceptible (%)	Resistant (%)	Non-susceptible (%)	No. tested isolates	Type of surveillance, population or samples[b]	Period for data collection	Year of publication or report
Bangladesh	National data not available							2013
Bangladesh	Publication (256)		0		139	Invasive isolates	2004–2007	2009
Bhutan	National data	0			13	Comprehensive	2012	2013
Democratic People's Republic of Korea	No information obtained for this report							
India	National data not available							2013
India	Publication (257)		5.6		776	Carriers	2004	2013
Indonesia	National data not available[d]							2013
Maldives	No information obtained for this report							
Myanmar	National data, incomplete							2013
Nepal	National data	48			225	Comprehensive	2012	2013
Sri Lanka	National data not available							2013
Thailand	National data	47			2581	Comprehensive	2012	2013
Timor-Leste	National data, incomplete, from national laboratory[e]	4					2010–2012	2013
International network	ANSORP[f]	4.6 (R + I[g])			2144	Non-meningitis pneumococcal infections	2008–2009	2012

a. National data refers to data returned on the questionnaires as defined in Annex 1. This definition does not imply that the data collected is representative for that country as a whole because information gaps are likely.

b. See Annex 1 for definitions.

c. "National data not available" means that there was information that no data were available; "No information obtained for this report" means that no information was obtained from authorities, networks or publications.

d. Some centres participate in some ANSORP (Asian Network for Surveillance of Resistant Pathogens) projects.

e. Data were provided, but no formal national data compilation was available.

f. Some centres from the following countries, territories and areas participate in some ANSORP projects: India, Indonesia, Japan, Malaysia, Philippines, Republic of Korea, Singapore, Sri Lanka, Saudi Arabia, Thailand, Viet Nam, in addition to China, Hong Kong SAR (Special Administrative Region) and Taiwan, China.

g. I=Intermediate.

Table A2.36 *Streptococcus pneumoniae:* **Resistance or non-susceptibility to penicillin Western Pacific Region**

Countries, territories and other areas or groupings	Data source[a, b, c]	Not specified whether resistant or non-susceptible (%)	Resistant (%)	Non-susceptible (%)	No. tested isolates	Type of surveillance, population or samples[b]	Period for data collection	Year of publication or report
Australia	National data	2.0			1831	Comprehensive	2007	2013
Brunei Darussalam	National data from hospital laboratory	15.4			76	Comprehensive	2012	2013
Cambodia	National data not available							2013
Cambodia	National data[d] collected from several sources by public health institute (NIPH). Pasteur Institute (PI)	0 (NIPH, surveillance network);		64 (NIPH, Hospital); 63.9 (PI)	17 (Surveillance network); 11 (Hospital); 47 (PI)	NIPH data: Sputum, blood (Surveillance network); Blood isolates (hospital); PI: Laboratory data (mixed patients)	2007–2013 (Surveillance network); 2007–2010 (Hospital); 2013 (PI)	2013
China	National data			1.9	420	Targeted	2010	2013
Cook Islands	No information obtained for this report							
Fiji	National data compilation not available							2013
Fiji	Institute surveillance[d,e]	1.1			86		2012	2013
Japan	National data	42.2		42.2	30 484	Comprehensive	2012	2013
Kiribati	National data				1	Comprehensive	2013	2013
Lao People's Democratic Republic	National data		66.7		3		2013	2013
Lao People's Democratic Republic	Institute surveillance		0		2	Comprehensive (Laboratory)	2011–2012	2013
Malaysia	National data			17.5	848	Comprehensive	2012	2013
Marshall Islands	National data not available							2013
Micronesia	National data	"Insignificant"			≤30	Comprehensive	2011	2013
Mongolia	Publication (99)		96.7		153	Community infections	2011	2013
Nauru	No information obtained for this report							
New Zealand	National data	14.9			2993	Comprehensive	2011	2013
Niue	No information obtained for this report							
Palau	No information obtained for this report							
Papua New Guinea	National data	30			10	Blood isolates	2012	2013
Philippines	National data	0			43	Comprehensive	2012	2013
Republic of Korea	National data	0[f]			270	Comprehensive	2011	2013
Republic of Korea	National network/ institute surveillance	89			347	Hospital samples	2012	2013
Samoa	National data	8			25		2011	2013
Singapore	National data not available							2013
Singapore	Publication (258)		44		147	Invasive infections	1997–2004	2008
Singapore	Publication (259)			0 (Non-meningitis)	186 (Non-meningitis)	Invasive infections	2000–2007	2009
Singapore	Publication (260)			69.5	59	Carriers (children)	(1997)– 2007–2008	2011
Solomon Islands	National data	47.0			30		2012	2013
Tonga	National data	0			30		2012	2013
Tuvalu	No information obtained for this report							

Countries, territories and other areas or groupings	Data source[a, b, c]	Not specified whether resistant or non-susceptible (%)	Resistant (%)	Non-susceptible (%)	No. tested isolates	Type of surveillance, population or samples[b]	Period for data collection	Year of publication or report
Vanuatu	No information obtained for this report							
Viet Nam	No information obtained for this report[g]							
International network	ANSORP[h]	4.6% (R + I[i])			2144	Non-meningitis pneumococcal infections	2008–2009	2012

a. National data refers to data returned on the questionnaires as defined in Annex 1. This definition does not imply that the data collected is representative for that country as a whole because information gaps are likely.

b. See Annex 1 for definitions.

c. "National data not available" means that there was information that no data were available; "No information obtained for this report" means that no information was obtained from authorities, networks or publications.

d. Data were provided, but no formal national data compilation was available.

e. Data from two hospitals aggregated.

f. Data aggregated from more than one surveillance source ("Hospitals" and "Clinics").

g. Some centres participate in some ANSORP (Asian Network for Surveillance of Resistant Pathogens) projects.

h. Some centres from the following countries, territories and areas participate in some ANSORP projects: India, Indonesia, Japan, Malaysia, Philippines, Republic of Korea, Singapore, Sri Lanka, Saudi Arabia, Thailand, Viet Nam, in addition to China, Hong Kong SAR (Special Administrative Region) and Taiwan, China.

i. I=intermediate.

Table A2.37 **Nontyphoidal *Salmonella* (NTS): Resistance to fluoroquinolones**
African region

Countries, territories and other areas or groupings	Data source[a, b, c]	Resistance (%)	No. tested isolates	Type of surveillance, population or samples[b]	Period for data collection	Year of publication or report
Algeria	No information obtained for this report					
Angola	No information obtained for this report					
Benin	National data not available					2013
Botswana	National data	1.6	61	Stool isolates	2012	2013
Burkina Faso	National data not available					2013
Burkina Faso	Publication (261)	1	25	Children with diarrhoea	2009–2010	2013
Burundi	National data	14.2	14		2012	2013
Cameroon	No information obtained for this report					
Cabo Verde	No information obtained for this report					
Central African Republic	National data	0	114			2013
Chad	No information obtained for this report					
Comoros	No information obtained for this report					
Congo	National data	1.65	61	Stool isolates	2012	2013
Côte d'Ivoire	No information obtained for this report					
Democratic Republic of the Congo	Publication (262)	1.3	79		2010–2011	2012
Equatorial Guinea	No information obtained for this report					
Eritrea	No information obtained for this report					
Ethiopia	National data	14	8			2013
Ethiopia	Publication (263)	0	37	Persons with and without diarrhoea	1992–1993	2008
Ethiopia	Publication (264)	8.9	214	Hospital patients		2008
Gabon	No information obtained for this report					
Gambia	National data not available					2013
Ghana	National data	0	9	All isolates	2013	2013
Ghana	Publication (265)	0	247	Clinical isolates	2002–2003	2011
Ghana	Publication (266)	0	113	Blood isolates, (children)	2007–2009	2010
Guinea	National data not available					2013
Guinea-Bissau	National data, incomplete		2	All isolates		2013
Kenya	National data, incomplete	2			2012	2013
Kenya	National network[d]	0	1	Targeted	2013	2013
Kenya	Publication (267)	0	23	Children with diarrhoea	2007	2008
Lesotho	National data	0	2		2012	2013
Liberia	National data	0	4	Targeted	2012	2013
Madagascar	No information obtained for this report					
Malawi	National data	0	4		2013	2013
Malawi	Publication (154)	0	22	Clinical isolates	2006–2007	2012
Mali	No information obtained for this report					
Mauritania	National data	35	68	All isolates	2013	2013
Mauritius	National data	3.2	124	All stool isolates	2012	2013
Mozambique	Publication (268)	0	40	Children under 5 years	2001–2003	2009
Namibia	National data	8	171		2012	2013
Niger	National data	0	1	Comprehensive	2013	2013
Nigeria	Publication (4)	30	30	Blood isolates children	2006–2008	2009
Rwanda	No information obtained for this report					
Sao Tome and Principe	National data not available					2013
Senegal	Publication (269)	0	62	AIDS patients	1996–2005	2008
Senegal	Publication (270)	0	249	Laboratory based	2004–2006	2008
Seychelles	No information obtained for this report					
Sierra Leone	No information obtained for this report					
South Africa	National data	3	2137	Comprehensive	2012	2013
South Sudan	National data not available					2013

Countries, territories and other areas or groupings	Data source[a, b, c]	Resistance (%)	No. tested isolates	Type of surveillance, population or samples[b]	Period for data collection	Year of publication or report
Swaziland	National data not available					2013
Togo	Publication (271)	0	51	Blood isolates (S. enterica serovars Enteritidis and Typhimurium)	1995–2004	2008
Uganda	National data	6.7	15	Comprehensive	2012	2013
Uganda	Publication (238)	0	42	HIV patients with blood stream infection	2006–2007	2010
United Republic of Tanzania	National data not available					2013
United Republic of Tanzania	Publication (272)	8	13	Febrile HIV-patients		2012
United Republic of Tanzania	Publication (17)	0	6	Hospitalized children with diarrhoea	2005–2006	2011
Zambia	National data	13.5	97	Targeted	2012	2013
Zimbabwe	National data	0	50	Comprehensive	2013	2013

a. National data refers to data returned on the questionnaires as defined in Annex 1. This definition does not imply that the data collected is representative for that country as a whole because information gaps are likely.

b. See Annex 1 for definitions.

c. "National data not available" means that there was information that no data were available; "No information obtained for this report" means that no information was obtained from authorities, networks or publications.

d. Global Disease Detection Center, Kenya/Division of Global Health Protection/Center for Global Health/CDC (US Centers for Disease Control and Prevention).

Table A2.38 Nontyphoidal *Salmonella* (NTS): Resistance to fluoroquinolones
Region of the Americas

Countries, territories and other areas or groupings	Data source[a, b, c]	Resistance (%)	No. tested isolates	Type of surveillance, population or samples[b]	Period for data collection	Year of publication or report
Antigua and Barbuda	No information obtained for this report					
Argentina	National data	3	452	Community isolates	2010	2013
Bahamas	No information obtained for this report					
Barbados	No information obtained for this report					
Belize	No information obtained for this report					
Bolivia (Plurinational State of)	National data	12	60	Community isolates	2010	2013
Brazil	National data	2	7221	Community isolates	2010	2013
Canada	National data	0	996	Laboratory samples	2011	2013
Chile	National data	0.3	384	Community isolates	2010	2013
Colombia	National data	0.4	240 (*S. enteritidis*); 217 (*S. typhimurium*)	*S. enterica* serovars *Enteritidis* and *Typhimurium*	2010	2013
Costa Rica	National data	0	2		2010	2013
Cuba	National data	0	20	Community isolates	2009	2013
Dominica	No information obtained for this report					
Dominican Republic	National data	3	26	Community isolates	2009	2013
Ecuador	National data	0	16	Community isolates	2010	2013
El Salvador	National data	0	21	Community isolates	2010	2013
Grenada	No information obtained for this report					
Guatemala	National data, incomplete [d]					2013
Guyana	No information obtained for this report					
Haiti	No information obtained for this report					
Honduras	National data	6	75	Community isolates	2010	2013
Jamaica	No information obtained for this report					
Mexico	National data	0	188	Community isolates	2010	2013
Nicaragua	National data	0	11	Community isolates	2010	2013
Panama	National data	10	102	Community isolates	2010	2013
Panama	National network	12	126		2010	2013
Paraguay	National data	0	116	Community isolates		2013
Peru	National data	96	42	Community isolates (*S. enterididis*)	2010	2013
Peru	National network	23	66	Comprehensive	2012	2013
Saint Kitts and Nevis	No information obtained for this report					
Saint Lucia	No information obtained for this report					
Saint Vicent and the Grenadines	No information obtained for this report					
Suriname	No information obtained for this report					
Trinidad and Tobago	Publication (*116*)	0	8	Hospitalized children	2007	2010
United States of America	National data	0	2474			2013
Uruguay	National data not available					2013

Countries, territories and other areas or groupings	Data source[a, b, c]	Resistance (%)	No. tested isolates	Type of surveillance, population or samples[b]	Period for data collection	Year of publication or report
Uruguay	Publication (*273*)	0	258	Only *Salmonella enterica* subspecies enterica serovar Typhimurium	1976–2000	2009
Venezuela (Bolivarian Republic of)	National data	0	44	Community isolates	2010	2013

a. National data refers to data returned on the questionnaires as defined in Annex 1. This definition does not imply that the data collected is representative for that country as a whole because information gaps are likely.
b. See Annex 1 for definitions.
c. "National data not available" means that there was information that no data were available; "No information obtained for this report" means that no information was obtained from authorities, networks or publications.
d. Serotype specific data available.

Table A2.39 Nontyphoidal *Salmonella* (NTS): Resistance to fluoroquinolones
Eastern Mediterranen Region

Countries, territories and other areas or groupings	Data source[a, b, c]	Resistance (%)	No. tested isolates	Type of surveillance, population or samples[b]	Period for data collection	Year of publication or report
Afghanistan	No information obtained for this report					
Bahrain	National data not available					2013
Djibouti	No information obtained for this report					
Egypt	National data not available					2013
Iran (Islamic Republic of)	National data	6.3	125	Invasive isolates		2013
Iraq	No information obtained for this report					
Jordan	National data	49.1	387	Comprehensive	2011	2013
Kuwait	National data from international publication (274)	1.6	247	Patients with diarrhoea and septicaemia.	2003–2005	2008
Lebanon	National data not available					2013
Libya	No information obtained for this report					
Libya	Publication (275)	63.1	19	Children with diarrhoea	2008	2011
Morocco	National data not available					2013
Morocco	Publication (276)	0	150		2000–2008	2010
Oman	National data	2	60	Comprehensive	2012	2013
Pakistan	National data, incomplete	15		Targeted		2013
Qatar	No information obtained for this report					
Saudi Arabia	Publication (277)	46	213	Hospital patients	2007–2009	2012
Somalia	No information obtained for this report					
Sudan	National data not available					2013
Syrian Arab Republic	National data not available					2013
Tunisia	No information obtained for this report					
United Arab Emirates[d]	National data	13.2	257	Comprehensive	2012	2013
United Arab Emirates	National data from international publication (274)	0.8	122	Patients with diarrhoea and septicaemia	2003–2005	2008
Yemen	Publication (278)	0.7	406	Patients with diarrhoea	2003–2005	2008
International network	ANSORP[e]	4.5	400		2003–2005	2009

a. National data refers to data returned on the questionnaires as defined in Annex 1. This definition does not imply that the data collected is representative for that country as a whole because information gaps are likely.

b. See Annex 1 for definitions.

c. "National data not available" means that there was information that no data were available; "No information obtained for this report" means that no information was obtained from authorities, networks or publications.

d. Data from United Arab Emirates originate from Abu Dhabi only.

e. Some centres from the following countries, territories and areas participate in some ANSORP (Asian Network for Surveillance of Resistant Pathogens) projects: India, Indonesia, Japan, Malaysia, Philippines, Republic of Korea, Singapore, Sri Lanka, Saudi Arabia, Thailand, Viet Nam, in addition to China, Hong Kong SAR (Special Administrative Region) and Taiwan, China.

Table A2.40 Nontyphoidal *Salmonella* (NTS): Resistance to fluoroquinolones
European Region

Countries, territories and other areas or groupings	Data source[a, b, c]	Resistance (%)	No. tested isolates	Type of surveillance, population or samples[b]	Period for data collection	Year of publication or report
Albania	National data not available					2013
Andorra	No information obtained for this report					
Armenia	National data not available					2013
Austria	National data	0.7	2235	All isolates	2011	2013
Azerbaijan	National data not available					2013
Belarus	No information obtained for this report					
Belgium	National data not available			All isolates	2011	2013
Belgium	Publication (*279*)	0	22		2000–2006	2011
Bosnia and Herzegovina	No information obtained for this report					
Bulgaria	National data not available				2011	2013
Croatia	National data	0	2858	Comprehensive	2012	2013
Cyprus	National data not available				2011	2013
Czech Republic	National surveillance	3.8	637	All isolates	2012	2013
Denmark	National data	14.6[d]	1149	All isolates	2010	2013
Estonia	National data	1.1	359	All isolates	2011	2013
Finland	National data	20.6	1978	All isolates	2012	2013
France	National data	9	1367	All isolates	2011	2013
Georgia	National data	0	16	All isolates	2012	2013
Germany	National data	1.1	1933	All isolates	2011	2013
Greece	National data	0	363	All isolates	2012	2013
Hungary	National data	0.1	697	All isolates	2011	2013
Iceland	National data	4.5	44	All isolates	2011	2013
Ireland	National data	1	304	All isolates	2011	2013
Israel	Publication (*280*)	13.3	1490		2002–2007	2012
Italy	National data	11.3	1522	All isolates	2011	2013
Kazakhstan	No information obtained for this report					
Kyrgyzstan	National data not available					2013
Latvia	National data	0	105	All isolates	2011	2013
Lithuania	National data	0.7	1800	All isolates	2011	2013
Luxembourg	National data	4.1	123	All isolates	2011	2013
Malta	National data	9.2	120	All isolates	2011	2013
Monaco	No information obtained for this report					
Montenegro	National data not available					2013
Netherlands	National data	10.2	1115	All isolates	2011	2013
Norway	National data	2.2	1245	All isolates	2011	2013
Poland	National data not available					2013
Portugal	National data not available					2013
Republic of Moldova	National data	4.2	310		2012	2013
Romania	National data	0.7	281	All isolates	2011	2013
Russian Federation	National data not available					2013
San Marino	No information obtained for this report					
Serbia	National data	8.7	1756	*S. enteritidis*	2004–2010	2013
Slovakia	National data	3.2	249	All isolates	2011	2013
Slovenia	National data	0.3	400	All isolates	2011	2013
Spain	National data	0.7	2110	All isolates	2011	2013
Sweden	National data	21	66	Blood isolates	2011	2013
Switzerland	National data	8	327	All isolates	2012	2013
Tajikistan	No information obtained for this report					
The former Yugoslav Republic of Macedonia	National data not available					2013
Turkey	National data	1.1	378	All isolates	2011	2013
Turkmenistan	No information obtained for this report					
Ukraine	No information obtained for this report					
United Kingdom	National data	17.6	9354	All isolates	2011	2013
Uzbekistan	No information obtained for this report					

a. National data refers to data returned on the questionnaires as defined in Annex 1. This definition does not imply that the data collected is representative for that country as a whole because information gaps are likely.

b. See Annex 1 for definitions.

c. "National data not available" means that there was information that no data were available; "No information obtained for this report" means that no information was obtained from authorities, networks or publications.

d. Proportion of non-wild type as resistance was interpreted using EUCAST ECOFF values, not clinical breakpoints.

Table A2.41 **Nontyphoidal *Salmonella* (NTS): Resistance to fluoroquinolones**
South East Asian Region

Countries, territories and other areas or groupings	Data source[a, b, c]	Resistance (%)	No. tested isolates	Type of surveillance, population or samples[b]	Period for data collection	Year of publication or report
Bangladesh	National data not available					2013
Bangladesh	Publication (*281*)	1.4	958	Patients with diarrhoea	2005–2008	2012
Bhutan	National data	0	5	Comprehensive	2011–2012	2013
Democratic People's Republic of Korea	No information obtained for this report					
India	National data not available[d]					2013
Indonesia	National data not available[d]					2013
Maldives	No information obtained for this report					
Myanmar	National data					2013
Nepal	National data	4	1102	Comprehensive	2012	2013
Sri Lanka	National data not available					2013
Thailand	National data	0.2 (nor); 4 (cip)	1483		2012	2013
Timor–Leste	National data not available					2013
International network	ANSORP[d]	4.5	400		2003–2005	2009

a. National data refers to data returned on the questionnaires as defined in Annex 1. This definition does not imply that the data collected is representative for that country as a whole because information gaps are likely.

b. See Annex 1 for definitions.

c. "National data not available" means that there was information that no data were available; "No information obtained for this report" means that no information was obtained from authorities, networks or publications.

d. Some centres from the following countries, territories and areas participate in some ANSORP (Asian Network for Surveillance of Resistant Pathogens) projects: India, Indonesia, Japan, Malaysia, Philippines, Republic of Korea, Singapore, Sri Lanka, Saudi Arabia, Thailand, Viet Nam, in addition to China, Hong Kong SAR (Special Administrative Region) and Taiwan, China.

Table A2.42 Nontyphoidal *Salmonella* (NTS): Resistance to fluoroquinolones
Western Pacific Region

Countries, territories and other areas or groupings	Data source[a, b, c]	Resistance (%)	No. tested isolates	Type of surveillance, population or samples[b]	Period for data collection	Year of publication or report
Australia	National data not available					2013
Brunei Darussalam	National data (hospital laboratory)	0	51	Comprehensive	2012	2013
Cambodia	National data[d] collected by public health institute (NIPH)	2.3	88	Blood and stool samples	2007–2013	2013
China	National data	11.9	177		2011	2013
Cook Islands	No information obtained for this report					
Fiji	National data compilation not available					2013
Fiji	Institute surveillance[d,e]	0.3	383		2012	2013
Japan	National data	2	1966	Comprehensive	2011	2013
Kiribati	National data	0	1	Comprehensive	2013	2013
Lao People's Democratic Republic	National data	1.3	75		2012–2013	2013
Lao People's Democratic Republic	Institute surveillance	9.1	11	Comprehensive	2011–2012	2013
Malaysia	National data	1.3	1787	Comprehensive	2012	2013
Marshall Islands	National data not available					2013
Micronesia	National data		≤30	Comprehensive	2011	2013
Mongolia	No information obtained for this report					
Nauru	No information obtained for this report					
New Zealand	National data	0.5	222	Clinical isolates		2013
Niue	No information obtained for this report					
Palau	No information obtained for this report					
Papua New Guinea	National data	33.3	15	Blood and stool isolates	2012	2013
Philippines	National data	14.3	98	Comprehensive	2012	2013
Republic of Korea	National data not available					2013
Republic of Korea	National network	0	38	Laboratory network, comprehensive	2012	2013
Samoa	National data	0	102	Blood and stool isolates	2011	2013
Singapore[f]	National data not available					2013
Solomon Islands	National data not available					2013
Tonga	National data not available					2013
Tuvalu	No information obtained for this report					
Vanuatu	No information obtained for this report					
Viet Nam	No information obtained for this report[f]					
International network	ANSORP[g]	4.5	400		2003–2005	2009

a. National data refers to data returned on the questionnaires as defined in Annex 1. This definition does not imply that the data collected is representative for that country as a whole because information gaps are likely.

b. See Annex 1 for definitions.

c. "National data not available" means that there was information that no data were available; "No information obtained for this report" means that no information was obtained from authorities, networks or publications.

d. Data were provided, but no formal national data compilation was available.

e. Data from two hospitals aggregated.

f. Some centres participate in some ANSORP (Asian Network for Surveillance of Resistant Pathogens) projects.

g. Some centres from the following countries, territories and areas participate in some ANSORP projects: India, Indonesia, Japan, Malaysia, Philippines, Republic of Korea, Singapore, Sri Lanka, Saudi Arabia, Thailand, Viet Nam, in addition to China, Hong Kong SAR (Special Administrative Region) and Taiwan, China.

Annex 2

Table A2.43 *Shigella* species: Resistance to fluoroquinolones
African Region

Countries, territories and other areas or groupings	Data source[a, b, c]	Resistance (%)	No. tested isolates	Type of surveillance, population or samples[b]	Period for data collection	Year of publication or report
Algeria	No information obtained for this report					
Angola	No information obtained for this report					
Benin	National data	0	1	Invasive	2012	2013
Botswana	National data	2.9	34	Stool samples	2012	2013
Burkina Faso	National data not available					2013
Burkina Faso	Publication (*261*)	0	16	Children with diarrhoea	2009–2010	2013
Burundi	National data not available					2013
Cameroon	No information obtained for this report					
Cabo Verde	No information obtained for this report					
Central African Republic	National data	0	60	Comprehensive	2012	
Chad	No information obtained for this report					
Comoros	No information obtained for this report					
Congo	National data not available					2013
Côte d'Ivoire	No information obtained for this report					
Democratic Republic of the Congo	No information obtained for this report					
Equatorial Guinea	No information obtained for this report					
Eritrea	No information obtained for this report					
Ethiopia	National data	0	7	Comprehensive	2012	2013
Ethiopia	Publication (*282*)	9.2	65	Patients with diarrrhoea, teaching hospital	2005	2008
Ethiopia	Publication (*263*)	0	76	Children with and without diarrhoea	1992–1993	2008
Ethiopia	Publication (*283*)	2.2	90	Hospital patients	2006–2008	2009
Ethiopia	Publication (*264*)	8.9	214	Hospital patients		2008
Gabon	No information obtained for this report					
Gambia	National data not available					2013
Ghana	National data not available					2013
Ghana	Publication (*284*)	0	5	Children with and without diarrhoea		2008
Guinea	National data not available					2013
Guinea-Bissau	National data not available					2013
Kenya	National data not available					2013
Kenya	National network[d]	0	1	Targeted	2013	2013
Kenya	Publication (*285*)	1	181	Population based surveillance	2006–2009	2009
Kenya	Publication (*286*)	1	224	Population based surveillance	2007–2011	2013
Lesotho	National data	0	1		2012	2013
Liberia	National data	0	3	Targeted	2012	2013
Madagascar	No information obtained for this report					
Malawi	National data not available					2013
Mali	No information obtained for this report					
Mauritania	National data not available					2013
Mauritius	National data	25	4	All stool isolates	2012	2013
Mozambique	Publication (*268*)	0	109	Children with diarrhoea	2001–2003	2009
Namibia	National data	1	58		2012	2013
Niger	National data not available					2013
Nigeria	No information obtained for this report					
Rwanda	No information obtained for this report					
Sao Tome and Principe	National data not available					2013
Senegal	Publication (*287*)	0.6	165	Outpatients	2004–2006	2008

Countries, territories and other areas or groupings	Data source[a, b, c]	Resistance (%)	No. tested isolates	Type of surveillance, population or samples[b]	Period for data collection	Year of publication or report
Seychelles	No information obtained for this report					
Sierra Leone	No information obtained for this report					
South Africa	National data	0.06	1639	Comprehensive	2012	2013
South Sudan	National data not available					2013
Swaziland	National data not available					2013
Togo	No information obtained for this report					
Uganda	National data	0	3	Comprehensive	2012	2013
United Republic of Tanzania	National data not available					2013
United Republic of Tanzania	Publication (*17*)	0	15	Hospitalized children with diarrhoea	2005–2006	2011
Zambia	National data	15.4	28	Targeted	2012	2013
Zimbabwe	National data	0	15	Comprehensive	2013	2013

a. National data refers to data returned on the questionnaires as defined in Annex 1. This definition does not imply that the data collected is representative for that country as a whole because information gaps are likely.

b. See Annex 1 for definitions.

c. "National data not available" means that there was information that no data were available; "No information obtained for this report" means that no information was obtained from authorities, networks or publications.

d. Global Disease Detection Center, Kenya/Division of Global Health Protection/Center for Global Health/CDC (US Centers for Disease Control and Prevention).

Annex 2

Table A2.44 *Shigella* species: Resistance to fluoroquinolones
Region of the Americas

Countries, territories and other areas or groupings	Data source[a, b, c]	Resistance (%)	No. tested isolates	Type of surveillance, population or samples[b]	Period for data collection	Year of publication or report
Antigua and Barbuda	No information obtained for this report					
Argentina	National data	0.1	2288	*S. flexneri* + *S. sonnei*	2010	2013
Bahamas	No information obtained for this report					
Barbados	No information obtained for this report					
Belize	No information obtained for this report					
Bolivia (Plurinational State of)	National data	3	122		2010	2013
Brazil	National data	1.3	77	Community isolates (*S. flexneri* + *S. sonnei*)	2010	2013
Canada	National data not available					2013
Canada	Publication (*288*)	14.9 (*S. sonnei*); 20.1 (*S. flexneri*)	222 (*S. sonnei*); 164 (*S. flexneri*)	Travel related cases	2002–2007	2010
Chile	National data	8	51	Community isolates (*S. flexneri*)	2010	2013
Colombia	National data	0	286	*S. flexneri* + *S. sonnei*	2010	2013
Costa Rica	National data	0	148	*S. boydii* + *S. flexneri* + *S. sonnei*	2010	2013
Cuba	National data	0	50	Community isolates	2009	2013
Dominica	No information obtained for this report					
Dominican Republic	National data	2	20	Community isolates	2009	2013
Ecuador	National data	0	55	*S. boydii* + *S. flexneri* + *S. sonnei*	2010	2013
El Salvador	National data	0	39	*S. flexneri* + *S. sonnei*	2010	2013
Grenada	No information obtained for this report					
Guatemala	National data	0	3	*S. flexneri*	2010	2013
Guyana	No information obtained for this report					
Haiti	No information obtained for this report					
Honduras	National data	4	52	Community isolates	2010	2013
Jamaica	No information obtained for this report					
Mexico	National data	0	2	Community isolates	2010	2013
Nicaragua	National data	0	6	Community isolates	2010	2013
Panama	National data	0	19	Community isolates	2010	2013
Panama	National network	3	27	Comprehensive	2011–2012	2013
Paraguay	National data	0	153	*S. flexneri* + *S. sonnei*	2010	2013
Peru	National data	0	121	*S. flexneri*	2010	2013
Peru	National network	1	117	Comprehensive	2012	2013
Saint Kitts and Nevis	No information obtained for this report					
Saint Lucia	No information obtained for this report					
Saint Vicent and the Grenadines	No information obtained for this report					
Suriname	No information obtained for this report					
Trinidad and Tobago	No information obtained for this report					
United States of America	National data	2	407		2010	2013
Uruguay	National data not available					2013
Uruguay	Publication (*289*)	0	51	Children with bloody diarrhoea	2001–2008	2010
Venezuela (Bolivarian Republic of)	National data	0	51	Community isolates	2010	2013

a. National data refers to data returned on the questionnaires as defined in Annex 1. This definition does not imply that the data collected is representative for that country as a whole because information gaps are likely.

b. See Annex 1 for definitions.

c. "National data not available" means that there was information that no data were available; "No information obtained for this report" means that no information was obtained from authorities, networks or publications.

Table A2.45 *Shigella* species: Resistance to fluoroquinolones
Eastern Mediterranean Region

Countries, territories and other areas or groupings	Data source[a, b, c]	Resistance (%)	No. tested isolates	Type of surveillance, population or samples[b]	Period for data collection	Year of publication or report
Afghanistan	No information obtained for this report					
Bahrain	National data not available					2013
Djibouti	No information obtained for this report					
Egypt	National data not available					2013
Iran (Islamic Republic of)	National data	2.7	260	Targeted	2012	2013
Iraq	No information obtained for this report					
Jordan	National data not available					2013
Kuwait	Publication (*290*)	0	42	Patients with diarrhoea	2003–2005	2010
Lebanon	National data not available					2013
Libya	No information obtained for this report					
Morocco	National data not available					2013
Oman	National data not available					2013
Oman	Publication (*291*)	0	91	Children	2000–2002	2008
Pakistan	National data, incomplete	5				2013
Pakistan	Publication (*292*)	3.3	394	Patients with diarrhoea	2002–2004	2009
Pakistan	Publication (*293*)	1.7	1573	Symptomatic	1996–2007	2009
Pakistan	Publication (*294*)	0	40	Children with diarrhoea		2011
Qatar	No information obtained for this report					
Saudi Arabia	No information obtained for this report[d]					
Somalia	No information obtained for this report					
Sudan	National data not available					2013
Sudan	Publication (*295*)	41.3	46	Patients with diarrhoea	2006–2007	2009
Syrian Arab Republic	National data not available					2013
Tunisia	No information obtained for this report					
United Arab Emirates	National data[f]	10.2	49	Comprehensive	2012	2013
Yemen	No information obtained for this report					
International network	ANSORP[f]	10	98	Comprehensive	2001–2004	2008

a. National data refers to data returned on the questionnaires as defined in Annex 1. This definition does not imply that the data collected is representative for that country as a whole because information gaps are likely.

b. See Annex 1 for definitions.

c. "National data not available" means that there was information that no data were available; "No information obtained for this report" means that no information was obtained from authorities, networks or publications.

d. Some centres participate in some ANSORP (Asian Network for Surveillance of Resistant Pathogens) projects.

e. Data from United Arab Emirates originate from Abu Dhabi only.

f. Some centres from the following countries, territories and areas participate in some ANSORP projects: India, Indonesia, Japan, Malaysia, Philippines, Republic of Korea, Singapore, Sri Lanka, Saudi Arabia, Taiwan, China, Thailand, Viet Nam, in addition to China, Hong Kong SAR (Special Administrative Region) and Taiwan, China.

Table A2.46 *Shigella* species: Resistance to fluoroquinolones
European Region

Countries, territories and other areas or groupings	Data source[a, b, c]	Resistance (%)	No. tested isolates	Type of surveillance, population or samples[b]	Period for data collection	Year of publication or report
Albania	National data not available					2013
Andorra	No information obtained for this report					
Armenia	National data not available					2013
Austria	National data	24.4	45	Stool samples	2011	2013
Azerbaijan	National data not available					2013
Belarus	No information obtained for this report					
Belgium	National data not available					2013
Belgium	Publication (279)	0	43	Returning travelers	2000–2006	2011
Belgium	Publication (296)	0	7307	Shigella sonnei isolates (national reference laboratory)	1990–2007	2009
Bosnia and Herzegovina	No information obtained for this report					
Bulgaria	National data not available					2013
Croatia	National data	13	24	Comprehensive		
Cyprus	National data not available					2013
Czech Republic	National data not available					2013
Denmark	National data not available					2013
Estonia	National data not available					2013
Finland	National data	46.9	98	Comprehensive	2012	2013
France	National data not available					2013
Georgia	National data	0	31	Comprehensive	2012	2013
Germany	National data not available					2013
Greece	National data	0	59	Comprehensive	2012	2013
Hungary	National data not available					2013
Iceland	National data not available					2013
Ireland	National data	13	30	Stool samples	2011	2013
Israel	No information obtained for this report					
Italy	National data not available					2013
Kazakhstan	No information obtained for this report					
Kyrgyzstan	National data not available					2013
Latvia	National data not available					2013
Lithuania	National data not available					2013
Luxembourg	National data not available					2013
Malta	National data not available					2013
Monaco	No information obtained for this report					
Montenegro	National data not available					2013
Netherlands	National data not available					2013
Norway	National data	14.4	111	Comprehensive	2011	2013
Poland	National data not available					2013
Portugal	National data not available					2013
Republic of Moldova	National data	9.2	324		2012	2013
Romania	National data not available					2013
Russian Federation	National data not available					2013
San Marino	No information obtained for this report					
Serbia	National data	0.5	382	Comprehensive	2005–2011	2013
Slovakia	National data not available					2013
Slovenia	National data not available					2013
Spain	National data not available					2013
Sweden	National data not available					2013
Switzerland	National data	13.2	53	Comprehensive	2012	2013
Tajikistan	No information obtained for this report					
The former Yugoslav Republic of Macedonia	National data not available					2013
Turkey	National data	0	108	Comprehensive	2011	2013
Turkmenistan	No information obtained for this report					
Ukraine	No information obtained for this report					
United Kingdom	National data not available					2013
Uzbekistan	No information obtained for this report					

a. National data refers to data returned on the questionnaires as defined in Annex 1. This definition does not imply that the data collected is representative for that country as a whole because information gaps are likely.

b. See Annex 1 for definitions.

c. "National data not available" means that there was information that no data were available; "No information obtained for this report" means that no information was obtained from authorities, networks or publications.

Table A2.47 *Shigella* species: Resistance to fluoroquinolones
South East Asian Region

Countries, territories and other areas or groupings	Data source[a, b, c]	Resistance (%)	No. tested isolates	Type of surveillance, population or samples[b]	Period for data collection	Year of publication or report
Bangladesh	National data not available					2013
Bangladesh	Publication (*281*)	8.5	634	Patients with diarrhoea	2005–2008	2012
Bhutan	National data not available					2013
Democratic People's Republic of Korea	No information obtained for this report					
India	National data not available					2013
India	Publication (*297*)	82	50	Children with diarrhoea	2006–2009	2012
India	Publication (*298*)	0	73	Children with diarrhoea	2009–2012	2012
India	Publication (*299*)	71	88	Stool samples	2003–2007	2008
India	Publication (*300*)	47.4	59	Children with diarrhoea	(2001–2006)–2007[d]	2010
India	Publication (*301*)	50	74	Patients with diarrhoea	2008–2010	2012
India	Publication (*302*)	48	154 (all years)	Patients with dysentery	(2002)–2007	2009
India	Publication (*303*)	11.2	71	Patients with diarrhoea	2008–2010	2013
Indonesia	National data not available[e]					2013
Maldives	No information obtained for this report					
Myanmar	National data not available					2013
Nepal	National data	17	14	Comprehensive	2012	2013
Nepal	Publication (*304*)	5.7	35	Children with diarrhoea	2007	2009
Nepal	Publication (*305*)	0	51	Traveller's diarrhoea	2001–2003	2011
Nepal	Publication (*306*)	17	41	NRL	2002–2004	2011
Sri Lanka	National data not available					2013
Thailand	National data, incomplete		76	Comprehensive	2012	2013
Timor-Leste	National data not available					2013
International network	ANSORP[f]	10	98	Comprehensive	2001–2004	2008

a. National data refers to data returned on the questionnaires as defined in Annex 1. This definition does not imply that the data collected is representative for that country as a whole because information gaps are likely.

b. See Annex 1 for definitions.

c. "National data not available" means that there was information that no data were available; "No information obtained for this report" means that no information was obtained from authorities, networks or publications.

d. For data from time periods of several years, or where data from a subset of year(s) were available, the format (2001)–2011, indicates the first year of data collection within parenthesis, and the most recent year with separate data outside the parenthesis.

e. Some centres participate in some ANSORP (Asian Network for Surveillance of Resistant Pathogens) projects.

f. Some centres from the following countries, territories and areas participate in some ANSORP projects: India, Indonesia, Japan, Malaysia, Philippines, Republic of Korea, Singapore, Sri Lanka, Saudi Arabia, Taiwan, China, Thailand, Viet Nam, in addition to China, Hong Kong SAR (Special Administrative Region) and Taiwan, China.

Annex 2

Table A2.48 *Shigella:* Resistance to fluoroquinolones
Western Pacific Region

Countries, territories and other areas or groupings	Data source[a, b, c]	Resistance (%)	No. tested isolates	Type of surveillance, population or samples[b]	Period for data collection	Year of publication or report
Australia	National data not available					2013
Brunei Darussalam	National data not available		0			2013
Cambodia	National data[d] collected from several sources by public health institute	11.8	76	Stool samples	2008–2013	2013
China	National data	27.9 (cip); 9.7 (lev)	308	Comprehensive	2011	2013
Cook Islands	No information obtained for this report					
Fiji	National data compilation not available					2013
Fiji	Institute surveillance[d,e]	0	102		2012	2013
Japan	National data not available					2013
Kiribati	National data not available					2013
Lao People's Democratic Republic	National data[d]	0	33		2013	2013
Malaysia	National data	2.9	35	All isolates	2012	2013
Marshall Islands	National data not available					2013
Micronesia	National data	"Insignificant"	≤30	Comprehensive	2011	2013
Mongolia	No information obtained for this report					
Nauru	No information obtained for this report					
New Zealand	National data not available					2013
Niue	No information obtained for this report					
Palau	No information obtained for this report					
Papua New Guinea	National data	0	53	Stool samples	2012	2013
Philippines	National data	44.4	9	Comprehensive	2012	2013
Republic of Korea	National data not available					
Samoa	National data	0	2	Stool samples	2011	2013
Singapore	National data not available					2013
Solomon Islands	National data not available					2013
Tonga	National data, incomplete	0			2012	2013
Tuvalu	No information obtained for this report					
Vanuatu	No information obtained for this report					
Viet Nam	Publication (*307*)	2	103	Stool samples	2006–2008	2009
International	ANSORP[g] (*308*)	10	98	Comprehensive	2001–2004	2008

cip, ciprofloxacin; lev, levofloxacin.

a. National data refers to data returned on the questionnaires as defined in Annex 1. This definition does not imply that the data collected is representative for that country as a whole because information gaps are likely.

b. See Annex 1 for definitions.

c. "National data not available" means that there was information that no data were available; "No information obtained for this report" means that no information was obtained from authorities, networks or publications.

d. Data were provided, but no formal national data compilation was available.

e. Data from two hospitals aggregated. One hospital included all isolates, the other hospital did not specify.

f. No information obtained, or incomplete.

g. Some centres from the following countries, territories and areas participate in some ANSORP projects: India, Indonesia, Japan, Malaysia, Philippines, Republic of Korea, Singapore, Sri Lanka, Saudi Arabia, Taiwan, China, Thailand, Viet Nam, in addition to China, Hong Kong SAR (Special Administrative Region) and Taiwan, China.

Table A2.49 *Neisseria gonorrhoeae:* Decreased susceptibility to third-generation cephalosporins[a]
African Region

Countries, territories and other areas or groupings	Data source[b, c, d]	Resistance (%)	No. tested isolates	Type of surveillance, population or samples[c]	Period for data collection	Year of publication or report
Algeria	No information obtained for this report					
Angola	No information obtained for this report					
Benin	National data, incomplete					2013
Botswana	National data not available					2013
Burkina Faso	National data not available					2013
Burundi	National data not available					2013
Cameroon	Data from international publication (*309*)	0	79		2004–2005	2008
Cabo Verde	No information obtained for this report					
Central African Republic	National data	0	1		2013	2013
Central African Republic	Data from international publication (*309*)	0	39		2004–2005	2008
Chad	No information obtained for this report					
Comoros	No information obtained for this report					
Congo	National data not available					2013
Côte d'Ivoire	Report to GASP[e]	"NC"	12	Sentinel site	2010	2013
Democratic Republic of the Congo	No information obtained for this report					
Equatorial Guinea	No information obtained for this report					
Eritrea	No information obtained for this report					
Ethiopia	National data not available					2013
Gabon	No information obtained for this report					
Gambia	National data not available					2013
Ghana	National data not available					2013
Guinea	National data not available					2013
Guinea-Bissau	Report to GASP	0	6			2013
Kenya	Publication (*310*)	0	168	Men undergoing circumcision	2002–2009	2011
Lesotho	Report to GASP	0	1		2012	2013
Liberia	National data not available					2013
Madagascar	Data from international publication (*309*)	0	126		2004–2005	2008
Malawi	National data	0	0	Comprehensive	2013	2013
Mali	No information obtained for this report					
Mauritania	Report to GASP	0	2	Comprehensive	2013	2013
Mauritius	Report to GASP	0	24	Comprehensive	2012	2013
Mozambique	Publication (*311*)	0	22	Cross-sectional study		2009
Namibia	Report to GASP	0	3		2012	2013
Niger	National data not available					2013
Nigeria	No information obtained for this report					
Rwanda	No information obtained for this report					
Sao Tome and Principe	National data not available					2013
Senegal	No information obtained for this report					
Seychelles	No information obtained for this report					
Sierra Leone	No information obtained for this report					
South Africa	Report to GASP	0	120	Comprehensive	2012	2013
South Sudan	National data not available					2013
Swaziland	National data not available					2013
Togo	No information obtained for this report					
Uganda	National data not available					2013
Uganda	Publication (*312*)	0	151		2007–2011	2012

Countries, territories and other areas or groupings	Data source[b, c, d]	Resistance (%)	No. tested isolates	Type of surveillance, population or samples[c]	Period for data collection	Year of publication or report
United Republic of Tanzania	National data not available					2013
Zambia	National data not available					2013
Zimbabwe	National data	12.3	57	Comprehensive	2012	2013

a. cfm, cefixim; cro, ceftriaxone
b. National data refers to data returned on the questionnaires as defined in Annex 1. This definition does not imply that the data collected is representative for that country as a whole because information gaps are likely.
c. See Annex 1 for definitions.
d. "National data not available" means that there was information that no data were available; "No information obtained for this report" means that no information was obtained from authorities, networks or publications.
e. GASP, Gonococcal Antimicrobial Surveillance Programme.

Table A2.50 *Neisseria gonorrhoeae:* Decreased susceptibility to third-generation cephalosporins[a]
Region of the Americas

Countries, territories and other areas or groupings	Data source[b, c, d]	Resistance (%)	No. tested isolates	Type of surveillance, population or samples[c]	Period for data collection	Year of publication or report
Antigua and Barbuda	No information obtained for this report					
Argentina	Report to GASP[e]	0	316	Sentinel site	2010	2013
Bahamas	No information obtained for this report					
Barbados	No information obtained for this report					
Belize	No information obtained for this report					
Bolivia (Plurinational State of)	National data not available					2013
Brazil	National data not available					2013
Canada	Report to GASP	31	155	Comprehensive	2010	2012
Chile	Report to GASP	0	508		2010	2013
Colombia	Report to GASP	Not tested	45		2010	2013
Costa Rica	National data not available					2013
Cuba	National data not available					2013
Dominica	No information obtained for this report					
Dominican Republic	National data	0	3			2013
Ecuador	Report to GASP	0	6		2010	2013
El Salvador	Report to GASP	0	14		2010	2013
Grenada	No information obtained for this report					
Guatemala	National data not available					2013
Guyana	No information obtained for this report					
Haiti	No information obtained for this report					
Honduras	National data not available					2013
Jamaica	No information obtained for this report					
Mexico	National data not available					2013
Nicaragua	National data not available					2013
Panama	Report to GASP	0	1		2010	2013
Panama	National network	0	10	Comprehensive	2011–2012	2013
Paraguay	National data	0	13		2010	2013
Peru	National data not available					2013
Saint Kitts and Nevis	No information obtained for this report					
Saint Lucia	No information obtained for this report					
Saint Vicent and the Grenadines	No information obtained for this report					
Suriname	No information obtained for this report					
Trinidad and Tobago	No information obtained for this report					
United States of America	National data – GISP[e] –reported to GASP	1.4 (cfm), 0.4 (cro)	5467	Comprehensive	2011	2012
Uruguay	National data not available					2013
Venezuela (Bolivarian Republic of)	Report to GASP	0	14		2010	2013
International	Publication (*313*)	7	110		2000–2009	2012

a. cfm, cefixim; cro, ceftriaxon.
b. National data refers to data returned on the questionnaires as defined in Annex 1. This definition does not imply that the data collected is representative for that country as a whole because information gaps are likely.
c. See Annex 1 for definitions.
d. "National data not available" means that there was information that no data were available; "No information obtained for this report" means that no information was obtained from authorities, networks or publications.
e. GASP, Gonococcal Antimicrobial Surveillance Programme.
f. GISP, Gonococcal Isolate Surveillance Project.

Table A2.51 *Neisseria gonorrhoeae:* **Decreased susceptibility to third-generation cephalosporins[a]**
Eastern Mediterranen region

Countries, territories and other areas or groupings	Data source[b, c, d]	Resistance (%)	No. tested isolates	Type of surveillance, population or samples[c]	Period for data collection	Year of publication or report
Afghanistan	No information obtained for this report					
Bahrain	Report to GASP[e]	0	41		2012	2013
Djibouti	No information obtained for this report					
Egypt	National data not available					2013
Iran (Islamic Republic of)	National data not available					2013
Iraq	No information obtained for this report					
Jordan	National data not available					2013
Kuwait	No information obtained for this report					
Lebanon	National data not available					2013
Libya	No information obtained for this report					
Morocco	Report to GASP	0	72	National survey	2009	2013
Oman	National data not available					
Pakistan	National data, incomplete	12		Targeted		2013
Pakistan	Publication (*314*)	0	106	Clinical samples	(1992)–2007–2009[f]	2011
Qatar	No information obtained for this report					
Saudi Arabia	Publication (*315*)	0	8	Random samples from pregnant women	2005–2006	2010
Somalia	No information obtained for this report					
Sudan	National data not available					2013
Syrian Arab Republic	National data not available					2013
Tunisia	No information obtained for this report					
United Arab Emirates	National data not available					2013
Yemen	No information obtained for this report					

a. cfm, cefixim; cro, ceftriaxon.
b. National data refers to data returned on the questionnaires as defined in Annex 1. This definition does not imply that the data collected is representative for that country as a whole because information gaps are likely.
c. See Annex 1 for definitions.
d. "National data not available" means that there was information that no data were available; "No information obtained for this report" means that no information was obtained from authorities, networks or publications.
e. GASP, Gonococcal Antimicrobial Surveillance Programme.
f. For data from time periods of several years, or where data from a subset of year(s) were available, the format (2001)–2011, indicates the first year of data collection within parenthesis, and the most recent year with separate data outside the parenthesis.

Table A2.52 *Neisseria gonorrhoeae:* Decreased susceptibility to third-generation cephalosporins[a]
European Region

Countries, territories and other areas or groupings	Data source[b, c, d]	Resistance (%)	No. tested isolates	Type of surveillance, population or samples[c]	Period for data collection	Year of publication or report
Albania	National data not available					2013
Andorra	No information obtained for this report					
Armenia	National data not available					2013
Austria	Report to EURO-GASP[e]	13.2	106	Comprehensive	2011	2013
Azerbaijan	National data not available					2013
Belarus	Publication (*316*)	0	80	Clinical isolates	2009	2011
Belgium	Report to EURO-GASP	0.9	110	Comprehensive	2011	2013
Bosnia and Herzegovina	No information obtained for this report					
Bulgaria	National data not available					2013
Croatia	National data not available					
Cyprus	Report to EURO-GASP	10	10	Comprehensive	2011	2013
Czech Republic	National data not available					2013
Denmark	Report to EURO-GASP	25	110	Comprehensive	2011	2013
Estonia	National data not available					2013
Finland	National data	2.1	145	Comprehensive	2011	2013
France	Report to EURO-GASP	0	109	Comprehensive	2011	2013
Georgia	National data not available					2013
Germany	Report to EURO-GASP	10.2	108	Comprehensive	2011	2013
Greece	Report to EURO-GASP	3.0	100	Comprehensive	2011	2013
Hungary	National data not available					2013
Iceland	National data not available					2013
Ireland	Report to EURO-GASP	3.1	64	Comprehensive	2011	2013
Israel	Publication (*317*)	0.0	406	STI patients	2002–2007	2010
Italy	Report to EURO-GASP	3.0	99	Comprehensive	2011	2013
Kazakhstan	No information obtained for this report					
Kyrgyzstan	National data not available					2013
Latvia	Report to EURO-GASP	0.0	28	Comprehensive	2011	2013
Lithuania	National data not available					2013
Luxembourg	National data not available					2013
Malta	Report to EURO-GASP	7.7	13	Comprehensive	2011	2013
Monaco	No information obtained for this report					
Montenegro	National data not available					2013
Netherlands	Report to EURO-GASP	0.0	217	Comprehensive	2011	2013
Norway	Report to EURO-GASP	1.3	77	Comprehensive	2011	2013
Poland	National data not available					2013
Portugal	Report to EURO-GASP	0.0	109	Comprehensive	2011	2013
Republic of Moldova	National data not available					2013
Romania	Report to EURO-GASP	15.4	26	Comprehensive	2011	2013
Russian Federation	Publication (*318*)	0.0	407	Surveillance sites	2010	2011
San Marino	No information obtained for this report					
Serbia	National data not available					2013
Slovakia	Report to EURO-GASP	36.3	113	Comprehensive	2011	2013
Slovenia	Report to EURO-GASP	36.8	19	Comprehensive	2011	2013
Spain	Report to EURO-GASP	15.0	100	Comprehensive	2011	2013
Sweden	Report to EURO-GASP	7.6	105	Comprehensive	2011	2013
Switzerland	National data	1.9	107	Targeted	2012	2013
Tajikistan	No information obtained for this report					
The former Yugoslav Republic of Macedonia	National data not available					2013
Turkey	National data not available					2013
Turkmenistan	No information obtained for this report					
Ukraine	No information obtained for this report					
United Kingdom	Report - GRASP[f]- to EURO-GASP	2.8	251	Comprehensive	2011	2013
Uzbekistan	No information obtained for this report					
International	International publication/EURO GASP (*319*)	0,0	1285	Laboratory study	2006–2008	2010

a. cro, ceftriaxon; cfm, cefixim.
b. National data refers to data returned on the questionnaires as defined in Annex 1. This definition does not imply that the data collected is representative for that country as a whole because information gaps are likely.
c. See Annex 1 for definitions.
d. "National data not available" means that there was information that no data were available; "No information obtained for this report" means that no information was obtained from authorities, networks or publications.
e. GASP, Gonococcal Antimicrobial Surveillance Programme. EURO-GASP data forwarded by ECDC (European Centre for Disease Prevention and Control) or from GASP.
f. GRASP, The Gonococcal Resistance to Antimicrobials Surveillance Programme.

Table A2.53 *Neisseria gonorrhoeae:* Decreased susceptibility to third-generation cephalosporins[a]
South East Asian Region

Countries, territories and other areas or groupings	Data source[b, c, d]	Resistance (%)	No. tested isolates	Type of surveillance, population or samples[c]	Period for data collection	Year of publication or report
Bangladesh	National data not available					2013
Bhutan	Report to GASP[e]	2.2	181		2010	2012
Bhutan	National data	0.16	1111	Comprehensive	2008–2012	2013
Democratic People's Republic of Korea	No information obtained for this report					
India	Report to GASP (*320*)	3.9	51	Comprehensive	2010	2012
Indonesia	Report to GASP	1,92 (cfm); 2.88 (cro)	218	Sex workers	2013	2013
Maldives	No information obtained for this report					
Myanmar	National data	18	22		2012	2013
Nepal	National data	0	7	Comprehensive	2012	2013
Sri Lanka	Report to GASP (*320*)	0	75	Comprehensive	2010	2012
Thailand	Report to GASP	0	213	Comprehensive	2012	2013
Timor-Leste	National data not available					2013

a. cfm, cefixim; cro, ceftriaxon.

b. National data refers to data returned on the questionnaires as defined in Annex 1. This definition does not imply that the data collected is representative for that country as a whole because information gaps are likely.

c. See Annex 1 for definitions.

d. "National data not available" means that there was information that no data were available; "No information obtained for this report" means that no information was obtained from authorities, networks or publications.

e. GASP, Gonococcal Antimicrobial Surveillance Programme.

Table A2.54 *Neisseria gonorrhoeae:* **Decreased susceptibility to third-generation cephalosporins**[a]
Western Pacific Region

Countries, territories and other areas or groupings	Data source[b, c, d]	Resistance (%)	No. tested isolates	Type of surveillance, population or samples[c]	Period for data collection	Year of publication or report
Australia	National data[e]	3.6 (urban), 0.4 (remote)	3647 (urban), 459 (remote)	Comprehensive	2012	2013
Brunei Darussalam	Report to GASP[f]	1.0	295	Comprehensive	2011	2013
Brunei Darussalam	National data	0.96	207	Comprehensive	2012	2013
Cambodia	National data not available					2013
Cambodia	Report to GASP	NI	6	Sentinel site	2010	2012
China	Report to GASP	21 (Mainland), 1.6 (Hong Kong SAR (Special Administrative Region))	1349 (Mainland); 1225 (Hong Kong SAR)	Comprehensive	2011	2013
China	National data	0.8 (Mainland), 3.8 (Hong Kong SAR)	NI (Mainland); 569 (Hong Kong SAR)		2006 (mainland), 2010 (Hong Kong)	
Cook Islands	No information obtained for this report					
Fiji	Report to GASP	0.4	541*		2010	2012
Japan	Report to GASP (*320*)	4.8	441	Comprehensive	2011	2013
Kiribati	National data	–	0			2013
Lao People's Democratic Republic	National data	0	24		2012–2013	2013
Malaysia	National data	1.8	109	Comprehensive	2012	2013
Marshall Islands	National data not available					
Micronesia	National data	"Insignificant"	<30	Comprehensive	2011	2013
Mongolia	Report to GASP	30.7	150		2010	2012
Nauru	No information obtained for this report					
New Caledonia	Report to GASP (*320*)	0	81	Comprehensive	2010	2012
New Zealand	Report to GASP (*320*)	3.2	317	Comprehensive	2010	2012
Niue	No information obtained for this report					
Palau	No information obtained for this report					
Papua New Guinea	National data not available					2013
Papua New Guinea	Report to GASP		0			2013
Philippines	Report to GASP (*320*)	0	34	Sentinel site	2011	
Republic of Korea	Data to GASP	25	64	Comprehensive	2011	2013
Republic of Korea	National data	0	61	Comprehensive	2011	2013
Republic of Korea	Surveillance network	0	91	Comprehensive	2012	2013
Samoa	National data	0	5	Sexually transmitted infection (STI) clinics	2011	2013
Singapore	Report to GASP	6.9	160	Comprehensive	2010	2012
Singapore	National data	14.1	148	STI clinics	2012	2013
Solomon Islands	National data	10	10		2012	2013
Tonga	Report to GASP (*320*)	0	4	Comprehensive	2010	2012
Tonga	National data, incomplete	0			2012	2013
Tuvalu	No information obtained for this report					
Vanuatu	No information obtained for this report					
Viet Nam	Report to GASP	1.3	75	Sentinel site	2011	2013

a. cro, ceftriaxone; cfm, cefixim.

b. National data refers to data returned on the questionnaires as defined in Annex 1. This definition does not imply that the data collected is representative for that country as a whole because information gaps are likely.

c. See Annex 1 for definitions.

d. "National data not available" means that there was information that no data were available; "No information obtained for this report" means that no information was obtained from authorities, networks or publications.

e. Data from two surveillance systems.

f. GASP, Gonococcal Antimicrobial Surveillance Programme.

A2.55 References

1. Borg MA, van de Sande-Bruinsma N, Scicluna E, de Kraker M, Tiemersma E, Monen J et al. Antimicrobial resistance in invasive strains of *Escherichia coli* from southern and eastern Mediterranean laboratories. *Clin Microbiol Infect*, 2008, 14(8):789-796. (http://www.ncbi.nlm.nih.gov/pubmed/18727803, accessed 7 April 2014).

2. Maina D, Paul Makau P, Nyerere A, Revathi G. Antimicrobial resistance patterns in ESBL producing *E. coli* and *K. pneumoniae* isolates in a private tertiary hospital, Kenya. *Histopathology*, 2012, 61:153-154. (http://www.hoajonline.com/microbiology/2052-6180/1/5, accessed 7 April 2014).

3. Randrianirina F, Vaillant L, Ramarokoto CE, Rakotoarijaona A, Andriamanarivo ML, Razafimahandry HC et al. Antimicrobial resistance in pathogens causing nosocomial infections in surgery and intensive care units of two hospitals in Antananarivo, Madagascar. *J Infect Dev Ctries*, 2010, 4(2):74-82. (http://www.ncbi.nlm.nih.gov/pubmed/20212337, accessed 12 January 2014).

4. Nwadioha S, Nwokedi I, Odimayo M, Okwori E, Kashibui E. Bacterial isolates in blood cultures of children with suspected septicaemia in a Nigerian tertiary hospital. *Internet J Inf Dis*, 2010, 8(1). (http://ispub.com/IJID/8/1/3350, accessed 7 April 2014).

5. Mordi R, Momoh M. A five year study on the susceptibility of isolates from various parts of the body. *Afr J Biotechnol*, 2008, 7(19):3401-3409. (http://www.ajol.info/index.php/ajb/article/view/59344, accessed 7 April 2014).

6. Okesola AO, Makanjuola O. Resistance to 3 generation cephalosporins and other antibiotics by Enterobacteriaceae in Western Nigeria. *Am J Infect Dis*, 2009, 5(1):17-20. (http://connection.ebscohost.com/c/articles/43899405/resistance-third-generation-cephalosporins-other-antibiotics-by-enterobacteriaceae-western-nigeria, accessed 7 April 2014).

7. Iroha IR, Adikwu MU, Esimone CO, Aibinu I, Amadi ES. Extended spectrum beta-lactamase ESBL in *E. coli* isolated from a tertiary hospital in Enugu State, Nigeria. *Pak J Med Sci*, 2009, 25(2):279-282. (http://www.pjms.com.pk/issues/aprjun109/article/article23.html, accessed 7 April 2014).

8. Nwadioha S, Nwokedi E, Jombo G, Kashibu E, Alao O. Antibiotics susceptibility pattern of uropathogenic bacterial isolates from community- and hospital-acquired urinary tract infections in a Nigerian tertiary hospital. *Internet J Inf Dis*, 2009, 8(1). (http://ispub.com/IJID/8/1/8393, accessed 1 February 2014).

9. Jombo G, Emanghe U, Amefule E, Damen J. Nosocomial and community acquired uropathogenic isolates of Proteus mirabilis and antimicrobial susceptibility profiles at a university hospital in Sub-Saharan Africa. *Asian Pac J Trop Med*, 2012:7-11. (http://www.apjtcm.com/zz/20121/3.pdf, accessed 7 April 2014).

10. Wariso KT, Siminialayi IM, Odigie JO. Pattern and antibiogram of urinary tract infection at the University of Port Harcourt Teaching Hospital. *Asian Pac J Trop Med*, 2010, 3(1):66-69.

11. Osazuwa F, Osazuwa E, Imade P, Dirisu J, Omoregie R, Okuonghae P et al. Occurrence of extended spectrum producing gram negative bacteria in HIV/AIDS infected patients with urinary and gastrointestinal tract infections in Benin metropolis. *Res J Pharm, Biol Chem Sci*, 2011, 2(2):230–234. (http://www.rjpbcs.com/pdf/2011_2%282%29/29.pdf, accessed 7 April 2014).

12. Imade PE, Eghafona NO. Incidence of bacteremia in antiretroviral-naive HIV-positive children less than five years of age in Benin City, Nigeria. *Libyan J Med*, 2010, 5. (http://www.ncbi.nlm.nih.gov/pubmed/21483552, accessed 19 January 2014).

13. Muvunyi CM, Masaisa F, Bayingana C, Mutesa L, Musemakweri A, Muhirwa G et al. Decreased susceptibility to commonly used antimicrobial agents in bacterial pathogens isolated from urinary tract infections in Rwanda: need for new antimicrobial guidelines. *Am J Trop Med Hyg*, 2011, 84(6):923-928. (http://www.ncbi.nlm.nih.gov/pubmed/21633029, accessed 7 April 2014).

14. Brink A, Feldman C, Richards G, Moolman J, Senekal M. Emergence of extensive drug resistance (XDR) among Gram-negative bacilli in South Africa looms nearer. *S Afr Med J*, 2008, 98(8):586-590. (http://www.ncbi.nlm.nih.gov/pubmed/18928032, accessed 7 April 2014).

15. Brink AJ, Botha RF, Poswa X, Senekal M, Badal RE, Grolman DC et al. Antimicrobial susceptibility of gram-negative pathogens isolated from patients with complicated intra-abdominal infections in South African hospitals (SMART Study 2004-2009): impact of the new carbapenem breakpoints. *Surg Infect*, 2012, 13(1):43-49. (http://www.ncbi.nlm.nih.gov/pubmed/22220506, accessed 7 April 2014).

16. Habte TM, Dube S, Ismail N, Hoosen AA. Hospital and community isolates of uropathogens at a tertiary hospital in South Africa. *S Afr Med J*, 2009, 99(8):584-587. (http://www.ncbi.nlm.nih.gov/pubmed/19908617, accessed 7 April 2014).

17. Moyo SJ, Gro N, Matee MI, Kitundu J, Myrmel H, Mylvaganam H et al. Age specific aetiological agents of diarrhoea in hospitalized children aged less than five years in Dar es Salaam, Tanzania. *BMC Pediatr*, 2011, 11:19. (http://www.ncbi.nlm.nih.gov/pubmed/21345186, accessed 7 April 2014).

18. Rossi F, Garcia P, Ronzon B, Curcio D, Dowzicky MJ. Rates of antimicrobial resistance in Latin America (2004-2007) and in vitro activity of the glycylcycline tigecycline and of other antibiotics. *Braz J Infect Dis*, 2008, 12(5):405-415. (http://www.scielo.br/scielo.php?script=sci_arttext&pid=S1413-86702008000500012&lng=en&nrm=iso&tlng=en, accessed 7 April 2014).

19. Gales AC, Castanheira M, Jones RN, Sader HS. Antimicrobial resistance among Gram-negative bacilli isolated from Latin America: results from SENTRY Antimicrobial Surveillance Program (Latin America, 2008-2010). *Diagn Microbiol Infect Dis*, 2012, 73(4):354-360. (http://www.ncbi.nlm.nih.gov/pubmed/22656912, accessed 7 April 2014).

20. Castro-Orozco R, Barreto-Maya AC, Guzmán-Álvarez H, Ortega-Quiroz RJ, Benítez-Peña L. Patrones de resistencia antimicrobiana en uropatogenos gramnegativos aislados de pacientes ambulatorios y hospitalizados Cartagena, 2005-2008. *Rev Salud Publica*, 2010, 12(6):1010-1019. (http://dx.doi.org/10.1590/S0124-00642010000600013, accessed 8 April 2014).

21. Murillo Llanes J, Varon J, Velarde Felix JS, Gonzalez-Ibarra FP. Antimicrobial resistance of *Escherichia coli* in Mexico: how serious is the problem? *J Infect Dev Ctries*, 2012, 6(2):126-131. (http://www.ncbi.nlm.nih.gov/pubmed/22337840, accessed 8 April 2014).

22. Morfin-Otero R, Tinoco-Favila J, Sader H, Salcido-Gutierrez L, Perez-Gomez H, Gonzalez-Diaz E et al. Resistance trends in gram-negative bacteria: surveillance results from two Mexican hospitals, 2005-2010. *BMC Res Notes*, 2012, 5:277. doi:10.1186/1756-0500-5-277.

23. Akpaka PE, Swanston WH. Phenotypic detection and occurrence of extended-spectrum beta-lactamases in clinical isolates of *Klebsiella pneumoniae* and *Escherichia coli* at a tertiary hospital in Trinidad & Tobago. *Braz J Infect Dis*, 2008, 12(6):516-520. (http://www.ncbi.nlm.nih.gov/pubmed/19287841, accessed 19 January 2014).

24. Seija V, Frantchez V, Pintos M, Bataglino MN, Torales M, Diaz A et al. Community acquired urinary tract infection and susceptibility profile of *Escherichia coli* to the main antimicrobial agents. *Rev Med Urug*, 2010, 26:14-24.

25. Villegas MV, Blanco MG, Sifuentes-Osornio J, Rossi F. Increasing prevalence of extended-spectrum-beta-lactamase among Gram-negative bacilli in Latin America--2008 update from the Study for Monitoring Antimicrobial Resistance Trends (SMART). *Braz J Infect Dis*, 2011, 15(1):34-39. (http://www.ncbi.nlm.nih.gov/pubmed/21412587, accessed 8 April 2014).

26. Al Shami Z. Occurence of ESBL in clinical isoltes of *Klebsiella pneumoniae* and Escheria coli in Al-Hakeem Teaching Hospital. *Kufa Med J*, 8(1):231-236.

27. Mahmood I, Jarjees Y, Satam Z. In vitro resistance to cephalosporins in women with bacterial urinary tract infections. *Iraqi Post Grad J*, 2012, 11:321-325.

28. Alshara MA. Uropathogens and their susceptibility patterns in children at Princess Rhmah Hospital, Jordan. *Jordan Med J*, 2011, 45(1):44-50.

29. Hammoud MS, Al-Taiar A, Thalib L, Al-Sweih N, Pathan S, Isaacs D. Incidence, aetiology and resistance of late-onset neonatal sepsis: a five-year prospective study. *J Paediatr Child Health*, 2012, 48(7):604-609.

30. Al Benwan K, Al Sweih N, Rotimi VO. Etiology and antibiotic susceptibility patterns of community- and hospital-acquired urinary tract infections in a general hospital in Kuwait. *Med Princ Pract*, 2010, 19(6):440-446.

31. Daoud Z, Afif C. *Escherichia coli* isolated from urinary tract infections of Lebanese patients between 2000 and 2009: Epidemiology and profiles of resistance. *Chemother Res Prac*, 2011, 2011:218431. (http://dx.doi.org/10.1155/2011/218431, accessed 8 April 2014).

32. Araj GF, Avedissian AZ, Ayyash NS, Bey HA, El Asmar RG, Hammoud RZ et al. A reflection on bacterial resistance to antimicrobial agents at a major tertiary care center in Lebanon over a decade. *J Med Liban*, 2012, 60(3):125-135. (http://www.ncbi.nlm.nih.gov/pubmed/23198452, accessed 8 April 2014).

Annex 2

33. Madani N, Rosenthal VD, Dendane T, Abidi K, Zeggwagh AA, Abouqal R. Health-care associated infections rates, length of stay, and bacterial resistance in an intensive care unit of Morocco: findings of the International Nosocomial Infection Control Consortium (INICC). *Int Arch Med*, 2009, 2(1):29. (http://www. ncbi.nlm.nih.gov/pubmed/19811636, accessed 19 January 2014).

34. Bouskraoui M, Ait Sab I, Draiss G, Bourrouss M, Sbihi M. [Epidemiology of urinary tract infection in children in Marrakech]. *Arch Pediatr*, 2010, 17 Suppl 4:S177-178. (http://www.ncbi.nlm.nih.gov/pubmed/20826328, accessed 19 January 2014).

35. Tagajdid MR, Boumhil L, Iken M, Adnaoui M, Benouda A. [Resistance to fluorquinolones and 3 generation cephalosporin of e coli isolated from urines]. *Med Mal Infect*, 2010, 40(2):70-73. doi:10.1016/j.medmal.2008.10.015.

36. Abdelmalek R, Kilani B, Kanoun F, Ammari L, Benaissa HT, Goubontini A et al. [Upper urinary tract infections in adults: about 261 episodes]. *Tunis Med*, 2010, 88(9):629-633. (http://www.ncbi.nlm.nih.gov/pubmed/20812174, accessed 8 April 2014).

37. Barguigua A, El Otmani F, Talmi M, Bourjilat F, Haouzane F, Zerouali K et al. Characterization of extended-spectrum ß-lactamase-producing *Escherichia coli* and *Klebsiella pneumoniae* isolates from the community in Morocco. *J Med Microbiol*, 2011, 60(Pt 9):1344-1352. doi:10.1099/jmm.0.032482-0.

38. Jameel N. Detection of AmpC beta lactamase in clinical isolates of Escheria coli among children. *Pak J Med Sci*, 2012, 28(5):12.

39. Sheik NA, Bashir K, Shafique AA, Khawaja S. An audit for microbiological surveillance and antimicrobial susceptibility in the intensive care unit. *Pak J Med Health Sci*, 2010, 4(2):93-96.

40. Zafar S, Baig N, Naqvi BS. Pathological threat of developing resistance againts broad spectrum antibiotcs. *Ann Abbasi Shaheed Hosp Karachi Med Dent Coll*, 2009, 14(1):58-65.

41. Akhtar N. Hospital acquired infections in a medical intensive care unit. *J Coll Physicians Surg Pak*, 2010, 20(6):386-390. doi:06.2010/JCPSP.386390.

42. Firdous R, Ahmed S, Chaudhary SA, Akhtar N. Evaluation of resistance to fluoroquinolones in clinical isolates of Escheria coli. *Medical Forum Monthly*, 2010, 21(5):54-60.

43. Mumtaz S, Ahmad M, Akhtar N, Hameed A. Extended spectrum beta lactamases in urinary gram negative bacilli and their susceptibility pattern. *Pak J Med Res*, 2008, 47(4):75-78.

44. Muhammad I, Uzma M, Yasmin B, Mehmood Q, Habib B. Prevalence of antimicrobial resistance and integrons in *Escherichia coli* from Punjab, Pakistan. *Braz J Microbiol*, 2011, 42(2):462-466. doi:10.1590/S1517-83822011000200008.

45. Mahajani S, Deshmukh A. Occurrence of ESBL and multiple drug resistance in UTI caused by *Escherichia coli*. *J Pure Appl Microbiol*, 2010, 4(1):257-261.

46. Hassan SA, Jamal SA, Kamal M. Occurrence of multidrug resistant and ESBL producing *E. coli* causing urinary tract infections. *J Basic Appl Sci*, 2011, 7(1):39-43.

47. Mumtaz S, Ahmad M, Aftab I, Akhtar N, ul Hassan M, Hamid A. Aerobic vaginal pathogens and their sensitivity pattern. *J Ayub Med Coll Abbottabad*, 2008, 20(1):113-117. (http://www.ncbi.nlm.nih.gov/pubmed/19024202, accessed 8 April 2014).

48. Bashir S, Sarwar Y, Ali A, Mohsin M, Saeed MA, Tariq A et al. Multiple drug resistance patterns in various phylogenetic groups of uropathogenic *E. coli* isolated from Faisalabad region of Pakistan. *Braz J Microbiol*, 2011, 42(4):1278-1283. doi:10.1590/S1517-83822011000400005.

49. Khan FY, Elshafie SS, Almaslamani M, Abu-Khattab M, El-Hiday AH, Errayes M et al. Epidemiology of bacteraemia in Hamad general hospital, Qatar: a one year hospital-based study. *Travel Med Infect Dis*, 2010, 8(6):377-387. doi:10.1016/j.tmaid.2010.10.004.

50. Al Johani S. Prevalence and antimicrobial susceptibility of extended spectrum beta-lactamase-producing *Escherichia coli* and *Klebsiella pneumoniae* in a tertiary care hospital. *Clin Microbiol Infect*, 2012, 18:761.

51. Al-Otaibi FE, Bukhari EE. Clinical and laboratory profiles of urinary tract infections caused by extended-spectrum beta-lactamase-producing *Escherichia coli* in a tertiary care center in central Saudi Arabia. *Saudi Med J*, 2013, 34(2):171-176. (http://www.ncbi.nlm.nih.gov/pubmed/23396464, accessed 8 April 2014).

52. Al-Tawfiq JA, Anani AA. Antimicrobial susceptibility pattern of bacterial pathogens causing urinary tract infections in a Saudi Arabian hospital. *Chemother*, 2009, 55(2):127-131. doi:10.1159/000198698.

53. Al Johani SM, Akhter J, Balkhy H, El-Saed A, Younan M, Memish Z. Prevalence of antimicrobial resistance among gram-negative isolates in an adult intensive care unit at a tertiary care center in Saudi Arabia. *Ann Saudi Med*, 2010, 30(5):364-369. doi:10.4103/0256-4947.67073.

54. Al-Saif MA, Al-Abdi SY, Samara JT, Al-Rahman NG, Mousa TA, Alabdulbaqi MA et al. Antibiotic sensitivity pattern of common community-acquired uropathogens in children in a Saudi tertiary care hospital. *Saudi Med J*, 2012, 33(5):565-567. (http://www.ncbi.nlm.nih.gov/pubmed/22588821, accessed 19 January 2014).

55. Khanfar HS, Bindayna KM, Senok AC, Botta GA. Extended spectrum beta-lactamases (ESBL) in *Escherichia coli* and *Klebsiella pneumoniae*: trends in the hospital and community settings. *J Infect Dev Ctries*, 2009, 3(4):295-299. (http://www.ncbi.nlm.nih.gov/pubmed/19759493, accessed 19 January 2014).

56. Sabra S, Abdel–Fattah M. Epidemiological and microbiological profile of nosocomial infection in Taif hospitals, KSA (2010–2011). *World J Med Sci*, 2012, 7(1):1-9. (http://www.idosi.org/wjms/7(1)12/1.pdf, accessed 8 April 2014).

57. Saeed NK, Kambal AM, El-Khizzi NA. Antimicrobial-resistant bacteria in a general intensive care unit in Saudi Arabia. *Saudi Med J*, 2010, 31(12):1341-1349. (http://www.ncbi.nlm.nih.gov/pubmed/21135998, accessed 19 January 2014).

58. Al-Harthi AA, Al-Fifi SH. Antibiotic resistance pattern and empirical therapy for urinary tract infections in children. *Saudi Med J*, 2008, 29(6):854-858. (http://www.ncbi.nlm.nih.gov/pubmed/18521464, accessed 19 January 2014).

59. Ibrahim ME, Bilal NE, Hamid ME. Increased multidrug resistant *Escherichia coli* from hospitals in Khartoum state, Sudan. *Afr Health Sci*, 2012, 12(3):368-375. (http://www.ncbi.nlm.nih.gov/pubmed/23382754, accessed 8 April 2014).

60. Al-Assil B, Mahfoud M, Hamzeh AR. Resistance trends and risk factors of extended spectrum ß-lactamases in *Escherichia coli* infections in Aleppo, Syria. *Am J Infect Control*, 2013, 41(7):597-600. doi:10.1016/j.ajic.2012.09.016.

61. Mkaouar D, Mahjoubi F, Mezghani S, Znazen A, Ktari S, Hammami A. [Resistance to third generation cephalosporins in Sfax hospitals, Tunisia (1999-2005)]. *Med Mal Infect*, 2008, 38(6):293-298. doi:10.1016/j.medmal.2007.

62. Ferjani A, Mkaddemi H, Tilouche S, Marzouk M, Hannechi N, Boughammoura L et al. [Epidemiological and bacteriological characteristics of uropathogen bacteria isolated in a pediatric environment]. *Arch Pediatr*, 2011, 18(2):230-234. doi:10.1016/j.arcped.2010.09.024.

63. Al-Dhaheri AS, Al-Niyadi MS, Al-Dhaheri AD, Bastaki SM. Resistance patterns of bacterial isolates to antimicrobials from 3 hospitals in the United Arab Emirates. *Saudi Med J*, 2009, 30(5):618-623. (http://www.ncbi.nlm.nih.gov/pubmed/19417958, accessed 30 January 2014).

64. Al-Zarouni M, Senok A, Rashid F, Al-Jesmi SM, Panigrahi D. Prevalence and antimicrobial susceptibility pattern of extended-spectrum beta-lactamase-producing Enterobacteriaceae in the United Arab Emirates. *Med Princ Pract*, 2008, 17(1):32-36. (http://www.ncbi.nlm.nih.gov/pubmed/18059098, accessed 19 January 2014).

65. Marian T, Plecko V, Vranes J, Mlinaric D, Bedenic B, Kalenic S. [Characterization of ESBL-producing *Escherichia coli* and *Klebsiella pneumoniae* strains isolated from urine of nonhospitalized patients in the Zagreb region]. [Article in Croatian]. *Med Glas*, 2010, 7:46-53. (http://www.ncbi.nlm.nih.gov/pubmed/20387724, accessed 8 April 2014).

66. Uzunović-Kamberovi S, Odobasić M, Husković A, Hutinović A, Ibranović N. Antibiotic resistance of coliform bacteria from community-acquired urinary tract infections in the Zenica-Doboj Canton, Bosnia and Herzegovina. *Med Glas*, 2010, 7(1):40-45. (http://www.ncbi.nlm.nih.gov/pubmed/20387723, accessed 8 April 2014).

67. Macharashvili N, Kourbatova E, Butsashvili M, Tsertsvadze T, McNutt LA, Leonard MK. Etiology of neonatal blood stream infections in Tbilisi, Republic of Georgia. *Int J Infect Dis*, 2009, 13(4):499-505. doi:10.1016/j.ijid.2008.08.020.

68. Chazan B, Raz R, Teitler N, Nitzan O, Edelstein H, Colodner R. Epidemiology and susceptibility to antimicrobials in community, hospital and long-term care facility bacteremia in northern Israel: a 6 year surveillance. *Isr Med Assoc J.*, 2009, 11(10):592-597. (http://www.ncbi.nlm.nih.gov/pubmed/20077944, accessed 8 April 2014).

69. Marchaim D, Zaidenstein R, Lazarovitch T, Karpuch Y, Ziv T, Weinberger M. Epidemiology of bacteremia episodes in a single center: increase in Gram-negative isolates, antibiotics resistance, and patient age. *Eur J Clin Microbiol Infect Dis*, 2008, 27(11):1045-1051. doi:10.1007/s10096-008-0545-z.

70. Newman N, Wattad E, Greenberg D, Peled N, Cohen Z, Leibovitz E. Community-acquired complicated intra-abdominal infections in children hospitalized during 1995-2004 at a paediatric surgery department. *Scand J Infect Dis*, 2009, 41(10):720-726. doi:10.1080/00365540903159261.

71. Hawser S, Hoban D, Bouchillon S, Badal R, Carmeli Y, Hawkey P. Antimicrobial susceptibility of intra-abdominal gram-negative bacilli from Europe: SMART Europe 2008. *Eur J Clin Microbiol Infect Dis*, 2011, 30(2):173-179. doi:10.1007/s10096-010-1066-0.

72. Khan SA, Feroz F, Noor R. Study of extended-spectrum (beta)-lactamase-producing bacteria from urinary tract infections in Bangladesh. *Tzu Chi Med J*, 2013, 25(1):39-42. doi:10.1016/j.tcmj.2013.01.008.

73. Dutta S, Hassan R, Rahman F, Jilani SA, Noor R. Study of antimicrobial susceptibility of clinically significant microorganisms isolated from selected areas of Dhaka, Bangladesh. *Bangladesh J Med Sci*, 2013, 12(1):34-42. (http://dx.doi.org/10.3329/bjms.v12i1.13351, accessed 8 April 2014).

74. Rizwan F, Monjur F, Asaduzzaman M, Nasrin N, Ghosh N, Samsuzzaman A et al. Antibiotic susceptibility patterns of uropathogens isolated from pediatric patients in a selected hospital of Bangladesh. *Int J Pharm Sci Rev Res*, 2012, 14(1):1-3.

75. Shahriar M, Hossain M, Kabir S. A survey on antimicrobial sensitivity pattern of different antibiotics on clinical isolates of *Escherichia coli* collected from Dhaka city, Bangladesh. *J App Sci Env Man*, 2010, 14(3):19-20. (http://dx.doi.org/10.4314/jasem.v14i3.61452, accessed 8 April 2014).

76. Datta S, Wattal C, Goel N, Oberoi JK, Raveendran R, Prasad KJ. A ten year analysis of multi-drug resistant blood stream infections caused by *Escherichia coli* & *Klebsiella pneumoniae* in a tertiary care hospital. *Indian J Med Res*, 2012, 135(6):907-912. (http://www.ncbi.nlm.nih.gov/pubmed/22825611, accessed 19 January 2014).

77. Anandkumar H, Srinivasa H, Kodliwadmath S, Raksha R. Symptomatic and asymptomatic urinary tract infection by *Escherichia coli* among pregnant women attending out patient clinic of obstetrics and gynecology. *J Pure Appl Microbiol*, 2011, 5(4):717-723.

78. Varaiya AY, Dogra JD, Kulkarni MH, Bhalekar PN. Extended-spectrum beta-lactamase-producing *Escherichia coli* and *Klebsiella pneumoniae* in diabetic foot infections. *Indian J Pathol Microbiol*, 2008, 51(3):370-372. (http://www.ncbi.nlm.nih.gov/pubmed/18723960, accessed 8 April 2014).

79. Agrawal P, Ghosh AN, Kumar S, Basu B, Kapila K. Prevalence of extended-spectrum beta-lactamases among *Escherichia coli* and *Klebsiella pneumoniae* isolates in a tertiary care hospital. *Indian J Pathol Microbiol*, 2008, 51(1):139-142. (http://www.ncbi.nlm.nih.gov/pubmed/18417887, accessed 8 April 2014).

80. Metri BC, Jyothi P, Peerapur BV. Detection of ESBL in *E. coli* and *K. pneumoniae* isolated from urinary tract infection. *Indian J Nephrol*, 2012, 22(5):401-402. doi:10.4103/0971-4065.103919.

81. Sinha P, Sharma R, Rishi S, Sood S, Pathak D. Prevalence of extended spectrum beta lactamase and AmpC beta lactamase producers among *Escherichia coli* isolates in a tertiary care hospital in Jaipur. *Indian J Pathol Microbiol*, 2008, 51(3):367-369. (http://www.ncbi.nlm.nih.gov/pubmed/18723959, accessed 8 April 2014).

82. Deshpande P, Vadwai V, Shetty A, Dalal R, Soman R, Rodrigues C. No NDM-1 carriage in healthy persons from Mumbai: reassuring for now. *J Antimicrob Chemother*, 2012, 67(4):1046-1047. doi:10.1093/jac/dkr580.

83. Ahmed SM, Jakribettu RP, Meletath SK, B A, Vpa S. Lower respiratory tract infections (LTRIs): An insight into the prevalence and the antibiogram of the gram negative, respiratory, bacterial agents. *J Clin Diagn Res*, 2013, 7(2):253-256. doi:10.7860/JCDR/2013/5308.2740.

84. Chen YH, Hsueh PR, Badal RE, Hawser SP, Hoban DJ, Bouchillon SK et al. Antimicrobial susceptibility profiles of aerobic and facultative Gram-negative bacilli isolated from patients with intra-abdominal infections in the Asia-Pacific region according to currently established susceptibility interpretive criteria. *J Infect*, 2011, 62(4):280-291. doi:10.1016/j.jinf.2011.02.009.

85. Eshwarappa M, Dosegowda R, Aprameya IV, Khan MW, Kumar PS, Kempegowda P. Clinico-microbiological profile of urinary tract infection in south India. *Indian J Nephrol*, 2011, 21(1):30-36. doi:10.4103/0971-4065.75226.

86. Gagneja D, Goel N, Aggarwal R, Chaudhary U. Changing trend of antimicrobial resistance among gram-negative bacilli isolated from lower respiratory tract of ICU patients: A 5-year study. *Indian J Crit Care Med*, 2011, 15(3):164-167. doi:10.4103/0972-5229.84900.

87. Hawser SP, Badal RE, Bouchillon SK, Hoban DJ. Antibiotic susceptibility of intra-abdominal infection isolates from Indian hospitals during 2008. *J Med Microbiol*, 2010, 59(Pt 9):1050-1054. doi:10.1099/jmm.0.020784-0.

88. Kumar P, Medhekar A, Ghadyalpatil NS, Noronha V, Biswas S, Kurkure P et al. The effect of age on the bacteria isolated and the antibiotic-sensitivity pattern in infections among cancer patients. *Indian J Cancer*, 2010, 47(4):391-396. doi:10.4103/0019-509X.73574.

89. Mandal J, Acharya NS, Buddhapriya D, Parija SC. Antibiotic resistance pattern among common bacterial uropathogens with a special reference to ciprofloxacin resistant *Escherichia coli*. *Indian J Med Res*, 2012, 136(5):842-849. (http://www.ncbi.nlm.nih.gov/pubmed/23287133, accessed 8 April 2014).

90. Mangaiarkkarasi A, Meher AR, Gopal R. Study of antimicrobial susceptibility pattern of *Escherichia coli* isolated from clinical specimens in a Teaching Hospital, Pondicherry. *Res J Pharm, Biol Chem Sci*, 2013, 4(1):1365-1371.

91. Pathak A, Marothi Y, Kekre V, Mahadik K, Macaden R, Lundborg CS. High prevalence of extended-spectrum (beta)-lactamase-producing pathogens: Results of a surveillance study in two hospitals in Ujjain, India. *Infect Drug Resist*, 2012, 5:65-73. doi:10.2147/IDR.S30043.

92. Patil A, Krishna B, Chandrasekhar M. Increasing burden of hospital acquired infections: Resistance to cephalosporin antibiotics among klebsiella and *Escherichia coli*. *J Ind Med Assoc*, 2009, 109(3):158-160. (http://www.ncbi.nlm.nih.gov/pubmed/22010583, accessed 8 April 2014).

93. Prakash S, Dayalan AJ, Edison N. Prevalence of bacteriuria in Jeyaseharan hospital of South India and their antibiogram. *Asian Pac J Trop Biomed*, 2011, 1:S105-S108. (http://dx.doi.org/10.1016/S2221-1691(11)60134-2, accessed 8 April 2014).

94. Gupta A, Sharma S, Arora A. Changing trends of in vitro antimicrobial resistance patterns in blood isolates in a tertiary care hospital over a period of 4 years. *Indian J Med Sci*, 2010, 64(11):485-492. doi:10.4103/0019-5359.102118.

95. Rubin D, Rajendra S. Prevalence of extended spectrum (beta)-lactamase (ESBL) producing *Escherichia coli* and Klebsiella isolated from various in patient department samples. *Int Res J Pharm*, 2012, 3(5):428-431.

96. Tantry BA, Rahiman S. Antibacterial resistance and trend of urinary tract pathogens to commonly used antibiotics in Kashmir Valley. *West Indian Med J*, 2012, 61(7):703-707. (http://www.ncbi.nlm.nih.gov/pubmed/23620968, accessed 19 January 2014).

97. Bandekar N. Bacteriology and antibiogram of burn infection at a Tertiary Care Center. *J Pure Appl Microbiol*, 2011, 5(2):781-786.

98. Moehario LH, Tjoa E, Kiranasari A, Ningsih I, Rosana Y, Karuniawati A. Trends in antimicrobial susceptibility of gram-negative bacteria isolated from blood in Jakarta from 2002 to 2008. *J Infect Dev Ctries*, 2009, 3(11):843-848. (http://www.ncbi.nlm.nih.gov/pubmed/20061679, accessed 8 April 2014).

99. Bao L, Peng R, Ren X, Ma R, Li J, Wang Y. Analysis of some common pathogens and their drug resistance to antibiotics. *Pak J Med Sci*, 2013, 29(1):135-139. doi:10.12669/pjms.291.2744.

100. Tan TY, Hsu LY, Koh TH, Ng LS, Tee NW, Krishnan P et al. Antibiotic resistance in gram-negative bacilli: A Singapore perspective. *Ann Acad Med Singapore*, 2008, 37(10):819-825.

101. Hsu LY, Tan TY, Tam VH, Kwa A, Fisher DA, Koh TH et al. Surveillance and correlation of antibiotic prescription and resistance of Gram-negative bacteria in Singaporean hospitals. *Antimicrob Agents Chemother*, 2010, 54(3):1173-1178. (http://www.ncbi.nlm.nih.gov/pubmed/19037514, accessed 8 April 2014).

102. Bahadin J, Teo SS, Mathew S. Aetiology of community-acquired urinary tract infection and antimicrobial susceptibility patterns of uropathogens isolated. *Singapore Med J*, 2011, 52(6):415-420. (http://www.ncbi.nlm.nih.gov/pubmed/21731993, accessed 19 January 2014).

103. Renuart AJ, Goldfarb DM, Mokomane M, Tawanana EO, Narasimhamurthy M, Steenhoff AP et al. Microbiology of urinary tract infections in Gaborone, Botswana. *PLoS ONE*, 2013, 8(3):e57776. doi:10.1371/journal.pone.0057776.

104. Kwashie A, Muibat AF, Modupe AI, Adejumoke B, Kehinde A. A survey of bacterial isolates cultured from apparently healthy individuals in South Western Nigeria. *Int J Trop Med*, 2012, 7(4):130-137. doi:10.3923/ijtmed.2012.130.137.

105. Oreh NC, Attamma AA. Prevalence and susceptibility patterns of urine isolates of escherichia coli to various fluoroquinolones in South-South Nigeria. *Pharmacoepidemiol Drug Saf*, 2012, 21:105-106.

106. Ngwai YB, Iliyasu H, Young E, Owuna G. Bacteriuria and antimicrobial susceptibility of e coli isolated from urine of asymptomatic university students in Keffi, Nigeria. *Jundishapur J Microbiol*, 2010, 5(1):323-327. doi:10.5812/kowsar.20083645.2372.

107. Inyang-Etoh PC, Udofia GC, Alaribe AAA, Udonwa NE. Asymptomatic bacteriuria in patients on antiretrovial drug therapy in Calabar. *J Med Sci*, 2009, 9(6):270-275.

108. Oladeinde BH, Omoregie R, Olley M, Anunibe JA. Urinary tract infection in a rural community of Nigeria. *N Am J Med Sci*, 2011, 3(2):75-77. doi:10.4297/najms.2011.375.

109. Omigie O, Okoror L, Umolu P, Ikuuh G. Increasing resistance to quinolones: A four-year prospective study of urinary tract infection pathogens. *Int J Gen Med*, 2009, 2:171-175. (http://www.ncbi.nlm.nih.gov/pubmed/20360901, accessed 19 January 2014).

110. Mordi RM, Borke ME, Isah A, Hugbo PG, Igeleke CL. The susceptibility of bacteria isolates from parts of the body to antibacterial agents at the University of Benin Teaching Hospital (U.B.T.H), Benin City, Edo State, Nigeria. *J Med Biomed Res*, 2012, 11(1):95-104. (http://www.ajol.info/index.php/jmbr/article/view/81367, accessed 8 April 2014).

111. Jombo G, Akpan S, Epoke J, Akaa P, Eyong K, Gyuse A. Antimicrobial susceptibility profile of community acquired and nosocomial isolates of *Escherichia coli* from clinical blood culture specimens at a Nigerian university teaching hospital. *Asian Pac J Trop Med*, 2010:662–665.

112. Okwori EE, Nwadioha SI, Jombo GTA, Nwokedi EOP, Odimayo MS. A comparative study of bacterial isolates from the urine samples of AIDS and non-AIDS patients in Benue, Nigeria. *Asian Pac J Trop Med*, 2010, 3(5):382-385. (http://dx.doi.org/10.1016/S1995-7645(10)60093-4, accessed 8 April 2014).

113. Kehinde A, Adedapo K, Aimakhu C, Odukogbe AT, Olayemi O, Salako B. Urinary pathogens and drug susceptibility patterns of urinary tract infections among antenatal clinic attendees in Ibadan, Nigeria. *J Obstet Gynaecol Res*, 2012, 38(1):280-284. doi:10.1111/j.1447-0756.2011.01635.x.

114. Bosch FJ, van Vuuren C, Joubert G. Antimicrobial resistance patterns in outpatient urinary tract infections--the constant need to revise prescribing habits. *S Afr Med J*, 2011, 101(5):328-331. (http://www.ncbi.nlm.nih.gov/pubmed/21837876, accessed 8 April 2014).

115. Arredondo-García JL, Amábile-Cuevas CF. High resistance prevalence towards ampicillin, co-trimoxazole and ciprofloxacin, among uropathogenic *Escherichia coli* isolates in Mexico City. *J Infect Dev Ctries*, 2008, 2(5):350-353. (http://www.ncbi.nlm.nih.gov/pubmed/19745501, accessed 8 April 2014).

116. Orrett FA, Changoor E, Maharaj N. Pediatric drug prescribing in a regional hospital in Trinidad. *J Chin Clin Med*, 2010, 5(3):157-163.

117. Buzayan M, Tobgi R, Taher I. Detection of extended spectrum ß-lactamases among urinary *Escherichia coli* and *Klebsiella pneumoniae* from two centres. *Jamahiriya Med J*, 2010, 10:10–16.

118. Mouti M. Profile of antimicrobial resistance of E coli strains isolated from urinary tract infections at IBN Sina hospital in Rabat. *Clin Chem Lab Med*, 2012, 50(4):A127. doi:10.1186/1755-7682-5-26.

119. Iffat W, Shoaib MH, Muhammad IN, Rehana, Tasleem S, Gauhar S. Antimicrobial susceptibility testing of newer quinolones against gram positive and gram negative clinical isolates. *Pak J Pharm Sci*, 2010, 23(3):245-249. (http://www.ncbi.nlm.nih.gov/pubmed/20566434, accessed 19 January 2014).

120. Akhtar N, Alqurashi AM, Abu Twibah M. In vitro ciprofloxacin resistance profiles among gram-negative bacteria isolated from clinical specimens in a teaching hospital. *J Pak Med Assoc*, 2010, 60(8):625-627. (http://www.ncbi.nlm.nih.gov/pubmed/20726190, accessed 8 April 2014).

121. Toumi A. Risk factors of fluoroquinolone resistance in community acquired acute pyelonephritis caused by E coli. *Clin Microbiol Infect*, 2012, 18:414-415.

122. Ben Hadj Khalifa A, Ben Hamouda H, Soua H, Braham H, Sfar M, Kheder M. [Bacteriological profile of maternofetal infections in Tunisian hospital]. *Med Mal Infect*, 2010, 40(3):180-182. doi:10.1016/j.medmal.2009.08.018.

123. Al Haddad A, Ghouth A, El-Hosseiny M. Microbial resistance in patients with urinary tract infections in Al Mukalla, Yemen. *Sudan J Med Sci*, 2010, 5(9):15-21. (http://dx.doi.org/10.4314/sjms.v5i2.57813, accessed 8 April 2014).

124. Taneja N, Rao P, Arora J, Dogra A. Occurrence of ESBL & Amp-C beta-lactamases & susceptibility to newer antimicrobial agents in complicated UTI. *Indian J Med Res*, 2008, 127(1):85-88. (http://www.ncbi.nlm.nih.gov/pubmed/18316858, accessed 19 January 2014).

125. Mathai E, Chandy S, Thomas K, Antoniswamy B, Joseph I, Mathai M et al. Antimicrobial resistance surveillance among commensal *Escherichia coli* in rural and urban areas in Southern India. *Trop Med Int Health*, 2008, 13(1):41-45. doi:10.1111/j.1365-3156.2007.01969.x.

126. Samal SK, Khuntia HK, Nanda PK, Satapathy CS, Nayak SR, Sarangi AK et al. Incidence of bacterial enteropathogens among hospitalized diarrhea patients from Orissa, India. *Jpn J Infect Dis*, 2008, 61(5):350-355. (http://www.ncbi.nlm.nih.gov/pubmed/18806340, accessed 8 April 2014).

127. Shahid M, Malik A, Akram M, Agrawal LM, Khan AU, Agrawal M. Prevalent phenotypes and antibiotic resistance in *Escherichia coli* and *Klebsiella pneumoniae* at an Indian tertiary care hospital: Plasmid-mediated cefoxitin resistance. *Int J Infect Dis*, 2008, 12(3):256-264. (http://www.ncbi.nlm.nih.gov/pubmed/17981482, accessed 23 January 2014).

128. Sureshkumar M, al. Gopinathan S, Rangachari Rajesh K, Priyadharsini I. Prevalence of ciprofoxacin resistance among gram-negative bacilli in a tertiary care hospital. *J Clin Diagn Res*, 2012, 6(2):180-181.

129. Dyar OJ, Hoa NQ, Trung NV, Phuc HD, Larsson M, Chuc NT et al. High prevalence of antibiotic resistance in commensal *Escherichia coli* among children in rural Vietnam. *BMC Infect Dis*, 2012, 12:92. doi:10.1186/1471-2334-12-92.

130. Olajubu F, Adetokunbo O, Ismail L, Bosede O, Anota Mopelola D. Pattern of hospital associated infections in a teaching hospital in Nigeria. *Asian Pacific J Trop Dis*, 2012, 2(SUPPL2):S869-S873. (http://www.apjtcm.com/zz/2012s2/65.pdf, accessed 8 April 2014).

131. Mawalla B, Mshana SE, Chalya PL, Imirzalioglu C, Mahalu W. Predictors of surgical site infections among patients undergoing major surgery at Bugando Medical Centre in Northwestern Tanzania. *BMC Surgery*, 2011, 11:21. doi:10.1186/1471-2482-11-21.

132. Superti SV, Augusti G, Zavascki AP. Risk factors for and mortality of extended-spectrum-beta-lactamase-producing *Klebsiella pneumoniae* and *Escherichia coli* nosocomial bloodstream infections. *Rev Inst Med Trop Sao Paulo*, 2009, 51(4):211-216. (http://www.ncbi.nlm.nih.gov/pubmed/19739001, accessed 8 April 2014).

133. Garza-González E, Llaca-Díaz J, Bosques-Padilla F, González G. Prevalence of multidrug-resistant bacteria at a tertiary-care teaching hospital in Mexico: special focus on *Acinetobacter baumannii*. *Chemother*, 2010, 56(4):275-279. doi:10.1159/000319903.

134. Al-Talib H, Al-Khateeb A, Al-Khalidi RN. Neonatal septicemia in neonatal intensive care units: Epidemiological and microbiological analysis of causative organisms and antimicrobial susceptibility. *Int Med J*, 2013; 20(1):36-40. *Int Med J*, 2013, 20(1):36-40.

135. Khan E, Ejaz M, Zafar A, Jabeen K, Shakoor S, Inayat R et al. Increased isolation of ESBL producing *Klebsiella pneumoniae* with emergence of carbapenem resistant isolates in Pakistan: Report from a tertiary care hospital. *J Pak Med Assoc*, 2010, 60(3):186-190. (http://www.ncbi.nlm.nih.gov/pubmed/20225774, accessed 8 April 2014).

136. Custović A, Zulcić-Naki V, Ascerić M, Hadzić S. Surveillance of intrahospital infections at the clinic for gynaecology and obstetrics. *Bosn J Basic Med Sci*, 2009, 9(1):66-70. (http://www.ncbi.nlm.nih.gov/pubmed/19284398, accessed 8 April 2014).

137. Monjur F, Rizwan F, Asaduzzaman M, Nasrin N, Ghosh NK, Apu AS et al. Antibiotic sensitivity pattern of causative organisms of neonatal septicemia in an urban hospital of Bangladesh. *Indian J Med Sci*, 2010, 64(6):265-271. doi:10.4103/0019-5359.99605.

138. Tagare A, Kadam S, Vaidya U, Deodha J, Pandit A. Multidrug resistant *Klebsiella pneumoniae* in NICU - what next? Trend of antibiotic resistance. *J Ped Infect Dis*, 2010, 5(2):119-124.

139. Ahmad S. Prevalence and antimicrobial susceptibility of extended spectrum a-lactamase producing klebsiella pneumonia at a microbiology diagnostic center in Kashmir. *Rawal Medical Journal*, 2009, 34(1):68-71. (http://www.scopemed.org/?mno=7221, accessed 8 April 2014).

140. Singhi S, Ray P, Mathew JL, Jayashree M, Dhanalakshmi. Nosocomial bloodstream infection in a pediatric intensive care unit. *Indian J Pediatr*, 2008, 75(1):25-30. (http://www.ncbi.nlm.nih.gov/pubmed/18245931, accessed 8 April 2014).

141. Solabannavar SS, Kardesai SG, Patil CS, Jayasimha VL, Vijayanath V. Bacteriological study of chronic obstructive pulmonary disease. *J Pure Appl Microbiol*, 2011, 5(2):865-868.

142. Chander A, Shrestha CD. Prevalence of extended spectrum beta lactamase producing *Escherichia coli* and *Klebsiella pneumoniae* urinary isolates in a tertiary care hospital in Kathmandu, Nepal. *BMC Res Notes*, 2013, 6:487. doi:10.1186/1756-0500-6-487.

143. Abreu A, Marques S, Monteiro Neto V, Carvalho R, Gonçalves A. Nosocomial infection and characterization of extended-spectrum ß-lactamases-producing Enterobacteriaceae in Northeast Brazil. *Rev Soc Bras Med Trop*, 2011, 44(4):441-446. (http://www.ncbi.nlm.nih.gov/pubmed/21860889, accessed 8 April 2014).

144. Araj G, Jaber F. In vitro activity of carbapenems against multidrugresistant gram-negative organisms at a tertiary care centre in Lebanon. *Clin Microbiol Infect*, 2012, 18:512-513.

145. Debby BD, Ganor O, Yasmin M, David L, Nathan K, Ilana T et al. Epidemiology of carbapenem resistant *Klebsiella pneumoniae* colonization in an intensive care unit. *Eur J Clin Microbiol Infect Dis*, 2012, 31(8):1811-1817. doi:10.1007/s10096-011-1506-5.

146. Wiener-Well Y, Rudensky B, Yinnon AM, Kopuit P, Schlesinger Y, Broide E et al. Carriage rate of carbapenem-resistant *Klebsiella pneumoniae* in hospitalised patients during a national outbreak. *J Hosp Infect*, 2010, 74(4):344-349. doi:10.1016/j.jhin.2009.07.022.

147. Bayram Y, Parlak M, Aypak C, Bayram I. Three-year review of bacteriological profile and antibiogram of burn wound isolates in Van, Turkey. *Int J Med Sci*, 2013, 10(1):19-23. doi:10.7150/ijms.4723.

148. Ahmad S, Alenzi FQ, Al-Juaid NF, Ahmed S. Prevalence and antibiotic susceptibility pattern of methicillin resistant *Staphylococcus aureus* at Armed Forces Hospital in Saudi Arabia. *Bangladesh Med Res Counc Bull*, 2009, 35(1):28-30. (http://www.ncbi.nlm.nih.gov/pubmed/19637545, accessed 8 April 2014).

149. Antri K, Rouzic N, Dauwalder O, Boubekri I, Bes M, Lina G et al. High prevalence of methicillin-resistant *Staphylococcus aureus* clone ST80-IV in hospital and community settings in Algiers. *Clin Microbiol Infect*, 2011, 17(4):526-532. doi:10.1111/j.1469-0691.2010.03273.x.

150. Truong H, Shah SS, Ludmir J, Twananana EO, Bafana M, Wood SM et al. *Staphylococcus aureus* skin and soft tissue infections at a tertiary hospital in Botswana. *S Afr Med J*, 2011, 101(6):413-416. (http://www.ncbi.nlm.nih.gov/pubmed/21920078, accessed 19 January 2014).

151. Schaumburg F, Biallas B, Ngoune Feugap E, Alabi AS, Mordmüller B, Kremsner PG et al. Carriage of encapsulated bacteria in Gabonese children with sickle cell anaemia. *Clin Microbiol Infect*, 2013, 19(3):235-241. doi:10.1111/j.1469-0691.2012.03771.x.

152. Schaumburg F, Ngoa UA, Kosters K, Kock R, Adegnika AA, Kremsner PG et al. Virulence factors and genotypes of *Staphylococcus aureus* from infection and carriage in Gabon. *Clin Microbiol Infect*, 2011, 17(10):1507-1513. doi:10.1111/j.1469-0691.2011.03534.x.

153. Gitaka A, .Wambugu, P. Mutua, F. Rajab, J. Bacterial isolates in post operative wounds and their antimicrobial susceptibility in Kenyatta National Hopsital, Kenya. *Histopathology*, 2012, 61:151.

154. Makoka MH, Miller WC, Hoffman IF, Cholera R, Gilligan PH, Kamwendo D et al. Bacterial infections in Lilongwe, Malawi: aetiology and antibiotic resistance. *BMC Infect Dis*, 2012, 12:67. doi:10.1186/1471-2334-12-67.

155. Akinkunmi EO, Lamikanra A. A study of the intestinal carriage of antibiotic resistant *Staphylococcus aureus* by Nigerian children. *Afr Health Sci*, 2012, 12(3):381-387. (http://www.ncbi.nlm.nih.gov/pubmed/23382756, accessed 19 January 2014).

156. Osazuwa F, Osazuwa E, Osime C, Igharo EA, Imade PE, Lofor P et al. Etiologic agents of otitis media in Benin city, Nigeria. *N Am J Med Sci*, 2011, 3(2):95-98. doi:10.4297/najms.2011.395.

157. Isibor JO, Samuel SO, Ehigiator EO, Inyang NJ, Igbinovia O. Plasmid-mediated methicillin-resistant *Staphylococcus aureus* in patients attending a tertiary health institution in Nigeria. *Pak J Med Sci*, 2011, 27(2):290-294.

158. Onanuga A, Awhowho GO. Antimicrobial resistance of *Staphylococcus aureus* strains from patients with urinary tract infections in Yenagoa, Nigeria. *J Pharm Bioallied Sci*, 2012, 4(3):226-230. doi:10.4103/0975-7406.99058.

159. Onanuga A, Temedie TC. Nasal carriage of multi-drug resistant *Staphylococcus aureus* in healthy inhabitants of Amassoma in Niger delta region of Nigeria. *Afr Health Sci*, 2011, 11(2):176-181. (http://www.ncbi.nlm.nih.gov/pubmed/21857847, accessed 19 January 2014).

160. Onwubiko NE, Sadiq N. Antibiotic sensitivity pattern of staphylococcus aureus from clinical isolates in a tertiary health institution in Kano, Northwestern Nigeria. *Pan Afr Med J*, 2011, 8(4). (http://www.panafrican-med-journal.com/content/article/8/4/full/, accessed 8 April 2014).

161. Ogunlesi TA, Ogunfowora OB, Osinupebi O, Olanrewaju DM. Changing trends in newborn sepsis in Sagamu, Nigeria: bacterial aetiology, risk factors and antibiotic susceptibility. *J Paediatr Child Health*, 2011, 47(1-2):5-11. (http://www.ncbi.nlm.nih.gov/pubmed/20973858, accessed 19 January 2014).

162. Nwankwo EO, Nasiru MS. Antibiotic sensitivity pattern of *Staphylococcus aureus* from clinical isolates in a tertiary health institution in Kano, Northwestern Nigeria. *Pan Afr Med J*, 2011, 8:4. doi:10.1111/j.1440-1754.2010.01882.x.

163. Okon KO, Shittu AO, Usman H, Adam N, Balogun ST, Adesina O. Epidemiology and characteristic pattern of methicillin–resistant *Staphylococcus aureus* recovered from tertiary hospitals in Northeastern, Nigeria. *Int J Trop Med*, 2011, 6(5):106–112. doi:10.3923/ijtmed.2011.106.112.

164. Okwori EE, Nwadioha S, Nwokedi E, Odimayo M, Jombo G. Bacterial pathogens and their antimicrobial susceptibility in Otukpo Benue state of Nigeria. *Asian Pac J Trop Biomed*, 2011, 1(S2):S261–S265. (http://www.apjtb.com/zz/2011s2/25.pdf, accessed 8 April 2014).

165. Kombaté K, Dagnra A, Saka B, Mouhari-Toure A, Akakpo S, Tchangaï-Walla K et al. [Prevalence of methicillin-resistant *Staphylococcus aureus* in community-acquired skin infections in Lome, Togo]. *Med Trop (Mars)*, 2011, 71(1):68-70. (http://www.ncbi.nlm.nih.gov/pubmed/21585096, accessed 8 April 2014).

166. Ojulong J, Mwambu T, Joloba M, Bwanga F, Kaddu-Mulindwa D. Relative prevalence of methicilin resistant staphylococcus aureus and its susceptibility pattern in Mulago Hospital, Kampala, Uganda. *Tanzan J Health Res*, 2009, 11(3):149-153. (http://www.bioline.org.br/request?th09026, accessed 23 January 2014).

167. Moremi N, Mshana SE, Kamugisha E, Kataraihya J, Tappe D, Vogel U et al. Predominance of methicillin resistant *Staphylococcus aureus* -ST88 and new ST1797 causing wound infection and abscesses. *J Infect Dev Ctries*, 2012, 6(8):620-625. doi:10.3855/jidc.2093.

168. De Almeida Cruz E, Pimenta F, Vanzato Palazzo I, da Costa Darini A, Gir E. [Prevalence of *Staphylococcus aureus* in saliva of healthcare workers]. *Colomb Med*, 2011, 42(S1):10–16. (http://colombiamedica.univalle.edu.co/index.php/comedica/article/view/815, accessed 8 April 2014).

169. Grothe C, da Silva Belasco AG, de Cassia Bittencourt AR, Vianna LA, de Castro Cintra Sesso R, Barbosa DA. Incidence of bloodstream infection among patients on hemodialysis by central venous catheter. *Rev Lat Am Enfermagem*, 2010, 18(1):73-80. (http://www.ncbi.nlm.nih.gov/pubmed/20428700, accessed 19 January 2014).

170. Prates KA, Torres AM, Garcia LB, Ogatta SF, Cardoso CL, Tognim MC. Nasal carriage of methicillin-resistant *Staphylococcus aureus* in university students. *Braz J Infect Dis*, 2010, 14(3):316-318. (http://www.ncbi.nlm.nih.gov/pubmed/20835520, accessed 4 February 2014).

171. Reiter KC, Machado AB, Freitas AL, Barth AL. High prevalence of methicillin-resistant *Staphylococcus aureus* with SCCmec type III in cystic fibrosis patients in southern Brazil. *Rev Soc Bras Med Trop*, 2010, 43(4):377-381. (http://www.ncbi.nlm.nih.gov/pubmed/20802934, accessed 23 January 2014).

172. Silva EC, Antas M, Monteiro BNA, Rabelo MA, Melo FL, Maciel MA. Prevalence and risk factors for *Staphylococcus aureus* in health care workers at a university hospital of Recife-PE. *Braz J Infect Dis*, 2008, 12(6):504-508. (http://www.ncbi.nlm.nih.gov/pubmed/19287839, accessed 31 March 2014).

173. Gales AC, Sader HS, Ribeiro J, Zoccoli C, Barth A, Pignatari AC. Antimicrobial susceptibility of gram-positive bacteria isolated in Brazilian hospitals participating in the SENTRY Program (2005-2008). *Braz J Infect Dis*, 2009, 13(2):90-98. (http://www.ncbi.nlm.nih.gov/pubmed/20140350, accessed 19 January 2014).

174. Sousa Junior F, Nunes E, Nascimento E, Oliveira S, Melo M, Fernandes M. Prevalence of methicillin-resistant Staphylococcus spp isolated in a teaching maternity hospital in the city of Natal, State of Rio Grande. [Article in Portuguese]. *Rev Soc Bras Med Trop*, 2009, 42(2):179-182. (http://www.ncbi.nlm.nih.gov/pubmed/19448938, accessed 8 April 2014).

Annex 2

175. Castro-Orozco R, Villafane-Ferrer LM, Alvarez-Rivera E, De Arco MM, Rambaut-Donado CL, Vitola-Heins GV. [Methicillin-resistant *Staphylococcus aureus* in children attending school in Cartagena, Colombia]. *Rev Salud Publica (Bogota)*, 2010, 12(3):454-463. (http://www.ncbi.nlm.nih.gov/pubmed/21311833, accessed 23 January 2014).

176. Olarte NM, Valderrama IA, Reyes KR, Garzon MI, Escobar JA, Castro BE et al. [Methicillin-resistant *Staphylococcus aureus* colonization in a Colombian hospital intensive care unit: phenotypic and molecular characterization]. *Biomedica*, 2010, 30(3):353-361. (http://www.ncbi.nlm.nih.gov/pubmed/21713337, accessed 19 January 2014).

177. Sosa Ávila L, Machuca Pérez M, Sosa Ávila C, González Rugeles C. [Methicillin-resistant *Staphylococcus aureus* infections in children in Bucaramanga Colombia]. *Rev. Univ. Ind. Santander, Salud*, 2010, 42(3):248-255.

178. Newnham MS, Brown H, Martin AC, Plummer JM, Mitchell DI, Cawich SO. Management of breast abscesses in Jamaican women is there need for a paradigm shift? *West Indian Med J*, 2012, 61(3):245-248. (http://www.ncbi.nlm.nih.gov/pubmed/23155981, accessed 19 January 2014).

179. Alvarez JA, Ramirez AJ, Mojica-Larrea M, Huerta Jdel R, Guerrero JD, Rolon AL et al. [Methicillin-resistant *Staphylococcus aureus* at a general hospital: epidemiological overview between 2000-2007]. *Rev Invest Clin*, 2009, 61(2):98-103. (http://www.ncbi.nlm.nih.gov/pubmed/19637723, accessed 8 April 2014).

180. Telechea H, Speranza N, Lucas L, Santurio A, Giachetto G, Algorta G et al. [Antibiotic consumption and antimicrobial susceptibility evolution in the Centro Hospitalario Pereira Rossell in methicillin resistant *Staphylococcus aureus* era]. *Rev Chilena Infectol*, 2009, 26(5):413-419. doi:/S0716-10182009000600003.

181. Pardo L, Vola M, Macedo-Vinas M, Machado V, Cuello D, Mollerach M et al. Community-associated methicillin-resistant *Staphylococcus aureus* in children treated in Uruguay. *J Infect Dev Ctries*, 2013, 7(1):10-16. doi:10.3855/jidc.2261.

182. Co EM, Keen EF 3rd, Aldous WK. Prevalence of methicillin-resistant staphylococcus aureus in a combat support hospital in Iraq. *Mil Med*, 2011, 176(1):89-93. (http://www.ncbi.nlm.nih.gov/pubmed/21305966, accessed 19 January 2014).

183. Udo EE, Al-Sweih N, Dhar R, Dimitrov TS, Mokaddas EM, Johny M et al. Surveillance of antibacterial resistance in *Staphylococcus aureus* isolated in Kuwaiti hospitals. *Med Princ Pract*, 2008, 17(1):71-75. (http://www.ncbi.nlm.nih.gov/pubmed/18059105, accessed 23 January 2014).

184. Buzaid N, Elzouki AN, Taher I, Ghenghesh KS. Methicillin-resistant *Staphylococcus aureus* (MRSA) in a tertiary surgical and trauma hospital in Benghazi, Libya. *J Infect Dev Ctries*, 2011, 5(10):723-726. (http://www.ncbi.nlm.nih.gov/pubmed/21997941, accessed 19 January 2014).

185. Elouennass M, Sahnoun I, Zrara A, Bajjou T, Elhamzaoui S. [Epidemiology and susceptibility profile of blood culture isolates in an intensive care unit (2002-2005)]. *Med Mal Infect*, 2008, 38(1):18-24. (http://www.ncbi.nlm.nih.gov/pubmed/18065180, accessed 8 April 2014).

186. Elhamzaoui S, Benouda A, Allali F, Abouqual R, Elouennass M. [Antibiotic susceptibility of *Staphylococcus aureus* strains isolated in two university hospitals in Rabat, Morocco]. *Med Mal Infect*, 2009, 39(12):891-895. doi:10.1016/j.medmal.2009.01.004.

187. Bukhari SZ, Ahmed S, Zia N. Antimicrobial susceptibility pattern of *Staphylococcus aureus* on clinical isolates and efficacy of laboratory tests to diagnose MRSA: a multi-centre study. *J Ayub Med Coll Abbottabad*, 2011, 23(1):139-142. (http://www.ncbi.nlm.nih.gov/pubmed/22830169, accessed 8 April 2014).

188. Mehdinejad M, Sheikh AF, Jolodar A. Study of methicilin resistance in staphylococcus aureus and species of coagulase negative staphylococci isolated from various clinical specimens. *Pak J Med Sci*, 2008, 24(5):719-724. (http://www.pjms.com.pk/issues/octdec108/article/article15.html, accessed 8 April 2014).

189. Akhtar N. Staphylococcal nasal carriage of health care workers. *J Coll Physicians Surg Pak*, 2010, 20(7):439 443. doi:07.2010/JCPSP.439443.

190. Moniri R. The prevalence of nasal carriage methicillin-resistant *Staphylococcus aureus* in hospitalized patients. *Pak J Med Sci*, 2009, 25(4):656-659.

191. Makkiya A. Community prevalence rate of methicillin resistant staphlococcus aureus (MRSA) associated with PVL among Qatar University students. *Am J Trop Med Hyg*, 2010, 83(5):309.

192. Ahmad S. Prevalence of *Staphylococcus aureus* colonization among healthcare workers at a specialist hospital in Saudi Arabia. *J Clin Diagn Res*, 2010, 4:2438-2441. (http://www.jcdr.net/articles/PDF/747/630-918_E(C)_F(P)_R(P)_PF_p.pdf, accessed 8 January 2014).

193. El Amin NM, Faidah HS. Methicillin-resistant *Staphylococcus aureus* in the western region of Saudi Arabia: prevalence and antibiotic susceptibility pattern. *Ann Saudi Med*, 2012, 32(5):513-516. doi:10.5144/0256-4947.2012.513.

194. Al Zamil FA, Al Saadi MM, Bokhary NA, Al Shamsa L, Al Alola S, Al Eissa Y. The clinical profile of childhood osteomyelitis: A Saudi experience. *J Pediatr Infect Dis*, 2008, 3(4):235-240. (http://iospress.metapress.com/content/l155764mt7p15807/, accessed 8 April 2014).

195. Asghar AH. Frequency and antibiotic susceptibility of gram-positive bacteria in Makkah hospitals. *Ann Saudi Med*, 2011, 31(5):462-468. doi:10.4103/0256-4947.84622.

196. Thabet L, Messadi A, Mbarek M, Turki A, Meddeb B, Ben Redjeb S. [Surveillance of multidrug resistant bacteria in a Tunisian hospital]. *Tunis Med*, 2008, 86(11):992-995. (http://www.ncbi.nlm.nih.gov/pubmed/19213491, accessed 8 April 2014).

197. Bouchoucha S, Drissi G, Trifa M, Saied W, Ammar C, Smida M et al. [Epidemiology of acute hematogenous osteomyelitis in children: a prospective study over a 32 months period]. *Tunis Med*, 2012, 90(6):473-478. (http://www.ncbi.nlm.nih.gov/pubmed/22693089, accessed 8 April 2014).

198. Thabet L, Turki A, Ben Redjeb S, Messadi A. [Bacteriological profile and antibiotic resistance of bacteria isolates in a burn department]. *Tunis Med*, 2008, 86(12):1051-1054. (http://www.ncbi.nlm.nih.gov/pubmed/19213512, accessed 23 January 2014).

199. Thabet L, Zoghlami A, Boukadida J, Ghanem A, Messadi AA. [Comparative study of antibiotic resistance in bacteria isolated from burned patients during two periods (2005-2008, 2008-2011) and in two hospitals (Hospital Aziza Othmana, Trauma and Burn Center)]. *Tunis Med*, 2013, 91(2):134-138. (http://www.ncbi.nlm.nih.gov/pubmed/23526277, accessed 8 April 2014).

200. Al Baidani ARH, El-Shouny WA, Shawa TM. Antibiotic susceptibility pattern of methicillin-resistant staphylococcus aureus in three hospitals at Hodeiah city. *Global J Pharmacol*, 2011, 5:105-111. (http://idosi.org/gjp/5(2)11/9.pdf, accessed 8 April 2014).

201. Bishara J, Goldberg E, Leibovici L, Samra Z, Shaked H, Mansur N et al. Healthcare-associated vs. hospital-acquired *Staphylococcus aureus* bacteremia. *Int J Infect Dis*, 2012, 16(6):e457-463. doi:10.1016/j.ijid.2012.02.009.

202. Mariievskyi VF, Poliachenko Iu V, Salmanov AH, Shpak IV, Doan SI. [Resistance to antibiotics of nosocomial cultures of *Staphylococcus aureus* in surgical departments of Ukraine in 2009 year]. *Klin Khir*, 2010, (9):31-35. (http://www.ncbi.nlm.nih.gov/pubmed/21105269, accessed 23 January 2014).

203. Batabyal B. Oral suffering and antimicrobial susceptibility of *Staphylococcus aureus* in a dental hospital in Kolkata, India. *Int J Pharm Bio Sci*, 2012, 3(4):620-629.

204. Chande CA, Shrikhande SN, Jain DL, Kapale S, Chaudhary H, Powar RM. Prevalence of methicillin-resistant *Staphylococcus aureus* nasopharyngeal carriage in children from urban community at Nagpur. *Indian J Public Health*, 2009, 53(3):196-198. (http://www.ncbi.nlm.nih.gov/pubmed/20108888, accessed 8 April 2014).

205. Dubey D, Dubeya D, Ratha S, Sahua MC, Pattnaikb L, Debataa NK et al. Surveillance of infection status of drug resistant *Staphylococcus aureus* in an Indian teaching hospital. *Asian Pac J Trop Med*, 2013, 3(2):133-142. (http://dx.doi.org/10.1016/S2222-1808(13)60057-2, accessed 8 April 2014).

206. Hanumanthappa AR. Methicillin resistant *Staphylococcus aureus* amongst the patients in burns unit. *J Pure Appl Microbiol*, 2012, 6(1):475-478.

207. Indian Network for Surveillance of Antimicrobial Resistance (INSAR) group I. Methicillin resistant *Staphylococcus aureus* (MRSA) in India: Prevalence & susceptibility pattern. *Indian J Med Res*, 2013, 137(2):363-369. (http://www.ncbi.nlm.nih.gov/pubmed/23563381, accessed 8 April 2014).

208. Kini AR, Shetty V, Kumar AM, Shetty SM, Shetty A. Community-associated, methicillin-susceptible, and methicillin-resistant *Staphylococcus aureus* bone and joint infections in children: experience from India. *J Pediatr Orthop, Part B*, 2013, 22(2):158-166. doi:10.1097/BPB.0b013e32835c530a.

Annex 2

209. Kumar S, Joseph N, Easow J, Singh R, Umadevi S, Pramodhini S et al. Prevalence and current antibiogram of staphylococci isolated from various clinical specimens in a tertiary care hospital in Pondicherry. *Internet J Microbiol*, 2012, 10(1). (http://ispub.com/IJMB/10/1/13868, accessed 8 April 2014).

210. Patted S, Chinagudi S, Soragavi V, Bhavi S. The prevalence of MRSA infection in orthopedic surgery in a medical college hospital: A 2–year analysis. *Biomed Res (India)*, 2013, 24(1):33-35.

211. Ramana KV, Mohanty SK, Wilson CG. *Staphylococcus aureus* colonization of anterior nares of school going children. *Indian J Pediatr*, 2009, 76(8):813-816. doi:10.1007/s12098-009-0159-1.

212. Rongpharpi SR, Hazarika NK, Kalita H. The prevalence of nasal carriage of *Staphylococcus aureus* among healthcare workers at a tertiary care hospital in assam with special reference to MRSA. *J Clin Diagn Res*, 2013, 7(2):257-260. doi:10.7860/JCDR/2013/4320.2741.

213. Kaistha N, Mehta M, Singla N, Garg R, Chander J. Neonatal septicemia isolates and resistance patterns in a tertiary care hospital of North India. *J Infect Dev Ctries*, 2010, 4(1):55-57. (http://www.ncbi.nlm.nih.gov/pubmed/20130381, accessed 23 January 2014).

214. Kalwaje EV, Munim F, Tellapragada C, Varma M, Edward LL, Mukhopadhyay C. Upsurge of MRSA bacteraemia in south Indian tertiary care hospital: An observational study on clinical epidemiology and resistance profile. *Int J Infect Dis*, 2012, Conference(var.pagings):e224. (http://dx.doi.org/10.1016/j.ijid.2012.05.827, accessed 29 January 2014).

215. Khanal LK, Jha BK. Prevalence of methicillin resistant *Staphylococcus aureus* (MRSA) among skin infection cases at a hospital in Chitwan, Nepal. *Nepal Med Coll J*, 2010, 12(4):224-228. (http://www.ncbi.nlm.nih.gov/pubmed/21744763, accessed 8 April 2014).

216. Easow J, Joseph N, Dhungel B, Chapagain B, Shivananda P. Blood stream infections among febrile patients attending a teaching hospital in Western Region of Nepal. *Aus Med J*, 2010, 3(10):633–637.

217. Kumari N, Mohapatra TM, Singh YI. Prevalence of Methicillin-resistant *Staphylococcus aureus* (MRSA) in a Tertiary-Care Hospital in Eastern Nepal. *JNMA J Nepal Med Assoc*, 2008, 47(170):53-56. (http://www.ncbi.nlm.nih.gov/pubmed/18709031, accessed 31 March 2014).

218. Tiwari HK, Das AK, Sapkota D, Sivrajan K, Pahwa VK. Methicillin resistant *Staphylococcus aureus*: prevalence and antibiogram in a tertiary care hospital in western Nepal. *J Infect Dev Ctries*, 2009, 3(9):681-684. (http://www.ncbi.nlm.nih.gov/pubmed/19858569, accessed 23 January 2014).

219. Rijal KR, Pahari N, Shrestha BK, Nepal AK, Paudel B, Mahato P et al. Prevalence of methicillin resistant *Staphylococcus aureus* in school children of Pokhara. *Nepal Med Coll J*, 2008, 10(3):192-195. (http://www.ncbi.nlm.nih.gov/pubmed/19253865, accessed 23 January 2014).

220. Sapkota K, Basnyat SR, Shrestha CD, Shrestha J, Dumre SP, Adhikari N. Prevalence of Methicillin Resistant *Staphylococcus aureus* (MRSA) in tertiary referral hospital in Nepal. *Int J Infect Dis*, 2010, 14:e347. (http://linkinghub.elsevier.com/retrieve/pii/S1201971210004236?showall=true, accessed 23 January 2014).

221. Shrestha B, Pokhrel B, Mohapatra T. Study of nosocomial isolates of *Staphylococcus aureus* with special reference to methicillin resistant *S. aureus* in a tertiary care hospital in Nepal. *Nepal Med Coll J*, 2009, 11(2):123-126. (http://www.ncbi.nlm.nih.gov/pubmed/19968154, accessed 23 January 2014).

222. Shrestha B, Pokhrel BM, Mohapatra TM. *Staphylococcus aureus* nasal carriage among health care workers in a Nepal Hospital. *Braz J Infect Dis*, 2009, 13(5):322. doi:10.1590/S1413-86702009000500001.

223. Gomes PLR, Malavige GN, Fernando N, Mahendra MHR, Kamaladasa SD, Seneviratne JKK et al. Characteristics of *Staphylococcus aureus* colonization in patients with atopic dermatitis in Sri Lanka. *Clin Exp Dermatol*, 2011, 36(2):195-200. doi:10.1111/j.1365-2230.2010.03962.x.

224. Lim LG, Tan XX, Woo SJ, Dan YY, Lee YM, Lai V et al. Risk factors for mortality in cirrhotic patients with sepsis. *Hepatol Int*, 2011, 5(3):800-807. doi:10.1007/s12072-011-9258-y.

225. Tali-Maamar H, Laliam R, Bentchouala C, Touati D, Sababou K, Azrou S et al. Reprint of: Serotyping and antibiotic susceptibility of Streptococcus pneumoniae strains isolated in Algeria from 2001 to 2010. *Vaccine*, 2012, 30:G25-G31. (http://dx.doi.org/10.1016/j.vaccine.2012.11.019, accessed 8 April 2014).

226. Borg MA, Tiemersma E, Scicluna E, van de Sande-Bruinsma N, de Kraker M, Monen J et al. Prevalence of penicillin and erythromycin resistance among invasive Streptococcus pneumoniae isolates reported by laboratories in the southern and eastern Mediterranean region. *Clin Microbiol Infect*, 2009, 15(3):232-237. doi:10.1111/j.1469-0691.2008.02651.x.

227. Mullan PC, Steenhoff AP, Draper H, Wedin T, Bafana M, Anabwani G et al. Etiology of meningitis among patients admitted to a tertiary referral hospital in Botswana. *Pediatr Infect Dis J*, 2011, 30(7):620-622. doi:10.1097/INF.0b013e318210b51e.

228. Bere LC, Simpore J, Karou SD, Zeba B, Bere AP, Bannerman E et al. Antimicrobial resistance and serotype distribution of Streptococcus pneumoniae strains causing childhood infection in Burkina Faso. *Pak J Biol Sci*, 2009, 12(18):1282-1286. (http://www.ncbi.nlm.nih.gov/pubmed/20384283, accessed 8 April 2014).

229. Ndip RN, Ntiege EA, Ndip LM, Nkwelang G, Akoachere JF, Akenji TN. Antimicrobial resistance of bacterial agents of the upper respiratory tract of school children in Buea, Cameroon. *J Health Popul Nutr*, 2008, 26(4):397-404. (http://www.ncbi.nlm.nih.gov/pubmed/19069618, accessed 23 January 2014).

230. Bercion R, Bobossi-Serengbe G, Gody JC, Beyam EN, Manirakiza A, Le Faou A. Acute bacterial meningitis at the 'Complexe Pédiatrique' of Bangui, Central African Republic. *J Trop Paediatr*, 2008, 54(2):125-128. (http://www.ncbi.nlm.nih.gov/pubmed/17906317, accessed 8 April 2014).

231. Erqou S, Kebede Y, Mulu A. Increased resistance of Streptococcus pneumoniae isolates to antimicrobial drugs, at a referral hospital in north-west Ethiopia. *Tropical Doctor*, 2008, 38(2):110-112. doi:10.1258/td.2007.006190.

232. Talbert AW, Mwaniki M, Mwarumba S, Newton CR, Berkley JA. Invasive bacterial infections in neonates and young infants born outside hospital admitted to a rural hospital in Kenya. *Pediatr Infect Dis J*, 2010, 29(10):945-949. doi:10.1097/INF.0b013e3181dfca8c.

233. Everett DB, Mukaka M, Denis B, Gordon SB, Carrol ED, van Oosterhout JJ et al. Ten years of surveillance for invasive Streptococcus pneumoniae during the era of antiretroviral scale-up and cotrimoxazole prophylaxis in Malawi. *PLoS ONE*, 2011, 6(3):e17765. doi:10.1371/journal.pone.0017765.

234. Mandomando I, Sigauque B, Morais L, Espasa M, Valles X, Sacarlal J et al. Antimicrobial drug resistance trends of bacteremia isolates in a rural hospital in southern Mozambique. *Am J Trop Med Hyg*, 2010, 83(1):152-157. doi:10.4269/ajtmh.2010.09-0578.

235. Kandakai-Olukemi YT, Dido MS. Antimicrobial resistant profile of Streptococcus pneumoniae isolated from the nasopharynx of secondary school students in Jos, Nigeria. *Ann Afr Med*, 2009, 8(1):10-13. (http://www.ncbi.nlm.nih.gov/pubmed/19763000, accessed 8 April 2014).

236. Ndiaye AG, Boye CS, Hounkponou E, Gueye FB, Badiane A. Antimicrobial susceptibility of select respiratory tract pathogens in Dakar, Senegal. *J Infect Dev Ctries*, 2009, 3(9):660-666. (http://www.ncbi.nlm.nih.gov/pubmed/19858566, accessed 8 April 2014).

237. Namayanja-Kaye GA, Namale A, Joloba ML, Salata RA. Outcome of patients with pneumococcal bacteremia at Mulago Hospital, Kampala. *Infect Dis Clin Prac*, 2009, 17(4):248. doi:10.1097/IPC.0b013e31819d85b1.

238. Mayanja BN, Todd J, Hughes P, Van der Paal L, Mugisha JO, Atuhumuza E et al. Septicaemia in a population-based HIV clinical cohort in rural Uganda, 1996-2007: incidence, aetiology, antimicrobial drug resistance and impact of antiretroviral therapy. *Trop Med Int Health*, 2010, 15(6):697-705. doi:10.1111/j.1365-3156.2010.02528.x.

239. Moyo SJ, Steinbakk M, Aboud S, Mkopi N, Kasubi M, Blomberg B et al. Penicillin resistance and serotype distribution of Streptococcus pneumoniae in nasopharyngeal carrier children under 5 years of age in Dar es Salaam, Tanzania. *J Med Microbiol*, 2012, 61(Pt 7):952-959. doi:10.1099/jmm.0.042598-0.

240. Benouda A, Ben Redjeb S, Hammami A, Sibille S, Tazir M, Ramdani-Bouguessa N. Antimicrobial resistance of respiratory pathogens in North African countries. *J Chemother*, 2009, 21(6):627-632. (http://www.ncbi.nlm.nih.gov/pubmed/20071285, accessed 8 April 2014).

241. Mudhune S, Wamae M, Network Surveillance for Pneumococcal Disease in the East African R. Report on invasive diseases and meningitis due to Haemophilus influenzae and streptococcus pneumonia from the network for surveillance of pneumococcal disease in the East African region. *Clin Infect Dis*, 2009, 48:S147-S152. doi:10.1086/596494.

242. Villaseñor-Sierra A, Lomas-Bautista M, Aguilar-Benavides S, Martinez-Aguilar G. Serotypes and susceptibility of Streptococcus pneumoniae strains isolated from children in Mexico. *Salud Publica Mex*, 2008, 50(4):330-333. (http://www.ncbi.nlm.nih.gov/pubmed/18670725, accessed 8 April 2014).

243. Johny M, Babelly M, Al-Obaid I, Al-Benwan K, Udo EE. Antimicrobial resistance in clinical isolates of Streptococcus pneumoniae in a tertiary hospital in Kuwait, 1997-2007: Implications for empiric therapy. *J Infect Public Health*, 2010, 3(2):60-66. doi:10.1016/j.jiph.2010.02.003.

244. Mokaddas E, Albert MJ. Impact of pneumococcal conjugate vaccines on burden of invasive pneumococcal disease and serotype distribution of Streptococcus pneumoniae isolates: an overview from Kuwait. *Vaccine*, 2012, 30 Suppl 6:G37-40. doi:10.1016/j.vaccine.2012.10.061.

245. Mokaddas EM, Rotimi VO, Albert MJ. Implications of Streptococcus pneumoniae penicillin resistance and serotype distribution in Kuwait for disease treatment and prevention. *Clin Vaccine Immunol*, 2008, 15(2):203-207. (http://www.ncbi.nlm.nih.gov/pubmed/18077618, accessed 23 January 2014).

246. Hanna-Wakim R, Chehab H, Mahfouz I, Nassar F, Baroud M, Shehab M et al. Epidemiologic characteristics, serotypes, and antimicrobial susceptibilities of invasive Streptococcus pneumoniae isolates in a nationwide surveillance study in Lebanon. *Vaccine*, 2012, 30:G11-G17. doi:10.1016/j.vaccine.2012.07.020.

247. Bouskraoui M, Soraa N, Zahlane K, Arsalane L, Doit C, Mariani P et al. [Study of nasopharyngeal colonization by Streptococcus pneumoniae and its antibiotics resistance in healthy children less than 2 years of age in the Marrakech region (Morocco)]. *Arch Pediatr*, 2011, 18(12):1265-1270. doi:10.1016/j.arcped.2011.08.028.

248. Benbachir M, Elmdaghri N, Belabbes H, Haddioui G, Benzaid H, Zaki B. Eleven-year surveillance of antibiotic resistance in Streptococcus pneumoniae in Casablanca (Morocco). *Microb Drug Resist*, 2012, 18(2):157-160. doi:10.1089/mdr.2011.0130.

249. Zafar A, Hussain Z, Lomama E, Sibille S, Irfan S, Khan E. Antibiotic susceptibility of pathogens isolated from patients with community-acquired respiratory tract infections in Pakistan--the active study. *J Ayub Med Coll Abbottabad*, 2008, 20(1):7-9. (http://www.ncbi.nlm.nih.gov/pubmed/19024175, accessed 8 April 2014).

250. Hussain T, Hayat A, Sosorburam T, Bontouraby S, Deo P, Pathak J et al. Pathological pattern and clinical presentation of Streptococcus pneumoniae among children in Pakistan: a retrospective study. *Int J Infect Dis*, 2011, 15(S1):S19. doi:10.1016/S1201-9712(11)60070-2.

251. Al Ayed MS, Hawan AA. Retrospective review of invasive pediatric pneumococcal diseases in a military hospital in the southern region of Saudi Arabia. *Ann Saudi Med*, 2011, 31(5):469-472. doi:10.4103/0256-4947.84623.

252. Shibl AM, Memish ZA, Al-Kattan KM. Antibiotic resistance and serotype distribution of invasive pneumococcal diseases before and after introduction of pneumococcal conjugate vaccine in the Kingdom of Saudi Arabia (KSA). *Vaccine*, 2012, 30 Suppl 6:G32-36. doi:10.1016/j.vaccine.2012.07.030.

253. Smaoui H, Amri J, Hajji N, Kechrid A. [Antimicrobial susceptibility and serotype distribution of streptococcus pneumoniae isolates in children in Tunis]. *Arch Pediatr*, 2009, 16(3):220-226. doi:10.1016/j.arcped.2008.12.015.

254. Al Shamahy HA. Prevalence of streptococcus pneumoniae carriage among healthy children in Yemen. *Emirates Med J*, 26(1):25-29.

255. Shibl A, Memish Z, Pelton S. Epidemiology of invasive pneumococcal disease in the Arabian Peninsula and Egypt. *Int J Antimicrob Agents*, 2009, 33(5):410 e411-419. doi:10.1016/j.ijantimicag.2008.08.012.

256. Saha SK, Naheed A, El Arifeen S, Islam M, Al-Emran H, Amin R et al. Surveillance for invasive Streptococcus pneumoniae disease among hospitalized children in Bangladesh: antimicrobial susceptibility and serotype distribution. *Clin Infect Dis*, 2009, 48:S75-S81. doi:10.1086/596544.

257. Lalitha MK, David T, Thomas K, Rapid Antimicrobial Resistance Study Group. Nasopharyngeal swabs of school children, useful in rapid assessment of community antimicrobial resistance patterns in Streptococcus pneumoniae and Haemophilus influenzae. *J Clin Epidemiol*, 2013, 66(1):44-51. doi:10.1016/j.jclinepi.2012.01.011.

258. Chong CY, Koh-Cheng T, Yee-Hui M, Nancy TW. Invasive pneumococcal disease in Singapore children. *Vaccine*, 2008, 26(27-28):3427-343. doi:10.1016/j.vaccine.2008.04.035.

259. Hsu LY, Lui SW, Lee JL, Hedzlyn HM, Kong DH, Shameen S et al. Adult invasive pneumococcal disease pre- and peri-pneumococcal conjugate vaccine introduction in a tertiary hospital in Singapore. *J Med Microbiol*, 2009, 58(Pt 1):101-104. doi:10.1099/jmm.0.003764-0.

260. Vasoo S, Singh K, Hsu LY, Chiew YF, Chow C, Lin RT et al. Increasing antibiotic resistance in Streptococcus pneumoniae colonizing children attending day-care centres in Singapore. *Respirology*, 2011, 16(8):1241-1248. doi:10.1111/j.1440-1843.2011.02036.x.

261. Bonkoungou IJ, Bonkoungou IJ, Haukka K, Österblad M, Hakanen AJ, Traoré AS, Barro N et al. Bacterial and viral etiology of childhood diarrhea in Ouagadougou, Burkina Faso. *BMC Pediatr*, 2013, 13:36. doi:10.1186/1471-2431-13-36.

262. Phoba MF, Lunguya O, Mayimon DV, Lewo di Mputu P, Bertrand S, Vanhoof R et al. Multidrug-resistant *Salmonella* enterica, Democratic Republic of the Congo. *Emerg Infect Dis*, 2012, 18(10):1692-1694. doi:10.3201/eid1810.120525.

263. Asrat D. Shigella and Salmonella serogroups and their antibiotic susceptibility patterns in Ethiopia. *East Mediterr Health J*, 2008, 14(4):760-767. (http://www.ncbi.nlm.nih.gov/pubmed/19166157, accessed 8 April 2014).

264. Yismaw G, Negeri C, Kassu A. A five-year antimicrobial resistance pattern of Shigella isolated from stools in the Gondar University hospital, northwest Ethiopia. *Tropical Doctor*, 2008, 38(1):43-45. doi:10.1258/td.2007.060215.

265. Newman MJ, Frimpong E, Donkor ES, Opintan JA, Asamoah-Adu A. Resistance to antimicrobial drugs in Ghana. *Infect Drug Resist*, 2011, 4:215-220. doi:10.2147/IDR.S21769.

266. Schwarz NG, Sarpong N, Hünger F, Marks F, Acquah SE, Agyekum A et al. Systemic bacteraemia in children presenting with clinical pneumonia and the impact of non-typhoid salmonella (NTS). *BMC Infect Dis*, 2010, 10:319. doi:10.1186/1471-2334-10-319.

267. Sang WK, Oundo V, Schnabel D. Prevalence and antibiotic resistance of bacterial pathogens isolated from childhood diarrhoea in four provinces of Kenya. *J Infect Dev Ctries*, 2012, 6(7):572-578. (http://www.ncbi.nlm.nih.gov/pubmed/22842944, accessed 8 April 2014).

268. Mandomando I, Jaintilal D, Pons MJ, Vallès X, Espasa M, Mensa L et al. Antimicrobial susceptibility and mechanisms of resistance in Shigella and Salmonella isolates from children under five years of age with diarrhea in rural Mozambique. *Antimicrob Agents Chemother*, 2009, 53(6):2450-2454. doi:10.1128/AAC.01282-08.

269. Seydi M, Soumare M, Sow AI, Diop SA, Sow I, Dieng AB et al. [Nontyphoidal Salmonella bacteremia cases in AIDS patients in a Dakar University Hospital (Senegal)]. *Med Mal Infect*, 2008, 38(1):25-28. (http://www.ncbi.nlm.nih.gov/pubmed/18093773, accessed 8 April 2014).

270. Sire JM, Garin B, Macondo EA. Low-level resistance to ciprofloxacin in non-Typhi Salmonella enterica isolated from human gastroenteritis in Dakar, Senegal (2004--2006). *Int J Antimicrob Agents*, 2008, 31(6):581-582. doi:10.1016/j.ijantimicag.2008.01.014.

271. Gbadoé AD, Lawson-Evi K, Dagnra AY, Guédénon K, Géraldo A, Djadou E et al. [Pediatric salmonellosis at the Tokoin's teaching hospital, Lomé (Togo)]. *Med Mal Infect*, 2008, 38(1):8-11. (http://www.ncbi.nlm.nih.gov/pubmed/18160240, accessed 8 April 2014).

272. Meremo A, Mshana SE, Kidenya BR, Kabangila R, Peck R, Kataraihya JB. High prevalence of non-typhoid salmonella bacteraemia among febrile HIV adult patients admitted at a tertiary Hospital, North-Western Tanzania. *Int Arch Med*, 2012, 5(1):28. doi:10.1186/1755-7682-5-28.

273. Macedo-Vinas M, Cordeiro NF, Bado I, Herrera-Leon S, Vola M, Robino L et al. Surveillance of antibiotic resistance evolution and detection of class 1 and 2 integrons in human isolates of multi-resistant Salmonella Typhimurium obtained in Uruguay between 1976 and 2000. *Int J Infect Dis*, 2009, 13(3):342-348. doi:10.1016/j.ijid.2008.07.012.

274. Rotimi VO, Jamal W, Pal T, Sonnevend A, Dimitrov TS, Albert MJ. Emergence of multidrug-resistant Salmonella spp. and isolates with reduced susceptibility to ciprofloxacin in Kuwait and the United Arab Emirates. *Diagn Microbiol Infect Dis*, 2008, 60(1):71-77. (http://www.ncbi.nlm.nih.gov/pubmed/17931817, accessed 19 January 2014).

275. Rahouma A, Klena JD, Krema Z, Abobker AA, Treesh K, Franka E et al. Enteric pathogens associated with childhood diarrhea in Tripoli-Libya. *Am J Trop Med Hyg*, 2011, 84(6):886-891. (http://www.ncbi.nlm.nih.gov/pubmed/21633024, accessed 2 February 2014).

276. Ohmani F, Khedid K, Britel S, Qasmaoui A, Charof R, Filali-Maltouf A et al. Antimicrobial resistance in Salmonella enterica serovar Enteritidis in Morocco. *J Infect Dev Ctries*, 2010, 4(12):804-809. (http://www.ncbi.nlm.nih.gov/pubmed/21252460, accessed 2 February 2014).

277. Somily AM, Sayyed SB, Habib HA, Al-Khattaf AS, Al Otabi FE, Shakoor Z et al. Salmonella isolates serotypes and susceptibility to commonly used drugs at a tertiary care hospital in Riyadh, Saudi Arabia. *J Infect Dev Ctries*, 2012, 6(6):478-482. (http://www.ncbi.nlm.nih.gov/pubmed/22706189, accessed 23 January 2014).

278. Al Robasi AA, Mohamed, MA. Al Osta, L. Nalidixic acid and ciprofloxacin resistance in non-typhoidal salmonella isolates in Sanaa city, Yemen. *J Barhrain Med Soc*, 2008, 20(1):15-20.

279. Bottieau E, Clerinx J, Vlieghe E, Van Esbroeck M, Jacobs J, Van Gompel A et al. Epidemiology and outcome of Shigella, Salmonella and Campylobacter infections in travellers returning from the tropics with fever and diarrhoea. *Acta Clin Belg*, 2011, 66(3):191-195. (http://www.ncbi.nlm.nih.gov/pubmed/21837926, accessed 8 April 2014).

280. Bassal R, Reisfeld A, Andorn N, Yishai R, Nissan I, Agmon V et al. Recent trends in the epidemiology of non-typhoidal Salmonella in Israel, 1999-2009. *Epidemiol Infect*, 2012, 140(8):1446-1453. doi:10.1017/S095026881100197X.

281. Ahmed D, Hoque A, Elahi MS, Endtz HP, Hossain MA. Bacterial aetiology of diarrhoeal diseases and antimicrobial resistance in Dhaka, Bangladesh, 2005-2008. *Epidemiol Infect*, 2012, 140(9):1678-1684. doi:10.1017/S0950268811002135.

282. Huruy K, Kassu A, Mulu A, Gebretsadik S, Andargie G, Tadesse T et al. High level of antimicrobial resistance in Shigella species isolated from diarrhoeal patients in University of Gondar Teaching Hospital, Gondar, Ethiopia. *Pharmacology Online*, 2008, 2:328-340.

283. Tiruneh M. Serodiversity and antimicrobial resistance pattern of Shigella isolates at Gondar University teaching hospital, Northwest Ethiopia. *Jpn J Infect Dis*, 2009, 62(2):93-97. (http://www.ncbi.nlm.nih.gov/pubmed/19305047, accessed 8 April 2014).

284. Djie-Maletz A, Reither K, Danour S, Anyidoho L, Saad E, Danikuu F et al. High rate of resistance to locally used antibiotics among enteric bacteria from children in Northern Ghana. *J Antimicrob Chemother*, 2008, 61(6):1315-1318. doi:10.1093/jac/dkn108.

285. Njuguna HN. Shigella serotypes and antibiotic sensitivity in an urban slum clinic in Nairobi. Kenya. *Am J Trop Med Hyg*, 2009, 81(5):20-21.

286. Njuguna HN, Cosmas L, Williamson J, Nyachieo D, Olack B, Ochieng JB et al. Use of population-based surveillance to define the high incidence of shigellosis in an urban slum in Nairobi, Kenya. *PLoS ONE*, 2013, 8(3):e58437. doi:10.1371/journal.pone.0058437.

287. Sire JM, Macondo EA, Perrier-Gros-Claude JD, Siby T, Bahsoun I, Seck A et al. Antimicrobial resistance in Shigella species isolated in Dakar, Senegal (2004-2006). *Jpn J Infect Dis*, 2008, 61(4):307-309. (http://www.ncbi.nlm.nih.gov/pubmed/18653976, accessed 9 April 2014).

288. Drews SJ, Lau C, Andersen M, Ferrato C, Simmonds K, Stafford L et al. Laboratory based surveillance of travel-related Shigella sonnei and Shigella flexneri in Alberta from 2002 to 2007. *Global Health*, 2010, 6:20. doi:10.1186/1744-8603-6-20.

289. Mota MI, Gadea MP, González S, González G, Pardo L, Sirok A et al. Bacterial pathogens associated with bloody diarrhea in Uruguayan children. *Rev Argent Microbiol*, 2010, 42(2):114-117. doi:10.1590/S0325-75412010000200009.

290. Jamal W, Rotimi VO, Pal T, Sonnevend A, Dimitrov TS. Comparative in vitro activity of tigecycline and other antimicrobial agents against Shigella species from Kuwait and the United Arab of Emirates. *J Infect Public Health*, 2010, 3(1):35-42. doi:10.1016/j.jiph.2009.10.001.

291. Patel PK, Mercy J, Shenoy J, Ashwini B. Factors associated with acute diarrhoea in children in Dhahira, Oman: a hospital-based study. *East Mediterr Health J*, 2008, 14(3):571-578. (http://www.ncbi.nlm.nih.gov/pubmed/18720621, accessed 9 April 2014).

292. Zafar A, Hasan R, Nizami SQ, von Seidlein L, Soofi S, Ahsan T et al. Frequency of isolation of various subtypes and antimicrobial resistance of Shigella from urban slums of Karachi, Pakistan. *Int J Infect Dis*, 2009, 13(6):668-672. doi:10.1016/j.ijid.2008.10.005.

293. Khan E, Jabeen K, Ejaz M, Siddiqui J, Shezad MF, Zafar A. Trends in antimicrobial resistance in Shigella species in Karachi, Pakistan. *J Infect Dev Ctries*, 2009, 3(10):798-802. (http://www.ncbi.nlm.nih.gov/pubmed/20009283, accessed 9 April 2014).

294. Bari M. Surveillance of antibiotic susceptibility patterns among Shigella species in stools of diarrheal children. *Medical Forum Monthly*, 2011, 22(4):16-20. (http://www.medforum.pk/index.php?option=com_content&view=article&id=416:surveillance-of-antibiotic-susceptibility-patterns-among-shigella-species-in-stools-of-diarrheal-children, accessed 9 April 2014).

295. Elhag WI, Saeed HA, Omer EFE, Path FRC. Bacterial etiology and antimicrobials susceptibility of diarrhea among displaced communities during 2006-2008. *Bahrain Med Bull*, 2009, 31(3). (http://www.bahrainmedicalbulletin.com/september_2009/bacterial_diarrhea.pdf, accessed 9 April 2014).

296. Vrints M, Mairiaux E, Van Meervenne E, Collard JM, Bertrand S. Surveillance of antibiotic susceptibility patterns among Shigella sonnei strains isolated in Belgium during the 18-year period 1990 to 2007. *J Clin Microbiol*, 2009, 47(5):1379-1385. doi:10.1128/JCM.02460-08.

297. Bhattacharya D, Sugunan AP, Bhattacharjee H, Thamizhmani R, Sayi DS, Thanasekaran K et al. Antimicrobial resistance in Shigella--rapid increase & widening of spectrum in Andaman Islands, India. *Indian J Med Res*, 2012, 135(3):365-370. (http://www.ncbi.nlm.nih.gov/pubmed/22561624, accessed 9 April 2014).

298. Dharmik PG, Gomashe AV, Wadher BJ. Surveillance of antibiotic susceptibility pattern among shigella flexneri strain isolated in Nagpur district during three years period, January 2009-January 2012. *Indian J Med Sci*, 2010, 64(11):493-500. doi:10.4103/0019-5359.102120.

299. Dhodapkar R, Acharya NS, Harish BN, Parija SC. Shigellosis in Puducherry. *Indian J Med Res*, 2008, 127(6):621-622. (http://www.ncbi.nlm.nih.gov/pubmed/18765885, accessed 9 April 2014).

300. Nandy S, Mitra U, Rajendran K, Dutta P, Dutta S. Subtype prevalence, plasmid profiles and growing fluoroquinolone resistance in Shigella from Kolkata, India (2001-2007): a hospital-based study. *Trop Med Int Health*, 2010, 15(12):1499-1507. doi:10.1111/j.1365-3156.2010.02656.x.

301. Mandal J, V G, Emelda J, S M, Parija SC. The recent trends of Shigellosis: A JIPMER perspective. *J Clin Diagn Res*, 2012, 6(9):1474-1477. doi:10.7860/JCDR/2012/4157.2536.

302. Srinivasa H, Baijayanti M, Raksha Y. Magnitude of drug resistant Shigellosis: A report from Bangalore. *Indian J Med Microbiol*, 2009, 27(4):358-360. doi:10.4103/0255-0857.55460.

303. Nath R, Saikia L, Choudhury G, Sharma D. Drug resistant Shigella flexneri in & around Dibrugarh, north-east India. *Indian J Med Res*, 2013, 137(1):183-186. (http://www.ncbi.nlm.nih.gov/pubmed/23481070, accessed 23 January 2014).

304. Pokharel M, Sherchand JB, Upreti HC, Katuwal A, Gauchan P. A perspective study on the etiology of diarrhea in children less than 12 years of age attending Kanti Children's Hospital. *J. Nepal Paediatr. Soc*, 2009, 29(1):10-16.

305. Pandey P, Bodhidatta L, Lewis M, Murphy H, Shlim DR, Cave W et al. Travelers' diarrhea in Nepal: an update on the pathogens and antibiotic resistance. *J Trav Med*, 2011, 18(2):102-108. doi:10.1111/j.1708-8305.2010.00475.x.

306. Kansakar P, Baral P, Malla S, Ghimire GR. Antimicrobial susceptibilities of enteric bacterial pathogens isolated in Kathmandu, Nepal, during 2002-2004. *J Infect Dev Ctries*, 2011, 5(3):163-168. (http://www.ncbi.nlm.nih.gov/pubmed/21444984, accessed 9 April 2014).

307. Vinh H, Nhu NT, Nga TV, Duy PT, Campbell JI, Hoang NV et al. A changing picture of shigellosis in southern Vietnam: shifting species dominance, antimicrobial susceptibility and clinical presentation. *BMC Infect Dis*, 2009, 9:204. doi:10.1186/1471-2334-9-204.

308. Kuo CY, Su LH, Perera J, Carlos C, Tan BH, Kumarasinghe G et al. Antimicrobial susceptibility of Shigella isolates in eight Asian countries, 2001-2004. *J Microbiol Immunol Infect*, 2008, 41(2):107-111. (http://www.ncbi.nlm.nih.gov/pubmed/18473096, accessed 9 April 2014).

309. Cao V, Ratsima E, Van Tri D, Bercion R, Fonkoua MC, Richard V et al. Antimicrobial susceptibility of Neisseria gonorrhoeae strains isolated in 2004-2006 in Bangui, Central African Republic; Yaoundé, Cameroon; Antananarivo, Madagascar; and Ho Chi Minh Ville and Nha Trang, Vietnam. *Sex Transm Dis*, 2008, 35(11):941-945. doi:10.1097/OLQ.0b013e31818318d8.

310. Mehta SD, Maclean I, Ndinya-Achola JO, Moses S, Martin I, Ronald A et al. Emergence of quinolone resistance and cephalosporin MIC creep in Neisseria gonorrhoeae isolates from a cohort of young men in Kisumu, Kenya, 2002 to 2009. *Antimicrob Agents Chemother*, 2011, 55(8):3882-3888. doi:10.1128/AAC.00155-11.

311. Apalata T, Zimba TF, Sturm WA, Moodley P. Antimicrobial susceptibility profile of Neisseria gonorrhoeae isolated from patients attending a STD facility in Maputo, Mozambique. *Sex Transm Dis*, 2009, 36(6):341-343. doi:10.1097/OLQ.0b013e3181982e3c.

312. Amito Florence P, Otim F, Okongo F, Ogwang M, Greco D. The prevalence and antibiotics susceptibility pattern of Neisseria gonorrhoeae in patients attending OPD clinics at St Mary's Hospital Lacor, Uganda. *J Prev Med Hyg*, 2012, 53(4):186-189. (http://www.ncbi.nlm.nih.gov/pubmed/23469585, accessed 9 April 2014).

313. Starnino S, Group G-LW, Galarza P, Carvallo M, Benzaken A, Ballesteros A et al. Retrospective analysis of antimircrobial susceptibility trends (2000-2009) in Neisseria gonorrhoeae isolates from countries in Latin America and the Caribean shows evolving resistance to ciprofloxacin, azithromycin and decreased susceptibility to ceftriaxone. *Sex Transm Dis*, 2012, 39(10):813-821. (http://www.ncbi.nlm.nih.gov/pubmed/23001269, accessed 9 April 2014).

314. Jabeen K, Nizamuddin S, Irfan S, Khan E, Malik F, Zafar A. Increasing trend of resistance to penicilin, tetracycline and fluoroquinoloe resistance in Neisseria gonorrhoeae from Pakistan (1992-2009). *J Trop Med*, 2011, 2011:960501. doi:10.1155/2011/960501.

315. Alzahrani AJ, Obeid OE, Hassan MI, Almulhim AA. Screening of pregnant women attending the antenatal care clinic of a tertiary hospital in eastern Saudi Arabia for Chlamydia trachomatis and Neisseria gonorrhoeae infections. *Indian J Sex Transm Dis*, 2010, 31(2):81-86. doi:10.4103/0253-7184.74976.

316. Glazkova S, Golparian D, Titov L, Pankratova N, Suhabokava N, Shimanskaya I et al. Antimicrobial susceptibility/resistance and molecular epidemiological characteristics of Neisseria gonorrhoeae in 2009 in Belarus. *APMIS*, 2011, 119(8):537-542. doi:10.1111/j.1600-0463.2011.02770.x.

317. Dan M, Mor Z, Gottliev S, Sheinberg B, Shohat T. Trends in antimicrobial susceptibility of Neisseria gonorrhoeae in Israel, 2002 to 2007, with special reference to fluoroquinolone resistance. *Sex Transm Dis*, 2010, 37(7):451-453. doi:10.1097/OLQ.0b013e3181cfca06.

318. Frigo N, Unemo M, Kubanova A, Kubanov A, Solomka V, Polevshikova S et al. Russian gonococcal antimicrobial susceptibility programme (RU-GASP) - resistance levels in 2010 and trends during 2005-2010 (Epidemiology poster session 1: STI trends: Neisseria gonorrhoeae: resistance: P1-S1.42). *Sex Transm Infect*, 2011, 87:A116-A117.

319. Cole MJ, Chisholm SA, Hoffmann S, Stary A, Lowndes CM, Ison CA et al. European surveillance of antimicrobial resistance in Neisseria gonorrhoeae. *Sex Transm Dis*, 2010, 86(6):427-432. doi:10.1136/sti.2010.044164.

320. Lahra MM. Surveillance of antibiotic resistance in Neisseria gonorrhoeae in the WHO Western Pacific and South East Asian Regions, 2010. *Commun Dis Intell Q Rep*, 2012, 36(1):95-100. (http://www.ncbi.nlm.nih.gov/pubmed/23153085, accessed 29 December 2013).

Annex 3
The burden of antibacterial resistance: a systematic review of published evidence (technical report on methods and detailed results)

A3.1 Methods

The strategy for building and analysing the evidence base for the burden of antimicrobial resistance consisted of two fundamental steps based on a predefined systematic review protocol:

(i) A broad systematic review of the available non-randomized evidence in the published literature for the outcomes specified in the protocol was undertaken. The systematic review was conducted in line with the *Cochrane handbook for systematic reviews of interventions* (1).

(ii) A meta-analysis was conducted comparing the available health and economic outcomes specified a priori for resistant and susceptible *Escherichia coli*, *Klebsiella pneumoniae* and *S. aureus* infections. Meta-analysis was done separately by resistance for each *E. coli*, *K. pneumoniae* and *S. aureus* outcome.

Population, intervention, comparator and outcome (PICO) statement

The population, intervention, comparator and outcome (PICO) statement is outlined in Table A3.1.

A3.1.1 Electronic search strategy

The literature search included the following bibliographic databases: MEDLINE and PubMed, Embase, the Centre for Reviews and Dissemination (DARE, NHS EED and HTA) databases, Web of Knowledge and Global Health (Ovid). Searches (from 1946) were run in March 2013. Where possible, searches were limited to human studies. No date or language limits were applied to the clinical or economics searches, but the search for existing reviews was limited to 2010 to present. The search terms used controlled vocabulary, such as the Medical Subject Headings (MeSH) terms: *Escherichia coli*, *Klebsiella pneumoniae* and *Staphylococcus aureus*, combined with MeSH terms for drug resistance, as well as additional keywords. Each database was searched for observational studies, economic and burden of illness studies, and recent systematic reviews. The comprehensive search strategy is available on request.

Table A3.1 Population, intervention, comparator and outcome elements for each investigated bacteria

Population	Patients with confirmed:		
	E. coli infection	*K. pneumonaie* infection	*S. aureus* infection
Intervention	Patients with:		
	3rd generation cephalosporin-resistant Fluoroquinolone-resistant	3rd generation cephalosporin-resistant Carbapenem-resistant	Methicillin-resistant
Comparator	3rd generation cephalosporin-susceptible Fluoroquinolone-susceptible	3rd generation cephalosporin-susceptible Carbapenem-susceptible	Methicillin-susceptible
Clinical outcomes (health burden)	Mortality (bacteria-attributable) Mortality (all-cause) 30-day mortality LOS in hospital PYLL	Other suggested outcomes ICU required Ventilator need Discharge (to home, care facility) Readmission	
Economic outcomes (economic burden)	Actual direct hospital costs for treating the patient (second-line drugs, investigations) Secondary costs for hospital/health care: contact testing, isolation room, staff cohorts LOS		
Outcomes (other)	Absenteeism Medical complications leading to physical impairment (short/long term)		
Included study types	All designs including case-series		
Subgroups of interest	Low- and middle-income countries Treatment setting		

ICU, intensive care unit; LOS, length of stay; PYLL, potential years of life loss.

Eligibility and study selection

Studies were included if the PICO criteria and type of study were appropriate. Selection eligibility criteria were applied to each title and abstract identified in the literature search by two independent reviewers in a standardized manner. Any uncertainties were resolved by discussion and consensus with a third review author. Any study passing the selection criteria was obtained in full-text format. The eligibility criteria were then applied and a final decision made for inclusion. The preliminary inclusion and exclusion criteria for consideration are provided below.

The study must be an approved design, and include:

- human patients with confirmed infection;

- data on outcomes of interest for both resistant and sensitive patients; and

- prospective or retrospective enrolment.

Studies were excluded if they were:

- reports of patients with colonization only (≤10% within a group allowable); or

- small numbers reported (e.g. <10 for a case-series).

Data extraction and management

All information was extracted using a standardized data abstraction form, which was developed, piloted and modified as necessary for this systematic review. Abstraction included the characteristics of study participants and the study itself, along with the relevant health and economic outcomes. All extracted data were checked for accuracy by two independent review authors.

Risk of bias assessment

Various quality assessment instruments were considered. The Newcastle-Ottawa Scale (NOS) (2) was used for assessing the quality of observational studies. This quality assessment instrument evaluates cohort studies along three dimensions: selection of cohorts, comparability of cohorts and ascertainment of outcome. Issues related specifically to observational studies – including confounding and selective analysis reporting – were carefully evaluated and incorporated into the analysis and interpretation.

Assessment of heterogeneity

Studies were assessed for both clinical and methodological diversity. Clinical diversity was assessed by checking that the patients, exposures and settings were not so different across studies that combining them would be inappropriate. Methodological diversity was assessed by checking that the studies were similar in terms of study design and risk of bias.

Once satisfied that the studies were minimally diverse (and hence that it made sense to pool them together in a meta-analysis), the statistical heterogeneity was assessed. If the effects observed across studies were inconsistent, and varied to a large extent, the results were again explored to assess whether the differences could be explained by some clinical or methodological feature.

Assessment of reporting bias

Reporting bias was assessed by constructing funnel plots, as well as bias indicators (e.g. Egger, Harbold-Egger) for each outcome.

Data synthesis

The data were first summarized descriptively. A meta-analysis was undertaken using fixed or random-effects models when data were available, sufficiently similar and of sufficient quality.

GRADE tables

Once the review was completed, Grading of Recommendations Assessment, Development and Evaluation (GRADE) tables were prepared using standard GRADE methodology. The quality of outcome measures was assessed using a standard GRADE approach as described by Guyatt et al. (3, 4) The assessment of the items identified in the GRADE risk of bias was based on the NOS assessment of the individual studies. The GRADE evidence table outcome measures were prepared using the GRADEpro program.[a] As described in the GRADE methodology, although evidence derived from observational studies was considered as low-quality evidence supporting an estimate of intervention effect, three factors could result in upgrading of the evidence – large effect, dose response and all plausible confounders or biases would result in an underestimate of the effect size. Ultimately, the quality of evidence for each outcome fell into four categories: very low, low, moderate and high.

---

[a] http://ims.cochrane.org/gradepro

A3.2 Results

Table A3.2 Complete overview of findings addressing the question: *Does the published scientific literature indicate that there is an inferior outcome in infections caused by the following bacteria if they are resistant to the following antibacterial drugs?*

| Parameter | E. coli | | K. pneumonae | | S. aureus |
	3rd generation cephalosporins	Fluoroquinolones	3rd generation cephalosporins	Carbapenems	Beta-lactam antibiotics (MRSA)
Outcome					
All-cause mortality	Yes (n = 16)	Yes (n = 8)	Yes (n = 14)	Yes (n = 11)	Yes (n = 107)
Bacterium-attributable mortality	Yes (n = 4)	No (n = 1)	Yes (n = 4)	No (n = 1)	Yes (n = 46)
30-day mortality	Yes (n = 11)	Yes (n = 5)	Yes (n = 7)	Yes (n = 3)	Yes (n = 16)
Intensive-care mortality	ND	ND	ND	No (n = 1)	Yes (n = 5)
LOS in hospital	No (n = 3)	No (n = 3)	No (n = 9)	Unclear (n = 3)[a]	Yes (n = 50)
Admission to ICU	No (n = 1)	Yes (n = 1)	Yes (n = 3)	ND	No (n = 17)
LOS in ICU	ND	ND	ND	No (n = 1)	Yes (n = 21)
Progression to septic shock	ND	Yes (n = 1)	No (n = 3)	ND	Yes (n = 21)
Postinfection LOS	No (n = 3)	ND	Yes (n = 4)	No (n = 1)	Yes (n = 27)
Transfer to other health-care facility	ND	ND	ND	No (n = 1)	Yes (n = 1)
Transfer to long-term care facility	ND	ND	ND	Unclear (n = 1)[b]	Yes (n = 1)
Attributable readmission	ND	ND	ND	ND	No (n = 6)
Attributable mechanical ventilation	ND	ND	ND	ND	No (n = 14)

ICU, intensive care unit; LOS, length of stay; MRSA, methicillin-resistant Staphylococcus aureus; *ND, no data.*

a. Data in two studies were inconsistent, and a third study could not be included in the analysis.

b. A small study found that there was not a significant increase in the risk of health-care facility transfer for patients with carbapenem-resistant *K. pneumoniae* infections; however, patients enrolled in this study may have come from long-term care facilities at the time of study enrollment, so this result may not be directly attributable to *K. pneumoniae*.

Health burden

Studies included in the systematic reviews for *E. coli* and *K. pneumoniae* (Table A3.2) were all conducted in countries classified as high or upper-middle-income status according to the 2013 World Bank member list of economies (*5*). Upper-middle countries include Argentina, Brazil, China, Hungary, Malaysia, Mexico, Romania, South Africa and Thailand. No studies were found that originated from, or studied populations, classified as low income.

Escherichia coli

The literature search identified 17 426 references possibly relevant for the question. Once duplicates were removed, 13 095 references remained, of which 425 were retrieved for full-text review. Ultimately, 12 studies (*6-17*) met the inclusion criteria for fluoroquinolone resistance and 25 studies (*7, 8, 10, 18-39*) for resistance to third-generation cephalosporins in *E. coli*. Three studies (*7, 8, 10*) were included in both *E. coli* reviews. Meta-analysis was done separately for fluoroquinolone and third-generation cephalosporin-resistant *E. coli* for each of the specified outcomes.

Infections caused by third-generation cephalosporin-resistant *Escherichia coli* infections

From the 25 included studies (Table A3.3) for infections with third-generation cephalosporin-resistant (including extended spectrum beta-lactamases [ESBL]-producing) *E. coli*, results were reported on the following health outcomes, in summary:

- **All-cause mortality:** There was a significant, more than twofold, increase in all-cause mortality in patients with cephalosporin-resistant *E. coli* infections (risk ratio [RR] 2.18, 95% confidence interval [CI]: 1.58 to 3.02, *P* < 0.00001). Data from 16 studies contributed to this estimate and the results were fairly inconsistent across the studies. (*8, 20-24, 26, 30, 32-39*).

- **Bacterium-attributable mortality:** There was a significant, more than twofold, increase in bacterium-attributable mortality for patients with cephalosporin-resistant *E. coli* infections (RR 2.02, 95% CI: 1.41 to 2.90, *P* 0.0001). Data from four studies contributed to this estimate and the results were consistent across the studies. (*18, 33, 34, 36*).

- **30-day mortality:** There was a significant, more than twofold, increase in risk of 30-day mortality in patients with cephalosporin-resistant *E. coli* infections (RR 2.19, 95% CI: 1.78 to 2.68, *P* < 0.00001). Data from 11 studies contributed to this estimate and the results were consistent across the studies. (*7, 10, 19, 25, 27-32, 35*).

- **Length of stay (LOS) in hospital:** There was no significant increase in LOS for patients with cephalosporin-resistant *E. coli* infections (mean difference [MD] 1.8 days, 95% CI: −1.3 to 5.0, *P* 0.26). The results were consistent across studies. Four studies reported on LOS (*23, 25, 36, 37*); for one study no standard deviation (SD) was available, and it could not be combined with the estimates of the other three studies (*25*).

- **Intensive care unit (ICU) admission:** Only one study (*32*) considered infection-attributable ICU admission, and there was no significant increase in risk for third-generation cephalosporin-resistant *E. coli* patients (RR 2.78, 95% CI: 0.58 to 13.20, *P* 0.20).

- **Postinfection LOS in hospital:** There was no significant increase in postinfection LOS for cephalosporin-resistant *E. coli* patients (MD 2.3 days, 95% CI: 0.25 to 4.90, *P* 0.08). Four studies reported on postinfection LOS (*19, 30, 35, 38*); for one study (*19*) no SD was available and it could not be combined with the estimates of the other three studies. The results were consistent across studies.

Fluoroquinolone-resistant *Escherichia coli* infections

All studies included were conducted in high-income countries. No studies were located from low-income or lower-middle-income countries. From the 12 included studies (*6-17*) (Table A3.4) results were reported on the following health outcomes comparing patients with fluoroquinolone-resistant *E. coli* to those with fluoroquinolone-susceptible *E. coli*, in summary:

- **All-cause mortality:** There was a significant increase in all-cause mortality for patients with fluoroquinolone-resistant *E. coli* infections, with over a twofold increase in risk of mortality (RR 2.11, 95% CI: 1.64 to 3.71, *P* < 0.00001). Data from eight studies contributed to this estimate and the results were consistent / similar across the studies. (*6, 8, 11, 13-17*).

- **Bacterium-attributable mortality:** Only one study (*11*) reported bacterium-attributable mortality. No bacterium-attributable mortality was observed in patients with fluoroquinolone-resistant or susceptible *E. coli*.

- **30-day mortality:** There was a significant increase in 30-day mortality for fluoroquinolone-resistant *E. coli* patients with over a twofold increase in risk (RR 2.16, 95% CI: 1.09 to 4.27, *P* 0.03). Data from five studies (*7, 9, 10, 12, 17*) contributed to this estimate and the results were somewhat inconsistent with the estimate from one study (*12*) that did not indicate greater 30-day mortality in patients with resistant infections.

- **LOS in hospital:** There was no significant increase in LOS for fluoroquinolone-resistant *E. coli* patients (MD 3.73, 95% CI: 3.49 to 10.94, *P* 0.31). However, data from the two studies (*11, 17*) that contributed to this estimate were inconsistent, with the estimate from one study indicating a significant increase in LOS (MD 7.8 days, 95% CI: 2.9 to 12.7) whereas the results of the other study were not significant (MD 0.40 days, 95% CI: −1.3 to 2.1). One additional study (*12*) was not included in the analysis due to missing information (SDs of the mean differences not reported).

- **ICU admission:** A single study (*9*) showed a significant twofold risk increase in infection-attributable ICU admission for fluoroquinolone-resistant *E. coli* patients (RR 2.40, 95% CI: 1.08 to 5.35, *P* 0.03).

- **Progression to septic shock:** Two studies (*9, 11*) reported on septic shock following *E. coli* infection. There was a significant increase in septic shock in patients with fluoroquinolone-resistant *E. coli* infections (RR 10.00, 95% CI: 1.19 to 84.36, *P* 0.03). This imprecise estimate was based on only one study (*9*),since no septic shock events occurred during the other study and the corresponding risk ratio (RR) was not estimable.

Klebsiella pneumoniae

The literature search identified 17 426 references possibly relevant for the question. Once duplicates were removed, 13 095 remained, of which 444 references were retrieved for full-text review. Ultimately, 24 studies (*29, 40-62*) met the inclusion criteria for third-generation cephalosporin *K. pneumoniae* and 13 studies (*63-75*) met the inclusion criteria for carbapenem-resistant *K. pneumoniae*.

Third-generation cephalosporin-resistant *Klebsiella pneumoniae* infections

Of the 24 included studies (Table A3.5) 13 were conducted in upper-middle-income countries and 10 in high-income countries, and a single study involved centres from mixed upper-middle- and high-income countries. From the included studies, results were reported on the following health outcomes for infections with third-generation cephalosporin-resistant (i.e. ESBL) *K. pneumoniae*, in summary:

- **All-cause mortality:** There was a significant increase in all-cause mortality for patients with infections caused by third-generation cephalosporin-resistant *K. pneumoniae* (RR 1.35, 95% CI: 1.14 to 1.61, *P* 0.0007). Data from 14 studies (*29, 40-42, 44-46, 48, 49, 51, 54, 58, 60, 61*) contributed to this estimate and the results were consistent across the studies.

- **Bacterium-attributable mortality:** There was a significant increase in bacterium-attributable mortality in patients with infections caused by third-generation *cephalosporin*-resistant *K. pneumoniae* (RR 1.93, 95% CI: 1.13 to 3.31, *P* 0.02). Data from four studies (*42, 46, 57, 62*) contributed to this estimate and the results were consistent across the studies.

- **30-day mortality:** There was a significant increase in 30-day mortality in patients with infections caused by third-generation cephalosporin-resistant *K. pneumoniae* (RR 1.45, 95% CI: 1.07 to 1.95, *P* 0.02). Data from seven studies (*29, 43, 47, 52, 53, 55, 56*) contributed to this estimate and the results were somewhat consistent across the studies.

- **LOS in hospital:** There was no significant increase in LOS in patients with infections caused by third-generation cephalosporin-resistant *K. pneumoniae* (MD 15.8 days, 95% CI: 2.6 to 34.2, *P 0.09*). Data from nine studies (*40, 41, 44, 48, 51-54, 59*) contributed to this estimate and the results were very inconsistent across the studies. In particular, one study (*54*) had a very large increase in LOS associated with third-generation cephalosporin-resistant *K. pneumoniae* (MD 46.6 days, 95% CI: 44.0 to 49.1). The results may be too inconsistent to pool into a single estimate, although all the results indicated an increase in total LOS.

- **ICU admission:** There was a significant increase in the risk of ICU admission for patients with infections caused by third-generation cephalosporin-resistant *K. pneumoniae* (RR 1.39, 95% CI: 1.08 to 1.80, *P* 0.01). Data from three studies (*40, 42, 52*) contributed to this estimate and the results were somewhat inconsistent across the studies, but all indicated an increased risk. Progression to septic shock: No relationship was found between third-generation cephalosporin-resistant K. pneumoniae and progression to septic shock (RR 0.99, 95% CI: 0.64 to 1.53, P 0.97). Data from three studies (*46, 50, 55*) contributed to this estimate and the results were consistent across the studies.

- **Postinfection LOS in hospital:** Two studies (*41, 54*) indicated a significant increase in postinfection LOS for patients with infections caused by third-generation cephalosporin-resistant *K. pneumoniae* (MD 20.1 days, 95% CI: 18.6 to 21.6 and MD 6.0 days, 95% CI: 2.7 to 9.3 respectively), and in two other studies (*49, 60*) there was also an increase (MD 18 days and MD 5 days), but the significance could not be assessed as the SDs were not provided. The results were too inconsistent to pool into a single estimate, although all the results indicated an increase in postinfection LOS.

Annex 3

Carbapenem-resistant *Klebsiella pneumoniae* infections

Published studies comparing carbapenem-resistant and susceptible *K. pneumoniae* infections generally came from high-income countries (n = 10). Only three studies were included from upper-middle-income countries, and there were no included studies from low- or lower-middle-income countries. From the included studies (Table A3.6) results were reported on the following health outcomes for infections with carbapenem-resistant *K. pneumoniae*, in summary:

- **All-cause mortality:** There was a significant increase in all-cause mortality for patients with carbapenem-resistant *K. pneumoniae* infections (RR 1.71, 95% CI: 1.35 to 2.18, *P* < 0.0001). Data from 11 studies (*63-68, 71-75*) contributed to this estimate and the results were somewhat consistent across the studies.

- **Bacterium-attributable mortality:** Only one small study reported bacterium-attributable mortality (*67*). Results showed that there was no significant increase in attributable mortality for patients with carbapenem-resistant *K. pneumoniae* infections (RR 1.98, 95% CI: 0.61 to 6.43, *P* 0.25).

- **30-day mortality:** There was a significant increase in 30-day mortality for patients with carbapenem-resistant *K. pneumoniae* infections (RR 1.51, 95% CI: 1.19 to 1.91, *P* < 0.0006). Data from three studies (*68-70*) contributed to this estimate and the results were consistent across the studies.

- **ICU mortality:** One small study (*67*) reported ICU mortality and found no significant increase in ICU mortality in patients with carbapenem-resistant *K. pneumoniae* infections (RR 1.39, 95% CI: 0.78 to 2.47, *P* 0.26).

- **LOS in hospital:** In two studies (*63, 68*), there was no significant increase in LOS for patients with carbapenem-resistant *K. pneumoniae* infections (MD 1.0 day, 95% CI: −11.9 to 13.8, *P* 0.88). However, data from the studies that contributed to this estimate were inconsistent. The estimate from one study (*68*) indicated a non-significant increase in LOS for carbapenem-resistant *K. pneumoniae* patients (MD 6 days, 95% CI: −1.4 to 13.4) and the results of the other study (*63*) indicated a non-significant decrease in LOS (MD −7.6 days, 95% CI: −23.1 to 7.9). A third study (*71*) could not be included in the analysis due to missing information (SDs of the mean differences not reported).

- **ICU LOS:** One small study (*71*) reported ICU LOS and found that patients with carbapenem-resistant *K. pneumoniae* infections had 0.7 days longer stay. However, its significance could not be determined since SDs were not reported.

- **Postinfection LOS:** One small study (*70*) reported postinfection LOS and found no significant increase in patients with carbapenem-resistant *K. pneumoniae* infections (MD 5 days, 95% CI: −21.7 to 31.7; *P* 0.71).

- **Transfer to other health-care facility:** One small study (*71*) reported transfer to another health-care facility and found no significant increase in the risk of health-care facility transfer for patients with carbapenem-resistant *K. pneumoniae* infections (RR 0.80, 95% CI: 0.17 to 3.75, *P* 0.78). However, patients enrolled in this study may have come from long-term care facilities at the time of study enrolment, so this result may not be directly attributable to *K. pneumoniae*.

- **Discharge to long-term care:** One small study (*71*) reported discharge to long-term care and found that there was a significant increase in the risk of long-term care discharge for patients with carbapenem-resistant *K. pneumoniae* infections (RR 2.31, 95% CI: 1.40 to 3.80, *P* 0.001). However, patients enrolled in this study may have come from long-term care facilities at the time of study enrolment, so this result may not be directly attributable to *K. pneumoniae*.

Staphylococcus aureus

Methicillin-resistant *Staphylococcus aureus* infections

The literature search identified 17 426 references possibly relevant for the question. Once duplicates were removed, 13 095 remained, of which 616 references were retrieved for full-text review. Ultimately, 147 studies (Table A3.7) met the inclusion criteria for *S. aureus* (*60, 76-221*).

Almost all of the included studies (n = 140, 95.2%) were conducted in upper-middle-income countries (n = 23, 15.6%) or high-income countries (n = 117, 79.6%). No studies included were conducted in low-income countries, and only two studies in lower-middle-income countries. Five studies included multiple countries, of which most were conducted in high-income countries.

Results were reported on the following health outcomes comparing patients with methicillin-resistant *S. aureus* (MRSA) to those with methicillin-susceptible *S. aureus* (MSSA), in summary:

- **All-cause mortality:** There was a significant increase in all-cause mortality for patients with MRSA infections (RR 1.61, 95% CI: 1.43 to 1.82, *P* < 0.00001). Data from 107 studies contributed to this estimate, and the results were somewhat consistent across the studies. Five studies could not be included in the effect estimate due to zero deaths reported in both MRSA and MSSA patients (*90, 141, 152, 213, 218*).

- **Bacterium-attributable mortality:** There was a significant increase in bacterium-attributable mortality for patients with MRSA infections (RR 1.64, 95% CI: 1.43 to 1.87, *P* < 0.00001). Data from 46 studies contributed to this estimate and the results were somewhat consistent across the studies. Two small studies (*106, 173*) not included in the effect estimate reported zero mortality in both the MRSA and MSSA patients enrolled.

- **30-day mortality:** There was a significant increase in 30-day mortality for patients with MRSA infections (RR 1.59, 95% CI: 1.33 to 1.91, *P* < 0.0.00001). Data from 16 studies (*78, 80, 81, 93, 115, 121, 148, 155, 172, 175, 189, 196, 201, 203, 211, 220*) contributed to this estimate and the results were somewhat consistent across the studies.

- **ICU mortality:** Five studies (*76, 112, 171, 196, 209*) reported ICU mortality and found that there was a significant increase in ICU mortality in patients with MRSA infections (RR 1.46, 95% CI: 1.23 to 1.74, *P* < 0.0001).

- **LOS in hospital:** 50 studies reported total LOS. There was a significant increase in LOS in patients with MRSA (MD 4.65, 95% CI: 2.96 to 6.33, *P* < 0.00001). However, results across studies were somewhat inconsistent. Eight studies (*85, 89, 92, 99, 128, 181, 203, 215*) could not be included in the analysis due to missing information (SDs not reported).

- **Postinfection LOS:** 27 studies reported a statistically significant increase in the mean difference of postinfection LOS (MD 3.12, 95% CI: 1.79 to 4.44, *P* < 0.00001); however, six studies (*60, 81, 91, 128, 143, 181*) could not be included in the analysis due to missing information (SDs not reported).

- **ICU LOS:** 21 studies reported a statistically significant increase in the mean difference in ICU LOS related to MRSA infection (MD 4.00, 95% CI: 2.12 to 5.87, *P* < 0.00001); however, three studies (*80, 99, 101*) could not be included in the analysis due to missing information (SDs not reported).

- **ICU admission:** In 17 studies, there was no significant increase in admission to ICU for patients with MRSA (RR 1.07, 95% CI: 0.92 to 1.25, *P* 0.36). However, data from the studies that contributed to this estimate were inconsistent. The estimate from one study (*195*) indicated a significant increase in ICU admission for MRSA patients (RR 2.12, 95% CI: 1.30 to 3.47) and the results of eight other studies (*102, 108, 137, 185, 193, 194, 212, 221*) indicated a non-significant increase in ICU admission. One study (*80*) indicated a statistically significant increase in ICU admission for MSSA (RR 0.33, 95% CI: 0.12 to 0.91), and six studies (*89, 93, 99, 120, 121, 129*) showed non-significant increases in MSSA patients admitted to ICU.

- **Progression to septic shock:** There was a significant increase in septic shock for patients with MRSA infections (RR 1.52, 95% CI: 1.24 to 1.88, *P* < 0.0001). Data from 21 studies contributed to this estimate and the results were consistent across the studies.

- **Mechanical ventilation:** There was no significant risk of requiring mechanical ventilation in 13 studies (*77, 93, 98, 99, 101, 102, 112, 137, 149-151, 164, 196*) (RR 1.07, 95% CI: 0.92 to 1.24, *P* 0.36) that compared MRSA and MSSA patients. However, data from the studies that contributed to this estimate were somewhat inconsistent.

- **Attributable readmission:** Six studies (*108, 120, 135, 148, 193, 217*) reported *S. aureus*-attributable readmissions to hospital following initial discharge. There was no significant increase in attributable readmission in patients with MRSA when compared to those with MSSA (RR 0.91, 95% CI: 0.67 to 1.23, *P* 0.53).

- **Discharge to long-term care:** A single study (*217*) showed a significant risk increase in discharge to long-term care for patients with MRSA (RR 1.54, 95% CI: 1.02 to 2.34, *P* 0.04) compared to those with MSSA.

- **Discharge to other health-care facility:** A single study (*207*) showed a significant, more than twofold, risk increase in discharge to long-term care for MRSA (RR 2.78, 95% CI: 1.40 to 5.55, *P* 0.004) compared to MSSA.

Table A3.3   Included study characteristics: Third-generation cephalosporin-resistant *Escherichia coli* (n = 25)

First author	Years	Countries, territories and other areas or grouping	Study design[a]	N resistant	N sensitive	Infection type	Duration of follow-up	Ages	Ref. no.
Ortega 2009	1991–2007	Spain	Prospective cohort	211	4547	Inpatients with bacteraemia	Death or discharge, death at 7 days, 30 days	All ages	(10)
Trecarichi 2009	2000–2007	Italy	Retrospective cohort	26	36	BSI in patients with haematological malignancies	30 days	≥15 years	(7)
Peralta 2007	1997–2005	Spain	Retrospective cohort	31	632	Bacteraemia/BSI – inpatient	In hospital	All ages	(8)
de Kraker 2011	2007–2008	13 European countries	Prospective parallel matched double cohort	111	1110	BSI, inpatients	Hospitalized, 30 days	≥18 years; all participants were 60+ for resistant and susceptible	(35)
Pena 2008	1996–2003	Spain	Retrospective cohort	100	100	Non-urinary mix of UTI, deep surgical site or intra-abdominal, bacteraemia (primary), bacterial peritonitis in cirrhotic patients, lower respiratory tract	NR, assume while in hospital	NR	(22)
Nicolas-Chanoine 2012	2008–2009	France	Prospective cohort	152	152	Hospitalized for at least 24 hours with infection – mostly (62%) UTI, other infections were from various deep sites - (for example. blood, surgical and respiratory infections)	NR, assume while in hospital	All ages	(24)
Ena 2006	1999–2004	Spain	Retrospective cohort	61	61	Inpatients and outpatients with UTI	NR	NR	(34)
Cornejo-Juarez 2012	2004–2009	Mexico	Retrospective cohort	100	100	Haematological malignancies with bacteraemia	60 days for death, longer for mean survival in alive patients	Unclear	(36)
Hsieh 2010	2005–2006	Taiwan, China	Retrospective cohort	19	385	Community-onset bacteraemia who visited the emergency department	30 days	All ages	(30)
Kang 2004	1998–2002	Republic of Korea	Retrospective cohort	5	10	Bacteraemic spontaneous bacterial peritonitis in patients with advanced liver cirrhosis	30 days	NR	(29)
Tumbarello 2010	2006	Italy	Retrospective cohort	37	97	Inpatients with BSI	Death or discharge and 21 days mortality	>18	(19)
Gudiol 2010	2006–2008	Spain	Prospective cohort	17	118	Hospitalized cancer/stem cell transplant patients with >1 episode of bacteraemia	7 days, 30 days	Adults	(32)

First author	Years	Countries, territories and other areas or grouping	Study design[a]	N resistant	N sensitive	Infection type	Duration of follow-up	Ages	Ref. no.
Apisarn-thanarak 2008	2003–2004	Thailand	Cohort	46	138	Community-onset infection inpatients	Looked back 1 year for risk factors, NR for mortality, assuming death or discharge	≥16	(37)
Ho 2002	1996–1998	China	Retrospective cohort	49	100	Bacteraemia with clinical features of sepsis	30 days mortality	NR but average age >73 in cases and controls	(31)
Melzer 2007	2003–2005	United Kingdom	Prospective cohort	46	308	Bacteraemia inpatients, community or hospital acquired; large majority (78%) were urinary tract infections	Discharge or death	≥16	(25)
Kang 2011	2010–2011	Republic of Korea	Retrospective cohort	108	100	Community-onset E. coli infections	30 days	15+	(27)
Khan 2010	2007–2008	Qatar	Prospective cohort	27	70	Bacteraemia, any type of acquisition, hospitalized	Death or discharge	Adults	(26)
Yan 2004	1999–2002	Taiwan, China	Cohort	30	60	E. coli BSI, inpatients	NR	≥18	(18)
Rodriguez-Bano 2010	2004–2006	Spain	Prospective cohort	95	188	Community-onset BSI	Until discharge or death	>14	(21)
Nussbaum 2013	2007–2009	USA (New York)	Retrospective cohort	34	66	Hospitalized patients with E. coli bacteraemia	In hospital	NR	(23)
Al-Otaibi 2013	2009–2011	Saudi Arabia	Retrospective cohort	113	226	Inpatients and outpatients with UTI	NR	All ages	(39)
Kang 2010	2008–2009	Republic of Korea	Retrospective cohort Post hoc analysis of subset of surveillance data	82	783	Community-onset bacteraemia	30 days	NR	(28)
Anunnatsiri 2012	2005–2006	Thailand	Retrospective cohort	32	113	Admitted with E. coli septicaemia (ESBL/non-ESBL)	72 hours and in hospital	>15 years	(38)
Garcia-Hernandez 2010	2006–2007	Spain	Cohort	34	119	Admitted patients with E. coli bacteraemia	7 days	Non-paediatric	(33)
Suankratay 2008	2004–2006	Thailand	Prospective cohort	35	76	Female patients hospitalized with acute pyelonephritis, community and nosocomial	72 hours and 14 days (but too many lost to report 14 days)	>15 years	(20)

BSI, bloodstream infection; ESBL, extended spectrum beta-lactamases; NR, not reported; USA, United States of America; UTI, urinary tract infection.

a. For some studies, the original study design may have been a case-control study assessing, for example, risk factors for infection. However, the authors also report for the case-control groups subsequent outcome data and, in this instance, for such outcomes the design would be considered a cohort.

Table A3.4 **Included study characteristics: Fluoroquinolone-resistant *Escherichia coli* (n = 12)**

First author	Years	Countries, territories and other areas or grouping	Study design[a]	N resistant	N sensitive	Focus/infection type	Duration of follow-up	Ages	Ref. no.
Cranendonk 2012	2008	Netherlands	Retrospective cohort	34	34	Inpatients with bacteraemia	During antimicrobial therapy and 6 months	All ages	(14)
Camins 2011	2000–2005	USA (Mississippi)	Retrospective cohort	93	93	Inpatients with bacteraemia	NR	Adults	(17)
Pepin 2009	2001–2007	Canada (Québec)	Cohort	93	186	Inpatients and outpatients with UTI	48 hours, 30 days	All ages	(9)
Ortega 2009	1991–2007	Spain	Prospective surveillance cohort	1300	3458	Inpatients with bacteraemia	Death or discharge	All ages	(10)
Trecarichi 2009	2000–2007	Italy	Retrospective cohort	39	23	BSI in patients with haematological malignancies	30 days	≥15 years	(7)
Peralta 2007	1997–2005	Spain	Retrospective cohort	125	538	Bacteraemia or BSI	Death or discharge	All ages but 72% >65 years	(8)
Huotari 2003	1997–1999	Finland	Retrospective cohort	51	102	Nosocomial, any *E. coli* infection	30 days	NR	(12)
van der Starre 2010	2004–2010	Netherlands	Prospective cohort	51	102	Community-onset febrile UTI	Unsure	Adults ≥18 years	(6)
Cereto 2008	2004–2005	Spain	Prospective cohort	18	29	Spontaneous bacterial peritonitis with cirrhosis	During hospitalization and at 3 months	Adults	(16)
Jeon 2012	2005–2008	Republic of Korea	Observational study	39	216	Women with uncomplicated acute pyelonephritis	4–7 days after start of therapy, 14–21 days after completion	>15 years	(11)
Garau 1999	1992–1997	Spain	Retrospective cohort	70	502	Bacteraemia (community and nosocomial)	Unsure	All ages	(13)
Cheong 2001	1993–1998	Republic of Korea	Retrospective cohort	40	80	Bacteraemia	Death or discharge	NR	(15)

BSI, bloodstream infection; NR, not reported; USA, United States of America; UTI, urinary tract infection.

a. For some studies, the original study design may have been a case-control study assessing, for example, risk factors for infection. However, the authors also report for the case-control groups subsequent outcome data and, in this instance, for such outcomes the design would be considered a cohort.

Table A3.5 Included study characteristics: Third-generation cephalosporin-resistant *Klebsiella pneumoniae* (n = 24)

First author	Years	Countries, territories and other areas or grouping	Study design[a]	N resistant	N sensitive	Infection type	Duration of follow-up	Ages	Ref. no.
Lee 2011	2002–2009	Republic of Korea	Retrospective cohort	32	192	Bacteraemia, community + health care associated	30 days	NR, 50% >65	(53)
Lin 2003	2001	Taiwan, China	Cohort	43	86	Community + nosocomial infections	Death or discharge	All ages	(52)
Loh 2006	2003–2004	Malaysia	Retrospective cohort	47	394	Respiratory tract infections	Death or discharge	≥12 years	(51)
Marra 2006	1996–2001	Brazil	Retrospective cohort	56	52	Nosocomial bacteraemia	15 days	All ages	(50)
Mosqueda-Gomez 2008	1993–2002	Mexico	Retrospective cohort	17	104	BSI	NR	Adults	(49)
Song 2009	2000–2006	Republic of Korea	Retrospective cohort	26	78	Advanced liver cirrhosis and spontaneous bacterial peritonitis	30 days	NR	(43)
Rebuck 2000	1997–1999	USA	Retrospective cohort	20	16	Hospitalized children who received liver transplants, intestinal transplants, or both	Death or discharge (max. 316 days)	Children	(44)
Kang 2006	1998–2002	Republic of Korea	Retrospective cohort	69	308	Nosocomial + community bacteraemia	30 days	>16 years	(56)
Huang 2007	2000–2002	China	Retrospective cohort	19	12	Neonates nosocomial infection	30 days	Neonates	(57)
Paterson 2004	1996–1997	Argentina, Australia, Belgium, Taiwan China, South Africa, Turkey and USA	Prospective cohort	78	175	Nosocomial bacteraemia	1 month	>16 years	(47)
Pillay 1998	1995–1996	South Africa	Prospective cohort	18	15	Nosocomial infection outbreak	NR	Neonates >48 hours old	(45)
BARTF 2002	1999	USA (Brooklyn)	Retrospective cohort	9	9	Nosocomial – UTI, respiratory tract infection, bacteraemia	NR	Adults	(60)
Tumbarello 2005	1999–2003	Italy	Retrospective cohort	48	99	Nosocomial + community bacteraemia	21 days	NR	(41)
Gomez 2006	1998	Brazil	Retrospective cohort	68	75	Nosocomial infection	21 days	>18 years	(58)
Demirdag 2010	2004–2005	Turkey	Retrospective cohort	52	52	Nosocomial + community infection	NR	NR	(59)
Kuo 2007	1992–2000	Taiwan, China	Retrospective cohort	54	54	Children with *K. pneumoniae* infections (community + nosocomial)	Death or discharge	Children	(54)
Kang 2004	2006–2009	Republic of Korea	Retrospective cohort	60	60	BSI (community + nosocomial)	30 days	NR	(29)
Tuon 2010	2006–2009	Brazil	Retrospective cohort	63	41	Bacteraemia	30 days	>12 years	(40)

First author	Years	Countries, territories and other areas or grouping	Study design[a]	N resistant	N sensitive	Infection type	Duration of follow-up	Ages	Ref. no.
Kang 2004	1998–2002	Republic of Korea	Retrospective cohort	10	20	Advanced liver cirrhosis and bacteraemia	30 days	Likely adults	(55)
Chiu 2005	2001	Taiwan, China	Retrospective cohort	15	16	Nosocomial enterobacterial infections in neonatal ICU	NR	Neonates	(61)
Ariffin 1999	1996–1997	(Malaysia (Kuala Lumpur)	Prospective cohort	16	15	Febrile neutropenic children with *K. pneumoniae* bacteraemia	NR	≤12 years	(62)
Pena 2001	1993–1995	Spain	Prospective cohort	45	42	Nosocomial bacteraemia, outbreak	NR	Adults	(46)
Szilagyi 2009	2005–2008	Hungary	Retrospective cohort	100	100	Nosocomial bacteraemia	NR	NR	(42)
Panhotra 2004	2001–2003	Saudi Arabia	Retrospective cohort	10	16	Nosocomial bacteraemia	NR	10–98 years	(48)

BSI, bloodstream infection; ICU, intensive care unit; NR, not reported; USA, United States of America; UTI, urinary tract infection.

a. For some studies, the original study design may have been a case-control study assessing, for example, risk factors for infection. However, the authors also report for the case-control groups subsequent outcome data and, in this instance, for such outcomes the design would be considered a cohort.

Table A3.6   Included study characteristics: Carbapenem-resistant *Klebsiella pneumoniae* (n = 12)

First author	Years	Countries, territories and other areas or grouping	Study design[a]	N resistant	N sensitive	Infection type	Duration of follow-up	Ages	Ref. no.
Liu 2011	2007–2009	Taiwan, China	Cohort	25	50	Bacteraemic inpatients	14 days, 28 days, in hospital	NR	(68)
Correa 2013	2006–2008	Brazil	Cohort	20	40	Health-care-associated infections	NR – assuming death or discharge	All ages	(75)
Falagas 2007	2000–2006	Greece	Cohort	53	53	Inpatients with infections	NR – assuming death or discharge	NR	(72)
Mouloudi 2010	2007–2008	Greece	Cohort	37	22	BSI in ICU patients	NR – assuming death or discharge	Adults	(67)
Patel 2008	2004–2006	USA (New York City)	Cohort	99	276	Inpatients with invasive infection	In hospital	Adults	(66)
Daikos 2006	2003–2004	Greece	Retrospective cohort	56	56	BSI in hospitalized patients	14 days	NR	(74)
Daikos 2009	2004–2006	Greece	Prospective cohort	14	148	BSI in hospitalized patients	Discharge or death	NR	(73)
Gaviria 2012	2009–2011	USA (West Virginia)	Cohort	19	38	General inpatients with infection	NR – assuming death or discharge	NR	(71)
Raviv 2012	2004–2007	Israel	Retrospective cohort	11	29	Lung transplant patients who acquire infection	1, 3, 6, 12 months	Adults ≥18 years	(65)
Shilo 2012	2006–2009	Israel (Jerusalem)	Cohort	135	127	Bacteriuria in hospitalized patients	Death or discharge	<14 years	(63)
Schwaber 2008	2003–2006	Israel	Cohort	48	56	Inpatients with infection	In hospital	Adults	(64)
Hussein 2012	2006–2008	Israel	Retrospective cohort	103	214	Inpatients with positive blood cultures	30 days	Adults ≥18	(70)
Lee 2011	2008–2009	China	Retrospective cohort	41	62	Patients with BSI	In hospital	NR	(69)

BSI, bloodstream infection; ICU, intensive care unit; NR, not reported; USA, United States of America.

a. For some studies, the original study design may have been a case-control study assessing, for example, risk factors for infection. However, the authors also report for the case-control groups subsequent outcome data and, in this instance, for such outcomes the design would be considered a cohort.

Table A3.7 Included study characteristics: Methicillin-resistant *Staphylococcus aureus* (n = 147)

First author	Years	Countries, territories and other areas or grouping	Study design[a]	N resistant	N sensitive	Infection type	Ages	Ref. no.
Abramson 1999	1993–1995	USA	Retrospective cohort	8	11	Inpatient BSI	>18 years	(221)
Allard 2008	1991–2005	Canada	Retrospective cohort	69	746	Bacteraemia	>18 years	(220)
Al-Nammari 2007	2000–2005	United Kingdom	Retrospective cohort	15	43	Haematogenous septic arthritis	>16 years	(219)
Al-Otaibi 2010	2005–2008	Saudi Arabia	Retrospective cohort	85	200	Children with invasive community-acquired MRSA; outpatients and some required hospitalization	0–18 years	(218)
Anderson 2009	1998–2003	USA	Matched outcomes study	150	128	Surgical site infection	NR	(217)
Arnold 2006	2000–2004	USA	Cohort	47	21	Paediatric acute haematogenous osteomyelitis and septic arthritis	Children	(216)
Austin 2003	1994–1995	Canada	Cohort	50	50	Inpatient bacteraemia	NR	(215)
Bader 2006	2003–2004	USA	Retrospective cohort	74	58	SA bacteraemia	Older adults	(214)
Baggett 2003	1998–2000	USA (Alaska, small rural setting)	Retrospective cohort	172	60	General outpatients and inpatients with SA skin infections	NR	(213)
Baraboutis 2011	1997–2001	USA	Cohort	127	170	Health-care-associated infections	NR	(212)
Bassetti 2011	2007	Italy	Case-control + cohort	89	76	Health-care-associated and community-acquired bacteraemia	NR	(211)
Bastug 2012	2006–2009	Turkey	Retrospective cohort	102	74	N bacteraemia	≥18	(210)
Ben-David 2009	2000–2003	USA	Retrospective cohort	95	87	N bacteraemia	NR	(209)
Blot 2002	1992–1998	Belgium	Retrospective cohort	47	38	Critically ill patients with bacteraemia	Adults	(208)
Burke 2009	2001–2006	USA (California)	Retrospective cohort	29	121	Inpatient children with SA bacteraemia	<18 years	(207)
Capitano 2003	1996–2000	USA	Retrospective cohort	41	49	SA infections in long-term care facility	Elderly	(206)
Carey 2010	2000–2007	USA (New York)	Retrospective cohort (chart)	49	123	Nosocomial ICU patients with MRSA/MSSA infections (BSI or SSTIs)	Infants	(205)
Carrillo-Marquez 2010	2001–2007	USA (Texas)	Prospective cohort	29	83	Children with SA-catheter-related bacteraemia	NR	(204)
Castillo 2012	2005–2008	Colombia	Retrospective cohort	186	186	Critically ill inpatients with SA bacteraemia	≥16 years	(203)

First author	Years	Countries, territories and other areas or grouping	Study design[a]	N resistant	N sensitive	Infection type	Ages	Ref. no.
Chan 2012	2006–2010	USA	Cohort	7090	8333	Haemodialysis end-stage renal disease outpatients with SA bacteraemia	NR	(202)
Chang 2003	1994–1996	USA	Prospective cohort	20	44	General SA bacteraemia patients with a subgroup who develop endocarditis	NR	(201)
Changchien 2011	2004–2008	Taiwan, China	Cohort	49	42	Postoperative patients with necrotizing fasciitis	NR	(200)
Chen 2010	2001–2007	Taiwan, China	Cohort	244	500	Community-onset bacteraemia	>15 years	(199)
Clancy 2005	2003	USA	Cohort	57	136	Community-acquired SA infection	All ages	(198)
Cofsky (BARTIF) 2002	1999	USA	Cohort	14	14	Nosocomial infections	NR	(60)
Combes 2004	Unclear	France	Cohort	74	97	SA ventilator-associated pneumonia patients with appropriate initial antibiotic therapy; all ICU patients	NR	(197)
Combes 2004	1989–2001	France	Cohort	73	145	SA poststernotomy mediastinitis patients (surgical) treated in ICU	NR	(196)
Conterno 1998	1991–1992	Brazil	Cohort	90	46	Bacteraemia	>14 years	(195)
Cosgrove	1997–2000	USA	Cohort	96	252	Inpatient bacteraemia	NR	(194)
Cowie 2005	2001	Canada	Retrospective cohort	22	15	Nosocomial infections in vascular surgery patients	NR	(193)
Cunney 1996	1991–1993	Ireland	Cohort	18	92	Nosocomial and community-acquired septicaemia	NR	(192)
Das 2007	2001–2002	United Kingdom	Prospective cohort	84	56	Bacteraemia	>18 years	(191)
Davis 2007	2003–2005	USA	Cohort	102	102	Patients with community-associated SA infections	NR	(190)
de Kraker 2011	2007–2008	13 European countries	Matched parallel cohort	248	618	Inpatients with laboratory-confirmed diagnosis of SA BSI	>18 years	(189)
de Oliveira 2002	1990–1991, 1995–1996	Brazil	Cohort	159	92	Bacteraemia	>14 years	(188)
Engemann 2003	1994–2000	USA	Cohort	121	165	Surgical site infection	NR	(187)
Erdem 2010	1996–2007	USA (Hawaii)	Cohort	26	14	Hospitalized children with community-acquired SA pneumonia	NR	(186)
Erdem 2010	1996–2007	USA	Retrospective cohort (chart)	15	47	Paediatric osteomyelitis	1 month–18 years	(185)

Annex 3

First author	Years	Countries, territories and other areas or grouping	Study design[a]	N resistant	N sensitive	Infection type	Ages	Ref. no.
Ernst 2005	1997–2001	USA	Case-control, control with cohort	21	21	Nosocomial bacteraemia	NR	(184)
Filice 2010	2004–2006	USA	Retrospective cohort	335	390	SA infection	NR	(183)
Fortunov 2006	2002–2004	USA	Retrospective cohort	61	28	Community-acquired infections in neonates	<30 days	(182)
French 1990	1984–1988	Hong Kong SAR	Cohort	74	80	Nosocomial bacteraemia	NR	(181)
Ganga 2009	2005–2006	USA	Cohort	163	90	Bacteraemia	Adults	(180)
Gerber 2009	2002–2007	USA	Retrospective cohort	29 309	28 485	SA infection in hospitalized children	<18 years	(179)
Gonzalez 1999	1990–1995	Spain	Prospective cohort	32	54	Bacteraemic pneumonia	NR	(178)
Graffunder 2002	1997–1999	USA	Cohort	121	123	Nosocomial SA infection	Adults	(177)
Greiner 2007	1999–2005	Germany	Retrospective cohort	28	81	BSI in patients with end-stage renal disease	NR	(176)
Guilarde 2006	2000–2001	Brazil	Cohort	61	50	BSI	>1 year	(175)
Haessler 2008	1998–2000	USA	Retrospective cohort	118	118	SA infections – inpatients and outpatients	>18 years	(174)
Hakim 2007	2000–2004	USA	Retrospective cohort (chart)	14	22	Bacteraemia in children	<18 years	(173)
Han 2012	2007–2009	USA	Retrospective cohort	190	202	Adult inpatients with SA bacteraemia	Adults	(172)
Hanberger 2011	2007	75 countries	Cohort	494	505	Infection in the ICU	NR	(171)
Harbarth 1998	1994–1995	Switzerland	Retrospective cohort + case-control	39	145	Bacteraemia	NR	(170)
Harbarth 1998	1994–1996	Switzerland	Matched case-control from cohort population	38	38	Bacteraemia	NR	(170)
Hawkins 2007	2001–2004	USA	Cohort	120	116	Hospitalized patients with bacteraemia	NR	(169)
Hawkshead 2009	1993–2005	USA	Unclear	21	27	Paediatric osteomyelitis	Children	(168)
Heo 2007	2000–2005	Republic of Korea – Seoul	Retrospective case-control and cohort	63	168	Bacteraemia in emergency department	NR	(167)
Hershow 1992	1989	USA	Retrospective cohort	22	22	Adults with nosocomial SA infection	≥18	(166)
Hill 2008	2000–2006	Belgium	Cohort	16	56	Infective endocarditis	NR	(165)

First author	Years	Countries, territories and other areas or grouping	Study design[a]	N resistant	N sensitive	Infection type	Ages	Ref. no.
Ho 2009	1997–2007	Australia	Cohort	21	60	Bacteraemia in critically ill patients	NR	(164)
Hsu 2004	1995–2002	Taiwan, China	Unclear	29	28	Infective endocarditis	NR	(163)
Hsu 2007	1995–2005	Taiwan, China	Unclear	48	75	Infective endocarditis	All ages	(162)
Huang 2008	2003–2004	USA	Cohort	127	127	Community-associated SA infection	NR	(161)
Hulten 2010	2001–2007	USA	Retrospective cohort	95	147	Nosocomial paediatric infection	Children	(160)
Isaacs 2004	1992–1999	Australia	Prospective surveillance cohort	65	223	SA sepsis in neonatal nurseries	Newborn	(159)
Jimenez 2013	2008–2010	Colombia	Cross-sectional	539	271	SA infections	16–60 years	(158)
Joo 2012	2007–2009	Republic of Korea (Seoul)	Case-control and cohort	84	84	Community-onset SA infection	NR	(157)
Kalwaje 2012	1 year	India	Cohort	38	32	Bacteraemia	NR	(156)
Kang 2010	2007–2006	Nine Asian countries	Cohort	2090	2859	Asian Network for Surveillance of Resistant Pathogens – SA infections	All ages	(155)
Khatib 2006	2002–2003	USA	Observational	174	168	Adult inpatients with bacteraemia	>18 years	(154)
Kim 2003	1998–2001	Republic of Korea (Seoul)	Retrospective cohort	127	111	Bacteraemia	NR	(153)
Kini 2013	2004–2008	India	Retrospective cohort (chart)	41	33	Paediatric bone and joint infections	8 months–17 years	(152)
Kopp 2004	1999–2000	USA	Retrospective cohort	36	36	SA infections	>2 years	(151)
Kuint 2007	1993–2003	Israel	Cohort	11[b]	12	Bacteraemia in neonatal ICU	Neonates	(150)
Kuint 2007	1993–2004	Israel	Cohort	20[c]	12	Bacteraemia in neonatal ICU	Neonates	(150)
Kuo 2007	2000–2005	Taiwan, China	Retrospective cohort (chart)	16	6	Endocarditis in haemodialysis patients	NR	(149)
Lawes 2012	2006–2010	United Kingdom (Scotland)	Retrospective cohort	208	659	All inpatients – assessing impact of screening for MRSA bacteraemia	NR	(148)
Lepelletier 2004	1994–2001	France	Unmatched case-control and cohort	24	64	ICU patients with nosocomial SA infections (respiratory, bacteraemia or urinary)	All ages	(147)
Lesens 2003	2001–2002	France	Cohort	53	113	Bacteraemia in adults	>18 years	(146)
Lesse 2006	1997–2003	USA (New York)	Cohort	15	24	Nursing home residents with SA bacteraemia	NR	(145)

First author	Years	Countries, territories and other areas or grouping	Study design[a]	N resistant	N sensitive	Infection type	Ages	Ref. no.
Lewis 1985	1980–1981	USA (Michigan)	Cohort	28	28	Community-acquired SA bacteraemia patients with history of parental drug use and abuse	NR	(144)
Lodise 2005	1999–2001	USA (Michigan)	Cohort	170	183	Inpatients with SA bacterium	NR	(143)
Manzur 2007	1999–2003	Spain	Cohort	50	98	Inpatients with SA BSI	NR	(142)
Martinez-Aguilar 2003	2000; 2001–2002	USA (Texas)	Cohort	46	53	Children with community-acquired SA infection	NR	(140)
Martinez-Aguilar 2004	2000–2002[d]	USA (Texas)	Cohort	31	28	Inpatient children with community-acquired SA and musculoskeletal infections	NR	(141)
Marty 1993	1982–1988	France	Case-control and cohort	14	14	Cancer inpatients with SA bacteraemia	All ages	(139)
McHugh 2004	1997–1999	USA (Washington)	Cohort	20	40	Inpatients with SA BSI confirmed by culture	NR	(138)
Mekontso-Dessap 2001	1996–2000	France	Cohort	15	26	Surgical patients developing SA poststernotomy mediastinitis	NR	(137)
Melzer 2003	1995–2000	United Kingdom (England)	Cohort	433	382	Inpatients and outpatients with nosocomial bacteraemia	Adults ≥16 years	(136)
Miller 2007	2004	USA (California)	Prospective cohort	70	47	Hospitalized patients discharged after community-acquired SA skin infection	NR	(135)
Mishaan 2005	2001–2003	USA (Texas)	Cohort	68	49	Paediatric patients with community-acquired SA infections and corresponding isolates	NR	(134)
Morikawa 2012	2004–2009	Japan	Cohort	68	83	Patients with acute SA pneumonia with thin-section chest CT exams	NR	(133)
Naves 2012	2006–2008	Brazil	Cohort	29	22	Non-ICU patients with SA BSI	NR	(132)
Nickerson 2006	2003–2004	Thailand	Cohort	36	121	Inpatients with SA bacteraemia (positive blood culture for SA)	NR	(130)
Nickerson 2009	2006–2007	Thailand	Cohort	27	71	SA bacteraemia patients	All ages	(131)
Ochoa 2005	2000–2001; 2002–2003	USA (Texas)	Cohort	159	80	Paediatric inpatients with SA infections	NR	(129)
O'Kane 1998	1993	Australia	Retrospective cohort (case)	32	73	SA bacteraemia patients	NR	(128)
Osmon 2004	2001–2002	USA (Missouri)	Prospective cohort	148	117	Hospitalized patients with SA bacteraemia	NR	(127)

First author	Years	Countries, territories and other areas or grouping	Study design[a]	N resistant	N sensitive	Infection type	Ages	Ref. no.
Ott 2010	2005–2007	Germany	Cohort	41	41	Inpatients with nosocomial SA pneumonia	NR	(126)
Park 2011	2003–2008	Republic of Korea	Cohort	53	53	Inpatients with SA bacteraemia	NR	(125)
Parvizi 2010	1998–2008	USA (Pennsylvania)	Cohort	231	160	Surgical patients with periprosthetic joint infection caused by SA	NR	(124)
Pasticci 2011	1988–2009	Italy	Cohort	13	49	Infective SA endocarditis	NR	(123)
Perovic 2006	1999–2002	South Africa	Cohort	105	344	Inpatients with SA bacteraemia	Adults	(122)
Ponce-de-Leon 2010	2003–2007	Mexico	Cohort	79	93	Inpatients with SA BSI	Adults ≥16 years	(121)
Popovich 2010	2000–2007	USA (Illinois)	Cohort	162	91	HIV-infected patients with community-acquired SSTIs	NR	(120)
Priest 2005	1994–2000	USA (North Carolina)	Cohort	11	24	Inpatients with SA haematogenous vertebral osteomyelitis	NR	(119)
Pujol 1996	1991–1992	Spain	Cohort	24	8	ICU patients with SA nasal carriage progressing to bacteraemia	NR	(117)
Pujol 1998	1990–1994	Spain	Cohort	41[e]	98	Mechanically ventilated ICU patients who developed SA pneumonia	NR	(118)
Quilty 2009	2004–2007	Australia	Cohort	5	5	Chemotherapy-induced febrile neutropenia patients with SA sepsis	NR	(116)
Rahikka 2011	2002–2010	Finland	Cohort	51	51	Inpatients with SA bacteraemia	NR	(115)
Rana 2012	2001–2008	USA (Ohio)	Cohort	22	12	Infants with positive SA blood culture	NR	(114)
Reed 2005	1996–2001	USA (North Carolina)	Cohort	54	89	Haemodialysis inpatients with end-stage renal disease and SA bacteraemia	NR	(113)
Rello 1994	1991–1993	Spain	Cohort	11	38	Mechanically ventilated patients who developed SA nosocomial infections in the lower respiratory tract	NR	(111)
Rello 2012	Unclear	Unclear	Cohort	E = 15; L = 5	E = 30; L = 6	ICU patients with hospital-acquired pneumonia or ventilator-associated pneumonia from SA	NR	(112)
Reshad 1994	1983–1991	Japan	Cohort	46	48	Patients with SA septicaemia	NR	(110)
Romero-Vivas 1995	1990–1993	Spain	Cohort	84	100	N SA bacteraemia patients	NR	(108, 109)

Annex 3

First author	Years	Countries, territories and other areas or grouping	Study design[a]	N resistant	N sensitive	Infection type	Ages	Ref. no.
Rubio-Terres 2010	2005	Spain	Cohort	121	245	SA bacteraemia patients	Adults ≥18 years	(108)
Saavedra-Lozano 2008	1999–2003	USA (Texas)	Cohort	36	72	Children inpatients with acute SA osteomyelitis	NR	(107)
Salgado 2007	1998–2004	USA (South Carolina)	Cohort	33[f]	12[g]	Patients with prosthetic joint infection from SA	NR	(106)
Selvey 2000	1992–1997	Australia	Cohort	188	316	Inpatients with nosocomial SA bacteraemia	NR	(105)
Shane 2012	2006–2008	USA (Maryland)	Cohort	88	228	Very low birth weight infants with SA bacteraemia and/or meningitis	NR	(104)
Shorr 2006	Unclear	France	Retrospective analysis of pooled, patient-level data from multiple clinical trials	38	69	ICU patients with SA ventilator-associated pneumonia	NR	(101)
Shorr 2006	2002–2003	USA	Cohort	95	59	Patients with early and late SA-related ventilator-associated pneumonia	NR	(103)
Shorr 2010	2005–2008	USA (Michigan)	Cohort	87	55	Patients with SA health-care-associated pneumonia	NR	(102)
Shurland 2007	1995–2003	USA (Maryland)	Retrospective cohort	193	245	Patients (majority veterans) with SA infections complicated by bacteraemia	Adults	(100)
Sicot 2013	1986–2010	France	Cohort	29	104	Inpatients with PVL-positive SA community-acquired necrotizing pneumonia	NR	(99)
Soriano 2000	1991–1998	Spain	Cohort	225	683	Patients with monocrobial SA bacteraemia	NR	(98)
Spindel 1995	1987–1991	USA (Oregon)	Cohort	28	40	Veterans' affairs nursing home care unit residents with SA infections	NR	(97)
Takayama 2010	1990–2006	Japan	Cohort	10	23	Patients with definite infective endocarditis	NR	(96)
Talon 2002	1997–1998	France	Prospective cohort	30	69	Inpatients with SA bacteraemia	NR	(95)
Tam 1988	1976–1985	Hong Kong SAR	Cohort	29	13	Neonates with severe SA infection	NR	(94)
Taneja 2010	2005–2008	USA (Michigan)	Cohort	55	73	Inpatients with SA community-acquired pneumonia	NR	(93)
Teterycz 2010	1996–2008	Switzerland	Retrospective cohort	44	58	Patients with orthopaedic implant infections	NR	(92)
Theodorou 2013	1989–2009	Germany	Cohort	33	41	Burn patients with SA bacteraemia	NR	(91)
Thomason 2007	2001–2005	USA (Texas)	Cohort	66	57	Children with SA neck abscesses	NR	(90)

First author	Years	Countries, territories and other areas or grouping	Study design[a]	N resistant	N sensitive	Infection type	Ages	Ref. no.
Tong 2009	2006–2007	Australia	Case-control and cohort	239	478	Patients with SA infections (combined with colonized – present data for both populations)	NR	(89)
Traverso 2010	2006–2008	Argentina	Cohort	17	22	Hospitalized patients with bacteraemia	NR	(88)
Trividic-Rumeau 2003	2000–2001	France	Cohort	21	22	Hospitalized patients with leg ulcers or foot wounds	NR	(87)
Truffault 2000	1996–1997	France	Cohort	39	20	ICU patients admitted for at least 48 hours with SA infection	NR	(86)
Tsai 2011	2003–2009	Taiwan, China	Cohort	29	26	Patients with necrotizing fasciitis caused by SA or *Vibrio vulnificus*	NR	(85)
Tumbarello 2002	1991–2000	Italy	Cohort	41	88	Bacteraemia in HIV-infected patients	>18 years	(84)
Viallon 2007	2003–2004	France	Retrospective cohort	93	145	SA infections in patients admitted to emergency department	NR	(83)
Wang CY 2012	2007	Taiwan, China	Cohort	10	7	SA in end-stage renal disease	NR	(82)
Wang FD 2008	1990–2004	Taiwan, China	Cohort	851	297	Patients with nosocomial SA bacteraemia	NR	(81)
Wehrhahn 2010	2 years	Australia	Prospective cohort	57	114	Invasive community-onset SA infection	All ages	(80)
Wolkewitz 2011	2005–2006	United Kingdom (Scotland)	Cohort	34	26	New hospital admission of health-care-associated SA bacteraemia	NR	(79)
Wyllie 2006	1997–2004[h]	United Kingdom (England)	Cohort	227	214	Inpatients with SA bacteraemia	Adults ≥18 years	(78)
Yoon 2005	1986–2004	Republic of Korea	Cohort	10	22	Patients with SA endocarditis	All ages	(77)
Zahar 2005	1997–2004	France	Cohort	69	65	Ventilator-associated pneumonia	Adults	(76)

BSI, bloodstream infection; CT, computed tomography; E, European Union group; ICU, intensive care unit; L, Latin American group; MRSA, methicillin-resistant Staphylococcus aureus; MSSA, methicillin-susceptible S. aureus; N, nosocomial; PVL, Panton-Valentine leukocidin; SA, S. aureus; SAR, Special Administrative Region; SSTI, skin and soft tissue infection: USA, United States of America.

a. For some studies, the original study design may have been a case-control study assessing, for example, risk factors for infection. However, the authors also report for the case-control groups subsequent outcome data and, in this instance, for such outcomes the design would be considered a cohort.
b. Community-associated MRSA only.
c. Multi-drug resistant MRSA only; same study by Kuint comparing different cases to same controls.
d. Excluding May 2000 and September 2 – October 15 2000.
e. All MRSA cases were late onset only.
f. 33 episodes in 31 patients; 7 prosthetic joint infection episodes in 7 patients were polymicrobial.
g. 12 episodes in 12 patients; 2 prosthetic joint infection episodes in 2 patients were polymicrobial.
h. 1997–2004 at one hospital; 1999–2004 at another.

Table A3.8 **GRADE table for third-generation cephalosporin-resistant *Escherichia coli***
Question: *Are clinical outcomes different in patients who are treated for third-generation cephalosporin (CEPH)-resistant E. coli when compared those treated for third-generation CEPH-sensitive E. coli?*

Quality assessment							No. of patients		Effect			
No. of studies	Design	Risk of bias	Inconsistency	Indirectness	Imprecision	Other considerations	CEPH-resistant	CEPH-sensitive	Relative (95% CI)	Absolute	Quality	Importance
All-cause mortality (follow-up 3 to 60 days[a]; assessed with: death events)												
16	Observational studies[b]	Serious[c]	No serious inconsistency	No serious indirectness	No serious imprecision	Strong association[d]	188/1007 (18.7%)	10.9%	RR 2.18 (1.58 to 3.02)	129 more per 1000 (from 63 more to 220 more)	⊕⊕◯◯ LOW	CRITICAL
Bacterium-attributable mortality (follow-up 30 to 60 days; assessed with: death events)												
4	Observational studies[e]	Serious[c]	No serious inconsistency	No serious indirectness	No serious imprecision	Reporting bias[f] Strong association[g]	53/225 (23.6%)	12.6%	RR 2.02 (1.41 to 2.90)	129 more per 1000 (from 52 more to 239 more)	⊕◯◯◯ VERY LOW	CRITICAL
30 day mortality (follow-up 7 to 30 days[e]; assessed with: death events)												
11	Observational studies	Serious[c]	No serious inconsistency	No serious indirectness	No serious imprecision	Strong association[g]	153/711 (21.5%)	10.4%	RR 2.19 (1.78 to 2.68)	124 more per 1000 (from 81 more to 175 more)	⊕⊕◯◯ LOW	CRITICAL
ICU admissions related to infection (follow-up mean 30 days; assessed with: number of patients admitted)												
1	Observational studies	Very serious[c]	No serious inconsistency	No serious indirectness	Very serious[h]	Reporting bias[i]	2/17 (11.8%)	4.2%	RR 2.78 (0.58 to 13.20)	75 more per 1000 (from 18 fewer to 512 more)	⊕◯◯◯ VERY LOW	IMPORTANT
Total LOS (follow-up median 60 days[e]; measured with: days; better indicated by lower values)												
4	Observational studies[b]	Serious[c]	No serious inconsistency	No serious indirectness	No serious imprecision	Reporting bias[f]	226	612	–	MD 1.8 days higher (1.3 lower to 5.0 higher)	⊕◯◯◯ VERY LOW	
Postinfection LOS (follow-up 3 to 30 days[e]; measured with: days; better indicated by lower values)												
4	Observational studies[b]	Serious[c]	No serious inconsistency	No serious indirectness	No serious imprecision	Reporting bias[f]	199	1705	–	MD 2.3 day higher (0.3 lower to 4.9 higher)	⊕◯◯◯ VERY LOW	

CEPH, cephalosporin; CI, confidence interval; ICU, intensive care unit; LOS, length of stay;, MD, mean difference; RR, relative risk.

a. Five studies did not report follow-up information; ambiguity in reporting follow-up information.
b. Majority of the studies are true cohort; for GRADE table all considered cohort.
c. Confounding is not properly adjusted.
d. Relative risk >2.
e. Lack of clarity in reporting duration of follow-up.
f. Only four studies identified.
g. Relative risk >2.
h. Single study with wide confidence interval.
i. Only three studies identified.

Table A3.9 GRADE table for fluoroquinolone-resistant *Escherichia coli*
Question: *Are clinical outcomes different in patients who are treated for fluoroquinolone (FQ)-resistant E. coli infection when compared to those treated for FQ-sensitive E. coli infection?*

No. of studies	Design	Risk of bias	Inconsistency	Indirectness	Imprecision	Other considerations	FQ-resistant	FQ-sensitive	Relative (95% CI)	Absolute	Quality[f]	Importance
All-cause mortality (follow-up 21 days to 6 years; assessed with: death events)												
8	Observational studies	Serious[b]	No serious inconsistency	No serious indirectness	No serious imprecision	Strong association[c]	96/470 (20.4%)	7.9%	RR 2.11 (1.64 to 2.71)	88 more per 1000 (from 51 more to 135 more)	⊕⊕○○ LOW	CRITICAL
Bacterium-attributable mortality (follow-up mean not available; assessed with: death events)												
1	Observational studies	Very serious[b]	No serious inconsistency	No serious indirectness	Very serious	Reporting bias[d]	0/30 (0%)	00%	–	–	⊕○○○ VERY LOW	
30 days mortality (follow-up 1 to 3 months[e]; assessed with: death events)												
5	Observational studies	Serious[b]	No serious inconsistency	No serious indirectness	No serious imprecision	Strong association[g]	203/1576 (12.9%)	7.8%	RR 2.16 (1.09 to 4.27)	90 more per 1000 (from 7 more to 255 more)	⊕⊕○○ LOW	CRITICAL
LOS in hospital (follow-up 21 days to 3 months; measured with: days; better indicated by lower values)												
3	Observational studies	Serious[b]	Serious[h]	No serious indirectness	Serious[i]	Reporting bias[j]	183	411	–	MD 3.7 days higher (3.5 lower to 10.9 higher)	⊕○○○ VERY LOW	NOT IMPORTANT
ICU admission (follow-up mean 60 days; assessed with: patients admitted)												
1	Observational studies	Very serious[b]	No serious inconsistency	No serious indirectness	No serious imprecision	Reporting bias[k] Strong association[g]	12/93 (12.9%)	5.40%	RR 2.4 (1.08 to 5.35)	76 more per 1000 (from 4 more to 235 more)	⊕○○○ VERY LOW	
Progression to septic shock (follow-up mean 21 days[l]; assessed with: number of patients progressed to septic shock)												
2	Observational studies	Very serious[b]	Serious	No serious indirectness	No serious imprecision	Reporting bias[k] Very strong association[g]	5/132 (3.8%)	0.25%	RR 10.00 (1.19 to 84.36)	22 more per 1000 (from 0 more to 208 more)	⊕○○○ VERY LOW	

CI, confidence interval; ICU, intensive care unit; FLQ, fluoroquinolone; LOS, length of stay; MD, mean difference; RR, relative risk.

a. In four studies follow-up information not available and ambiguity in reporting.
b. Confounding in majority of the studies a concern and/or small sample size.
c. Relative risk >2.
d. Just two studies identified.
e. Not available in one study.
f. High – randomized trials or double-upgraded observational studies; Moderate – downgraded randomized trials or upgraded observational studies; low – double-downgraded randomized trials or observational studies; Very low – triple-downgraded randomized trials; or downgraded observational studies; or case series/case reports.
g. Relative risk >2 or >5.
h. Disparity in effect size: of three studies; one shows no effect and in one effect size is not estimable.
i. Effect size varies across the studies by a wide margin.
j. Only three studies identified.
k. Single study identified.
l. In one study follow-up not reported.
l. Two studies identified.

Table A3.10 **GRADE table for third-generation cephalosporin-resistant *Klebsiella pneumoniae***
Question: *Are clinical outcomes different in patients who are treated for third-generation cephalosporin (CEPH)-resistant K. pneumoniae when compared to those treated for third-generation CEPH-sensitive K. pneumoniae infection?*

Quality assessment							No. of patients		Effect			
No. of studies	Design	Risk of bias	Inconsistency	Indirectness	Imprecision	Other considerations	CEPH-resistant	CEPH-sensitive	Relative (95% CI)	Absolute	Quality	Importance
All-cause mortality (follow-up 21 to 316 days[a]; assessed with: death events)												
14	Observational studies	Serious[b]	No serious inconsistency	No serious indirectness	No serious imprecision	None	183/574 (31.9%)	211/1041 (20.3%)	RR 1.35 (1.14 to 1.61)	71 more per 1000 (from 28 more to 124 more)	⊕◯◯◯ VERY LOW	CRITICAL
Bacterium-attributable mortality (follow-up mean 30 days[c]; assessed with: death events)												
4	Observational studies	Serious[b]	No serious inconsistency	No serious indirectness	No serious imprecision	Reporting bias[d]	36/180 (20.0%)	17/169 (10.1%)	RR 1.93 (1.13 to 3.31)	94 more per 1000 (from 13 more to 232 more)	⊕◯◯◯ VERY LOW	CRITICAL
30 days mortality (follow-up 30 days; assessed with: death events)												
7	Observational studies	Serious[b]	No serious inconsistency	No serious indirectness	No serious imprecision	None	96/318 (30.2%)	193/919 (21%)	RR 1.45 (1.07 to 1.95)	95 more per 1000 (from 15 more to 200 more)	⊕◯◯◯ VERY LOW	CRITICAL
Total LOS in hospital (follow-up 21 to 316 days[e]; measured with: number of days; better indicated by lower values)												
9	Observational studies	Serious[b]	No serious inconsistency	No serious indirectness	Serious[f]	None	369	950	–	MD 15.8 days higher (2.6 lower to 34.2 higher)	⊕◯◯◯ VERY LOW	IMPORTANT
Postinfection LOS in hospital (follow-up 25 to 30 days[g]; measured with: number of days; better indicated by lower values)												
4	Observational studies	Very serious[b]	Serious[h]	No serious indirectness	No serious imprecision	Reporting bias[i]	128	266	–	MD 13.1 days higher (0.7 lower to 26.9 higher)[j]	⊕◯◯◯ VERY LOW	IMPORTANT
Infection-related ICU admission (follow-up mean 30 days[g]; assessed with: number of patients admitted to ICU due to infection)												
3	Observational studies	Very serious[b]	No serious inconsistency	No serious indirectness	No serious imprecision	Reporting bias[d]	155/206 (75.2%)	121/227 (53.3%)	RR 1.39 (1.08 to 1.80)	208 more per 1000 (from 43 more to 426 more)	⊕◯◯◯ VERY LOW	
Progression to septic shock (follow-up mean 30 days; assessed with: number of patients went into septic shock)												
3	Observational studies	Very serious[b]	Serious[h]	No serious indirectness	Serious[f]	Reporting bias[d]	33/161 (20.5%)	32/154 (20.8%)	RR 0.99 (0.64, 1.53)	208 fewer per 1000 (from 208 fewer to 208 fewer)		

CEPH, cephalosporin; CI, confidence interval; ICU, intensive care unit; LOS, length of stay; MD, mean difference; RR, relative risk.

a. In eight studies the follow-up is not reported or unclear.
b. Cohort studies; issues related to confounding are not addressed adequately; follow-up is not reported or unclear.
c. In three studies follow-up not reported.
d. <5 studies; and all studies are small.
e. In five studies follow-up is unclear or not reported.
f. Wide confidence intervals.
g. Two studies not reported or unclear.
h. Effect size varies from no effect to large effect.
i. Only four studies identified.
j. Results too inconsistent to pool into a single estimate; although all the results indicated an increase for CEPH-resistant.

Table A3.11 GRADE table for carbapenem-resistant *Klebsiella pneumoniae*
Question: *Are clinical outcomes different in patients who are treated for carbapenem (CARB)-resistant K. pneumoniae when compared to those treated for CARB-sensitive K. pneumoniae infection?*

No. of studies	Design	Risk of bias	Inconsistency	Indirectness	Imprecision	Other considerations	Carba-resistant	Cepha-sensitive	RR (95% CI)	Absolute	Quality	Importance
All-cause mortality (follow-up 14 days to 1 year[d]; assessed with: death events)												
11	Observational studies	Serious[a]	No serious inconsistency	No serious indirectness	No serious imprecision	None	198/517 (38.3%)	208/895 (23.2%)	RR 1.71 (1.35 to 2.18)	165 more per 1000 (from 81 more to 274 more)	⊕◯◯◯ VERY LOW	CRITICAL
Bacterium-attributable mortality (follow-up not reported; assessed with: death events)												
1	Observational studies	Very serious[a]	No serious inconsistency	No serious indirectness	Serious[b]	Reporting bias[c]	10/37 (27%)	3/22 (13.6%)	RR 1.98 (0.61 to 6.43)	134 more per 1000 (from 53 fewer to 740 more)	⊕◯◯◯ VERY LOW	CRITICAL
30 days mortality (follow-up 28 to 30 days, not reported in one study; assessed with: death events)												
3	Observational studies	Serious[a]	No serious inconsistency	No serious indirectness	No serious imprecision	Reporting bias[e]	76/169 (45%)	97/326 (29.8%)	RR 1.51 (1.19 to 1.91)	152 more per 1000 (from 57 more to 271 more)	⊕◯◯◯ VERY LOW	CRITICAL
ICU mortality (follow-up not available; assessed with: death events)												
1	Observational studies	Very serious[a]	no serious inconsistency	No serious indirectness	Serious[b]	Reporting bias[c]	21/37 (56.8%)	9/22 (40.9%)	RR 1.39 (0.78 to 2.47)	160 more per 1000 (from 90 fewer to 601 more)	⊕◯◯◯ VERY LOW	
Total LOS in hospital (follow-up 28 days not available in two studies; measured with: number of days; better indicated by lower values)												
3	Observational studies	Serious[a]	Serious[f]	No serious indirectness	Serious[g]	Reporting bias[e]	179	215	–	MD 1.0 day higher (11.9 lower to 13.8 higher)	⊕◯◯◯ VERY LOW	IMPORTANT
Postinfection LOS (follow-up mean 30 days; measured with: number of days; better indicated by lower values)												
1	Observational studies	Very serious[a]	No serious inconsistency	No serious indirectness	Serious[g]	Reporting bias[c]	103	214	–	MD 5.0 days higher (21.7 lower to 31.7 higher)	⊕◯◯◯ VERY LOW	IMPORTANT
Discharge to long-term care facility (follow-up not available; assessed with: number of patients discharged)												
1	Observational studies	Serious[a]	No serious inconsistency	No serious indirectness	No serious imprecision	Reporting bias[h] strong association[i]	15/19 (78.9%)	13/38 (34.2%)	RR 2.31 (1.40 to 3.80)	448 more per 1000 (from 137 more to 958 more)	⊕◯◯◯ VERY LOW	
Transfer to other health care facility (follow-up not available; assessed with: number of patients transferred)												
1	Observational studies	Very serious[a]	No serious inconsistency	No serious indirectness	Serious[g]	Reporting bias[c]	2/19 (10.5%)	5/38 (13.2%)	RR 0.80 (0.17 to 3.75)	26 fewer per 1000 (from 109 fewer to 362 more)	⊕◯◯◯ VERY LOW	

CARB, carbapenem; CEPH, cephalosporin; CI, confidence interval; ICU, intensive care unit; LOS, length of stay;, MD, mean difference; RR, relative risk.

a. Cohort study; confounding is not addressed.
b. Single study with wide confidence interval.
c. Single study.
d. Follow-up not reported in eight studies.
e. Three studies less than 5.
f. I² =59%; wide variation in effect size across studies.
g. Wide confidence interval.
h. No explanation was provided.
i. RR>2.

Table A3.12 GRADE table for MRSA
Question: *Are clinical outcomes different in patients who are treated for MRSA infection when compared to those treated for MSSA infection?*

Quality assessment							No. of patients		Effect			
No. of studies	Design	Risk of bias	Inconsistency	Indirectness	Imprecision	Other considerations	MRSA	MSSA	Relative (95% CI)	Absolute	Quality	Importance
All-cause mortality (assessed with: death events)												
107	Observational studies	Serious[a]	No serious inconsistency	No serious indirectness	No serious imprecision	None	2448/37537 (6.5%)	6.4%	RR 1.61 (1.43 to 1.82)	39 more per 1000 (from 28 more to 52 more)	⊕◯◯◯ VERY LOW	CRITICAL
Bacterium-attributable mortality (assessed with: death events)												
46	Observational studies	Serious[a]	No serious inconsistency	No serious indirectness	No serious imprecision	None	958/3646 (26.3%)	893/5271 (16.9%)	RR 1.64 (1.43 to 1.87)	108 more per 1000 (from 73 more to 147 more)	⊕◯◯◯ VERY LOW	CRITICAL
30 days mortality (assessed with: death events)												
16	Observational studies	Serious[a]	No serious inconsistency	No serious indirectness	No serious imprecision	None	1271/4549 (27.9%)	939/6346 (14.8%)	RR 1.59 (1.33 to 1.91)	87 more per 1000 (from 49 more to 135 more)	⊕◯◯◯ VERY LOW	CRITICAL
ICU mortality (assessed with: death events)												
5	Observational studies	Serious[a]	No serious inconsistency	No serious indirectness	No serious imprecision	None	220/751 (29.3%)	171/838 (20.4%)	RR 1.46 (1.23 to 1.74)	94 more per 1000 (from 47 more to 151 more)	⊕◯◯◯ VERY LOW	CRITICAL
Total LOS in hospital (measured with: days; better indicated by lower values)												
50	Observational studies	Serious[a]	No serious inconsistency	No serious indirectness	No serious imprecision	None	33 705	33 675	–	MD 4.65 higher (2.96 to 6.33 higher)	⊕◯◯◯ VERY LOW	CRITICAL
Postinfection LOS (measured with: days; better indicated by lower values)												
27	Observational studies	Serious[a]	No serious inconsistency	No serious indirectness	No serious imprecision	None	2539	2785	–	MD 3.12 higher (1.79 to 4.44 higher)	⊕◯◯◯ VERY LOW	CRITICAL
ICU LOS (measured with: days; better indicated by lower values)												
21	Observational studies	Serious[a]	No serious inconsistency	No serious indirectness	No serious imprecision	None	1211	1699	–	MD 4.00 higher (2.12 to 5.87 higher)	⊕◯◯◯ VERY LOW	IMPORTANT
Readmission (assessed with: number of patients readmitted)												
6	Observational studies	Serious[a]	Serious[b]	No serious indirectness	No serious imprecision	None	189/733 (25.8%)	241/1185 (20.3%)	RR 0.91 (0.67 to 1.23)	18 fewer per 1000 (from 67 fewer to 47 more)	⊕◯◯◯ VERY LOW	IMPORTANT
ICU admission (assessed with: number of patients admitted to ICU)												
17	Observational studies	Serious[a]	Serious[b]	No serious indirectness	No serious imprecision	None	364/1397 (26.1%)	461/1936 (23.8%)	RR 1.07 (0.92 to 1.25)	17 more per 1000 (from 19 fewer to 60 more)	⊕◯◯◯ VERY LOW	IMPORTANT
Progression to septic shock (assessed with: patients progressed to septic shock)												
21	Observational studies	Serious[a]	No serious inconsistency	No serious indirectness	No serious imprecision	None	275/1756 (15.7%)	354/3559 (9.9%)	RR 1.52 (1.24 to 1.88)	52 more per 1000 (from 24 more to 88 more)	⊕◯◯◯ VERY LOW	IMPORTANT

Quality assessment							No. of patients		Effect			
No. of studies	Design	Risk of bias	Inconsistency	Indirectness	Imprecision	Other considerations	MRSA	MSSA	Relative (95% CI)	Absolute	Quality	Importance
Mechanical ventilation (assessed with: number of patients put on mechanical ventilator)												
14	Observational studies	Serious[a]	No serious inconsistency	No serious indirectness	No serious imprecision	None	340/713 (47.7%)	407/1329 (30.6%)	RR 1.07 (0.92 to 1.24)	21 more per 1000 (from 24 fewer to 73 more)	⊕◯◯◯ VERY LOW	IMPORTANT
Discharge to long-term care facility (assessed with: number of patients discharger to long-term care)												
1	Observational studies	Serious[a]	No serious inconsistency	No serious indirectness	No serious imprecision	Reporting bias[c]	47/150 (31.3%)	26/128 (20.3%)	RR 1.54 (1.02 to 2.34)	110 more per 1000 (from 4 more to 272 more)	⊕◯◯◯ VERY LOW	CRITICAL
Discharge to other health care facility (assessed with: number of patients discharged to other health–care facility)												
1	Observational studies	Very serious[a]	No serious inconsistency	No serious indirectness	No serious imprecision	Reporting bias[c]	10/29 (34.5%)	15/121 (12.4%)	RR 2.78 (1.4 to 5.55)	221 more per 1000 (from 50 more to 564 more)	⊕◯◯◯ VERY LOW	IMPORTANT

CI, confidence interval; ICU, intensive care unit; LOS, length of stay; MD, mean difference; MRSA, methicillin-resistant Staphylococcus aureus; MSSA, methicillin-susceptible S. aureus; RR, relative risk.

a. Confounding was not taken into account in all studies and/or sample size was very small in some studies.
b. Wide variation in effect size across studies.
c. Single study.

Table A3.13 **Complete overview of findings on costs addressing the question:**
Does the published scientific literature support that there is an excess costs outcome in infections caused by the following bacteria if they are resistant to the following antibacterials, respectively?

First author	Total no.		Data, unit of cost	Resources costed	Resistant cost	Susceptible cost	Reported cost differential	PICO outcomes
	Sensitive	Resistant						
E. coli	ESBL	Non-ESBL						
Apisarnthanarak 2008 (37)	46	138	Median, USD ($)	**Hospital costs accrued after infection** (direct and indirect costs required to provide health-care services and medications)	$528 (43–3173)	$194 (53–1861)		Crude mortality
Tumbarello 2010 (19)	37	97	Mean, euros (€)	**Total hospital costs:** direct health care costs (total expenditures incurred by the hospital to provide services or goods for each patient with a bloodstream infection)	€13 709 ±16 312	€8683 ±6683	Cost difference related to ESBL production vs non-ESBL production (by BSI case): €5026 vs €4322 2006 US$ 6314 vs 5429	Postinfection LOS; 21 days mortality
				Medical care	€1964 ±417	€1134 ±83		
				Nursing care	€3894 ±1078	€2001 ±163		
				Pharmacy services (all drugs)	€933 ±1706	€848 ±1434		
				Diagnostic testing (includes laboratory and imaging studies)	€2373 ±2734	€1760 ±1974		
				Support services (includes food service, laundry, maintenance, security, etc.)	€1674 ±1983	€1016 ±723		
				Others (includes utilities, admission/ discharge, depreciation, and overhead costs)	€2869 ±2676	€1921 ±2152		
				Antimicrobial drug treatment (also accounted for in pharmacy services above)	€763 ±437	€474 ±270		
S. aureus	MRSA	MSSA						
Anderson 2009 (217)	150 (144 had financial data)	128 (127 had financial data)	Median IQR, USD ($) 2003 (All hospital charges were adjusted to reference year 2003 by inflating charges from prior years at a 3% annual rate)	**Hospital charges** (Including readmissions); no further details reported	$79 029 (38 113, 127 846)	$55 667 (22 201, 86 757)	Attributable difference least squares mean (IQR) Unadjusted: $36 379 (13 509, 59 250) Adjusted (*surgical duration >75th NNIS percentile, ASA score >3, procedure at tertiary care hospital, Charlson score >3, surgery on same day as admission, and coronary artery bypass graft surgery*): $24 113	Readmission within 90 days; post-procedure LOS; LOS attributable to SSI

First author	Total no.		Data, unit of cost	Resources costed	Resistant cost	Susceptible cost	Reported cost differential	PICO outcomes
	Sensitive	Resistant						
Ben-David 2009 (209)	95	87	USD ($) 2003	**Total hospital actual cost** (As opposed to charges) BSI occurred while in ICU BSI occurred while in general unit	ICU: 113 852 (48 961–55 001) Non-ICU: 53 409 (32 945–84 053)	ICU: 42 137 (32 388–74 781) Non-ICU: 35 131 (18 340–50 896)	P < .001 P .005	LOS after infection; ICU LOS after infection
				Subtotal hospital cost after BSI BSI occurred while in ICU BSI occurred while in general unit	ICU: 51 492 (24 535–104 499) Non-ICU: 23 690 (13 545–43 375)	ICU: 17 603 (10 228–42 117) Non-ICU: 18 152 (11 091–33 202)	P < .001 P .3	
				Daily hospital cost after BSI BSI occurred while in ICU BSI occurred while in general unit (Subtotal and daily hospital costs also available for pre-infection hospitalization)	ICU: 2894 (1902–3553) Non-ICU: 1756 (1329–2113)	ICU: 2042 (1487–2472) Non-ICU: 1565 (1227–1882)	P .005 P .1	
Capitano 2003 (206)	41	49	Median (range), USD ($) 2003	**All infection-related costs incurred by long-term care facility** Total pharmaceutical: infection-related medication acquisition, determination of drug levels, pharmacist dispensing, pharmacist monitoring, adverse effect, and nursing medication administration costs	$332 (17–1552)	$269 (49–1216)	Authors state total cost associated with MRSA was 1.95 X greater P .425	Relapse
				Infection management: Infection-related microbiological cultures, laboratories, X-rays, ambulance transfers and isolation costs	$562 (31–2457)	$93 (14–912)	P < .001	
				Physician care: Infection-related consulting physician fee and primary physician care	$248 (0–2078)	$184 (0–1736)	P .227	
				Nursing care: Nursing and certified nursing assistant care	$1347 (399–4847)	$610 (102–2550)	P .001	
				Total infection cost: The sum of all previously defined associated costs	$2607 (849–8895)	$1332 (268–7265)	P < .001	

First author	Total no.		Data, unit of cost	Resources costed	Resistant cost	Susceptible cost	Reported cost differential	PICO outcomes
	Sensitive	Resistant						
Cosgrove 2005 (194)	96	252	Median IQR, USD ($)	**Total hospital charges:** (From the hospital's billing system) starting on day of bacteraemia through to discharge	$26 424 ($14 006–$50 484)	$19 212 ($9999–$36 548)	Mean attributable MRSA $6916	LOS postinfection
				Hospital costs: Estimated by adjusting charges using the overall Medicare cost-to-charge ratio for institution	$14 655 ($7768–$27 998)	$10 655 ($5545–$20 270)	$3836 = median charge or cost for MSSA bacteraemia X multiplicative effect for increased charges or costs due to MRSA bacteraemia	
Engemann 2003 (*187*)	121	165	Median IQR, mean USD ($)	**Hospital costs** (Hospital charges as direct cost data were not available); 90 day postoperative period	$92 363 (40 198, 136 479) $118 415	$52 791 (29 074, 91 805) $73 165	MRSA associated with 1.19-fold increase in median hospital cost (*P* .03) (adjusting for duration of surgery, hospital, length of hospitalization before infection, length of ICU stay before infection, renal disease, diabetes)	Post-surgery, postinfection and postinfection ICU
Erdem 2010 (*185*)	15	47	Median IQR, USD ($)	**Hospital costs:** Patient billing charges; no other info available	$44 000 (37 000, 106 000)	$22 000 (14 000, 40 000)	*P* .0045	LOS (after infection); ICU admission (after infection); septic shock (after admission)

First author	Total no.		Data, unit of cost	Resources costed	Resistant cost	Susceptible cost	Reported cost differential	PICO outcomes
	Sensitive	Resistant						
Filice 2010 (*183*)	335	390	Median (range), USD ($) 2007	**Total cost:**	$34 657 ($11 517–$98 287)	$15 923 ($5270–$45 684)	*P* < .001	Postinfection LOS; postinfection ICU LOS; septic shock Use and cost data were collected from the VA Decision Support System – all direct and indirect costs of care, including services provided by contracted non-VA providers. The costs and services were quantified for each day during the 6 months after onset of SA illness. As well, they conducted interviews to estimate costs incurred by patients or third-party payers for care received from sources outside the Minneapolis VA Medical Center
				INPATIENT TREATMENT: (Includes room and board, patient acuity costs, nutrition, and some identified in-hospital medical care costs)				
				Overall inpatient costs	$26 274 ($4531–$86,974)	$6748 ($0–$35 089）	*P* < .001	
				Basic inpatient costs	$16 416 ($2661–$54 180)	$3820 ($0–$21 913)	*P* < .001	
				Inpatient antimicrobial agents	$142 ($6–$508)	$21 ($0–$337)	*P* < .001	
				Other drugs	$1530 ($242–$5502)	$406 ($0–$2394)	*P* < .001	
				Laboratory tests	$1002 ($179–$2749)	$362 ($0–$1249)	*P* < .001	
				Imaging	$1048 ($0–$5453)	$227 ($0–$1597)	*P* < .001	
				Surgical procedures	$0 ($0–$3432)	$0 ($0–$378)	*P* .02	
				PMR	$0 ($0–$731)	$0 ($0–$98)	*P* < .001	
				Mental, social and spiritual	$459 ($33–$1280)	$80 ($0–$750)	*P* < .001	
				Haemodialysis	$0 ($0–$0)	$0 ($0–$0)	*P* .42	
				Other (Includes home care costs while the patient was hospitalized, inpatient fee-basis costs, and other noncategorized costs)	$1307 ($9–$5818)	$100 ($0–$1980)	*P* < .001	
				OUTPATIENT TREATMENT: Overall outpatient costs	$4322 ($1395–$9438)	$4495 ($2076–$8979)	*P* .30	
				Outpatient basic clinic costs	$1169 ($345–$2494)	$1344 ($626–$2571)	*P* .05	
				Outpatient antimicrobial agents	$2 ($0–$28)	$7 ($0–$32)	*P* .01	

First author	Total no.		Data, unit of cost	Resources costed	Resistant cost	Susceptible cost	Reported cost differential	PICO outcomes
	Sensitive	Resistant						
Filice 2010 (*183*)				Other drugs	$766 ($41–$1979)	$793 ($173–$1678)	P .72	Postinfection LOS; postinfection ICU LOS; septic shock Use and cost data were collected from the VA Decision Support System – all direct and indirect costs of care, including services provided by contracted non-VA providers. The costs and services were quantified for each day during the 6 months after onset of SA illness. As well, they conducted interviews to estimate costs incurred by patients or third-party payers for care received from sources outside the Minneapolis VA Medical Center
				Laboratory tests	$171 ($0–$450)	$232 ($95–$484)	P .005	
				Imaging	$95 ($0–$446)	$146 ($0–$506)	P .04	
				Surgical procedures	$0 ($0–$374)	$44 ($0–$451)	P .13	
				PMR	$0 ($0–$0)	$0 ($0–$0)	P .75	
				Mental, social and spiritual	$0 ($0–$108)	$0 ($0–$83)	P .09	
				Haemodialysis	$0 ($0–$0)	$0 ($0–$0)	P .63	
				Other (Includes costs for outpatient observation [room and board, acuity, nutrition, and some costs incurred while patient was under observation status], outpatient fee-basis costs, and other noncategorized costs)	$661 ($51–$2106)	$652 ($158–$1976)	P .37	
Kopp 2004 (151)	36	36	Median IQR, USD ($)	Hospital cost:	$16 575 ($7275–$89 157)	$12 862 ($5292–$36 471)	P 0.11	Mechanical ventilation; total LOS; total ICU LOS Paper does not specify if costs are included for post infection period only
				Hospital charge:	$50 059 ($22 200–$215 752)	$40 102 ($14 775–$112 278)	P 0.162	

First author	Total no.		Data, unit of cost	Resources costed	Resistant cost	Susceptible cost	Reported cost differential	PICO outcomes
	Sensitive	Resistant						
Lepelletier 2004 (*147*)	24	64	Mean, euros (€)	**Cost of hospitalization** = (LOS) x (Average price/day in ICU)	€37 278 (6344–121 329)	€27 755 (7930–121 329)		Total LOS; mortality
				Cost of antibiotic therapy = (total dosage of each molecule received by the patient) x (corresponding unit price)	€184 (8–1202)	€72 (2–350)		
				Cost of medical care per patient: used a model relating to the Omega score (measures medical costs in euros by giving a score based on how long the patient was in the ICU, whether they had a surgical procedure or invasive radiology); this model does not include fixed costs or staff costs	€12 345 (1255–26 260)	€10 632 (2207–24 351)		
Lodise 2005 (*143*)	170	183	Continuous variable log transformed and expressed as mean (95% CI), USD ($)	**Overall cost of hospitalization after onset of SA bacteraemia,** includes fixed indirect costs, variable direct costs, fixed direct costs Fixed indirect: from departments that do not provide direct patient care services (ie. housekeeping, medical records, billing, etc); Variable direct: cost of patient care services (ie. nursing staff, medications, etc.); Fixed direct: not captured in patient care services (ie. administration, clerical support, building overhead, etc.)	$22 735 Excludes patients that died secondary to SA bacteraemia	$11 205 Excludes patients that died secondary to SA bacteraemia		Post LOS; mortality (attributable)
				Adjusted cost – SA bacteraemia, used ANCOVA to analyse mean group difference while adjusting for confounding variables (APACHE II score at onset of SA bacteraemia, ICU at onset of SA bacteraemia, and hospital-acquired SA bacteraemia, hospital days prior to onset of SA bacteraemia, and intravenous drug use source of SA bacteraemia)	$21 577 (17 061–27 290)	$11 668 (9550–14 223)		

First author	Total no.		Data, unit of cost	Resources costed	Resistant cost	Susceptible cost	Reported cost differential	PICO outcomes
	Sensitive	Resistant						
McHugh 2004 (*138*)	20	40	USD ($)	**Total charge during hospitalization**	$45 920	$9699		Total LOS; mortality
				Cost per patient–day of hospitalization	$5878	$2073		
				Cost per patient–day for patients with low CMI* (≤2) [less severe illness] *CMI (case mix index) cost: weighted measure of severity of illness (average of 2 for the study patients and is greater than the general population [1 is the average])	$2715	$2462		
				Cost per patient–day for patients with high CMI (>2) [poorer health status]	$9744	$4442	$5302	
Ott 2010 (*126*)	41	41	Median IQR, euros (€)	**Overall costs per patient**	€60 684 (23 127–93 468)	€38 731 (15 365–47 814)		Post LOS; total LOS; ICU LOS; mortality
				Cost of nursing staff	€14 424	€9389	–	
				Cost of assistant medical technicians	€5813	€3551		
				Cost for pharmacy	€5533	€1165		
				Cost for medical products	€5408	€3533		
				Median costs attributable to methicillin resistance in SA pneumonia per patient (different in costs of the matched pairs)	–	–	€17 281 (–929–53 541)	
				Reimbursement per patient	€47 480 (21 082–81 302)	€32 369 (11 853–48 048)	–	
				Loss per patient (financial loss per patient for the hospital) = costs–reimbursement	€11 701 (2203–21 981)	€2662 (–2103–617)	–	
				Loss attributable to methicillin resistance in SA pneumonia per patient (difference of median loss of the matched pairs)	–	–	€4418 (–1905–22 035)	

First author	Total no.		Data, unit of cost	Resources costed	Resistant cost	Susceptible cost	Reported cost differential	PICO outcomes
	Sensitive	Resistant						
Park 2011	53	53	2008 USD ($)	**Total hospital costs** (includes cost of hospital stay, laboratory tests, care and treatments)* *Cost of hospital stay = cost from administration, clerical support, housekeeping and medical records); Cost of care = cost of physician care, nursing care, and consultations; Treatment costs = total drug costs, costs of materials (catheters and implanted devices) and costs of procedures (operations, dialysis, respiratory care, rehabilitation)	$9369.6 ±12 911.5	$8355.8 ±8959.3		Post LOS; total LOS; mortality Note 3
				Basic inpatient costs	$1957.1 ±2518.8	$1649.8 ±1749.5		
				Laboratory tests	$1463.3 ±2057.6	$1694.1 ±2192.5		
				Imaging	$446.9 ±641.7	$622.7 ±817.4		
				Drugs	$3485.9 ±6277.2	$2692.0 ±3722.2		
				Haemodialysis	$729.6 ±1235.1	$476.2 ±970.7		
				Surgical procedure	$68.1 ±218.1	$203.1 ±393.4		
				Consultation	$147.9 ±171.2	$155.4 ±169.8		
				Others	$1031.8 ±1617.9	$874.8 ±1219.8		
Parvizi 2010 (*124*)	231	160	2009 USD ($)	**In-hospital costs**	$107 264 ±110 953	$68 053 ±50 354		Total LOS Data also available for cost per procedure (resection, re-vision, re-im-plantation; dealing with prosthetic join infection patients)
				Cost per hospital stay	$30 580 ±31 752	$22 779 ±18 385		
				Cost per hospital day	$3173 ±2850	$3473 ±2269		

First author	Total no.		Data, unit of cost	Resources costed	Resistant cost	Susceptible cost	Reported cost differential	PICO outcomes
	Sensitive	Resistant						
Reed 2005 (*113*)	54	89	2001 USD ($)	**Cost of index hospitalization** (includes costs incurred before positive blood culture) = inpatients costs and physician fees for initial inpatient stay	Mean = $28 297 ±23 619 Median (min–max) = $21 322 (12 315–34 933)	Mean = $16 066 ±16 337 Median (min–max) = $12 908 (7920–18 174)		Total LOS; post LOS; ICU LOS; in-hospital and 12 weeks mortality; 12 weeks relapse; discharge to home or other long-term care facility Note 5
				Total cost during 12 weeks (only 14.8% of MRSA and 12.4% of MSSA patients were rehospitalized within 12 weeks) = costs of index hospitalization + costs for outpatient care and rehospitalizations related to SA bacteraemia or its sequelae	Mean = $32 655 ±25 313 Median (min–max) = $25 968 (13 072–45 008)	Mean = $18,803 ±17,929 Median (min–max) = $15 017 (8960–20 053)		
Rubio-Terres 2010 (*108*)	121	245	Mean, euros (€)	**Total cost per episode of bacteraemia** (base value of the use of resources and of the unit cost) – includes cost of empirical antibiotic, targeted antibiotic, complementary tests, hospitalization/ ICU, and consultations and intravenous administration)	€11 044.59	€9839.25	€1205.34	Total LOS; ICU LOS; crude and attributable mortality; ICU admission; readmission
				Cost of hospitalization/ ICU (included in total cost above)	€8703.86	€6917.51	€1786.35	
				Empirical antibiotic	€51.05	€36.69	€14.36	
				Targeted antibiotic	€285.12	€128.55	€156.57	
				Complementary tests	€1820.50	€2572.44	€–751.94	
				Consultations and intravenous administration	€184.06	€184.06	€0	

First author	Total no.		Data, unit of cost	Resources costed	Resistant cost	Susceptible cost	Reported cost differential	PICO outcomes
	Sensitive	Resistant						
Shorr 2006 (*103*)	95	59	Median IQR, USD ($)	**Total cost** = (operating cost/charge ratio + capital cost/charge ratio) x total charge Operating cost = (hospital specific cost/charge ratio) x hospital total charges Computed total costs by taking component charges for the hospital stay (pharmacy, laboratory, bed day, etc.) and multiplied them by the Medicare cost-to-charge ratios. These were summed to derive total costs	$40 734 (18 347– 71 064)	$36 523 (15 539– 72 080)	$7731 (–8393– +23 856) Attributable excess cost from multivariate analysis of MRSA vs MSSA after controlling for surgical and trauma status, time of onset of ventilator-associated pneumonia and admission severity	Total LOS; crude mortality
Shorr **2010** (102)	87	55	USD ($)	**Total hospital charges for all services provided between hospital admission and discharge**	Mean = $98 170 ±94 707 Median = $70 028	Mean = $104 121 ±91 314 Median = $71 186		Total LOS; mortality; ICU admission; receipt of mechanical ventilation
Taneja **2010** (93)	55	73	USD ($)	**Total hospital charges for all services provided between hospital admission and discharge**	Mean = $117 489 ±132 164 Median = $71 868	Mean = $135 784 ±170 046 Median = $84 593		Total LOS; in-hospital and 30 days mortality (for those discharged); receipt of mechanical ventilation; ICU admission

ASA, American Society of Anesthesiologists; BSI, bloodstream infection; CI, confidence interval; CMI, case mix index ; ESBL, extended spectrum beta-lactamases; ICU, intensive care unit; IQR, interquartile range; LOS, length of stay; MRSA, methicillin-resistant S. aureus; MSSA, methicillin-susceptible S. aureus; NNIS, National Nosocomial Infections Surveillance; PICO, population; intervention; comparison; outcome; SA, S. aureus; SSI, surgical site infections; VA, veterans affairs.

Annex 3

A3.3 References

1. Higgins J, Green S. *Cochrane handbook for systematic reviews of interventions, version 5.1.0.* West Sussex, Wiley-Blackwell, A John Wiley & Sons, Ltd, 2011.

2. GA Wells BS, D O'Connell, J Peterson, V Welch, M Losos, P Tugwell, The Newcastle-Ottawa Scale (NOS) for assessing the quality of nonrandomised studies in meta-analyses. *www.medecine.mcgill.ca*, 2000.

3. Guyatt GH, Oxman AD, Vist GE, Kunz R, Falck-Ytter Y, Alonso-Coello P et al. GRADE: An emerging consensus on rating quality of evidence and strength of recommendations. *BMJ (Clinical Research Ed.)*, 2008, 336(7650):924-926. (http://www.ncbi.nlm.nih.gov/entrez/query.fcgi?cmd=Retrieve&db=PubMed&dopt=Citation&list_uids=18436948, accessed 29 January 2014).

4. Guyatt G, Oxman AD, Akl EA, Kunz R, Vist G, Brozek J et al. GRADE guidelines: 1. Introduction-GRADE evidence profiles and summary of findings tables. *J Clin Epidemiol*, 2011, 64(4):383-394. doi:10.1136/bmj.39489.470347.AD.

5. The World Bank. World Bank List of Economies. 2013 (July). (http://data.worldbank.org/about/country-classifications/country-and-lending-groups, accessed 29 January 2014).

6. van der Starre WE, van Nieuwkoop C, Paltansing S, van't Wout JW, Groeneveld GH, Becker MJ et al. Risk factors for fluoroquinolone-resistant *Escherichia coli* in adults with community-onset febrile urinary tract infection. *J Antimicrob Chemother*, 2010, 66(3):650-656. doi:10.1093/jac/dkq465.

7. Trecarichi EM, Tumbarello M, Spanu T, Caira M, Fianchi L, Chiusolo P et al. Incidence and clinical impact of extended-spectrum-beta-lactamase (ESBL) production and fluoroquinolone resistance in bloodstream infections caused by *Escherichia coli* in patients with hematological malignancies. *J Infect*, 2009, 58(4):299-307. doi:10.1016/j.jinf.2009.02.002.

8. Peralta G, Sanchez MB, Garrido JC, De Benito I, Cano ME, Martinez-Martinez L et al. Impact of antibiotic resistance and of adequate empirical antibiotic treatment in the prognosis of patients with *Escherichia coli* bacteraemia. *J Antimicrob Chemother*, 2007, 60(4):855-863. (http://www.ncbi.nlm.nih.gov/pubmed/17644532, accessed 9 April 2014).

9. Pepin J, Plamondon M, Lacroix C, Alarie I. Emergence of and risk factors for ciprofloxacin-gentamicin-resistant *Escherichia coli* urinary tract infections in a region of Quebec. *Can J Infect Dis Med Microbiol*, 2009, 20(4):e163-168. (http://www.ncbi.nlm.nih.gov/pubmed/21119795, accessed 29 January 2014).

10. Ortega M, Marco F, Soriano A, Almela M, Martinez JA, Munoz A et al. Analysis of 4758 *Escherichia coli* bacteraemia episodes: predictive factors for isolation of an antibiotic-resistant strain and their impact on the outcome. *J Antimicrob Chemother*, 2009, 63(3):568-574. doi:10.1093/jac/dkn514.

11. Jeon J, Kim K, Han WD, Song SH, Park KU, Rhee JE et al. Empirical use of ciprofloxacin for acute uncomplicated pyelonephritis caused by *Escherichia coli* in communities where the prevalence of fluoroquinolone resistance is high. *Antimicrob Agents Chemother*, 2012, 56(6):3043-3046. (http://dx.doi.org/10.1128/AAC.06212-11, accessed 29 January 2014).

12. Huotari K, Tarkka E, Valtonen V, Kolho E. Incidence and risk factors for nosocomial infections caused by fluoroquinolone-resistant *Escherichia coli*. *Eur J Clin Microbiol Infect Dis*, 2003, 22(8):492-495. (http://www.ncbi.nlm.nih.gov/pubmed/12884069, accessed 9 April 2014).

13. Garau J, Xercavins M, Rodriguez-Carballeira M, Gomez-Vera JR, Coll I, Vidal D et al. Emergence and dissemination of quinolone-resistant *Escherichia coli* in the community. *Antimicrob Agents Chemother*, 1999, 43(11):2736-2741. (http://www.ncbi.nlm.nih.gov/pubmed/10543756, accessed 9 April 2014).

14. Cranendonk DR, van der Valk M, Langenberg ML, van der Meer JT. Clinical consequences of increased ciprofloxacin and gentamicin resistance in patients with *Escherichia coli* bacteraemia in the Netherlands. *Scand J Infect Dis*, 2012, 44(5):363-368. doi:10.3109/00365548.2011.641506.

15. Cheong HJ, Yoo CW, Sohn JW, Kim WJ, Kim MJ, Park SC. Bacteremia due to quinolone-resistant *Escherichia coli* in a teaching hospital in South Korea. *Clin Infect Dis*, 2001, 33(1):48-53. (http://www.ncbi.nlm.nih.gov/entrez/query.fcgi?cmd=Retrieve&db=PubMed&dopt=Citation&list_uids=11389494, accessed 29 January 2014).

16. Cereto F, Herranz X, Moreno E, Andreu A, Vergara M, Fontanals D et al. Role of host and bacterial virulence factors in *Escherichia coli* spontaneous bacterial peritonitis. *Eur J Gastroen Hepat*, 2008, 20(9):924-929. doi:10.1097/MEG.0b013e3282fc7390.

17. Camins BC, Marschall J, DeVader SR, Maker DE, Hoffman MW, Fraser VJ. The clinical impact of fluoroquinolone resistance in patients with E coli bacteremia. *J Hosp Med*, 2011, 6(6):344-349. doi:10.1002/jhm.877.

18. Yan JJ, Ko WC, Wu JJ, Tsai SH, Chuang CL. Epidemiological investigation of bloodstream infections by extended spectrum cephalosporin-resistant *Escherichia coli* in a Taiwanese teaching hospital. *J Clin Microbiol*, 2004, 42(7):3329-3332. doi:10.1128/JCM.42.7.3329-3332.2004.

19. Tumbarello M, Spanu T, Di Bidino R, Marchetti M, Ruggeri M, Trecarichi EM et al. Costs of bloodstream infections caused by *Escherichia coli* and influence of extended-spectrum-beta-lactamase production and inadequate initial antibiotic therapy. *Antimicrob Agents Chemother*, 2010, 54(10):4085-4091. doi:10.1128/AAC.00143-10.

20. Suankratay C, Jutivorakool K, Jirajariyavej S. A prospective study of ceftriaxone treatment in acute pyelonephritis caused by extended-spectrum beta-lactamase-producing bacteria. *J Med Assoc Thai*, 2008, 91(8):1172-1181. (http://www.ncbi.nlm.nih.gov/entrez/query.fcgi?cmd=Retrieve&db=PubMed&dopt=Citation&list_uids=18788687, accessed 29 January 2014).

21. Rodriguez-Bano J, Picon E, Gijon P, Hernandez JR, Ruiz M, Pena C et al. Community-onset bacteremia due to extended-spectrum beta-lactamase-producing *Escherichia coli*: risk factors and prognosis. *Clin Infect Dis*, 2010, 50(1):40-48. doi:10.1086/649537.

22. Pena C, Gudiol C, Calatayud L, Tubau F, Dominguez MA, Pujol M et al. Infections due to *Escherichia coli* producing extended-spectrum beta-lactamase among hospitalised patients: factors influencing mortality. *J Hosp Infect*, 2008, 68(2):116-122. doi:10.1016/j.jhin.2007.11.012.

23. Nussbaum A, Mariano N, Colon-Urban R, Modeste RA, Zahid S, Wehbeh W et al. Microbiologic and Clinical Comparison of Patients Harboring *Escherichia coli* Blood Isolates with and without Extended-Spectrum ß-Lactamases. *Advances in Infectious Diseases*, 2013, Vol.3 No 1.:50-54.

24. Nicolas-Chanoine MH, Jarlier V, Robert J, Arlet G, Drieux L, Leflon-Guibout V et al. Patient's origin and lifestyle associated with CTX-M-producing *Escherichia coli*: a case-control-control study. *PLoS ONE [Electronic Resource]*, 2012, 7(1):e30498. doi:10.1371/journal.pone.0030498.

25. Melzer M, Petersen I. Mortality following bacteraemic infection caused by extended spectrum beta-lactamase (ESBL) producing *E. coli* compared to non-ESBL producing *E. coli*. *J Infect*, 2007, 55(3):254-259. (http://www.ncbi.nlm.nih.gov/pubmed/17574678, accessed 9 April 2014).

26. Khan FY, Elshafie SS, Almaslamani M, Abu-Khattab M, El-Hiday AH, Errayes M et al. Epidemiology of bacteraemia in Hamad general hospital, Qatar: a one year hospital-based study. *Travel Med Infect Dis*, 2010, 8(6):377-387. (http://www.sciencedirect.com/science/journal/14778939, accessed 19 January 2014).

27. Kang CI, Wi YM, Lee MY, Ko KS, Chung DR, Peck KR et al. Epidemiology and risk factors of community onset infections caused by extended-spectrum beta-lactamase-producing *Escherichia coli* strains. *J Clin Microbiol*, 2011, 50(2):312-317.

28. Kang CI, Song JH, Chung DR, Peck KR, Ko KS, Yeom JS et al. Risk factors and treatment outcomes of community-onset bacteraemia caused by extended-spectrum beta-lactamase-producing *Escherichia coli*. *Int J Antimicrob Agents*, 2010, 36(3):284-287. doi:10.1128/JCM.06002-11.

29. Kang CI, Kim SH, Park WB, Lee KD, Kim HB, Oh MD et al. Clinical outcome of bacteremic spontaneous bacterial peritonitis due to extended-spectrum beta-lactamase-producing *Escherichia coli* and *Klebsiella pneumoniae*. *Korean J Intern Med*, 2004, 19(3):160-164. (http://www.ncbi.nlm.nih.gov/pubmed/15481607, accessed 9 April 2014).

30. Hsieh CJ, Shen YH, Hwang KP. Clinical implications, risk factors and mortality following community-onset bacteremia caused by extended-spectrum -lactamase (ESBL) and non-ESBL producing *Escherichia coli*. *J Microbiol, Immunol Infect*, 2010, 43(3):240-248.

31. Ho PL, Chan WM, Tsang KW, Wong SS, Young K. Bacteremia caused by *Escherichia coli* producing extended-spectrum beta-lactamase: a case-control study of risk factors and outcomes. *Scand J Infect Dis*, 2002, 34(8):567-573. (http://www.ncbi.nlm.nih.gov/pubmed/12238570, accessed 9 April 2014).

32. Gudiol C, Calatayud L, Garcia-Vidal C, Lora-Tamayo J, Cisnal M, Duarte R et al. Bacteraemia due to extended-spectrum beta-lactamase-producing *Escherichia coli* (ESBL-EC) in cancer patients: clinical features, risk factors, molecular epidemiology and outcome. *J Antimicrob Chemother*, 2010, 65(2):333-341. (http://dx.doi.org/10.1093/jac/dkp411, accessed 29 January 2014).

33. Garcia Hernandez A, Garcia-Vazquez E, Gomez GJ, Canteras M, Hernandez-Torres A, Ruiz GJ. [Predictive factors of ESBL versus non-ESBL *Escherichia coli* bacteraemia and influence of resistance on the mortality of the patients]. [Spanish]. *Med Clin (Barc)*, 2010, 136(2):56-60. doi:10.1016/j.medcli.2010.05.014.

34. Ena J, Arjona F, Martinez-Peinado C, Lopez-Perezagua MM, Amador C. Epidemiology of urinary tract infections caused by extended-spectrum beta-lactamase-producing *Escherichia coli. Urology*, 2006, 68(6):1169-1174. (http://www.ncbi.nlm.nih.gov/pubmed/17169640, accessed 9 April 2014).

35. de Kraker ME, Davey PG, Grundmann H, BURDEN study group. Mortality and hospital stay associated with resistant *Staphylococcus aureus* and *Escherichia coli* bacteremia: estimating the burden of antibiotic resistance in Europe. *PLoS Med*, 2011, 8(10):e1001104. doi:10.1371/journal.pmed.1001104.

36. Cornejo-Juarez P, Perez-Jimenez C, Silva-Sanchez J, Velazquez-Acosta C, Gonzalez-Lara F, Reyna-Flores F et al. Molecular analysis and risk factors for *Escherichia coli* producing extended-spectrum beta-lactamase bloodstream infection in hematological malignancies. *PLoS ONE*, 2012, 7(4):e35780. (http://dx.doi.org/10.1371/journal.pone.0035780, accessed 29 January 2014).

37. Apisarnthanarak A, Kiratisin P, Saifon P, Kitphati R, Dejsirilert S, Mundy LM. Predictors of mortality among patients with community-onset infection due to extended-spectrum beta-lactamase-producing *Escherichia coli* in Thailand. *Infect Control Hosp Epidemiol*, 2008, 29(1):80-82. doi:10.1086/524321.

38. Anunnatsiri S, Towiwat P, Chaimanee P. Risk factors and clinical outcomes of extended spectrum beta-lactamase (ESBL)-producing *Escherichia coli* septicemia at Srinagarind University Hospital, Thailand. *Southeast Asian J Trop Med Public Health*, 2012, 43(5):1169-1177. (http://www.ncbi.nlm.nih.gov/pubmed/23431823, accessed 9 April 2014).

39. Al-Otaibi FE, Bukhari EE. Clinical and laboratory profiles of urinary tract infections caused by extended-spectrum beta-lactamase-producing *Escherichia coli* in a tertiary care center in central Saudi Arabia. *Saudi Med J*, 2013, 34(2):171-176. (http://www.ncbi.nlm.nih.gov/pubmed/23396464, accessed 9 April 2014).

40. Tuon FF, Kruger M, Terreri M, Penteado-Filho SR, Gortz L. Klebsiella ESBL bacteremia-mortality and risk factors. *Braz J Infect Dis*, 2011, 15(6):594-598. (http://www.ncbi.nlm.nih.gov/pubmed/22218521, accessed 9 April 2014).

41. Tumbarello M, Spanu T, Sanguinetti M, Citton R, Montuori E, Leone F et al. Bloodstream infections caused by extended-spectrum-beta-lactamase-producing *Klebsiella pneumoniae*: risk factors, molecular epidemiology, and clinical outcome. *Antimicrob Agents Chemother*, 2006, 50(2):498-504. (http://www.ncbi.nlm.nih.gov/pubmed/16436702, accessed 9 April 2014).

42. Szilagyi E, Fuzi M, Borocz K, Kurcz A, Toth A, Nagy K. Risk factors and outcomes for bloodstream infections with extended-spectrum beta -lactamase-producing *Klebsiella pneumoniae* ; Findings of the nosocomial surveillance system in Hungary. *Acta Microbiologica et Immunologica Hungarica*, 2009, 56(3):251-262.

43. Song KH, Jeon JH, Park WB, Park SW, Kim HB, Oh MD et al. Clinical outcomes of spontaneous bacterial peritonitis due to extended-spectrum beta-lactamase-producing *Escherichia coli* and Klebsiella species: a retrospective matched case-control study. *BMC Infect Dis*, 2009, 9:41. doi:10.1186/1471-2334-9-41.

44. Rebuck JA, Olsen KM, Fey PD, Langnas AN, Rupp ME. Characterization of an outbreak due to extended-spectrum beta-lactamase-producing *Klebsiella pneumoniae* in a pediatric intensive care unit transplant population. *Clin Infect Dis*, 2000, 31(6):1368-1372. (http://www.ncbi.nlm.nih.gov/pubmed/11096004, accessed 9 April 2014).

45. Pillay T, Pillay DG, Adhikari M, Sturm AW. Piperacillin/tazobactam in the treatment of *Klebsiella pneumoniae* infections in neonates. *Am J Perinatol*, 1998, 15(1):47-51. (http://www.ncbi.nlm.nih.gov/pubmed/9475688, accessed 9 April 2014).

46. Pena C, Pujol M, Ardanuy C, Ricart A, Pallares R, Linares J et al. An outbreak of hospital-acquired *Klebsiella pneumoniae* bacteraemia, including strains producing extended-spectrum beta-lactamase. *J Hosp Infect*, 2001, 47(1):53-59. (http://www.ncbi.nlm.nih.gov/pubmed/11161899, accessed 9 April 2014).

47. Paterson DL, Ko WC, Von Gottberg A, Mohapatra S, Casellas JM, Goossens H et al. International Prospective Study of *Klebsiella pneumoniae* Bacteremia: Implications of Extended-Spectrum beta-Lactamase Production in Nosocomial Infections. *Ann Intern Med*, 2004, 140(1):26-32. (http://www.ncbi.nlm.nih.gov/pubmed/14706969, accessed 9 April 2014).

48. Panhotra BR, Saxena AK, Al-Ghamdi AM. Extended-spectrum beta-lactamase-producing *Klebsiella pneumoniae* hospital acquired bacteremia. Risk factors and clinical outcome. *Saudi Med J*, 2004, 25(12):1871-1876. (http://www.ncbi.nlm.nih.gov/pubmed/15711657, accessed 9 April 2014).

49. Mosqueda-Gomez JL, Montano-Loza A, Rolon AL, Cervantes C, Bobadilla-del-Valle JM, Silva-Sanchez J et al. Molecular epidemiology and risk factors of bloodstream infections caused by extended-spectrum beta-lactamase-producing *Klebsiella pneumoniae* A case-control study. *Int J Infect Dis*, 2008, 12(6):653-659. doi:10.1016/j.ijid.2008.03.008.

50. Marra AR, Wey SB, Castelo A, Gales AC, Cal RG, Filho JR et al. Nosocomial bloodstream infections caused by *Klebsiella pneumoniae*: impact of extended-spectrum beta-lactamase (ESBL) production on clinical outcome in a hospital with high ESBL prevalence. *BMC Infect Dis*, 2006, 6:24. doi:10.1186/1471-2334-6-24.

51. Loh LC, Nor Izran Hanim Bt Abdul S, Rosdara Masayuni Bt Mohd S, Raman S, Thayaparan T, Kumar S. Hospital Outcomes of Adult Respiratory Tract Infections with Extended-Spectrum B-Lactamase (ESBL) Producing Klebsiella Pneumoniae. *Malays J Med Sci*, 2007, 14(2):36-40. (http://www.ncbi.nlm.nih.gov/pmc/articles/PMC3442624/, accessed 9 April 2014).

52. Lin MF, Huang ML, Lai SH. Risk factors in the acquisition of extended-spectrum beta-lactamase *Klebsiella pneumoniae*: a case-control study in a district teaching hospital in Taiwan. *J Hosp Infect*, 2003, 53(1):39-45. (http://www.ncbi.nlm.nih.gov/pubmed/12495684, accessed 9 April 2014).

53. Lee JA, Kang CI, Joo EJ, Ha YE, Kang SJ, Park SY et al. Epidemiology and clinical features of community-onset bacteremia caused by extended-spectrum -lactamase-producing *Klebsiella pneumoniae*. *Microb Drug Resist*, 2011, 17(2):267-273.

54. Kuo KC, Shen YH, Hwang KP. Clinical implications and risk factors of extended-spectrum beta-lactamase-producing *Klebsiella pneumoniae* infection in children: a case-control retrospective study in a medical center in southern Taiwan. *J Microbiol, Immunol Infect*, 2007, 40(3):248-254. (http://www.ncbi.nlm.nih.gov/pubmed/17639166, accessed 9 April 2014).

55. Kang CI, Kim SH, Kim DM, Park WB, Lee KD, Kim HB et al. Risk factors for and clinical outcomes of bloodstream infections caused by extended-spectrum beta-lactamase-producing *Klebsiella pneumoniae*. *Infect Control Hosp Epidemiol*, 2004, 25(10):860-867.

56. Kang CI, Kim SH, Bang JW, Kim HB, Kim NJ, Kim EC et al. Community-acquired versus nosocomial *Klebsiella pneumoniae* bacteremia: clinical features, treatment outcomes, and clinical implication of antimicrobial resistance. *J Korean Med Sci*, 2006, 21(5):816-822. doi:10.3346/jkms.2006.21.5.816.

57. Huang Y, Zhuang S, Du M. Risk factors of nosocomial infection with extended-spectrum beta-lactamase-producing bacteria in a neonatal intensive care unit in China. *Infection*, 2007, 35(5):339-345. (http://www.ncbi.nlm.nih.gov/pubmed/17721736, accessed 9 April 2014).

58. Gomes CC, Vormittag E, Santos CR, Levin AS. Nosocomial infection with cephalosporin-resistant *Klebsiella pneumoniae* is not associated with increased mortality. *Infect Control Hosp Epidemiol*, 2006, 27(9):907-912. (http://www.ncbi.nlm.nih.gov/pubmed/16941314, accessed 9 April 2014).

59. Demirdag K, Hosoglu S. Epidemiology and risk factors for ESBL-producing *Klebsiella pneumoniae*: a case control study. *J Infect Dev Ctries*, 2010, 4(11):717-722. (http://www.ncbi.nlm.nih.gov/pubmed/21252449, accessed 9 April 2014).

60. Cofsky R, Vangala K, Haag R, Recco R, Maccario E, Sathe S et al. The cost of antibiotic resistance: Effect of resistance among *Staphylococcus aureus*, *Klebsiella pneumoniae*, *Acinetobacter baumannii*, and *Pseudomonas aeruginosa* on length of hospital stay. *Infect Control Hosp Epidemiol*, 2002, 23(2):106-108. (http://www.ncbi.nlm.nih.gov/pubmed/11893146, accessed 9 April 2014).

61. Chiu S, Huang YC, Lien RI, Chou YH, Lin TY. Clinical features of nosocomial infections by extended-spectrum beta-lactamase-producing Enterobacteriaceae in neonatal intensive care units. *Acta Paediatrica*, 2005, 94(11):1644-1649. (http://www.ncbi.nlm.nih.gov/pubmed/16303704, accessed 9 April 2014).

62. Ariffin H, Navaratnam P, Mohamed M, Arasu A, Abdullah WA, Lee CL et al. Ceftazidime-resistant *Klebsiella pneumoniae* bloodstream infection in children with febrile neutropenia. *Int J Infect Dis*, 2000, 4(1):21-25. (http://www.ncbi.nlm.nih.gov/entrez/query.fcgi?cmd=Retrieve&db=PubMed&dopt=Citation&list_uids=10689210, accessed 29 January 2014).

63. Shilo S, Assous MV, Lachish T, Kopuit P, Bdolah-Abram T, Yinnon AM et al. Risk factors for bacteriuria with carbapenem-resistant *Klebsiella pneumoniae* and its impact on mortality: a case-control study. *Infection*, 2013, 41(2):503-509. doi:10.1007/s15010-012-0380-0.

64. Schwaber MJ, Klarfeld-Lidji S, Navon-Venezia S, Schwartz D, Leavitt A, Carmeli Y. Predictors of carbapenem-resistant *Klebsiella pneumoniae* acquisition among hospitalized adults and effect of acquisition on mortality. *Antimicrob Agents Chemother*, 2008, 52(3):1028-1033. doi:10.1128/AAC.01020-07.

65. Raviv Y, Shitrit D, Amital A, Fox B, Bakal I, Tauber R et al. Multidrug-resistant *Klebsiella pneumoniae* acquisition in lung transplant recipients. *Clin Transpl*, 2012, 26(4):E388-E394. doi:10.1111/j.1399-0012.2012.01671.x.

66. Patel G, Huprikar S, Factor SH, Jenkins SG, Calfee DP. Outcomes of carbapenem-resistant *Klebsiella pneumoniae* infection and the impact of antimicrobial and adjunctive therapies. *Infect Control Hosp Epidemiol*, 2008, 29(12):1099-1106. doi:10.1086/592412.

67. Mouloudi E, Protonotariou E, Zagorianou A, Iosifidis E, Karapanagiotou A, Giasnetsova T et al. Bloodstream infections caused by metallo--lactamase/*Klebsiella pneumoniae* carbapenemase-producing *K. pneumoniae* among intensive care unit patients in Greece: risk factors for infection and impact of type of resistance on outcomes. *Infect Control Hosp Epidemiol*, 2010, 31(12):1250-1256. doi:10.1086/657135.

68. Liu SW, Chang HJ, Chia JH, Kuo AJ, Wu TL, Lee MH. Outcomes and characteristics of ertapenem-nonsusceptible *Klebsiella pneumoniae* bacteremia at a university hospital in Northern Taiwan: a matched case-control study. *J Microbiol, Immunol Infect*, 2012, 45(2):113-119. (http://dx.doi.org/10.1016/j.jmii.2011.09.026, accessed 9 April 2014).

69. Lee NY, Wu JJ, Lin SH, Ko WC, Tsai LH, Yan JJ. Characterization of carbapenem-nonsusceptible *Klebsiella pneumoniae* bloodstream isolates at a Taiwanese hospital: clinical impacts of lowered breakpoints for carbapenems. *Eur J Clin Microbiol Infect Dis*, 2012, 31(8):1941-1950. doi:10.1007/s10096-011-1525-2.

70. Hussein K, Raz-Pasteur A, Finkelstein R, Neuberger A, Shachor-Meyouhas Y, Oren I et al. Impact of carbapenem resistance on the outcome of patients' hospital-acquired bacteraemia caused by *Klebsiella pneumoniae*. *J Hosp Infect*, 2013, 83(4):307-313. doi:10.1016/j.jhin.2012.10.012.

71. Gaviria D, Greenfield V, Bixler D, Thomas CA, Ibrahim SM, Kallen A et al. Carbapenem-resistant klebsiella pneumoniae associated with a long-term--care facility - west Virginia, 2009-2011. *Morb Mortal Wkly Rep*, 2011, 60(41):1418-1420.

72. Falagas ME, Rafailidis PI, Kofteridis D, Virtzili S, Chelvatzoglou FC, Papaioannou V et al. Risk factors of carbapenem-resistant *Klebsiella pneumoniae* infections: a matched case control study. *J Antimicrob Chemother*, 2007, 60(5):1124-1130 (http://www.ncbi.nlm.nih.gov/pubmed/17884829, accessed 9 April 2014).

73. Daikos GL, Petrikkos P, Psichogiou M, Kosmidis C, Vryonis E, Skoutelis A et al. Prospective observational study of the impact of VIM-1 metallo-beta-lactamase on the outcome of patients with *Klebsiella pneumoniae* bloodstream infections. *Antimicrob Agents Chemother*, 2009, 53(5):1868-1873. doi:10.1128/AAC.00782-08.

74. Daikos GL, Karabinis A, Paramythiotou E, Syriopoulou VP, Kosmidis C, Avlami A et al. VIM-1-producing *Klebsiella pneumoniae* bloodstream infections: analysis of 28 cases. *Int J Androl*, 2007, 29(4):471-473.

75. Correa L, Martino MD, Siqueira I, Pasternak J, Gales AC, Silva CV et al. A hospital-based matched case-control study to identify clinical outcome and risk factors associated with carbapenem-resistant *Klebsiella pneumoniae* infection. *BMC Infect Dis*, 2013, 13:80. doi:10.1186/1471-2334-13-80.

76. Zahar JR, Clec'h C, Tafflet M, Garrouste-Orgeas M, Jamali S, Mourvillier B et al. Is methicillin resistance associated with a worse prognosis in *Staphylococcus aureus* ventilator-associated pneumonia? *Clin Infect Dis*, 2005, 41(9):1224-1231. (http://www.ncbi.nlm.nih.gov/pubmed/16206094, accessed 9 April 2014).

77. Yoon HJ, Choi JY, Kim CO, Kim JM, Song YG. A comparison of clinical features and mortality among methicillin-resistant and methicillin-sensitive strains of *Staphylococcus aureus* endocarditis. *Yonsei Med J*, 2005, 46(4):496-502. doi:10.3349/ymj.2005.46.4.496.

78. Wyllie DH, Crook DW, Peto TE. Mortality after *Staphylococcus aureus* bacteraemia in two hospitals in Oxfordshire, 1997-2003: cohort study. [Erratum appears in BMJ. 2006 Sep 2; 333(7566):468]. *BMJ (Clinical Research Ed.)*, 2006, 333(7562):281. (http://www.ncbi.nlm.nih.gov/pubmed/16798756, accessed 9 April 2014).

79. Wolkewitz M, Frank U, Philips G, Schumacher M, Davey P, group Bs. Mortality associated with in-hospital bacteraemia caused by *Staphylococcus aureus*: a multistate analysis with follow-up beyond hospital discharge. *J Antimicrob Chemother*, 2011, 66(2):381-386. doi:10.1093/jac/dkq424.

80. Wehrhahn MC, Robinson JO, Pearson JC, O'Brien FG, Tan HL, Coombs GW et al. Clinical and laboratory features of invasive community-onset methicillin-resistant *Staphylococcus aureus* infection: a prospective case-control study. *Eur J Clin Microbiol Infect Dis*, 2010, 29(8):1025-1033. doi:10.1007/s10096-010-0973-4.

81. Wang FD, Chen YY, Chen TL, Liu CY. Risk factors and mortality in patients with nosocomial *Staphylococcus aureus* bacteremia. *Am J Infect Control*, 2008, 36(2):118-122. doi:10.1016/j.ajic.2007.02.005.

82. Wang CY, Wu VC, Wang WJ, Lin YF, Lin YH, Chen YM et al. Risk factors for nasal carriage of methicillin-resistant *Staphylococcus aureus* among patients with end-stage renal disease in Taiwan. *J Formos Med Assoc*, 2012, 111(1):14-18. doi:10.1016/j.jfma.2012.01.001.

83. Viallon A, Marjollet O, Berthelot P, Carricajo A, Guyomarc'h S, Robert F et al. Risk factors associated with methicillin-resistant *Staphylococcus aureus* infection in patients admitted to the ED. *Am J Emerg Med*, 2007, 25(8):880-886. (http://www.ncbi.nlm.nih.gov/pubmed/17920971, accessed 9 April 2014).

84. Tumbarello M, de Gaetano DK, Tacconelli E, Citton R, Spanu T, Leone F et al. Risk factors and predictors of mortality of methicillin-resistant *Staphylococcus aureus* (MRSA) bacteraemia in HIV-infected patients. *J Antimicrob Chemother*, 2002, 50(3):375-382. (http://www.ncbi.nlm.nih.gov/pubmed/12205062, accessed 9 April 2014).

85. Tsai YH, Wen-Wei HR, Huang KC, Huang TJ. Comparison of necrotizing fasciitis and sepsis caused by Vibrio vulnificus and *Staphylococcus aureus*. *J Bone Joint Surg Am*, 2011, 93(3):274-284. doi:10.2106/JBJS.I.01679.

86. Truffault A, Mimoz O, Karim A, Edouard A, Nordmann P, Samii K. [Colonization by methicillin-resistant *Staphylococcus aureus* is a predictive factor for the resistance phenotype of an infectious strain of *S. aureus*]. [French]. *Ann Fr Anesth*, 2000, 19(3):151-155.

87. Trividic-Rumeau M, Bouyssou-Gauthier ML, Mounier M, Sparsa A, Blaise S, Bedane C et al. [Methicilline-sensitive and methicilline-resistant *Staphylococcus aureus* related morbidity in chronic wounds: a prospective study]. [French]. *Ann Dermatol Venereol*, 2003, 130(6-7):601-605. (http://www.ncbi.nlm.nih.gov/pubmed/13679695, accessed 9 April 2014).

88. Traverso F, Peluffo M, Louge M, Funaro F, Suasnabar R, Cepeda R. [Impact of methicillin resistance on mortality and surveillance of vancomycin susceptibility in bacteremias caused by *Staphylococcus aureus*]. [Spanish]. *Rev Argent Microbiol*, 2010, 42(4):274-278. doi:10.1590/S0325-75412010000400007.

89. Tong SY, Bishop EJ, Lilliebridge RA, Cheng AC, Spasova-Penkova Z, Holt DC et al. Community-associated strains of methicillin-resistant *Staphylococcus aureus* and methicillin-susceptible *S. aureus* in indigenous Northern Australia: epidemiology and outcomes. *J Infect Dis*, 2009, 199(10):1461-1470. doi:10.1086/598218.

90. Thomason TS, Brenski A, McClay J, Ehmer D. The rising incidence of methicillin-resistant *Staphylococcus aureus* in pediatric neck abscesses. *Otolaryngol Head Neck Surg*, 2007, 137(3):459-464. (http://www.ncbi.nlm.nih.gov/pubmed/17765776, accessed 9 April 2014).

91. Theodorou P, Lefering R, Perbix W, Spanholtz TA, Maegele M, Spilker G et al. *Staphylococcus aureus* bacteremia after thermal injury: The clinical impact of methicillin resistance. *Burns*, 2013, 39(3):404-412. doi:10.1016/j.burns.2012.12.006.

92. Teterycz D, Ferry T, Lew D, Stern R, Assal M, Hoffmeyer P et al. Outcome of orthopedic implant infections due to different staphylococci. *Int J Infect Dis*, 2010, 14(10):e913-e918. doi:10.1016/j.ijid.2010.05.014.

93. Taneja C, Haque N, Oster G, Shorr AF, Zilber S, Kyan PO et al. Clinical and economic outcomes in patients with community-acquired *Staphylococcus aureus* pneumonia. *J Hosp Med*, 2010, 5(9):528-534. doi:10.1002/jhm.704.

94. Tam AY, Yeung CY. The changing pattern of severe neonatal staphylococcal infection: a 10-year study. *Aust Paediatr J*, 1988, 24(5):275-279. (http://www.ncbi.nlm.nih.gov/pubmed/3265869, accessed 9 April 2014).

95. Talon D, Woronoff-Lemsi MC, Limat S, Bertrand X, Chatillon M, Gil H et al. The impact of resistance to methicillin in *Staphylococcus aureus* bacteremia on mortality. *Eur J Int Med*, 2002, 13(1):31-36. (http://dx.doi.org/10.1016/S0953-6205%2801%2900189-3, accessed 29 January 2014).

96. Takayama Y, Okamoto R, Sunakawa K. Definite infective endocarditis: clinical and microbiological features of 155 episodes in one Japanese university hospital. *J Formos Med Assoc*, 2010, 109(11):788-799. doi:10.1016/S0929-6646(10)60124-6.

97. Spindel SJ, Strausbaugh LJ, Jacobson C. Infections caused by *Staphylococcus aureus* in a Veterans' Affairs nursing home care unit: a 5-year experience. *Infect Control Hosp Epidemiol*, 1995, 16(4):217-223. (http://www.ncbi.nlm.nih.gov/pubmed/7636169, accessed 9 April 2014).

98. Soriano A, Martinez JA, Mensa J, Marco F, Almela M, Moreno-Martinez A et al. Pathogenic significance of methicillin resistance for patients with *Staphylococcus aureus* bacteremia. *Clin Infect Dis*, 2000, 30(2):368-373. (http://www.ncbi.nlm.nih.gov/pubmed/10671343, accessed 9 April 2014).

99. Sicot N, Khanafer N, Meyssonnier V, Dumitrescu O, Tristan A, Bes M et al. Methicillin resistance is not a predictor of severity in community-acquired *Staphylococcus aureus* necrotizing pneumoniaresults of a prospective observational study. *Clin Microbiol Infect*, 2013, 19(3):E142-E148. doi:10.1111/1469-0691.12022.

100. Shurland S, Zhan M, Bradham DD, Roghmann MC. Comparison of mortality risk associated with bacteremia due to methicillin-resistant and methicillin-susceptible *Staphylococcus aureus*. *Infect Control Hosp Epidemiol*, 2007, 28(3):273-279. (http://www.ncbi.nlm.nih.gov/pubmed/17326017, accessed 9 April 2014).

101. Shorr AF, Tabak YP, Gupta V, Johannes RS, Liu LZ, Kollef MH. Morbidity and cost burden of methicillin-resistant *Staphylococcus aureus* in early onset ventilator-associated pneumonia. *Crit Care (London, England)*, 2006, 10(3):R97. (http://www.ncbi.nlm.nih.gov/pubmed/16808853, accessed 9 April 2014).

102. Shorr AF, Haque N, Taneja C, Zervos M, Lamerato L, Kothari S et al. Clinical and economic outcomes for patients with health care-associated *Staphylococcus aureus* Pneumonia. *J. Clin. Microbiol.* 2010, 48(9): 3258-3262. doi:10.1128/JCM.02529-09.

103. Shorr AF, Combes A, Kollef MH, Chastre J. Methicillin-resistant *Staphylococcus aureus* prolongs intensive care unit stay in ventilator-associated pneumonia, despite initially appropriate antibiotic therapy. *Crit Care Med*, 2006, 34(3):700-706. (http://www.ncbi.nlm.nih.gov/pubmed/16505656, accessed 9 April 2014).

104. Shane AL, Hansen NI, Stoll BJ, Bell EF, Sanchez PJ, Shankaran S et al. Methicillin-resistant and susceptible *Staphylococcus aureus* bacteremia and meningitis in preterm infants. *Pediatrics*, 2012, 129(4):e914-e922. doi:10.1542/peds.2011-0966.

105. Selvey LA, Whitby M, Johnson B. Nosocomial methicillin-resistant *Staphylococcus aureus* bacteremia: is it any worse than nosocomial methicillin-sensitive *Staphylococcus aureus* bacteremia? *Infect Control Hosp Epidemiol*, 2000, 21(10):645-648. (http://www.ncbi.nlm.nih.gov/pubmed/11083180, accessed 9 April 2014).

106. Salgado CD, Dash S, Cantey JR, Marculescu CE. Higher risk of failure of methicillin-resistant *Staphylococcus aureus* prosthetic joint infections. *Clin Orthop Relat Res*, 2007, 461:48-53. (http://www.ncbi.nlm.nih.gov/pubmed/17534195, accessed 9 April 2014).

107. Saavedra-Lozano J, Mejias A, Ahmad N, Peromingo E, Ardura MI, Guillen S et al. Changing trends in acute osteomyelitis in children: impact of methicillin-resistant *Staphylococcus aureus* infections. *J Pediatr Orthop*, 2008, 28(5):569-575. doi:10.1097/BPO.0b013e31817bb816.

108. Rubio-Terres C, Garau J, Grau S, Martinez-Martinez L. Cast of Resistance Study Group. Cost of bacteraemia caused by methicillin-resistant vs. methicillin-susceptible *Staphylococcus aureus* in Spain: a retrospective cohort study. *Clin Microbiol Infect*, 2010, 16(6):722-728. doi:10.1111/j.1469-0691.2009.02902.x.

109. Romero-Vivas J, Rubio M, Fernandez C, Picazo JJ. Mortality associated with nosocomial bacteremia due to methicillin-resistant *Staphylococcus aureus*. *Clin Infect Dis*, 1995, 21(6):1417-1423. (http://www.ncbi.nlm.nih.gov/pubmed/8749626, accessed 9 April 2014).

110. Reshad K, Tanaka F, Sekine T, Maesako N, Masui K, Oka K et al. [A prospective study of septic episodes due to *Staphylococcus aureus* and the background of the patients]. [Japanese]. *Kansenshogaku Zasshi - J Jpn Assoc Infect Dis*, 1994, 68(2):171-176. (http://www.ncbi.nlm.nih.gov/pubmed/8151141, accessed 9 April 2014).

111. Rello J, Torres A, Ricart M, Valles J, Gonzalez J, Artigas A et al. Ventilator-associated pneumonia by *Staphylococcus aureus*. Comparison of methicillin-resistant and methicillin-sensitive episodes. *Am J Respir Crit Care Med*, 1994, 150(6:Pt 1):t-9. (http://www.ncbi.nlm.nih.gov/pubmed/0007952612, accessed 9 April 2014).

112. Rello J, Molano D, Villabon M, Reina R, Rita-Quispe R, Previgliano I et al. Differences in hospital- and ventilator-associated pneumonia due to *Staphylococcus aureus* (methicillin-susceptible and methicillin-resistant) between Europe and Latin America: A comparison of the EUVAP and LATINVAP study cohorts. *Med Intensiva*, 2012. doi:10.1016/j.medin.2012.04.008.

113. Reed SD, Friedman JY, Engemann JJ, Griffiths RI, Anstrom KJ, Kaye KS et al. Costs and outcomes among hemodialysis-dependent patients with methicillin-resistant or methicillin-susceptible *Staphylococcus aureus* bacteremia. *Infect Control Hosp Epidemiol*, 2005, 26(2):175-183. (http://www.ncbi.nlm.nih.gov/pubmed/15756889, accessed 9 April 2014).

114. Rana D, Abughali N, Kumar D, Super DM, Jacobs MR, Kumar ML. *Staphylococcus aureus*, including community-acquired methicillin-resistant *S. aureus*, in a level III NICU: 2001 to 2008. *Am J Perinatol*, 2012, 29(6):401-408. doi:10.1055/s-0032-1304819.

115. Rahikka P, Syrjanen J, Vuento R, Laine J, Huttunen R. Meticillin-resistant *Staphylococcus aureus* (MRSA) bacteraemia in Tampere University Hospital: a case-control study, Finland October 2002 to January 2010. *Eur Surveill: Euro Comm Dis Bull*, 2011, 16(35):2011. (http://www.eurosurveillance.org/ViewArticle.aspx?ArticleId=19958, accessed 9 April 2014).

116. Quilty S, Kwok G, Hajkowicz K, Currie B. High incidence of methicillin-resistant *Staphylococcus aureus* sepsis and death in patients with febrile neutropenia at Royal Darwin Hospital. *Int Med J*, 2009, 39(8):557-559. doi:10.1111/j.1445-5994.2009.02003.x.

117. Pujol M, Pena C, Pallares R, Ariza J, Ayats J, Dominguez MA et al. Nosocomial *Staphylococcus aureus* bacteremia among nasal carriers of methicillin-resistant and methicillin-susceptible strains. *Am J Med*, 1996, 100(5):509-516. (http://www.ncbi.nlm.nih.gov/pubmed/8644762, accessed 9 April 2014).

118. Pujol M, Corbella X, Pena C, Pallares R, Dorca J, Verdaguer R et al. Clinical and epidemiological findings in mechanically-ventilated patients with methicillin-resistant *Staphylococcus aureus* pneumonia. *Eur J Clin Microbiol Infect Dis*, 1998, 17(9):622-628. (http://www.ncbi.nlm.nih.gov/pubmed/9832263, accessed 9 April 2014).

119. Priest DH, Peacock JE, Jr. Hematogenous vertebral osteomyelitis due to *Staphylococcus aureus* in the adult: clinical features and therapeutic outcomes. *South Med J*, 2005, 98(9):854-862. (http://www.ncbi.nlm.nih.gov/pubmed/16217976, accessed 9 April 2014).

120. Popovich KJ, Weinstein RA, Aroutcheva A, Rice T, Hota B. Community-associated methicillin-resistant *Staphylococcus aureus* and HIV: intersecting epidemics. *Clin Infect Dis*, 2010, 50(7):979-987. doi:10.1086/651076.

121. Ponce-de-Leon A, Camacho-Ortiz A, Macias AE, Landin-Larios C, Villanueva-Walbey C, Trinidad-Guerrero D et al. Epidemiology and clinical characteristics of *Staphylococcus aureus* bloodstream infections in a tertiary-care center in Mexico City: 2003-2007. *Rev Invest Clin*, 2010, 62(6):553-559. (http://www.ncbi.nlm.nih.gov/pubmed/21416781, accessed 9 April 2014).

122. Perovic O, Koornhof H, Black V, Moodley I, Duse A, Galpin J. *Staphylococcus aureus* bacteraemia at two academic hospitals in Johannesburg. *S Afr Med J*, 2006, 96(8):714-717. (http://www.ncbi.nlm.nih.gov/pubmed/17019494, accessed 9 April 2014).

123. Pasticci MB, Moretti A, Stagni G, Ravasio V, Soavi L, Raglio A et al. Bactericidal activity of oxacillin and glycopeptides against *Staphylococcus aureus* in patients with endocarditis: looking for a relationship between tolerance and outcome. *Ann Clin Microbiol Antimicrob*, 2011, 10:26. doi:10.1186/1476-0711-10-26.

124. Parvizi J, Pawasarat IM, Azzam KA, Joshi A, Hansen EN, Bozic KJ. Periprosthetic joint infection: the economic impact of methicillin-resistant infections. *J Arthroplasty*, 2010, 25(6:Suppl):Suppl-7. doi:10.1016/j.arth.2010.04.011.

125. Park SY, Son JS, Oh IH, Choi JM, Lee MS. Clinical impact of methicillin-resistant *Staphylococcus aureus* bacteremia based on propensity scores. *Infection*, 2011, 39(2):141-147. doi:10.1007/s15010-011-0100-1.

126. Ott E, Bange FC, Reichardt C, Graf K, Eckstein M, Schwab F et al. Costs of nosocomial pneumonia caused by meticillin-resistant *Staphylococcus aureus*. *J Hosp Infect*, 2010, 76(4):300-303. doi:10.1016/j.jhin.2010.07.007.

127. Osmon S, Ward S, Fraser VJ, Kollef MH. Hospital mortality for patients with bacteremia due to *Staphylococcus aureus* or *Pseudomonas aeruginosa*. *Chest*, 2004, 125(2):607-616. (http://www.ncbi.nlm.nih.gov/pubmed/14769745, accessed 9 April 2014).

128. O'Kane GM, Gottlieb T, Bradbury R. Staphylococcal bacteraemia: the hospital or the home? A review of *Staphylococcus aureus* bacteraemia at Concord Hospital in 1993. *Aust N Z J Med*, 1998, 28(1):23-27. (http://www.ncbi.nlm.nih.gov/pubmed/9544382, accessed 9 April 2014).

129. Ochoa TJ, Mohr J, Wanger A, Murphy JR, Heresi GP. Community-associated methicillin-resistant *Staphylococcus aureus* in pediatric patients. *Emerg Infect Dis*, 2005, 11(6):966-968. doi:10.3201/eid1106.050142.

130. Nickerson EK, Wuthiekanun V, Day NP, Chaowagul W, Peacock SJ. Meticillin-resistant *Staphylococcus aureus* in rural Asia. *Lancet Infect Dis*, 2006, 6(2):70-71. (http://www.ncbi.nlm.nih.gov/pubmed/16439325, accessed 9 April 2014).

131. Nickerson EK, Hongsuwan M, Limmathurotsakul D, Wuthiekanun V, Shah KR, Srisomang P et al. *Staphylococcus aureus* bacteraemia in a tropical setting: patient outcome and impact of antibiotic resistance. *PLoS ONE [Electronic Resource]*, 2009, 4(1):e4308. doi:10.1371/journal.pone.0004308.

132. Naves KS, Vaz da Trindade N, Gontijo Filho PP. Methicillin-resistant *Staphylococcus aureus* bloodstream infection: risk factors and clinical outcome in non-intensive-care units. *Rev Soc Bras Med Trop*, 2012, 45(2):189-193.

133. Morikawa K, Okada F, Ando Y, Ishii R, Matsushita S, Ono A et al. Meticillin-resistant *Staphylococcus aureus* and meticillin-susceptible *S. aureus* pneumonia: comparison of clinical and thin-section CT findings. *Br J Radiol*, 85(1014):e168-e175. doi:10.1259/bjr/65538472.

134. Mishaan AM, Mason EO, Jr., Martinez-Aguilar G, Hammerman W, Propst JJ, Lupski JR et al. Emergence of a predominant clone of community-acquired *Staphylococcus aureus* among children in Houston, Texas. *Pediatr Infect Dis J*, 2005, 24(3):201-206. (http://www.ncbi.nlm.nih.gov/pubmed/15750454, accessed 9 April 2014).

135. Miller LG, Quan C, Shay A, Mostafaie K, Bharadwa K, Tan N et al. A prospective investigation of outcomes after hospital discharge for endemic, community-acquired methicillin-resistant and -susceptible *Staphylococcus aureus* skin infection. *Clin Infect Dis*, 2007, 44(4):483-492. (http://www.ncbi.nlm.nih.gov/pubmed/17243049, accessed 9 April 2014).

136. Melzer M, Eykyn SJ, Gransden WR, Chinn S. Is methicillin-resistant *Staphylococcus aureus* more virulent than methicillin-susceptible *S. aureus*? A comparative cohort study of British patients with nosocomial infection and bacteremia. *Clin Infect Dis*, 2003, 37(11):1453-1460. (http://www.ncbi.nlm.nih.gov/pubmed/14614667, accessed 9 April 2014).

137. Mekontso-Dessap A, Kirsch M, Brun-Buisson C, Loisance D. Poststernotomy mediastinitis due to *Staphylococcus aureus*: Comparison of methicillin-resistant and methicillin-susceptible cases. *Clin Infect Dis*, 2001, 32(6):877-883. doi:10.1086/319355.

138. McHugh CG, Riley LW. Risk factors and costs associated with methicillin-resistant *Staphylococcus aureus* bloodstream infections. *Infect Control Hosp Epidemiol*, 2004, 25(5):425-430. (http://www.ncbi.nlm.nih.gov/pubmed/15188850, accessed 9 April 2014).

139. Marty L, Flahault A, Suarez B, Caillon J, Hill C, Andremont A. Resistance to methicillin and virulence of *Staphylococcus aureus* strains in bacteriemic cancer patients. *Intensive Care Medicine*, 1993, 19(5):285-289. (http://www.ncbi.nlm.nih.gov/pubmed/0008408938, accessed 9 April 2014).

140. Martinez-Aguilar G, Hammerman WA, Mason, Jr., Kaplan SL. Clindamycin treatment of invasive infections caused by community-acquired, methicillin-resistant and methicillin-susceptible *Staphylococcus aureus* in children. *Pediatr Infect Dis J*, 2003, 22(7):593-598. (http://dx.doi.org/10.1097/00006454-200307000-00006, accessed 29 January 2014).

141. Martinez-Aguilar G, Avalos-Mishaan A, Hulten K, Hammerman W, Mason EO, Jr., Kaplan SL. Community-acquired, methicillin-resistant and methicillin-susceptible *Staphylococcus aureus* musculoskeletal infections in children. *Pediatr Infect Dis J*, 2004, 23(8):701-706. (http://www.ncbi.nlm.nih.gov/pubmed/15295218, accessed 9 April 2014).

142. Manzur A, Vidal M, Pujol M, Cisnal M, Hornero A, Masuet C et al. Predictive factors of meticillin resistance among patients with *Staphylococcus aureus* bloodstream infections at hospital admission. *J Hosp Infect*, 2007, 66(2):135-141. (http://www.ncbi.nlm.nih.gov/pubmed/17513007, accessed 9 April 2014).

143. Lodise TP, McKinnon PS. Clinical and economic impact of methicillin resistance in patients with *Staphylococcus aureus* bacteremia. *Diagn Microbiol Infect Dis*, 2005, 52(2):113-122. (http://www.ncbi.nlm.nih.gov/pubmed/15964499, accessed 9 April 2014).

144. Lewis E, Saravolatz LD. Comparison of methicillin-resistant and methicillin-sensitive *Staphylococcus aureus* bacteremia. *Am J Infect Control*, 1985, 13(3):109-114.

145. Lesse AJ, Mylotte JM. Clinical and molecular epidemiology of nursing home-associated *Staphylococcus aureus* bacteremia. *Am J Infect Control*, 2006, 34(10):642-650. (http://www.ncbi.nlm.nih.gov/pubmed/17161739, accessed 9 April 2014).

146. Lesens O, Methlin CH, Y., Remy V, Martinot M, Bergin C, Meyer P et al. Role of comorbidity in mortality related to *Staphylococcus aureus* bacteremia: a prospective study using the Charlson weighted index of comorbidity. *Infect Control Hosp Epidemiol.*, 2003, Dec; 24(12):890-6. (http://www.ncbi.nlm.nih.gov/pubmed/14700403, accessed 9 April 2014).

147. Lepelletier D, Ferreol S, Villers D, Richet H. [Methicillin-resistant *Staphylococcus aureus* nosocomial infections in ICU: risk factors, morbidity and cost]. [French]. *Pathol Biol*, 2004, 52(8):474-479. (http://www.ncbi.nlm.nih.gov/pubmed/15465267, accessed 9 April 2014)

148. Lawes T, Edwards B, Lopez-Lozano JM, Gould I. Trends in *Staphylococcus aureus* bacteraemia and impacts of infection control practices including universal MRSA admission screening in a hospital in Scotland, 2006-2010: retrospective cohort study and time-series intervention analysis. *BMJ Open*, 2012, 2(3):2012. doi:10.1136/bmjopen-2011-000797.

149. Kuo CB, Lin JC, Peng MY, Wang NC, Chang FY. Endocarditis: impact of methicillin-resistant *Staphylococcus aureus* in hemodialysis patients and community-acquired infection. *J Microbiol, Immunol Infect*, 2007, 40(4):317-324. (http://www.ncbi.nlm.nih.gov/pubmed/17712466, accessed 9 April 2014).

150. Kuint J, Barzilai A, Regev-Yochay G, Rubinstein E, Keller N, Maayan-Metzger A. Comparison of community-acquired methicillin-resistant *Staphylococcus aureus* bacteremia to other staphylococcal species in a neonatal intensive care unit. *Eur J Pediatr*, 2007, 166(4):319-325. (http://www.ncbi.nlm.nih.gov/pubmed/17051356, accessed 9 April 2014).

151. Kopp BJ, Nix DE, Armstrong EP. Clinical and economic analysis of methicillin-susceptible and -resistant *Staphylococcus aureus* infections. *Ann Pharmacother*, 2004, 38(9):1377-1382.

152. Kini AR, Shetty V, Kumar AM, Shetty SM, Shetty A. Community-associated, methicillin-susceptible, and methicillin-resistant *Staphylococcus aureus* bone and joint infections in children: experience from India. *J Pediatr Orthop, Part B*, 2013, 22(2):158-166. doi:10.1097/BPB.0b013e32835c530a.

153. Kim SH, Park WB, Lee KD, Kang CI, Kim HB, Oh MD et al. Outcome of *Staphylococcus aureus* bacteremia in patients with eradicable foci versus noneradicable foci. *Clin Infect Dis*, 2003, 37(6):794-799. (http://www.ncbi.nlm.nih.gov/pubmed/12955640, accessed 9 April 2014).

154. Khatib R, Johnson LB, Fakih MG, Riederer K, Khosrovaneh A, Shamse TM et al. Persistence in *Staphylococcus aureus* bacteremia: incidence, characteristics of patients and outcome. *Scand J Infect Dis*, 2006, 38(1):7-14. (http://www.ncbi.nlm.nih.gov/pubmed/16338832, accessed 9 April 2014).

155. Kang CI, Song JH, Chung DR, Peck KR, Ko KS, Yeom JS et al. Clinical impact of methicillin resistance on outcome of patients with *Staphylococcus aureus* infection: a stratified analysis according to underlying diseases and sites of infection in a large prospective cohort. *J Infect*, 2010, 61(4):299-306. doi:10.1016/j.jinf.2010.07.011.

156. Kalwaje EV, Munim F, Tellapragada C, Varma M, Edward LL, Mukhopadhyay C. Upsurge of MRSA bacteraemia in south Indian tertiary care hospital: An observational study on clinical epidemiology and resistance profile. *Int J Infect Dis*, 2012, Conference(var.pagings):e224. (http://dx.doi.org/10.1016/j.ijid.2012.05.827, accessed 29 January 2014).

157. Joo EJ, Chung DR, Ha YE, Park SY, Kim HA, Lim MH et al. Clinical predictors of community-genotype ST72-methicillin-resistant *Staphylococcus aureus*-SCCmec type IV in patients with community-onset *S. aureus* infection. *J Antimicrob Chemother*, 2012, 67(7):1755-1759. doi:10.1093/jac/dks120.

158. Jimenez JN, Ocampo AM, Vanegas JM, Rodriguez EA, Mediavilla JR, Chen L et al. A comparison of methicillin-resistant and methicillin-susceptible *Staphylococcus aureus* reveals no clinical and epidemiological but molecular differences. *Int J Med Microb*, 2013, 303(2):76-83. doi:10.1016/j.ijmm.2012.12.003.

159. Isaacs D, Fraser S, Hogg G, Li HY. *Staphylococcus aureus* infections in Australasian neonatal nurseries. *Arch Dis Child Fetal Neonatal Ed*, 2004, 89(4):F331-F335. (http://www.ncbi.nlm.nih.gov/pubmed/15210669, accessed 9 April 2014).

160. Hulten KG, Kaplan SL, Lamberth LB, Slimp K, Hammerman WA, Carrillo-Marquez M et al. Hospital-acquired *Staphylococcus aureus* infections at Texas Children's Hospital, 2001-2007. *Infect Control Hosp Epidemiol*, 2010, 31(2):183-190. doi:10.1086/649793.

161. Huang H, Cohen SH, King JH, Monchaud C, Nguyen H, Flynn NM. Injecting drug use and community-associated methicillin-resistant *Staphylococcus aureus* infection. *Diagn Microbiol Infect Dis*, 2008, 60(4):347-350. doi:10.1016/j.diagmicrobio.2007.11.001.

162. Hsu RB, Lin FY. Methicillin resistance and risk factors for embolism in *Staphylococcus aureus* infective endocarditis. *Infect Control Hosp Epidemiol*, 2007, 28(7):860-866. (http://www.ncbi.nlm.nih.gov/pubmed/17564990, accessed 9 April 2014).

163. Hsu RB, Chu SH. Impact of methicillin resistance on clinical features and outcomes of infective endocarditis due to *Staphylococcus aureus*. *Am J Med Sci*, 2004, 328(3):150-155.

164. Ho K, Robinson O, J. Risk factors and outcomes of methicillin-resistant *Staphylococcus aureus* bacteraemia in critically ill patients: a case control study. *Anaesth Intens Care*, 2009, 37(3):457-63. (http://www.ncbi.nlm.nih.gov/pubmed/19499868, accessed 9 April 2014).

165. Hill EE, Peetermans WE, Vanderschueren S, Claus P, Herregods MC, Herijgers P. Methicillin-resistant versus methicillin-sensitive *Staphylococcus aureus* infective endocarditis. *Eur J Clin Microbiol Infect Dis*, 2008, 27(6):445-450. (http://dx.doi.org/10.1007/s10096-007-0458-2, accessed 29 January 2014).

166. Hershow RC, Khayr WF, Smith NL. A comparison of clinical virulence of nosocomially acquired methicillin-resistant and methicillin-sensitive *Staphylococcus aureus* infections in a university hospital. [Review] [25 refs]. *Infect Control Hosp Epidemiol*, 1992, 13(10):587-593.

167. Heo ST, Peck KR, Ryu SY, Kwon KT, Ko KS, Oh WS et al. Analysis of methicillin resistance among *Staphylococcus aureus* blood isolates in an emergency department. *J Korean Med Sci*, 2007, 22(4):682-686. (http://www.ncbi.nlm.nih.gov/pubmed/17728510, accessed 9 April 2014).

168. Hawkshead JJ, III, Patel NB, Steele RW, Heinrich SD. Comparative severity of pediatric osteomyelitis attributable to methicillin-resistant versus methicillin-sensitive *Staphylococcus aureus*. *J Pediatr Orthop*, 2009, 29(1):85-90. doi:10.1097/BPO.0b013e3181901c3a.

169. Hawkins C, Huang J, Jin N, Noskin GA, Zembower TR, Bolon M. Persistent *Staphylococcus aureus* bacteremia: an analysis of risk factors and outcomes. *Arch Intern Med*, 2007, 167(17):1861-1867. (http://www.ncbi.nlm.nih.gov/pubmed/17893307, accessed 9 April 2014).

170. Harbarth S, Rutschmann O, Sudre P, Pittet D. Impact of methicillin resistance on the outcome of patients with bacteremia caused by *Staphylococcus aureus*. *Arch Intern Med*, 1998, 158(2):182-189. (http://www.ncbi.nlm.nih.gov/pubmed/9448557, accessed 9 April 2014).

171. Hanberger H, Walther S, Leone M, Barie PS, Rello J, Lipman J et al. Increased mortality associated with methicillin-resistant *Staphylococcus aureus* (MRSA) infection in the intensive care unit: results from the EPIC II study. *Int J Antimicrob Agents*, 2011, 38(4):331-5. doi:10.1016/j.ijantimicag.2011.05.013.

172. Han JH, Bilker WB, Edelstein PH, Mascitti KB, Lautenbach E. Derivation and validation of clinical prediction rules for reduced vancomycin susceptibility in *Staphylococcus aureus* bacteraemia. *Epidemiol Infect*, 2012, 141(1):165-173. doi:10.1017/S0950268812000295.

173. Hakim H, Mylotte JM, Faden H. Morbidity and mortality of Staphylococcal bacteremia in children. *Am J Infect Control*, 2007, 35(2):102-105. (http://www.ncbi.nlm.nih.gov/pubmed/17327189, accessed 9 April 2014).

174. Haessler S, Mackenzie T, Kirkland KB. Long-term outcomes following infection with meticillin-resistant or meticillin-susceptible *Staphylococcus aureus*. *J Hosp Infect*, 2008, 69(1):39-45. doi:10.1016/j.jhin.2008.01.008.

175. Guilarde AO, Turchi MD, Martelli CM, Primo MG. *Staphylococcus aureus* bacteraemia: incidence, risk factors and predictors for death in a Brazilian teaching hospital. *J Hosp Infect*, 2006, 63(3):330-336. (http://www.ncbi.nlm.nih.gov/pubmed/16713018, accessed 9 April 2014).

176. Greiner W, Rasch A, Kohler D, Salzberger B, Fatkenheuer G, Leidig M. Clinical outcome and costs of nosocomial and community-acquired *Staphylococcus aureus* bloodstream infection in haemodialysis patients. *Clin Microbiol Infect*, 2007, 13(3):264-268. (http://www.ncbi.nlm.nih.gov/pubmed/17391380, accessed 9 April 2014).

177. Graffunder EM, Venezia RA. Risk factors associated with nosocomial methicillin-resistant *Staphylococcus aureus* (MRSA) infection including previous use of antimicrobials. *J Antimicrob Chemother*, 2002, 49(6):999-1005. (http://www.ncbi.nlm.nih.gov/pubmed/12039892, accessed 9 April 2014).

178. Gonzalez C, Rubio M, Romero-Vivas J, Gonzalez M, Picazo JJ. Bacteremic pneumonia due to *Staphylococcus aureus*: A comparison of disease caused by methicillin-resistant and methicillin-susceptible organisms. *Clin Infect Dis*, 1999, 29(5):1171-1177. (http://www.ncbi.nlm.nih.gov/pubmed/10524959, accessed 9 April 2014).

179. Gerber JS, Coffin SE, Smathers SA, Zaoutis TE. Trends in the incidence of methicillin-resistant *Staphylococcus aureus* infection in children's hospitals in the United States. *Clin Infect Dis*, 2009, 49(1):65-71. doi:10.1086/599348.

180. Ganga R, Riederer K, Sharma M, Fakih MG, Johnson LB, Shemes S et al. Role of SCCmec type in outcome of *Staphylococcus aureus* bacteremia in a single medical center. *J Clin Microbiol*, 2009, 47(3):590-595.

181. French GL, Cheng AF, Ling JM, Mo P, Donnan S. Hong Kong strains of methicillin-resistant and methicillin-sensitive *Staphylococcus aureus* have similar virulence. *J Hosp Infect*, 1990, 15(2):117-125. (http://www.ncbi.nlm.nih.gov/pubmed/1969433, accessed 9 April 2014).

182. Fortunov RM, Hulten KG, Hammerman WA, Mason EO, Jr., Kaplan SL. Community-acquired *Staphylococcus aureus* infections in term and near-term previously healthy neonates. *Pediatrics*, 2006, 118(3):874-881 doi:10.1542/peds.2006-0884.

183. Filice GA, Nyman JA, Lexau C, Lees CH, Bockstedt LA, Como-Sabetti K et al. Excess costs and utilization associated with methicillin resistance for patients with *Staphylococcus aureus* infection. *Infect Control Hosp Epidemiol*, 2010, 31(4):365-373. doi:10.1086/651094.

184. Ernst EJ, Raley G, Herwaldt LA, Diekema DJ. Importance of control group selection for evaluating antimicrobial use as a risk factor for methicillin-resistant *Staphylococcus aureus* bacteremia. *Infect Control Hosp Epidemiol*, 2005, 26(7):634-637. (http://www.ncbi.nlm.nih.gov/pubmed/16092744, accessed 9 April 2014).

185. Erdem G, Salazar R, Kimata C, Simasathien T, Len KA, Bergert L et al. *Staphylococcus aureus* osteomyelitis in Hawaii. *Clin Pediatr*, 2010, 49(5):477-484. doi:10.1177/0009922809352805.

186. Erdem G, Bergert L, Len K, Melish M, Kon K, DiMauro R. Radiological findings of community-acquired methicillin-resistant and methicillin-susceptible *Staphylococcus aureus* pediatric pneumonia in Hawaii. *Pediatr Radiol*, 2010, 40(11):1768-1773. (http://dx.doi.org/10.1007/s00247-010-1680-0, accessed 29 January 2014).

187. Engemann JJ, Carmeli Y, Cosgrove SE, Fowler VG, Bronstein MZ, Trivette SL et al. Adverse clinical and economic outcomes attributable to methicillin resistance among patients with *Staphylococcus aureus* surgical site infection. *Clin Infect Dis*, 2003, 36(5):592-598. (http://www.ncbi.nlm.nih.gov/pubmed/12594640, accessed 9 April 2014).

188. de Oliveira CL, Wey SB, Castelo A. *Staphylococcus aureus* bacteremia: comparison of two periods and a predictive model of mortality. *Braz J Infect Dis*, 2002, 6(6):288-297. (http://www.ncbi.nlm.nih.gov/pubmed/12585972, accessed 9 April 2014).

189. de Kraker ME, Wolkewitz M, Davey PG, Koller W, Berger J, Nagler J et al. Burden of antimicrobial resistance in European hospitals: excess mortality and length of hospital stay associated with bloodstream infections due to *Escherichia coli* resistant to third-generation cephalosporins. *J Antimicrob Chemother*, 2011, 66(2):398-407. doi:10.1093/jac/dkq412.

190. Davis SL, Perri MB, Donabedian SM, Manierski C, Singh A, Vager D et al. Epidemiology and outcomes of community-associated methicillin-resistant *Staphylococcus aureus* infection. *J Clin Microbiol*, 2007, 45(6):1705-1711. (http://www.ncbi.nlm.nih.gov/pubmed/17392441, accessed 9 April 2014).

191. Das I, O'Connell N, Lambert P. Epidemiology, clinical and laboratory characteristics of *Staphylococcus aureus* bacteraemia in a university hospital in United Kingdom.[Erratum appears in J Hosp Infect. 2007 Jun; 66(2):199]. *J Hosp Infect*, 2007, 65(2):117-123. (http://www.ncbi.nlm.nih.gov/pubmed/17145105, accessed 9 April 2014).

192. Cunney RJ, McNamara EB, alAnsari N, Smyth EG. Community and hospital acquired *Staphylococcus aureus* septicaemia: 115 cases from a Dublin teaching hospital. *J Infect*, 1996, 33(1):11-13. (http://www.ncbi.nlm.nih.gov/pubmed/8842988, accessed 9 April 2014).

193. Cowie SE, Ma I, Lee SK, Smith RM, Hsiang YN. Nosocomial MRSA infection in vascular surgery patients: impact on patient outcome. *Vasc Endovasc Surg*, 2005, 39(4):327-334. (http://www.ncbi.nlm.nih.gov/pubmed/16079941, accessed 9 April 2014).

194. Cosgrove SE, Qi Y, Kaye KS, Harbarth S, Karchmer AW, Carmeli Y. The impact of methicillin resistance in *Staphylococcus aureus* bacteremia on patient outcomes: mortality, length of stay, and hospital charges. *Infect Control Hosp Epidemiol*, 2005, 26(2):166-174. (http://www.ncbi.nlm.nih.gov/pubmed/15756888, accessed 9 April 2014).

195. Conterno LO, Wey SB, Castelo A. Risk factors for mortality in *Staphylococcus aureus* bacteremia. *Infect Control Hosp Epidemiol*, 1998, 19(1):32-37. (http://www.ncbi.nlm.nih.gov/pubmed/9475347, accessed 9 April 2014).

196. Combes A, Trouillet JL, Joly-Guillou ML, Chastre J, Gibert C. The impact of methicillin resistance on the outcome of poststernotomy mediastinitis due to *Staphylococcus aureus*. *Clin Infect Dis*, 2004, 38(6):822-829. (http://www.ncbi.nlm.nih.gov/pubmed/14999626, accessed 9 April 2014).

197. Combes A, Luyt CE, Fagon JY, Wollf M, Trouillet JL, Gibert C et al. Impact of methicillin resistance on outcome of *Staphylococcus aureus* ventilator-associated pneumonia. *Am J Respir Crit Care Med*, 2004, 170(7):786-792. (http://www.ncbi.nlm.nih.gov/pubmed/15242840, accessed 9 April 2014).

198. Clancy MJ, Graepler A, Breese PE, Price CS, Burman WJ. Widespread emergence of methicillin resistance in community-acquired *Staphylococcus aureus* infections in Denver. *South Med J*, 2005, 98(11):1069-1075. (http://www.ncbi.nlm.nih.gov/pubmed/16351027, accessed 9 April 2014).

199. Chen SY, Wang JT, Chen THH, Lai MS, Chie WC, Chien KL et al. Impact of traditional hospital strain of methicillin-resistant *Staphylococcus aureus* (MRSA) and community strain of MRSA on mortality in patients with community-onset S aureus bacteremia. *Medicine*, 2010, 89(5):285-294. (http://dx.doi.org/10.1097/MD.0b013e3181f1851e, accessed 29 January 2014).

200. Changchien CH, Chen YY, Chen SW, Chen WL, Tsay JG, Chu C. Retrospective study of necrotizing fasciitis and characterization of its associated methicillin-resistant *Staphylococcus aureus* in Taiwan. *BMC Infect Dis*, 2011, 11:297. doi:10.1186/1471-2334-11-297.

201. Chang FY, MacDonald BB, Peacock JE Jr., Musher DM, Triplett P, Mylotte JM et al. A prospective multicenter study of *Staphylococcus aureus* bacteremia: incidence of endocarditis, risk factors for mortality, and clinical impact of methicillin resistance. *Medicine*, 2003, 82(5):322-332. (http://www.ncbi.nlm.nih.gov/pubmed/14530781, accessed 9 April 2014).

202. Chan KE, Warren HS, Thadhani RI, Steele DJ, Hymes JL, Maddux FW et al. Prevalence and outcomes of antimicrobial treatment for *Staphylococcus aureus* bacteremia in outpatients with ESRD. *J Am Soc Nephrol*, 2012, 23(9):1551-1559. doi:10.1681/ASN.2012010050.

203. Castillo JS, Leal AL, Cortes JA, Alvarez CA, Sanchez R, Buitrago G et al. Mortality among critically ill patients with methicillin-resistant *Staphylococcus aureus* bacteremia: a multicenter cohort study in Colombia. *Rev Panam Salud Publica*, 2012, 32(5):343-350. (http://www.ncbi.nlm.nih.gov/pubmed/23338691, accessed 9 April 2014).

204. Carrillo-Marquez MA, Hulten KG, Mason EO, Kaplan SL. Clinical and molecular epidemiology of *Staphylococcus aureus* catheter-related bacteremia in children. *Pediatr Infect Dis J*, 2010, 29(5):410-414. doi:10.1097/INF.0b013e3181c767b6.

205. Carey AJ, Long SS. *Staphylococcus aureus*: a continuously evolving and formidable pathogen in the neonatal intensive care unit. 2010. (http://tinyurl.com/mea2vhc, accessed 29 January 2014).

206. Capitano B, Leshem OA, Nightingale CH, Nicolau DP. Cost effect of managing methicillin-resistant *Staphylococcus aureus* in a long-term care facility. *J Am Geriatr Soc*, 2003, 51(1):10-16. (http://www.ncbi.nlm.nih.gov/pubmed/12534839, accessed 9 April 2014).

207. Burke RE, Halpern MS, Baron EJ, Gutierrez K. Pediatric and neonatal *Staphylococcus aureus* bacteremia: epidemiology, risk factors, and outcome. *Infect Control Hosp Epidemiol*, 2009, 30(7):636-644. doi:10.1086/597521.

208. Blot SI, Vandewoude KH, Hoste EA, Colardyn FA. Outcome and attributable mortality in critically Ill patients with bacteremia involving methicillin-susceptible and methicillin-resistant *Staphylococcus aureus*. *Arch Intern Med*, 2002, 162(19):2229-2235. (http://www.ncbi.nlm.nih.gov/pubmed/12390067, accessed 9 April 2014).

209. Ben-David D, Novikov I, Mermel LA. Are there differences in hospital cost between patients with nosocomial methicillin-resistant *Staphylococcus aureus* bloodstream infection and those with methicillin-susceptible *S. aureus* bloodstream infection? *Infect Control Hosp Epidemiol*, 2009, 30(5):453-460. doi:10.1086/596731.

210. Bastug A, Yilmaz GR, Kayaaslan B, Akinci E, Bodur H. Risk factors for mortality in patients with nosocomial *Staphylococcus aureus* bacteremia. *Turkish J Med Sci*, 2012, 42(SUPPL.1):1222-1229. doi:10.1111/j.1469-0691.2011.03679.x.

211. Bassetti M, Trecarichi EM, Mesini A, Spanu T, Giacobbe DR, Rossi M et al. Risk factors and mortality of healthcare-associated and community-acquired *Staphylococcus aureus* bacteraemia. *Clin Microbiol Infect*, 2012, 18(9):862-869.

212. Baraboutis IG, Tsagalou EP, Papakonstantinou I, Marangos MN, Gogos C, Skoutelis AT et al. Length of exposure to the hospital environment is more important than antibiotic exposure in healthcare associated infections by methicillin-resistant *Staphylococcus aureus*: a comparative study. *Braz J Infect Dis*, 2011, 15(5):426-435. (http://www.ncbi.nlm.nih.gov/pubmed/22230848, accessed 9 April 2014).

213. Baggett HC, Hennessy TW, Leman R, Hamlin C, Bruden D, Reasonover A et al. An outbreak of community-onset methicillin-resistant *Staphylococcus aureus* skin infections in southwestern Alaska. *Infect Control Hosp Epidemiol*, 2003, 24(6):397-402. (http://www.ncbi.nlm.nih.gov/pubmed/12828314, accessed 9 April 2014).

214. Bader MS. *Staphylococcus aureus* bacteremia in older adults: predictors of 7-day mortality and infection with a methicillin-resistant strain. *Infect Control Hosp Epidemiol*, 2006, 27(11):1219-1225. (http://www.ncbi.nlm.nih.gov/pubmed/17080380, accessed 9 April 2014).

215. Austin TW, Austin MA, Coleman B. Methicillin-resistant/methicillin-sensitive *Staphylococcus aureus* bacteremia. *Saudi Med J*, 2003, 24(3):256-260. (http://www.ncbi.nlm.nih.gov/pubmed/12704499, accessed 9 April 2014).

216. Arnold SR, Elias D, Buckingham SC, Thomas ED, Novais E, Arkader A et al. Changing patterns of acute hematogenous osteomyelitis and septic arthritis: emergence of community-associated methicillin-resistant *Staphylococcus aureus*. *J Pediatr Orthop*, 2006, 26(6):703-708. (http://www.ncbi.nlm.nih.gov/pubmed/17065930, accessed 9 April 2014).

217. Anderson DJ, Kaye KS, Chen LF, Schmader KE, Choi Y, Sloane R et al. Clinical and financial outcomes due to methicillin resistant *Staphylococcus aureus* surgical site infection: a multi-center matched outcomes study. *PLoS ONE [Electronic Resource]*, 2009, 4(12):e8305 doi:10.1371/journal.pone.0008305.

218. Al-Otaibi F, Bukhari E. Community-acquired methicillin-resistant *Staphylococcus aureus* in outpatient children assisted at a university hospital in Saudi Arabia: a 3-year study (2005-2008). *J Pediatr Infect Dis*, 2010, 5(4):369-376. (http://iospress.metapress.com/content/d853041635808721/, accessed 9 April 2014).

219. Al-Nammari SS, Bobak P, Venkatesh R. Methicillin resistant *Staphylococcus aureus* versus methicillin sensitive *Staphylococcus aureus* adult haematogenous septic arthritis. *Arch Orthop Trauma Surg*, 2007, 127(7):537-542. (http://www.ncbi.nlm.nih.gov/pubmed/17260151, accessed 9 April 2014).

220. Allard C, Carignan A, Bergevin M, Boulais I, Tremblay V, Robichaud P et al. Secular changes in incidence and mortality associated with *Staphylococcus aureus* bacteraemia in Quebec, Canada, 1991-2005. *Clin Microbiol Infect*, 2008, 14(5):421-428. doi:10.1111/j.1469-0691.2008.01965.x.

221. Abramson MA, Sexton DJ. Nosocomial methicillin-resistant and methicillin-susceptible *Staphylococcus aureus* primary bacteremia: at what costs? *Infect Control Hosp Epidemiol*, 1999, 20(6):408-411. (http://www.ncbi.nlm.nih.gov/pubmed/10395142, accessed 9 April 2014).

APPENDICES

Appendix 1
Questionnaires used for data collection

Ap1.1 Questionnaire and data template for national antimicrobial resistance (AMR) surveillance

	Surveillance data				Type of source for data (tick for each resistance) (to understand if there is one common national report on AMR or several sources for information for the different bacteria)					Contact information
1/ Resistance rates	Year	Resistance rate (%)	Figure based on following number of tested isolates (if given)	Comprehen-sive (all isolates), or targeted, (e.g. only invasive isolates) surveillance?	AMR report to govern-ment?	AMR report/ compilation at national body institute, reference lab or similar.	Report of mandatory surveillance, Communi-cable diseases act or similar.	Other national/ regional report on AMR situation	No, there is no national compila-tion on AMR of this resistance, please tick and continue under 2 below	Please provide name of body/institute and name + e-mail to focal point/contact person(s) for the information
E. coli (3rd gen. cephalosporins)										
E. coli (fluoroquinolones)										
K. pneumoniae (3rd gen. cephalosporins)										
K. pneumoniae (carbapenems)										
Salmonella spp (fluoroquinolones)										
Shigella spp (fluoroquinolones)										
N. gonorrhoeae (decreased susceptibility to 3rd gen. cephalosporins)										
S. pneumoniae (penicillin resistance, oxacillin)										
S. aureus (methicillin, MRSA)										
2/ Additional info on surveillance of antibacterial resistance in your country	Provide name/adress/web-page/email of body/institute and focal point/contact person(s) in other surveillance network(s) or other centers engaged in ABR surveillance in your country									

Appendix 1

Ap1.2 Questionnaire and data template for antimicrobial resistance (AMR) surveillance networks

1/	General information on network/ institution		
	Name of network/ institution		
	Name and e-mail to contact person		
	Address to web-page (if any)		
	Geographical coverage (i.e. in which country, or if several countries, which participating countries)?		
	Number of sites participating? If in several countries, please specify per country		
	Is the resistance rate figure based on inclusion of all clinical isolates (comprehensive, write C) or limited to only a subset of isolates, write S, and in case of «S» also which types of isolates (e.g. blood, ICU etc). In any case (C or S), please state whether screening samples are included or not.		
	Are resistance results based on quantitative data (MIC, zone diameters) or on qualitative (i.e. SIR)?		
	Which breakpoint standards are used (CLSI, EUCAST, OTHER)		
	Does a majority of the laboratories, or the institution, generating data have an internal QA-strategy ?		
	Does a majority of the laboratories in the network, or the institution, participate in external QA?		
	Does a majority of laboratories, or the institution, enter data in a digital system in their own lab (Y/N)?		Is WHONET used for this purpose (y/n)
	Does the participants in the network, or the institution, transfer data to coordinator digitally (y/n)?		Does network coordinator manage data in WHONET (y/n)?

2/ Resistance rates

Bacteriae	Antibiotic class	Please enter compound you use for testing	Year data collected	% resistance	Number of tested isolates:
E. coli	3rd generation cephalosporins				
E. coli	quinolones, preferably fluoroquinolones				
K. pneumoniae	3rd generation cephalosporins				
K. pneumoniae	carbapenems				
P. aeruginosa	carbapenems				
Salmonella spp (non-typhi)	quinolones, preferably fluoroquinolones				
Shigella spp	quinolones, preferably fluoroquinolones				
S. aureus, (MRSA)	oxacillin/cefoxitin				
S. pneumoniae	non-susceptible to penicillin				
S. pneumoniae	co-trimoxazole				
N. gonorrhoeae	decreased susceptibility to 3rd gen. cephalosporins				

3/ Please provide in the cells below additional information on other surveillance network(s) or other centers engaged in ABR surveillance in your country

Name of focal point/ contact person		
Web-page of network or institution		
Additional information or comments		

Appendix 1

Appendix 2
WHO tools to facilitate surveillance of antibacterial resistance

The following are some of the key WHO tools, documents and recommendations addressing surveillance of antimicrobial resistance (AMR), in particular, antibacterial resistance (ABR). Other documents specifically address surveillance of resistance in the disease-specific programmes on tuberculosis (TB), malaria, HIV and influenza, and are cited in the respective sections of this report.

Ap2.1 WHONET

WHONET is freely available database software for the management and analysis of microbiology laboratory data with a special focus on the analysis of AST results. WHONET supports ABR surveillance, including data-sharing, but it is not a surveillance network.

Development and dissemination of the software is guided by two objectives:

- enhancing the use of data for local needs; and

- promoting local, national, regional and global collaborations through the exchange of data and sharing of experiences.

Continuing development of the software depends critically on the expressed needs and feedback of users around the world in a number of fields. Current features of WHONET include:

- data entry of clinical and microbiological information from routine diagnostic testing or from research studies;

- data capture from existing laboratory information systems and susceptibility test instruments into WHONET using the BacLink data import module of WHONET;

- modular configuration allowing for the customization of the software for local clinical, research and epidemiological needs;

- analysis of laboratory findings, including isolate line listings, AST statistics, studies of multidrug-resistance patterns, microbiological and epidemiological alert notifications, and hospital and community outbreak detection;

- integrated susceptibility test interpretation guidelines for most standardized testing methodologies;

- simple data file structure and output formats compatible with major database, spread sheet, statistical and word processing software; and

- software use in interactive mode for ad hoc analyses, or automated mode for regularly scheduled analyses and notifications.

The WHONET software can be downloaded from the WHO website.[a] WHONET runs on all modern versions of Microsoft Windows (Windows 98 and later); it can also be run on Linux and Macintosh computers using Windows emulators. Currently, most facilities use WHONET 5.6, a desktop version of the software that is suitable for use on individual computers or in local area networks (LANs). A new web-based version of WHONET (WHONET 2013) is currently being pilot tested. It permits remote secure data entry into centralized databases hosted by surveillance network coordinators. Access to data analysis features is configurable by database administrators, and can support both open data access without passwords (e.g. of aggregate statistics and charts) and restricted password-protected access (e.g. selective access to appropriate data subsets only by network participants).

The software is multilingual and currently available in Bulgarian, Chinese, English, Estonian, French, German, Greek, Indonesian, Italian, Japanese, Mongolian, Norwegian, Portuguese, Russian, Spanish, Thai and Turkish.

____

[a] http://www.who.int/medicines/areas/rational_use/AMR_WHONET_SOFTWARE/en/

Ap2.2 Guiding WHO documents for surveillance of AMR

General and comprehensive recommendations

http://www.who.int/drugresistance/WHO_Global_
Strategy.htm/en/

WHO Global Strategy for Containment of Antimicrobial Resistance (2001) (1)

The strategy provides a framework of interventions to slow the emergence and reduce the spread of antimicrobial-resistant microorganisms through:

- reducing the disease burden and the spread of infection;
- improving access to appropriate antimicrobials;
- improving use of antimicrobials;
- strengthening health systems and their surveillance capacities;
- enforcing regulations and legislation; and
- encouraging the development of appropriate new drugs and vaccines.

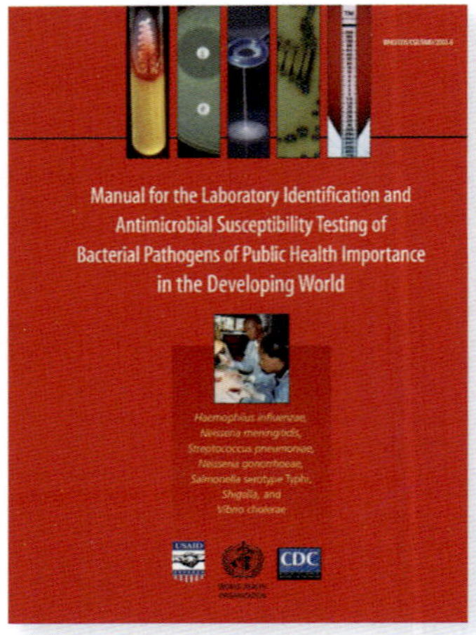

http://www.who.int/world-health-day/2011/
policybriefs/en/index.html

World Health Day 2011: policy briefs (2011) (2)

In the six-point policy package, WHO called on all key stakeholders to act and take responsibility in six main areas to combat antimicrobial resistance:

- develop and implement a comprehensive, financed national plan
- strengthen surveillance and laboratory capacity
- ensure uninterrupted access to essential medicines of assured quality
- regulate and promote rational use of medicines
- enhance infection prevention and control
- foster innovation and research and development for new tools.

Antimicrobial susceptibility testing

http://www.who.int/csr/resources/publications/
drugresist/en/IAMRmanual.pdf

Manual for the laboratory identification and antimicrobial susceptibility testing of bacterial pathogens of public health importance in the developing world (2003) (3)

This manual describes the tests needed to confirm the identification and antimicrobial susceptibility profile of seven bacterial pathogens of public health importance causing outbreaks of pneumonia, meningitis, enteric disease and gonorrhoea. A set of appendices provides more detail on such topics as media and reagents, primary isolation, packaging and shipping of infectious material, and preservation and storage of isolates. The manual is intended for use in a reference laboratory or national central laboratory that is adequately resourced and staffed.

Surveillance of antimicrobial resistance

http://whqlibdoc.who.int/hq/2002/WHO_CDS_CSR_DRS_2001.5.pdf

Surveillance standards for antimicrobial resistance (2002) (4)

The document is a brief manual covering the core microbiological and epidemiologal principles relevant for surveillance of antimicrobial resistance. Special attention is given to confounding factors that may undermine the validity of results from such programmes. A separate section contains protocols for integrated surveillance of communicable diseases and resistance.

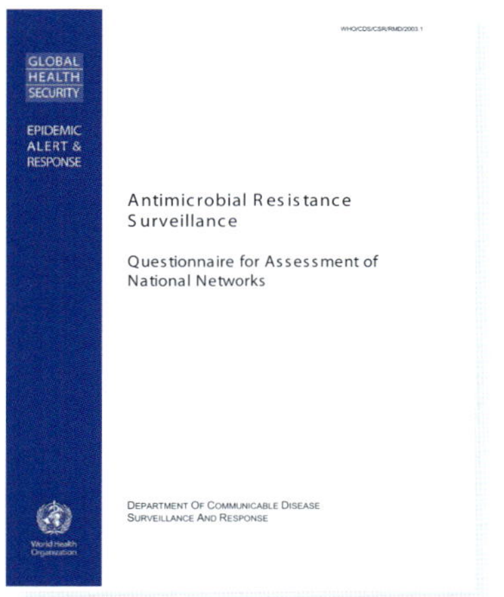

http://www.who.int/drugresistance/whocdscsrrmd20031.pdf

Antimicrobial resistance surveillance: Questionnaire for assessment of national networks (2003) (5).

The questionnaire is one component of a strategy for quality assessment. Component I aims to provide a means for laboratory networks currently active in antimicrobial resistance surveillance to assess the status of the individual laboratories in the network with respect to:

- basic laboratory capacity and infrastructure (Part 1);

- the ability to isolate and identify bacterial isolates (Part 2); and

- the performance of antimicrobial susceptibility testing (Part 3).

Component II is a tool for evaluating the network coordinating centre and the overall functioning of the surveillance network.

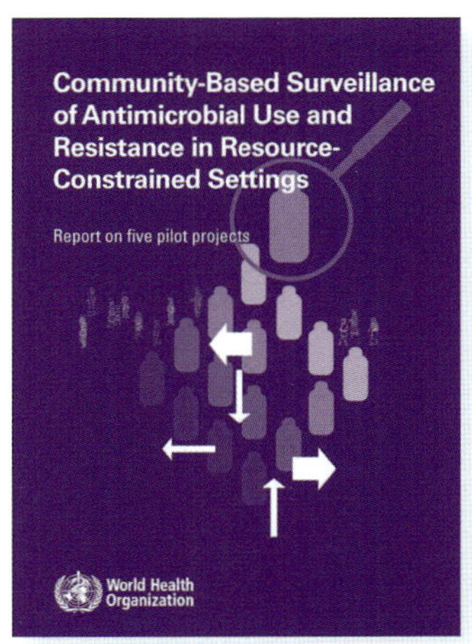

http://apps.who.int/medicinedocs/en/m/abstract/Js16168e/

Community-based surveillance of antimicrobial use and resistance in resource-constrained settings. Report on five pilot projects (2009) (6)

Integrated surveillance of antimicrobial resistance and use at all levels of health care is an essential component of any programme to contain antimicrobial resistance. There is currently no standard methodology for conducting community-based surveillance in resource-constrained settings. This document describes five pilot surveillance projects that were set up in India (three sites) and South Africa (two sites), with the aim of developing a model for undertaking integrated community-based surveillance in resource-constrained settings and generating baseline data.

Regional documents

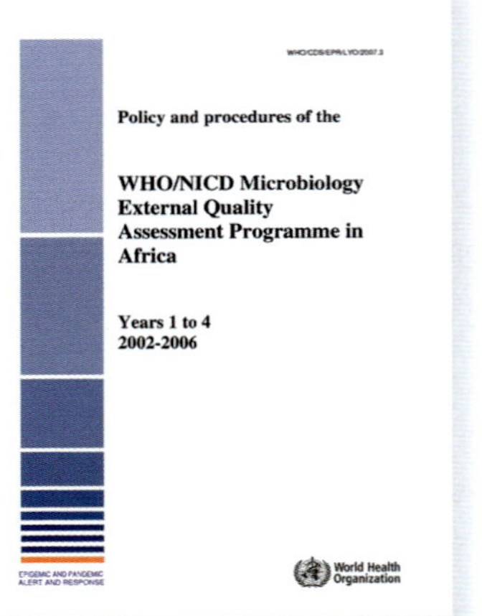

http://www.who.int/csr/ihr/lyon/Policy_procedures_eqa_en.pdf

Policy and procedures of the WHO/NICD Microbiology External Quality Assessment Programme in Africa (1.42M) (2007) *(7)*

The programme has served as a model for regional and national external quality assessment (EQA) within Africa and beyond. The purpose of the document is to:

- describe the WHO/National Institute for Communicable Diseases (NICD) microbiology EQA programme;

- describe current policies and procedures;

- provide samples of technical documents; and

- summarize previous surveys of laboratory capacity to detect certain infectious agents.

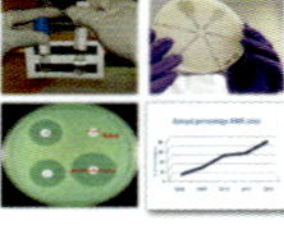

http://apps.who.int/medicinedocs/documents/s20135en/
s20135en.pdf

Guide for establishing laboratory-based surveillance for antimicrobial resistance (2013) *(8)*

The WHO Regional Office for Africa developed this guide to facilitate establishment of laboratory-based surveillance for priority bacterial diseases in the WHO African Region.

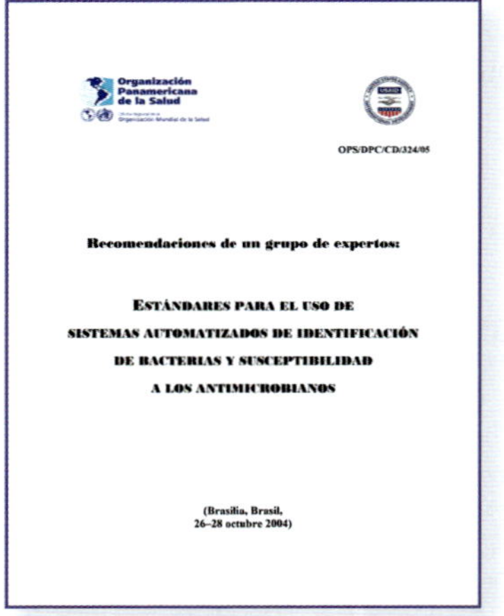

http://www1.paho.org/common/Display.asp?
Lang=E&RecID=10980

Recommendations of a group of experts: Standards for the use of automated identification systems for bacteria and susceptibility to antimicrobials. Brasilia, Brazil, 26–28 October 2004 (2005) *(9)*

Ap2.3 ICD 10 codes for antimicrobial resistance

The *International statistical classification of diseases and related health problems* 10th Revision (ICD-10) Version for 2010 (*10*) provides in chapter XXII *"Codes for special purposes"* (U00-U89). One of these sections addresses *"bacterial agents resistant to antibiotics"*. These were updated in 2009 and implemented in 2013 (*11*) as follows:

U82   Resistance to beta-lactam antibiotics Use additional code (B95-B98), if desired, to identify agents resistant to beta-lactam antibiotic treatment.

U82.0   Resistance to penicillin Resistance to amoxicillin, ampicillin

U82.1   Resistance to methicillin Resistance to cloxacillin flucloxacillin, oxacillin

U82.2   Extended spectrum beta-lactamase (ESBL) resistance

U82.8   Resistance to other beta-lactam antibiotics

U82.9   Resistance to beta-lactam antibiotics, unspecified

U83   Resistance to other antibiotics: Use additional code (B95-B98), if desired, to identify agents resistant to other antibiotic treatment.

U83.0   Resistance to vancomycin U83.1. Resistance to other vancomycin-related antibiotics

U83.2   Resistance to quinolones

U83.7   Resistance to multiple antibiotics

U83.8   Resistance to other single specified antibiotics

U83.9   Resistance to unspecified antibiotics. Resistance to antibiotics NOS

Note: These categories should never be used in primary coding. They are provided for use as supplementary or additional codes when it is desired to identify the antibiotic to which a bacterial agent is resistant, in bacterial infection classified elsewhere.

It is possible to make some tailored amendments for national purposes. For example, South Africa assigned the codes U51 and U52 to *multidrug-resistant tuberculosis* (MDR-TB) and *extensively drug-resistant tuberculosis* (XDR-TB) respectively, and added these to the *tuberculosis* (A15-A19) broad group of causes of death (*12*).

Ap2.4 References

1. *WHO Global Strategy for Containment of Antimicrobial Resistance*. Geneva, World Health Organization (WHO), 2001. (http://www.who.int/drugresistance/WHO_Global_Strategy.htm/en/, accessed 23 January 2014).

2. *World Health Day policy briefs*. Geneva, World Health Organization, 2011. (http://www.who.int/world-health-day/2011/policybriefs/en/index.html, accessed 27 December 2013).

3. *Manual for the laboratory identification and antimicrobial susceptibility testing of bacterial pathogens of public health importance in the developing world*. Geneva, Centers for Disease Control and Prevention and World Health Organization, 2003. (http://www.who.int/csr/resources/publications/drugresist/en/IAMRmanual.pdf, accessed 6 January 2014).

4. *Surveillance standards for antimicrobial resistance*. Geneva, World Health Organization, 2002. (http://whqlibdoc.who.int/hq/2002/WHO_CDS_CSR_DRS_2001.5.pdf, accessed 23 January 2014).

5. *Antimicrobial resistance surveillance: Questionnaire for assessment of national networks*. Geneva, World Health Organization, 2003. (http://www.who.int/drugresistance/whocdscsrrmd20031.pdf, accessed 10 December 2013).

6. *Community-based surveillance of antimicrobial use and resistance in resource-constrained settings. Report on five pilot projects*. Geneva, World Health Organization, 2009. (http://apps.who.int/medicinedocs/en/m/abstract/Js16168e/, accessed 23 January 2014).

7. *Policy and procedures of the WHO/NICD Microbiology External Quality Assessment Programme in Africa: Years 1 to 4 (2002–2006)*. WHO/CDS/EPR/LYO/2007.3, Geneva, World Health Organization, 2007. (http://www.who.int/csr/ihr/lyon/Policy_procedures_eqa_en.pdf, accessed 23 January 2014).

8. *Guide for establishing laboratory-based surveillance for antimicrobial resistance*. Disease surveillance and response programme area Disease Prevention and Control cluster, Brazzaville, Africa, World Health Organization ICD Regional Office for Africa, 2013. (http://apps.who.int/medicinedocs/documents/s20135en/s20135en.pdf, accessed 2 December 2013).

9.   *Recommendations of a group of experts: Standards for the use of automated identification systems for bacteria and susceptibility to antimicrobials (Brasilia, Brazil, 26–28 October 2004).* Pan American Health Organization, World Health Organization, 2005. (http://www1.paho.org/common/Display.asp?Lang=E&RecID=10980, accessed 23 January 2014).

10. *International statistical classification of diseases and related health problems 10th revision (ICD-10)* World Health Organization, 2010. (http://apps.who.int/classifications/icd10/browse/2010/en#/U80, accessed 31 July 2013).

11. *Cumulative official updates to the ICD-10.* World Health Organization, 2013. (http://www.who.int/classifications/icd/updates/Official_WHO_updates_combined_1996_2012_Volume_1.pdf, accessed 10 December 2013).

12. *Mortality and causes of death in South Africa, 2010: Findings from death notification.* Statistical release, Pretoria, South Africa, Statistics South Africa, 2013. (http://www.statssa.gov.za/publications/p03093/p030932010.pdf, accessed 10 December 2013).

Appendix 3
Additional international antibacterial resistance surveillance networks

Surveillance networks have been developed for different reasons, including professional initiatives, time-limited projects, and commercial or security purposes. Some of these networks have (or have had) activities in several WHO regions. Identified networks or initiatives collecting ABR data for non-commercial purposes in more than one country are listed below.

Ap3.1 Networks performing general surveillance of antibacterial resistance

AFHSC-GEIS[a] is the Global Emerging Infections Surveillance & Response System (GEIS) operated by the US Armed Forces Health Surveillance Center (AFHSC). It includes a programme for surveillance of antimicrobial resistant organisms from which some data on ABR have been published (*1*).

The Asian Network for Surveillance of Resistant Pathogens (ANSORP[b]) –– is an independent, non-profit nongovernmental international collaborative research group on AMR and infectious diseases in the Asian-Pacific region. ANSORP is based in the Republic of Korea, which is a member of the Asia Pacific Foundation for Infectious Diseases (APFID). ANSORP includes collaborators from 123 hospitals in 14 countries, territories and areas.[c] The ANSORP network has studied various bacteria and the etiology of infectious diseases syndromes during different time periods. Current areas of interest, involving multinational collaboration, include community-acquired methicillin-resistant *Staphylococcus aureus* (CA-MRSA), community-acquired pneumonia, hospital-acquired pneumonia, multidrug-resistant Gram-negative pathogens, and drug-resistant *Streptococcus pneumoniae* and disease burden of pneumococcal infections.

The Antibiotic Resistance Surveillance and Control in the Mediterranean Region (ARMed) was a 4-year project financed by the European Commission's Directorate General for Research during 2003–2007. Centres from Cyprus, Egypt, Jordan, Malta (coordinator), Morocco, Tunisia and Turkey participated and presented data on ABR in the region (*2*). The activity ceased when funding terminated.

The BSAC Resistance Surveillance Project[d] monitors antibacterial drug resistance in England, Wales, Scotland, Northern Ireland and the Republic of Ireland. Bacterial isolates are collected by a network of laboratories in these countries. Central laboratory services for the programme are provided by Public Health England.

The US CDC Global Disease Detection programe[e] has recently conducted AMR surveillance activities in 10 countries, as part of capacity-building related to surveillance, response and control of emerging infectious diseases, including AMR. Most activities are country-specific. In Egypt, a recent research project included university and a few public hospitals for surveillance of hospital-acquired infections and ABR. Systematic surveillance for antimicrobial resistance has been conducted on population-based surveillance platforms in Kenya, Guatemala and Thailand.

The WHO Gonococcal Antimicrobial Surveillance Programme (GASP) was established in 1992 in the Western Pacific Region, and since then a global laboratory network has been developed to coordinate gonococcal antimicrobial resistance surveillance, monitor longitudinal trends in antimicrobial resistance and provide data to inform treatment guidelines. In each WHO region there is a GASP coordinating laboratory that works in partnership with the corresponding WHO regional office. The regional coordinating laboratory provides technical support to countries to strengthen laboratory capacity, and an external quality assessment programme including maintenance and distribution of the WHO panels of *N. gonorrhoeae* reference strains for quality assurance (*3*).

Médecins Sans Frontières (MSF) is a medical nongovernmental organization working in more than 60 countries to assist people whose survival is threatened by violence, neglect or catastrophe. MSF collects data on bacterial resistance among

---

[a] http://www.afhsc.mil/geisAntiMicro (accessed 16 October 2013)
[b] http://www.ansorp.org/06_ansorp/ansorp_01.htm (accessed 16 October 2013)
[c] India, Indonesia, Japan, Malaysia, Philippines, Republic of Korea, Saudi Arabia, Singapore, Sri Lanka, Thailand, Viet Nam, in addition to China, Hong Kong SAR and Taiwan, China
[d] http://www.bsacsurv.org (accessed 16 October 2013)

[e] http://www.cdc.gov/globalhealth/gdder/gdd (accessed 16 October 2013)

some patient groups in some locations of activity, in area where most of this data are missing (e.g. rural, displaced population, war zone). To compile local data, MSF is developing and increasing its current network capacity focusing on orthopaedic hospitalized patients from the Middle East region, and malnourished children in sub-Saharan Africa. MSF findings in several countries around the world raise concerns about the high proportions of ABR in sampled patients in emergency settings.[a]

The Pasteur Institute has an international network of 32 institutes, which has a project "CHARLI" (*Children's Antibiotic Resistant infections in Low-Income countries: an international cohort study*) for which the main objective is to assess the incidence as well as the medical and economic consequences of severe childhood and neonatal infections caused by ABR bacteria.[b]

RusNet[c] is based in the Russian Federation and is coordinated by the Institute of Antimicrobial Chemotherapy (IAC) of the Smolensk State Medical Academy, Scientific Center on Monitoring Antimicrobial Resistance, and the Interregional Association for Clinical Microbiology and Antimicrobial Chemotherapy (IACMAC). RusNet collects the national data for the Russian Federation; it also has collaboration with a few centres in four other countries.[d] Presently the network has 21–42 participating sites (depending on study). Collected samples are classified according to diagnosis and whether they originate from community or hospital-acquired infections.

The commercially driven surveillance networks or projects that have previously delivered data on ABR in support of drug development and marketing – for example, SENTRY, MYSTIC and SMART – were not approached during preparation of this report. According to another recent mapping, most of these networks are no longer active (4).

The list of internationally active surveillance networks is probably incomplete. Further mapping of national and regional networks, including additional specific pathogen-based networks, is required for better understanding of the full range of current activities worldwide, and identification of further opportunities for coordination and collaboration.

---

[a] http://www.msf.org/search?keyword=resistance
[b] http://www.pasteur-international.org/ip/easysite/pasteur-international-en/
scientific-activities/projects (accessed 18 December 2013)
[c] http://antibiotics.ru/index.php?newlang=eng (accessed 16 October 2013)

[d] Belarus, Kazakhstan, Moldova and the Ukraine

Ap3.2 References

1. Meyer WG, Pavlin JA, Hospentha lD, Murray CK, Jerke. K, Hawksworth A et al. Antimicrobial resistance surveillance in the AFHSC-GEIS network. *BMC Public Health*, 2011. doi:10.1186/1471-2458-11-S2-S8.

2. Borg M, Cookson B, Zarb P, Scicluna E. Antibiotic resistance surveillance and control in the Mediterranean region: report of the ARMed Consensus Conference. *J Infect Dev Ctries*, 2009, 3(9):654-659. (http://www.ncbi.nlm.nih.gov/pubmed/19858565, accessed 9 April 2014).

3. Unemo M, Fasth O, Fredlund H, Limnios A, Tapsall J. Phenotypic and genetic characterization of the 2008 WHO *Neisseria gonorrhoeae* reference strain panel intended for global quality assurance and quality control of gonococcal antimicrobial resistance surveillance for public health purposes. *J Antimicrob Chemother*, 2009, 63(6):1142-1151. doi:10.1093/jac/dkp098.

4. Grundmann H, Klugman K, Walsh T, Ramon-Pardo P, Sigauque B, Khan W et al. A framework for global surveillance of antibiotic resistance. doi:10.1016/j.drup.2011.02.007.